KV-335-926

The City
in
West Europe

The City in West Europe

D. Burtenshaw
M. Bateman
Department of Geography
Portsmouth Polytechnic
and
G. J. Ashworth
Geografisch Instituut
Rijksuniversiteit Groningen

JOHN WILEY & SONS
Chichester · New York · Brisbane · Toronto

British Library Cataloguing in Publication Data:

Burtenshaw, David
The city in West Europe.
1. City planning—Europe, Western
I. Title II. Bateman, Michael, *b. 1944*
III. Ashworth, Gregory John
711'.4'094 80–41589

ISBN 0 471 27929 3

Typeset by Computacomp (UK) Ltd, Fort William, Scotland, and printed in the United States of America by Vail-Ballou Press, Inc., Binghampton, N.Y.

Contents

Preface and Acknowledgements

The nature of this book, indeed the fact that it was written at all, is a result of our joint experiences as teachers, researchers and citizens. Our attempts to explain to students over a number of years in various institutions the nature of change in the contemporary European city revealed a gap in the existing literature. When faced with this problem, each of us independently could find no existing book which fitted the needs of our students. There were and are many excellent British, American and Continental works on the problems and policies of individual European cities and countries, and rather fewer good syntheses of international experiences in particular aspects of urban policy-making. While acknowledging our debt to these writers (we hope adequately in our references), we still feel that the comparative view of European urban planning has been inadequately presented.

From the outset, we have attempted to provide a comparative view of West European urban development and planning, which has grown out of our previous research into office developments, retailing and urban recreation, particularly applied to West Germany, France and the Low Countries. Our fortuitous presence together on the staff of Portsmouth Polytechnic demonstrated to us both the weaknesses of our individual topical approaches and the value of close collaboration on a collective project. We acknowledge that the shape of the book still owes much to our particular specialist views. Equally it must be said that we are all three, intellectual 'children of the 1960s', whose optimism about the efficacy of planning has survived the disappointments of the 1970s. In addition, our writing has been coloured by an increasing awareness, gleaned from contact with our European colleagues, that assumptions and models derived from North American studies are not only simplistic in the European context, but at times quite erroneous. Cities in West Europe remain distinct, just as the approaches to their planning remain distinct. We strongly believe that the qualities inherent in this distinctiveness make the city in West Europe an attractive and highly amenable place in which to live.

The delimitation of a geographical area of study and the selection of examples from within it, must inevitably be somewhat arbitrary. We are content to give prominence to the ideas and applications developed in Britain, France, Germany, Italy, the Low Countries and Scandinavia, as forming the core of our West Europe, supplemented by occasional reference to Iberia, Greece, Austria, Switzerland and Ireland. We are less happy about excluding reference to the countries of Eastern Europe, since they both shared the heritage of cities in West Europe and have made their contribution to the European tradition. Their more recent development, however, has meant that they have become distinct from cities in West Europe and this is acknowledged by the existence of a sister volume edited by F. E. I. Hamilton and R. A. French on *The Socialist City*.

On a more technical note, we have adopted the use of anglicized spellings of place-names where they exist. Although this is at the risk of offending our European colleagues outside Britain, it was our inevitable compromise necessary if we were to avoid the problems of Liège, *Luik* or *Luttich*, or even Milan, *Milano* or *Mailand*!

Our approach to each of the aspects of urban life owes much to the continuing debate amongst geographers on the role of our subject in the making of public policy. We have taken it as axiomatic that the geographical investigation of the city must begin with the attempt to trace and understand the patterns and processes of urban life, and then to move, without a clearly envisaged gap, to consider the impacts of the policies of public and private bodies on these patterns. The optimistic assumptions about both the efficacy of planning, broadly defined to include a much wider range of spatial policies than is handled by most city planners, and the role of an applied geography, are obvious to us and we make no apology for them. If this is seen as a naïvety, contrary to the spirit of the times, it is in our eyes morally preferable to what has been termed the 'structural trap of informed inactivity'.

In writing this book, we have received the help and support of many individuals and organizations throughout West Europe and it would be an impossible task to single out even a selection from amongst them. Every reference that we quote and each city that we name must remain as a recognition of the assistance which has been willingly and patiently given wherever we journeyed or wrote during the past five years. For a part of this travelling we are indebted to the assistance given by Portsmouth Polytechnic, and by the Social Science Research Council which together with the *Deutsche Forschungs Gemeinschaft* financed one visit to West Germany.

Closer to home we are conscious of a debt to our departmental colleagues and to our students in places as far apart as Portsmouth, Groningen and Ottawa for their willingness to listen and to discuss aspects of the work as well as to contribute corrections and examples. Ray Riley and John-Louis Smith in Portsmouth, Jan Dekker and Jan Ten Brummelhuis in Groningen have always offered us the benefit of their advice. Our research assistants in Portsmouth, Miriam Boyle and Alistair Drummond, were tireless in their pursuit of even the most obscure references and information, even if it entailed frequent visits to such places as St Étienne! The quality of the maps is a better tribute to the work of the Cartographic Unit in the Department of Geography at Portsmouth than this all-too-brief acknowledgement. The numerous drafts of the manuscript were patiently deciphered by Sandra Winterbotham over many an evening and weekend. We hope that those who have helped us in so many ways will feel recompensed by the result, but of course any shortcomings must be firmly attributed to us alone. No acknowledgement would be complete without mention of our gratitude for the advice which we received during the early stages of the project from Michael Coombs, and in the later stages from Celia Bird, our editors, whose patience was quite remarkable!

Finally we would like to thank and dedicate our efforts to our teachers and students—those who have taught us and those we have taught.

Introduction

The basic thesis of this book is that the cities of West Europe have sufficient in common to justify the use of the term 'West European City', and are sufficiently distinct in important respects to render examination of the common elements worthwhile. In this examination of the city in West Europe, three broad approaches have been taken, represented by the three parts of this book. In the first part, we concentrate on the philosophies, histories and processes which have made the West European city system rich in internal variety yet distinct from that of the rest of western industrialized urban society.

We examine in the first chapter the various guiding themes of urban planning which have stemmed from a wide variety of national cultures and are rooted in varying depths of urban experience. It is against this diverse background that West Europe has produced a large number of architects, planners and urban visionaries, whose thinking has found physical expression in the cities of Europe. In Chapter 2 we have traced the history of some of these traditions through the works, both literary and architectural, of 'household names' such as Haussmann, Howard, Le Corbusier, Sitte, Geddes and Cerda. The social composition and patterning of the West European city does not fit easily into the models of urban social structure that have been derived from North American, or even Australian, experience. In Chapter 3 we examine a selection of studies of social morphology, social processes and social change in cities as diverse as Sunderland, Helsinki, Rome and Arnhem. We hope in this way to show that the critical influences on the urban social system and its expression in the morphology of the city are significantly different from those implied in the 'North American' models. The length of the historical experience, the variety of social welfare policies and differences in the value placed on the various possible lifestyles offered by the city, will, again, underpin the explanation of the distinctiveness of Europe.

If we are to sustain the thesis of distinctiveness, it is necessary to examine those policies which are tending to maintain the unique flavour of urban life in Europe, or which constitute a peculiarly European response to a more widespread trend. The second, and largest, part of the book examines policies towards various aspects of the city's development. It is not intended to be an all-encompassing inventory of policy-making in cities but an attempt to synthesize the policies from diverse examples in those fields of urban planning and management where West European cities have made significant contributions towards solving the various problems resulting from urban change in the period since 1945.

Although cities have always been service centres there has been a notable shift in the last decade away from employment in the secondary sector so that in most cities between 60 and 70 per cent of the workforce is employed in tertiary and quaternary occupations. The rapid expansion of financial services, the growing scale of company activities and the growth of the national and local civil service to administer the increase in legislation, have all contributed to the heavy demands for new office development. The growth of higher education and research have had a similar impact on not only the traditional academic centres such as Munich, Cambridge or Groningen, but also on smaller towns such as Umeå, Stirling and Winchester.

In the retailing field there have been pressures for locational change deriving both from changes in the structure of the industry and changes in the behaviour of customers.The new wealth of postwar European society, and the new consumption patterns that the resulting lifestyles have encouraged, has occurred at the same time as fundamental change in the economics and management structures of shops. The consequence of such trends in location have been resisted by the established interests in the city-centre high streets, and often also by the conservation interest. Chapter 4 examines various planning responses to such developments in the retailing and office sectors of the urban economy.

Part of the reason for the dispersal shared by the 'suburbanization' of shops and offices, has been the shrinkage of distance effected by the widespread use of the motorcar. Its benefits were more quickly appreciated than its costs, and policies designed to accommodate its use have generally been superseded by policies of restraint on private transport use and support for alternative public transport services. Chapter 5 traces variations in this trend and the emergence of transport systems distinctively different from those devised to meet the needs of the North American city.

Housing policies are the third set of planning policies to be discussed. In this field widely different policies have been derived as a result of differences in traditional national approaches to the provision, finance, design and maintenance of the housing stock. Nevertheless there are a number of policies which are sufficiently similar to merit comparative study. The production of large areas of 'social' housing, often on the urban periphery, was a similar response with common consequences whether in Sarcelles, Sloetermeer, Becontree or Perlach. Similarly, the renovation of old housing stock and the reappraisal of its value, has led to 'gentrification' in response to similar opportunities presented in the Île St Louis, Trastevere, Portico d'Ottavia, or Islington.

An obvious difference between the cities of Europe and those of the new world, is that the former contain relict buildings and street patterns which are valued by tourist and citizen alike as giving interest and identity to the urban scene. Many of the changes in the economic functions, housing provision and transport use discussed above were seen to threaten this historic heritage. Chapter 7 traces the growth of a response to this threat mainly in the last fifteen years and argues that conservation planning can no longer be seen as a simple matter of preservation but has implications for many other aspects of urban life, and involves a choice between priorities, lifestyles and values. The lessons of Edinburgh new town, the Parisian

Marais, Stockholm's Gamla Stan or Bologna's *centro storico* have an application far beyond the widely different cultural and historical environments from which they were derived.

It is not possible to conceive of a European architectural heritage without considering how the enjoyment of that heritage is made accessible to Europeans. Thus planning for tourism and planning for conservation must be reconciled despite the pressures that visitors themselves can place upon the heritage that they have come to experience. We hope therefore that Chapters 7 and 8 will be viewed together. The rapid growth of the major cities of Europe as tourist attractions and the development of extensive tourist districts have posed problems to planners which have only recently been appreciated.

Cities have always been centres of leisure and entertainment for citizens as well as visitors, but since the war, increased disposable income, leisure time and personal mobility have intensified demands for facilities as diverse as theatres, sports halls, parks and open spaces. Chapter 9 takes the view that recreation planning has ceased to be an incidental embellishment to the town plan, but is occupying an increasing share of urban resources, planners' attention, and citizens' expectations. In addition the recreational demands of urban populations provide the most important functional link between the city and its more rural surroundings.

The third part of the book synthesizes the sectoral policies described above by means of an examination of the city plan as a whole. Initially in Chapter 10 we return to the *leitmotifs* of history, nationality and ideology in an examination of national urban systems, and the involved question of the relationship of city planning to the regional and national planning policies. This acts as a necessary preliminary to the understanding of the structure plans of individual cities. The major West European metropolitan centres, Europe's 'world cities' have been the subject of frequent scrutiny, as for example by Hall in 1966, 1977 and 1978. Chapter 11 examines again the places of both the unicentric capitals such as London, Paris, Copenhagen and Brussels, as well as the multicentric city regions of the Rhine–Ruhr and West Netherlands, with the intention of distinguishing between the common features of planning policy and the unique characteristics of individual cities.

The attention paid by international commentators to the 'world cities' has not been matched by an equal attention to the plans of the non-primate urban areas (Chapter 12). These are both more numerous and more varied but equally reflect the themes that are the subject of this book, as well as shaping the living environment of the majority of Europeans. Although there is clearly a great variety of responses to the individual circumstances of this large and motley collection of cities, it is possible to group them into 'families of plans' and thus draw more general conclusions. Part three concludes with a review of what is perhaps West Europe's most distinctive contribution to urban planning—the new town (Chapter 13).

The task of examining the cities of Europe is a forbidding one not least because of the number of urban centres involved in this rich heartland of urban society. It must be emphasized that our attempt has not been to create an exhaustive catalogue of urban experience in Europe. Selection has been necessary to illustrate our major themes, entailing the inclusion of examples from some countries at the expense of others. Our reasoning is straightforward and rests simply on the fact that West Europe offers so many cities across such a broad spectrum that no examination could be totally exhaustive. We hope that our selection is not unrepresentative of West European urban society but adequately reflects both the overall distinctiveness and the internal variety of the urban system which is the overriding thesis of this book.

The problems facing the planners of the West European city are formidable and the policies created for their solution are on only rare occasions obviously and immediately successful. The fact, however, that an increasing number of citizens are taking a critical interest in the actions of the politicians and the planners upon their environment, and that consequently this participation is being given statutory recognition in almost all the countries of West Europe in the 1970s, is a cause for optimism. This interest implies both a belief that the European city provides a congenial environment for living, and a growing determination that its distinctive qualities are worth some effort to preserve. This also is the philosophy of the authors and the *raison d'être* for this book.

List of Tables

List of Figures

Part I

CHAPTER 1

The Role of History, Nation and Ideology

The use of the term 'the West European City' strongly implies that the cities of the subcontinent have characteristics in common which give them a distinctiveness setting them apart from cities developed elsewhere. It is a paradox that, in a large part, this distinctiveness is a result of the variety of historical experiences which have contributed to the physical fabric in which citizens live, work and play. In many cases it is the history of the nation or, occasionally the nations, in which a particular town has been situated that have shaped the town's development from age to age. Each stage in national development has, in its turn, brought about corresponding changes in the form and functions of towns and cities. In this way the city in West Europe becomes a palimpsest representing the physical expression in the built environment of successive ideologies at each point of development. However, the changes have not occurred simultaneously throughout West Europe and therefore part of this urban distinctiveness has resulted from the differential effects of policies and social movements.

The historical experience has been sharp and dramatic for many cities. In some cases, for instance, it involved the loss of an imperial role with consequent effects on the imperial city. In 1919 as a result of the Treaties of St Germain and Trianon, Vienna was transformed from the capital of an empire of 52 million persons to the capital of a dismembered country with approximately one-tenth of its former population. More recently we can point to West Berlin as an exclave of the Federal Republic of Germany, divested of its capital status by the events of the 'cold war', and divided and distinct from East Berlin, now Hauptstadt Berlin, the capital of the German Democratic Republic. The last vestiges of Berlin's role remain in the Tiergarten or with the boundaries of 1920 Berlin even if the immediate past was less than glorious. For other cities the dramatic change took the form of the truncation of a trading hinterland as in Londonderry in 1920, Hamburg and Lübeck in 1945 or Trieste at the same time. In other cases, the dramatic changes were more frequent as the nation-states of Europe fought over the cultural shatter belt between the French and German peoples. Saarbrücken's national allegiance has oscillated for the past century. Only since 1960 has the city or its near neighbours in the Saarland been an integral part of West Germany. From 1945 until 1960 French laws, customs, education and urban development fashioned the Saarland towns and built a university modelled on the French pattern of higher education. This was not the first period of French domination since, as cities in the League of Nations Territory of the Saarland, they were subject to French administration from 1920 until 1935. Before that Saarlouis and Saarbrücken had been under French control for a short time in the Napoleonic Wars. The history of other cities in Alsace-Lorraine, such as Metz and Strasbourg, has also been affected by the oscillations of the international boundary over the past century. Boundary changes have left Vyborg in Denmark with a similar imprint of changed national allegiance. The more one penetrates history from the recent past, the greater are the number of cities affected by the changing political map of Europe.

In contrast, other cities have had greatness thrust upon them by the course of history. The relatively sudden promotion of Dublin from the role of a provincial capital to that of the capital of a new republic in 1920 is a case in point. Bonn enjoyed a similar fate a quarter of a century later when it became the temporary capital of the western zones of Germany. While the former was the logical choice, the latter was a mere university town of no great urban status compared with its rivals such as Kassel, or Stuttgart or its near neighbour Cologne. Yet today Bonn–Bad Godesberg is a fascinating mixture of government offices, nestling in a suburban sprawl surrounding the old town of Bonn and its elegant spa neighbour.

Violent change as the consequence of war and revolution is a strong theme in the development of the city in West Europe. Frequently the fear of war or revolution has had a lasting effect on the form of our cities. The changes in military technology in the medieval period resulted in equally rapid alterations to the defences of cities. The imprint of these defences on the present urban fabric is unmistakable. As the cities grew in population and as the technology of war improved so new defences were planned and built while the old walls frequently vanished to be sites for parks and boulevards. Even as late as the nineteenth century Palmerston's fear of a French attack on Portsmouth dictated fortifications which affected subsequent city form and development. The forts and defences remain prominent features in the townscape, serving a varied role as recreational open spaces, museums, sites for industrial estates and, more recently, superstores, while a select few retain their military function. Similarly the French mistrust of the Prussians produced comparable military works around Verdun.

The imprints of past defence are indeed commonplace over much of urban Europe often in towns which were never directly involved in military action. Without question, however, war has destroyed the fabric of many cities twice in this century and has been the catalyst from which new approaches to urban growth or changes have emerged. The whole concept of the Lijnbaan pedestrianized shopping centre of Rotterdam was formulated during the darker days of the Second World War. Abercrombie was conceiving his plan for Greater London in a period when large areas of that city were being razed to the ground by enemy incendiary bombs. Frequently 40 per cent and more of the buildings in German cities were destroyed by allied bombing in the latter stages of that war. Other cities throughout West Europe bore the scars of war to a greater or lesser extent. Le Havre, Coventry and Antwerp were among some of those that were severely devastated. Spanish cities had suffered a similar fate in the Civil War so that the opportunities to build anew existed in part of Teruel.

On the other hand, the neutrality maintained by Sweden and Switzerland meant that cities and towns in those two countries remained unscathed during the twentieth century. It was left to the violence of the bulldozer and the developer to alter the fabric of Stockholm or Zürich. Perhaps neutrality has been a prominent factor in the success of building conservation in these two countries.

It is out of the ashes of 1945 that many ideas for urban development sprung as a part of the new free Europe that was to grow from the ruins of war. The development of so many fundamental attitudes to urban life, urban development and future urban change are embodied in that period of the new Europe. The ideas that were embodied in Gravier's seminal work *Paris et le désert français* which was published in 1947 were conceived in Vichy France (Gravier 1947). In Britain the founding of the welfare state, the new town movement and the self-congratulatory Festival of Britain epitomized the optimism born of years of sacrifice.

When one is examining the imprint of history, it is not solely the landmarks of national history that have fashioned the modern city. At the more local scale the redefinition of urban boundaries in areas of strong allegiance to particular towns can have a lasting impact. The creation of modern Hamburg in 1938 is a case in point. The modern city is the product of a major boundary change which absorbed the Prussian city of Altona. To this day Altona has a separate identity; the trains to Hamburg invariably terminate there and the shopping centre is still an important regional centre within greater Hamburg. In Italy many of the regional planning boundaries, which in turn affect city planning, were derived from the pre-existing states of the Italian peninsula rather than from areas specifically designed for effective planning.

History can also be viewed as an important aspect of our urban cultural heritage from the point of view of the buildings that were the product of each age. The variety of architectural responses to social conditions in the past are not the subject of this text although they are an integral part of the variety of forms that comprise the city. As Kormoss (1976) stated 'It is one of the consequences of the historic, geographic, linguistic and philosophic diversity of Europe which turns it into a very rich region with a very important heritage'. It is somewhat surprising therefore to note authors who have criticized approaches to the reconstruction of previous building forms in the years after 1945 as being 'anti-progressive and anti-innovation' (Holzner, 1970). Such a view represents the extreme application of cultural blinkers to the understanding of West European urbanism, with the resultant misunderstanding of the role of the built environment in our distinctive European heritage.

The development of cities has followed a far from common path through time. Industrialization, for instance, came earlier to Britain and Belgium with consequent effects on town growth and form that are not found to the same degree in France, Germany or Spain. Late industrialization, the advent of railways prior to industrialization and the coming of electric power so quickly after the 'takeoff' to industrialization has made German cities very distinct from their British counterparts. Industries that migrated to the coalfield cities and towns in Britain remained *in situ* in German towns. The railways penetrated closer to the medieval core of German cities and linked the preindustrial towns and states rather than focusing on the needs of industrial exploitation. German cities developed tram systems very early in their period of industrial growth thus reducing the need to concentrate the workforce close to the point of employment. So the industrial colonies, while being both a distinctive characteristic and a product of their times, were more 'open' than their British or Belgian counterparts.

A recurring theme in this book is the interplay between the city as an expression of the nation-state, and the city as a product of international forces. The former condition tends towards the production of distinctly national city systems, while the latter leads towards increasing uniformity across political boundaries. Hall (1977) contends this to be a common process with a simple timelag between different systems, with all countries moving inexorably towards a single model. In the case of housing policies (see Chapter 6), the national view is so dominant in our opinion that the policies cannot be compared unless the national variations are noted. Similarly the consideration of city planning policies seems incomplete without some reference to the relationships between national, regional and urban planning (see Chapter 10). On the other hand the international aspects of office location and tourism are important factors in any consideration of economic change (see Chapter 4) or tourism (see Chapter 8). Obviously the international role of cities is a major consideration in any overview of the planning strategies for both the national capitals and other cities that traditionally aspire to international status such as Frankfurt, Zürich, Geneva and Strasbourg.

The impact of the national political system is unmistakable in its effect on the national urban system. Centralized nation states have created strong, dominant primate cities such as London and Paris. Architectural and planning innovations tended to spread from the core city to towns on the national periphery. The primate city is the centre of perceived wisdom and through the activities of the inhabitants and organizations housed there, not least of which is central government, proceeds to reinforce the perceived centralized wisdom. In France the ideas of Haussmann, Le Corbusier and the more recent new town planners were initially Parisian ideas which later spread to the provincial towns. The architectural ideas of Georgian England originated in London and were copied, modified and improved on throughout the United Kingdom. Ideas emerged from Copenhagen to be instituted in the towns of the Jutland peninsular. On the other hand, countries with a strong tradition of provincial separatism produced a less clearly defined urban hierarchy. In Italy the relict capitals of Turin, Venice and Naples are serious rivals to the status of Rome, while Milan has acquired many of the trappings of an economic, if not a political, national capital city. Similarly the separate national identities of Castile, Catalonia and the Basque country have produced Madrid, Barcelona and Bilbao respectively, competing with the older products of a moslem culture, Seville and Granada, which dominated the Spanish urban system until the recent past. In Belgium the severity of the cultural schism has led to both restrictions on the growth of Brussels and the identification of many Belgians with either Antwerp or Liège rather than the legal capital.

If London and Paris are the products of a history of centralized government, the cities of Austria, West Germany and Switzerland reflect the role of federalism. In Switzerland there are five dominant cities in the urban hierarchy. Bern, the national capital is the fourth largest, following Zürich, Geneva and Basle, with Lausanne only slightly smaller. Apart from these there are also Lugano, the cultural capital of the Italian-speaking Ticino, the industrial centres of Biel, Winterthur and St Gallen and important cantonal capitals such as Schaffhausen, Fribourg and Lucerne.

The German federal tradition and the partition and occupation of the Reich encouraged the similar development of a multicentred urban system. In this case, the tradition has a long history stretching back to the small princedoms which characterized the central European region prior to German unification, each with its own capital such as Bamburg, Brunswick, Fulda and Oldenburg. The old capital of the Reich, Berlin, is divided and both politically and physically isolated from the Federal Republic. Both Hamburg and Munich could lay claim to being the largest city whilst Kiel, Hannover Dusseldorf, Mainz, Wiesbaden, Bremen, Stuttgart and Saarbrücken are all *Land* capitals, many much larger than Bonn, the federal capital. In addition, Frankfurt can claim, with justice, to be the financial capital and major centre of international communications. In contrast, Austria does possess a dominant capital city, but like its neighbour its federal status has enabled the *Land* capitals such as Bregenz, Linz, Salzburg and Klagenfurt to possess a broader range of employment opportunities than similarly sized cities in France.

The 'world city' fulfilling international functions and shaped by forces beyond the nation state is not a recent phenomenon. Government of the world, or a substantial portion of it, has been exercized from Rome, Madrid, Lisbon, Paris, Brussels and London. International trade and its financing has been concentrated in Venice, Antwerp, Amsterdam and London in successive centuries from the fifteenth to the nineteenth. Financial prowess in the world today is claimed by London, Paris, Frankfurt, Zürich and Luxembourg City. Similarly, more recently the movement in Europe towards establishing international governmental institutions and the contemporaneous growth of the multinational corporations has increased the international role of selected cities. The antecedents for some centres are now rooted deep in history; Vienna was a congress centre in 1814–15, Berlin in 1870 and Paris in 1918. The International Court of Justice at The Hague, the League of Nations in Geneva, the Council of Europe in Strasbourg, the various organs of the European Community in Brussels, Strasbourg and Luxembourg City are only the largest of a multiplicity of similar international organizations to be found in West Europe's world cities. To these must be added the efforts of cities such as Vienna and Helsinki to establish themselves as neutral international conference centres to rival the traditional position held by Geneva.

Besides the international organs of government the world cities have set about attracting the multinational office complexes, the international banks and financial activities that are part of the world city image. The dreams of de Gaulle to create a centre to rival Manhattan are enshrined in the whole concept of the new office node of La Défense. The airport which bears his name at Roissy and the modernized telecommunications system based on Paris are part and parcel of the same dream. All the main financial centres have seen the development of new office buildings each frequently more lofty than its predecessor housing the major international banking groups. The National Westminster tower in London and the Deutsche Bank, ıesdner Bank and Commerz Bank towers in Frankfurt illustrate the demand for prestige city-centre buildings in the world of banking, a trend that has been backed by the city authorities. The most spectacular growth in this sector has been reserved for Luxembourg City where the number of banks represented in the city has risen from fifteen in 1960 to 74 in 1974 and 108 in 1979. The Boulevard Royale today is nicknamed *la royauté de l'argent* for its occupants are, among others, Crédit Lyonnais, Banque National de Paris, Banque Internationale, Japan Bank, Houston Bank, Bank of America, Bank of Boston, Kredietbank, and IBM. No visitor to Dusseldorf can fail to notice the presence of Japanese interests in the city, for the Japanese have chosen that city as a centre for their West European activities. A short walk north from the Bank of England in London will introduce the pedestrian to a whole new set of Middle Eastern banking groups. Similarly the international role of the major cities as tourist centres for the wealth of the Middle East countries and Japan is unmistakable on any visit to Paris or London. Hotels can be patronized, thanks to package tours, and clientèle from particular countries. Even tourist 'souvenir honeypots' such as Harrods, Marks and Spencer and Marble Arch in London have attracted retail activities and banking concerned almost exclusively with the needs of the tourists. These are the trappings of world city status.

It was the new international status that produced a powerful backlash in many cities against the type, form and social consequences of development. The takeover of the Westend district of Frankfurt by tertiary businesses encouraged by the city government because it raised the revenues of the city was violently opposed by protesters. Bloody clashes did have their effects because the city relented at the same time as the gains from property development disappeared and the process was halted. Similar protests have taken place in other cities throughout Europe making cities more conscious of the heritage that has to be sacrificed for international status. Other powerful protest lobbies have gained strength from these successes and therefore anti-motorway lobbies and anti-nuclear power movements have opposed city and national development policies. Symbolic of this growing strength is the success gained by the ecologist 'Green Party' in the 1979 elections in Bremen when they achieved in excess of the 5 per cent of the votes required to guarantee some proportional representation in the *Land* government. 'Ecology against urbanism' is the classic dichotomy now seen by researchers in France (Mathieu, 1977).

Alongside the experience of history and the role of national and international identity the third theme that emerges in cities throughout the continent is the impact of ideology whether conservative, ecological, feudal or socialist. Past ideologies have created cities that are memorials to the divine monarch, such as Versailles, to the imperial mission, Vienna, and to utilitarianism and the pursuit of profit, Manchester. It has been suggested that the morphology of the city is not only a product of the civilization that it houses but also a factor in the creation of that civilization (Sacco, 1976). At a more prosaic level it is clear that in cities such as Stockholm, Gothenburg or Helsinki attitudes towards conservation, social housing provision and public transport reflect the contemporary dominant social-democratic ideology of the Scandinavian countries. In contrast, the development of many West German cities in the immediate postwar period occurred within the framework of a social-market economy and a certain rejection of planning resulting from the experience of twelve years of National Socialism. The result was weak central direction and wide scope for local initiative. In liberal-conservative (Christian democrat) cities such as Cologne, little attempt was made to control urban development for many years while in other cities such as Essen and Bochum the reactions of local government was quite different (Blacksell, 1968).

It is not solely in the modern period that relationships can be drawn between the dominant ideologies and value systems and the nature of urban development. Sjoberg (1960) saw cities in preindustrial Europe as the product of their societies whether they be the community of merchants at a market point noted by Jones (1966) and Pirenne (1925), or an agricultural-based primary civilization, or the quarters of a medieval city created by the Guilds and political rivalry (Vance, 1978). No matter what forces created these towns, wealth was concentrated at the centre and declined towards the periphery (Langton, 1978). The precapitalist modes of production produced a distinctive urban morphology.

By the eighteenth century many of the preindustrial towns had become the homes of the absolute ruler while in some cases new residential towns had been created for the princes such as Karlsruhe and the productive functions were dispersed to the rural areas for the convenience of the *Land* (Lichtenberger, 1972). During the industrial period many of the same towns developed industrial suburbs and altered in character as the new *laissez-faire* ideology dominated the ideas of city builders. Thus the Baroque heart of Nancy was surrounded by industrial housing dating particularly from the years between 1871 and 1914. At the same period new industrial towns sprung up throughout West Europe to exploit the new resources for industry and the economies of scale that technology had made available given a concentration of the labour force. Vance's (1977) depiction of the 'generalized' suburbs of the Lancashire mill towns, the *villes minières*, and the Ruhr, as the products of this liberal industrial phase of city growth, seems to be most apt. All of these towns and cities today are the cores of the mid-twentieth-century welfare state cities with their peripheral social housing and their inner area redevelopment and refurbishing programmes. Thus many cities have acquired the buildings and street plans from periods of contrasting ideologies and possess a richness derived from this variety. The preindustrial burger town could develop into the capital of a principality and a *Land* capital like Munich or remain a museum like Arundel in Southern England. Industrial towns have also developed to achieve regional importance like Birmingham or Essen, or a locally important status such as Merthyr Tydfil or Volklingen. Alternatively they can become museums to an ideology such as Millom in Cumbria or Thiers in central France. Only the new towns and satellite towns are the product of the twentieth-century welfare state, and whether some of these will grow accumulating the artefacts of changing ideologies while others remain as museums of mid-twentieth-century urban ideals is for future generations to discover. What is certain is that the imprint of ideologies on cities is far from even.

Other particular features of West European urban morphology can be viewed as the product of particular ideological conditions. Lichtenberger (1976) notes that the apartment is a product of the Italian renaissance cities that spread initially to France and Austria. Today it is a form of housing common throughout Europe, praised in some quarters and decried in others, although the nature of the apartment has been modified to accommodate the contrasting housing needs of the stratified central Parisian society and the social housing needs of the lower socio-economic groups in the inner suburbs of London or the outermost fringes of Cologne. The crowded housing conditions of the nineteenth-century industrial city are viewed in a similar vein by Vance (1977). For him the back-to-back housing of Leeds, the Glasgow tenements and the single-room apartments of the European mainland were all responses to the needs for a labour force located adjacent to the mill. This strengthened class segregation between the mean terraces of the workers and the more substantial villas or town houses of the bourgeoisie.

It is notable that since 1945 the dominant ideology of government has been more stable in some countries than others. It is possible to recognize countries such as Britain which have suffered from relatively violent oscillations in their dominant political ideology compared with the greater stability of the coalition governments of the continental countries. While there have been changes in the dominant political ideology in Germany, Spain and Sweden, they have been a single change rather than a succession of oscillating and damaging swings. Consequently, British policies on housing tenure, new town expansion, inner-city renewal and regional development have often become political symbols to be changed when power changes hands. Some would go so far as to suggest that this lack of coherent goals for society in general and British cities in particular, has slowed down the urban change and development process compared with that of France or Scandinavia where the continuity of environmental policies is more apparent despite changes in the details of policies. Even at the local level, sudden changes in local political control can lead to sharp reversals of policy, as is illustrated in Chapter 5 in the case of public transport.

It must be acknowledged, however, that there is an influential school of thought which claims that the oscillations between more or less reformist parties, or between reformist and conservative parties, does little to alter the fundamentally central role of the capitalist mode of production on urban development. National and local politicians, whether they are labelled social democrat, christian democrat or liberal will still depend on the institutions of the capitalist money market or the 'property machine' for the financing of all developments, whether public or private (Ambrose and Colenutt, 1975). Thus commentators such as Castells, Harvey (1973) and Lefebre (1968) adopt a very critical stance on urban change even when such change is ostensibly beneficial, such as urban renewal in central Paris. For instance, Castells (1978) sees the role of the new express metro (RER) as providing commuters/workers from the poorer suburbs of the east of Paris for the multinational offices clustered in western Paris.

On the other hand, we would maintain that the various shades of ideological commitment contribute towards those very differences in national, regional and local policy which make the character of the city in West Europe so distinct. If Castells's view is simplistic, that of Berry (1973), who sees West Europe as a group of identical redistributive welfare states, does no justice to the widely differing social and political experiences of countries as diverse as Ireland and Sweden or Portugal and Austria. The simple dichotomies of the Marxist and the Americanized view of the world are valuable teaching devices and theoretical constructs from which to begin analysis. However, the variety of built environments, policy goals and responses, whether for separate sectors of the city, such as housing, or for the city as a whole in the form of structure plans, are proof of the distinctiveness of the city in West Europe. It is distinct because it is the product of a variety of histories in a large number of countries each with its own evolving ideological position.

It can be argued, or believed as an article of faith, that a future European Union will bring about a set of more uniform urban policies from Gibraltar to Tromsö. While numerous references in the following pages to the publications of international organizations bear witness to the steps being made in this direction, there is also another tide flowing in Europe towards the smaller rather than the larger political unit. The city is frequently at the heart of such regionalist movements as is Bilbao for the Basques, Edinburgh for the Scots and Bozen for the Tyroleans. Whether regionalist movements can succeed in producing cities that reflect the dominance of local ideologies and cultures is a problem for the future.

Three interrelated themes of historical experience, national identity and political ideology together account for both the variety and the continuing distinctiveness of the West European city. The approach is unashamedly 'very historicist, very European and very French; the city is the product of history, the reflection of society, the action of man upon space' (Castells, 1976).

CHAPTER 2

The European Tradition of Urban Planning

Over the centuries the cities of Europe have inspired men from Plato to Castells to describe their deficiencies and to eulogize about the means of providing the best form of urban life for the future citizens. This tradition of concern for the built environment, unmatched elsewhere in the world, has produced a whole series of approaches to urban planning. These approaches are as diverse as the backgrounds of their authors but it is possible to trace several lineages within West Europe that still have an important impact on policies and plans.

Such masterly reflections on urban architecture, history and planning as the works of Curl, Gutkind, Lavedan, Mumford and Vance do not agree on all the relationships through time and it is not our intention to replicate their work (Curl, 1970; Gutkind, 1969–72; Lavedan, 1959; Mumford, 1961; and Vance, 1977). However glorious the urban past might have been, we are not attempting to describe the heritage of the built environment but rather to highlight those movements, theories and theorists that have had an influence on the urban planner in the second half of the twentieth century. Most European nations have been blessed with urban theorists or urbanists and their ideas have been diffused from Austria, France, Great Britain or Italy with increasing rapidity especially in the past 100 years. In the past century, in particular, a handful of such theorists have become famous beyond West Europe and their ideas modified and translated into bricks and mortar by subsequent architects. Unlike the earlier city planners the greatest urban theorists of the nineteenth and twentieth century have few of their own designs as living memorials to their influential theories.

It is possible to trace five separate urban planning traditions within West Europe, namely: authoritarian, organic, romantic, technocratic utopian and utopian. These traditions while obviously distinct at various times do blur into one another especially in the period since 1945. Others have discussed the deficiencies but have not actually planned the future city and these theorists can also be given a rightful place in the tradition of urban thinkers as socialists. It is the underlying thesis of some commentators that many movements are the product of their time and that emphasizing the individual who fashions a movement rather than the individual who is produced by a movement, is placing the wrong emphasis on the individual. The traditions of European urban theorists and their lineages that are traced in this chapter are but one way of viewing what is a complex history. However, this particular perspective does aid the comprehension of some of the policies that can be seen in cities today.

The Authoritarian Tradition

Perhaps the longest tradition is that of the authoritarian planner although this is the most maligned today. Rather than reason on the layout of the city this tradition has tended to follow the views of one man, or an élite that seemed essential, given the conditions of the time. Little scope was permitted for debate or if there was debate it was to no avail. The earliest traditions were that of the gridiron layout credited to Hippodamus by Aristotle and the radial pattern described by Vitruvius in the first Century A.D. (Kirk, 1953). From the dawn of the Renaissance radial forms were utilized in conjunction with the new technologies of fortifications by Alberti, who said 'once the site is chosen everything *must* conform'. Scamozzi, Martini and Averlino all conceived the city as a perfect whole, adopting Renaissance concepts of geometrical perfection, illustrated in Averlino's description of the imaginary city of Sforzinda. The gridiron appeared also as an authoritarian creation in the *bastide* towns such as Villeneuve-sur-Lot in south-west France and Edward I's implantations in Wales such as Flint (Figure 2.1).

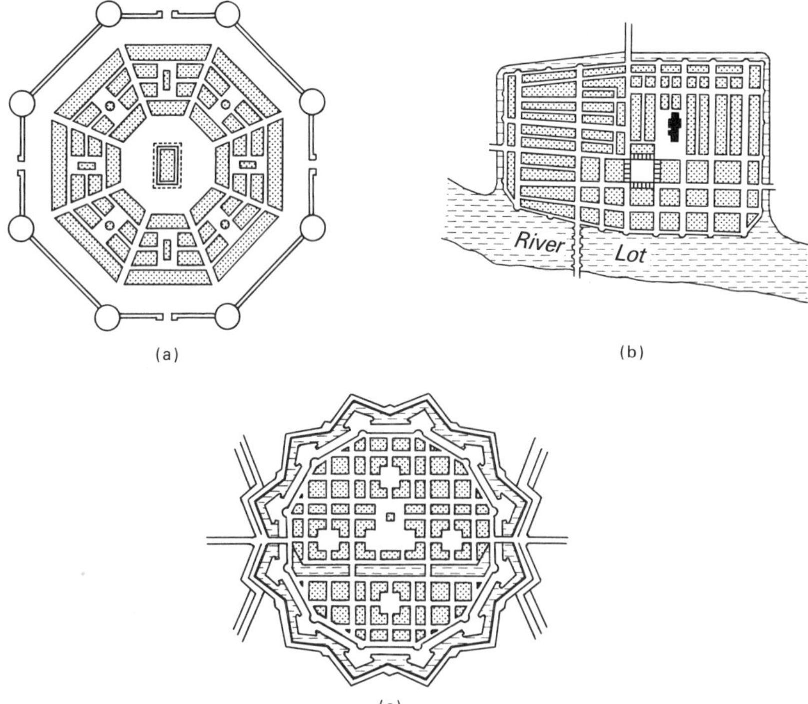

Figure 2.1 Early town plans in the authoritarian tradition: (a) Vitruvius; (b) bastide—Villeneuve-sur-Lot; (c) Scamozzi's ideal town, 1615

The high point of geometric authoritarianism came in the sixteenth century. In Italy, Scamozzi designed a gridiron town within a polygon of defensive walls which was eventually built as the Venetian frontier town of Palma Nova. Vascari developed this design further to incorporate both gridiron and radials within the defensive polygon. The ideas spread into France in the form of increasingly stellar-shaped defences that were employed by Vauban as the perimeter to the designs of Longwy, Neuf Brisach and Montlouis and elements of plans for Strasbourg, Lille, Brest and La Rochelle. Military needs overshadowed all other considerations at least until the advances of military technology made each design in its turn obsolete.

The tradition of the grand design which had diffused northwards was embodied in Wren's plan for London after the Great Fire of 1666 which was to replace wooden London, but little was to be realized in comparison with the grand designs that had emerged in Place Royale (Place des Vosges) in Paris or the baroque grand design of Place Stanislas in Nancy (Lavedan, 1959). At Versailles Louis XIV, with the assistance of the architect Le Vau, transformed a village that his father has popularized into an urban monument to the greatness of France. Other monuments to the greatness of the regime or the ruler appeared in Karlsruhe, Berlin, Copenhagen (Amalienborg) and Lisbon.

By the nineteenth century perhaps the best example of this strong tradition comes from France in the work of Haussmann for the third empire. Haussmann's imprint on central Paris was never completed but the scale of his enterprise is still amazing. It has also been suggested that Napoleon III actually ordered much of the work himself and used the ideas of Napoleon I which were culled in turn from the Artists Plan of 1780. Nevertheless, the works attributed to Haussmann were motivated by a mixture of military considerations (control of the 'mob'), the need to provide employment for the mob, and vanity which provided monumental embellishments. The new boulevards which cut across the streets of medieval Paris can be seen clearly in the area of Arc de Triomphe – Étoile. Other radials such as the Boulevards Magenta and St Michel and ring routes such as the Boulevard St Germain were conceived as part of his plan (Figure 2.2). Haussmann was able to use powers of compulsory acquisition in order to create the boulevards and 22 urban parks in a city that had none in 1850. The Bois de Boulogne was transformed under his direction and new landscaped squares such as the Place des Arts et Métiers (1857) and the Place des Invalides (1865) were created. Water supplies were improved and mature trees were transplanted into the boulevards instantly reducing their harshness (Reau, 1954; and Sutcliffe, 1970).

Haussmann's influence spread to other French cities. In Lyons Väisse built Rue Impériale and other new streets while other schemes were initiated in Avignon, Marseilles, Montpellier, Rouen and Toulouse. His influence spread to Brussels where Anspach masterminded a new 2 km boulevard, transformed the Notre Dame-des-Neiges quarter and acquired the Bois de la Cambre for the city. The Haussmann tradition was reflected in Viviani's copies in Rome, now obliterated, while in Stockholm, Lindhagen's 1866 plan was plainly influenced by the same source. The Spanish architect Cerda developed a Haussmann-like plan for the expansion of Barcelona in 1859 (Wurzer, 1976). At the same time similar autocratically inspired plans were being developed in Vienna under the auspices of Franz Joseph I, where an urban development commission began to prepare plans for the city's *Ringstrassenzone*.

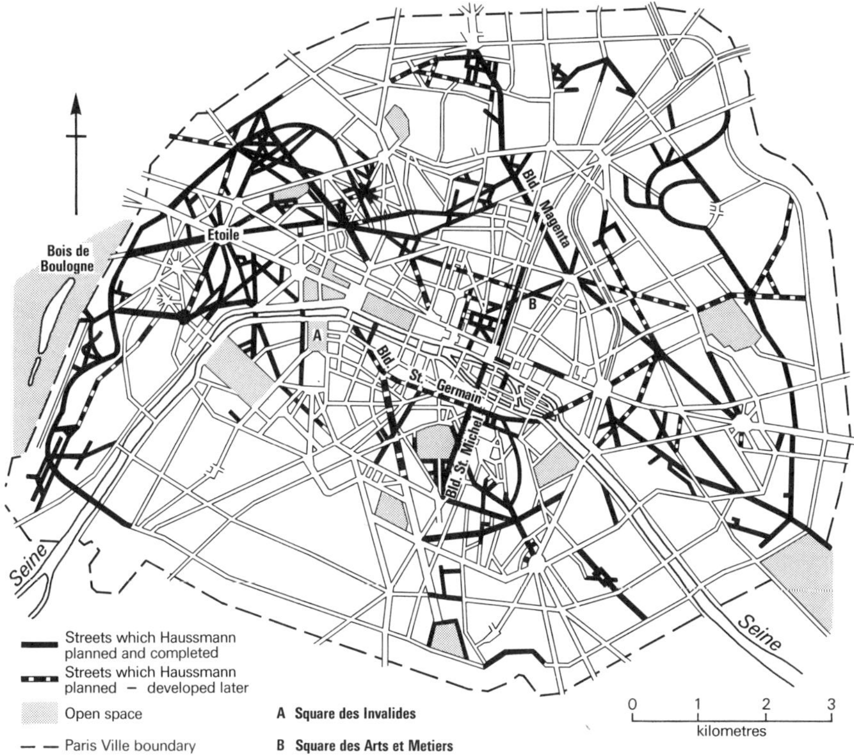

Figure 2.2 Haussmann's imprint on Paris (reproduced by permission from Les Travaux d'Haussmann, *Les Grandes villes du Monde, Paris*, no. 3, 483, 23rd April 1968)

By the interwar period 1919–39 geometric authoritarianism had been superseded in most of West Europe by other traditions that we will examine below. But during the Fascist era, however, the tradition reappeared in some of the schemes of the time. In general the authoritarian tradition was reinforced by the monumentalism of the building schemes proposed by Fascist architects. The construction of Via della Conciliazione in Rome and the demolition of Spina dei Borghi, a much more appropriate route to the Piazza San Pietro is one example of the ill-conceived schemes designed to replace entire districts with showpiece monumentalism. Broad avenues and outsize civic centres replaced the traditional old neighbourhoods in Rome and Taranto.

In Berlin similar monumentalist plans were laid by Speer and known as *Die grosse Strasse* a 7 km north–south avenue leading from the Tiergarten to Schöneberg lined by the 'grandiose façadism' and 'debased neo-classicism' of the new monuments to the Fascist state (Curl, 1970). Only a small section was realized before destruction and the second east–west axis with its shops and offices was never realized (Dahne and Dahl, 1975). Likewise the new towns of Nazi Germany, Wolfsburg and Salzgitter Lebenstadt contained formal layouts to house the workforce for the Volkswagen works and the Hermann Goering steel works respectively. The spacious layout with ample garden areas was in keeping with the 'blood and soil' ideology of the régime.

Madrid's plan which followed the end of the long civil war (1936–39) was very much in the authoritarian tradition. Long avenues along which elements of the falangist city were arranged, were a feature of the 1941 *Plan General de Urbanization de Madrid*. The working class were to be firmly segregated in this plan, which otherwise adapted ideas from earlier plans, into suburban belts of misery (Wynn and Smith, 1978).

Since 1945 the strictly authoritarian tradition has had very little influence within West Europe although it is very much present in many of the plans of the postwar East European states. Only in Spain were plans produced with the same authoritarian ideals including schemes to decentralize people to new towns around six cities. These ran into problems of coordination between physical and economic planning that were characteristic of most Spanish planning. On the other hand some French planners have expressed the view that on a limited scale the authoritarian tradition was very much present in Gaullist France. The creation, despite opposition, of a spectacular office centre (La Défense) or the building of the Charles de Gaulle airport at Roissy were pressed through. The same planners have strongly suggested that President Pompidou's desire to create a new arts centre in the heart of Paris (Pompidou Centre, Beaubourg) at the expense of Nanterre where it was originally proposed to locate the centre, is another example of the authoritarian tradition in French urban planning. Authoritarian traditions reigned in Portuguese planning until 1974 but very little was achieved in the form of definite plans. The authoritarian tradition in West Europe can be seen as the expression in the built environment of the political ideologies of the right ranging from the autocratic heads of states to fascists and to the liberal conservative governments.

The Utilitarian Tradition

The utilitarian tradition was a product of *laissez-faire* economics and the rise of nineteenth-century capitalism. It resulted in urban developments which were predominantly functional and subservient to the demands of an industrial economy born of free enterprise. It is more difficult to identify individuals connected with this urban tradition because its very essence derived from nineteenth-century social attitudes and the lack of concern that created the 'tunnel backs', *villes minières*, *zijnwijken* and *kolonien* of the nineteenth-century city. In many cities the worst examples of *laissez-faire* building abutted onto the architecturally better products of the age. Thus in London the poor conditions of Somers Town were separated from the better housing at Fig's Mead by a changed street layout. Others built gates and barriers into their schemes to keep out unwanted incursions from the slum areas (Choay, 1969).

The contribution of the utilitarian tradition in the nineteenth century was twofold. First, it gave birth to legislation to control the worst environmental evils that had been created by the prevalent social attitudes. In Great Britain the 1875 Health Act was the first significant step in compulsory legislation setting up the Boards of Health whose activities raised suburban housing standards. Belgium introduced laws to enable property for redevelopment to be compulsorily purchased thus controlling the unhealthy housing environments. Similar laws were enacted in Italy between 1865 and 1885, and in France after the turn of the century. Secondly, the movement gave birth to its antithesis, the tradition of utopian thought that reached its zenith by the beginning of the twentieth century.

In the twentieth century the utilitarian tradition continued to have an impact albeit in changed form. The *lotissements* of Paris, and the unregulated spread of suburban housing, often in ribbons along arterial routes, in the London suburbs were examples of the new forms of *laissez-faire* urban growth. It is also possible to detect the role of *laissez-faire* increasing in the 1980s in Great Britain with proposals to remove many of the building regulations from local authority housing schemes. Since 1945 the unplanned sprawl that characterizes the Bonn urban area is another example of a continuing tradition which is more frequently observed in the commentaries and reports of the plans of physical planners and architects who pay allegiance to other planning traditions.

The Utopian Tradition

Utopian thinkers have been contributing to urban planning ever since towns were first built. This particular tradition has been exceedingly strong in West Europe thanks to the influence of one man, Ebenezer Howard. Howard, however, acknowledges the fact that the ideas which he developed in *Tomorrow: a Peaceful Path to Real Reform* in 1898 (Howard, 1946) were based on ideas gleaned from a long tradition of utopian thinking. Normally Plato's ideals for city government, and the Socratic moral values from which they are derived, are regarded as one of the earliest statements in the utopian tradition. In 1516 Thomas More's *Utopia* discussed the ideal city of material abundance linked to work and participation, including a novel scheme of rotating city and country living. The second-home boom of the twentieth century had been forecast! In addition, More gave some attention to the recreation function of the urban periphery (Meyerson, 1961).

As early as the late eighteenth century, idealism in urban planning had returned as a response to the social and environmental conditions produced in the early years of the industrial revolution. Owen's scheme published in 1816 concentrated on the physical structure of the community as a compromise solution within the confines of the industrial system that he abhorred. His model creation which failed at Orbiston, Lanark, like many others that followed, was small. Fourier's *phalanstères* were a similar creation in France which was utilized in Godin's work at Guise thus giving birth to the technocratic utopian tradition which we will discuss below.

Owen's ideas led to a series of new settlements designed to alleviate the horrors of life in the industrial city. Salt's Saltaire, Morris's Morriston, Griffith's Griffithstown (cheek by jowl with Cwmbran), Ackroyd's Ackroyden, Lever's Port Sunlight, Cadbury's Bournville and Rowntree's New Earswick are a few such settlements in Britain. In Prussia the colonies developed by Krupp in the Ruhr also attempted to follow new ideals for urban living. In contrast, J. S. Buckingham's 'Victoria' was a very austere urban design that never reached fruition. Others such as Cabet, Bellamy, Morris, Ruskin, Disraeli, Engels, H. G. Wells and Zola contributed both directly and indirectly through novels to the growing body of literature that acknowledged the problems of urban life in nineteenth-century Europe.

Howard acknowledged Ruskin's influence on his own thoughts as well as the impact of Buckingham's unsuccessful Victoria which, like the garden city which it preceded, was to be set in 'a large agricultural estate' (Howard, 1946). To Howard the garden city was the ideal combination of the benefits of rural and urban living. Howard then describes his garden city in great detail including perhaps the most publicized diagrams in the history of planning (Figure 2.3). The garden city which would have grown as a colony of 32 000 in the countryside, was also the vehicle through which Howard was able to forecast both the extension of municipal enterprise in all fields and the need to have teamwork to create fluid plans. The final chapter illustrates the way in which London's problems would be alleviated by his urban programme to achieve a so-called 'polynuclear city'.

Letchworth was the city that transformed much of Howard's dream into reality although it lacked any municipal enterprise, being developed by private developers. Here, Parker and Unwin soon grasped the essence of Howard's ideals and built what Osborne has described as 'a faithful fulfilment of Howard's essential ideas' (Howard, 1946). Welwyn Garden City was begun in 1919 on Howard's own initiative and remains as a museum to his genius and a permanent memorial to his undoubtedly fundamental contribution to West European urban thinking.

The ideas of Howard were gradually diffused in Britain partly by Parker, by Unwin in his book *Town Planning in Practice* (1909) and by Geddes who, in his work, acknowledges a debt to Parker to whom he was related. Governmental reports, such as those of Marley (HMSO, 1935), Barlow (HMSO, 1940) and Reith (HMSO, 1946), saw the need for new settlements to provide for the growing population and new industries although the *raison d'être* of the new town had diverged increasingly from the basic Howardian concept. Abercrombie's Greater London Plan in 1944 also contained similar proposals for new towns. Garden cities, *gartenstädte*, *cité-jardins* began to be built throughout West Europe following the translation of *Garden Cities of Tomorrow* into French in 1917. Letchworth, Welwyn and later Hampstead Garden Suburb were the models on which the architects and planners based their own garden cities adjusted to each nation's need. Schmitthener planned a garden suburb at Staaken near Berlin in 1913. In 1925 Floréal, a garden city, was built in Boitsfort near Brussels. Bernoulli was responsible for developing a Swiss garden suburb which was built in the Hirzbrunnen area of Basle between 1924 and 1930 (Gubler, 1975). In Germany Metzendorf acknowledged his debt to Howard when he designed Margarethenhöhe (Essen) for the Krupp family, while in Frankfurt, (Romerstadt) May was building a *Gartenstadt*. Howard's ideas were used in Finland by Saarinen. In Mediterranean Europe a garden suburb, Milanino, was built 8 km outside of Milan as early as 1910. Other Italian garden cities such as Tiepolo and Campo dei Fiori were developed after the First World War (Whittick, 1974). As early as 1912 Montoliu had founded a garden city movement in Spain which eventually influenced plans developed for Madrid in 1924 and the 1929 *Plan*

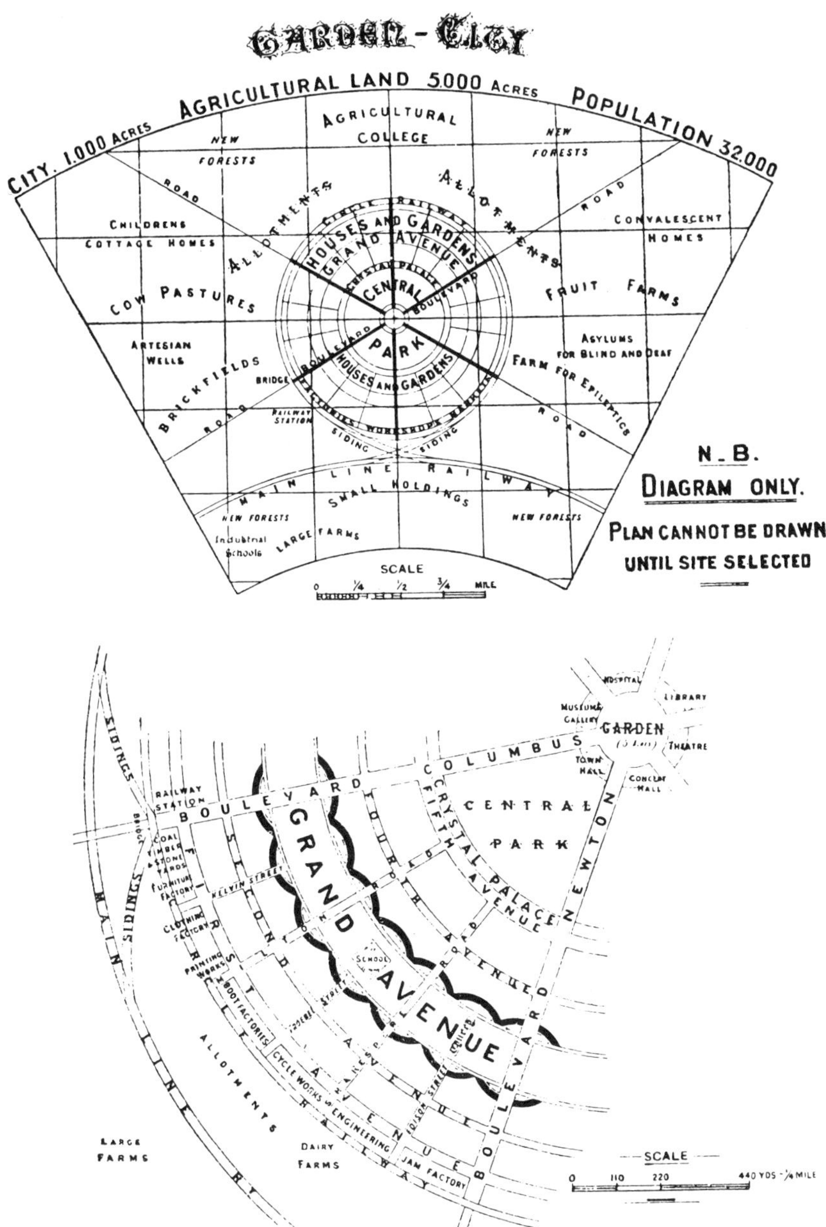

Figure 2.3 Howard's garden city proposals, 1898 (reprinted by permission of Faber and Faber from *Garden Cities of Tomorrow* by Ebenezer Howard)

de Extension designed by Zuazo and Mercadal and Jansen, one of Sitte's disciples. Throughout Europe, therefore, Howard's ideas were persued, although Merlin (1969) notes that those which came closest to his ideals were in Scandinavia.

Whether the new town can be seen as a further link in the utopian tradition is a matter of debate. Certainly the new town is not the same as the garden city in terms of its ethos, financing or size. The British new towns were more controlled though not strictly municipal ventures. Decentralization from London to the eight towns around the capital was very much in the Howardian tradition that Abercrombie, Barlow and Reith had followed. The plans that emerged after the 1946 Act did represent the realistic attempts by the new planners of post-1945 socialist Britain to create urban utopias. Perhaps the most publicized of all the plans were those of Gibberd for Harlow in 1947, which set a pattern for urban planning that wed transatlantic ideas on movement to social planning concepts from Europe in the context of the site conditions of Harlow (Figure 2.4).

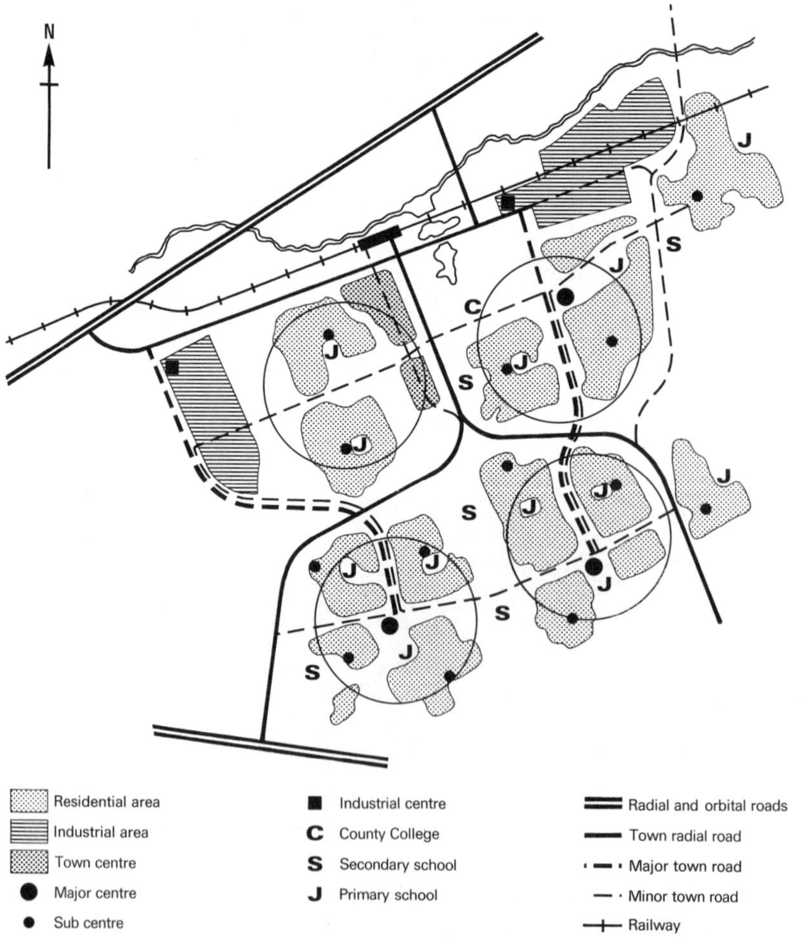

Figure 2.4 Gibberd's plan for Harlow new town, 1947 (reproduced by permission of Lund Humphries Publishers Ltd.)

The ready adoption of the new town formula for urban growth in the third quarter of the twentieth century is expanded in Chapter 13. Modifications of the formula to suit the needs and ideas of almost all the nations were designed and built. Many cases, as we shall see, were taken from other traditions and fused to provide the new town utopias suited to that culture.

Howard's utopian vision is a landmark in West European urban thinking. There are few urban thinkers whose ideas have been copied and modified as extensively. The themes of controlling metropolitan growth, decentralization, self-contained urban community and green belts are all part of what he called his 'unique combination of proposals'. His work represents the high point in a distinctly European contribution to urban planning whose origins are part of the European urban tradition and whose effects have been felt worldwide. The utopian tradition also had its offshoots of which the technocratic utopian movement was the strongest.

The Romantic Tradition

A tradition whose zenith was contemporaneous with that of Howard was the romantic tradition of urban planning. It was a direct result of the feeling of horror at the industrial revolution's impact on urban form on the one hand, and on the other, a reaction to the authoritarians' impact on the beautiful capitals of Europe. Camillo Sitte, whose work was published a decade before Howard's, was its main authority. He wrote his classic, *Der Städtebau*, in 1889 partly as a result of the Emperor Franz Joseph's 'haussmannization' of the *Ringstrasse* in Vienna, an act that Sitte condemned. By analysing the spatial organization and aesthetic values of cities and city planners in the past he began to identify the fundamental role of space in the city. He attempted to analyse the connection between elements in townscapes and saw the need for enclosed spaces which are characterized by irregularity, imagination and symmetry. In so doing he challenged abstract city planning and by reference to examples culled from his extensive travels such as the work of Alberti or Louis XIV he tried to introduce aesthetic values into urban planning. Streets, squares and plazas are analysed before he prescribed his solutions for modern city plans so that 'the monumental centre of a large city could be redesigned artistically in accordance with the teachings of history and the model of beautiful old towns' (Sitte, 1965).

Sitte's emphasis on aesthetic values was readily adopted in Germany and Austria as an antidote to autocratic planning. His ideas were utilized directly in plans for Salzburg and Vienna (Figure 2.5) and indirectly in plans for Altona, Munich and Flensburg by Henrici and by Pulzer in extensions to Darmstadt, Wiesbaden and Mainz. Sitte's work was translated into French in 1902 but his sole influence in that linguistic region was the preservation of the total townscape of the Grande Place, Brussels by Buls (Choay, 1969). Le Corbusier mocked the man and his thoughts perhaps accounting for his poor reception in France.

In Britain Sitte's ideas were first used by Unwin in designing Letchworth after the translation of his *Der Städtebau* into French (the English edition did not appear until 1965). Unwin brought together both the aesthetic values of the romantic tradition and those of the utopian garden city. Geddes also recognized Sitte's contributions to

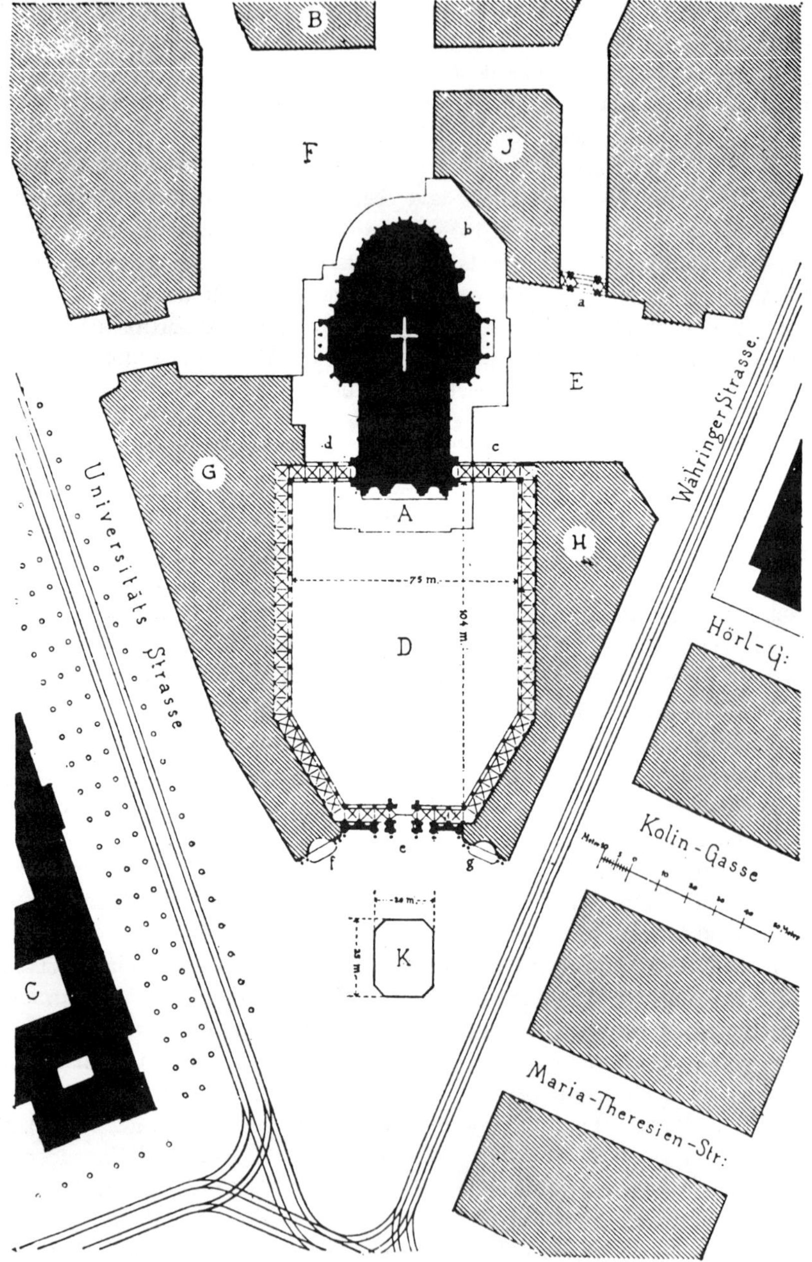

Figure 2.5 Sitte's plan for part of the Western *Ringstrasse*, Vienna. (Letters refer to suggested buildings)

urban planning. Perhaps the most deliberate use of Sitte's work, however, has always been in Scandinavia. In Finland for instance, the German architect Engel incorporated Sitte's ideas in his plans while the early twentieth-century plans for many Swedish cities, such as new developments around Gothenburg, placed great emphasis on detail that owes much to Sitte's ideas. Van Eesteren's plan for Amsterdam also possessed all the detailed studies that are the hallmark of Sitte's followers. In Spain Jansen was able to bring Sitte's ideas to bear on the 1929 Madrid plan.

Sitte's emphasis on town planning as a creative art had dragged urban planning out of the narrow confines of authoritarianism and uncoordinated utilitarian policies. It represented a parallel reaction to that of Howard especially in central Europe, and, like Howard's work, it has continued to influence West European urban planning theory almost a century later. Once again building and planning could be an art form.

The Technocratic Utopian Tradition

The origins of this tradition are inextricably bound up with the utopian plans of the eighteenth and nineteenth centuries in which the concept that every urban activity is open to a technical analysis is developed. In the same way the machines that form the heart of a town's industrial production was considered to be the proper core to a town. Technological power has formed the basis of this tradition from Francis Bacon onwards. Thus the earliest scheme, Ledoux's Chaux-les-Salines (1773), placed the factory at the centre of the industrial town. A second more influential origin to the technocratic tradition was Fourier's *phalanstère* (1829), a vast château-like structure to house his utopian community. Fourier's work attracted a similar interest in France to that accorded to Owen in Britain and his influence was acknowledged by subsequent writers including Marx. In 1871 Godin attempted to turn Fourier's ideas into reality at Guise but the rigidity of the system meant that it was not designed for the rapid social and technological changes of the nineteenth century despite the fame accorded to the Guise *Familistère*. Goransson's steel works village at Sandviken is another parallel, less grandiose scheme which dates from 1860.

By the turn of the century another design for the *cité industrielle*, a utopian vision of the industrial age seen through French eyes, had been propounded by Garnier. In his city the land-use zoning was strict and separate industrial, residential, hospital and central service areas were isolated by green zones (Figure 2.6). On the plans the built forms were monotonously repetitious and lacking the grandiose scale of the *phalanstère*. It was a pragmatic design that made the maximum use of known building and transport technologies. One plan in existence that acknowledges Garnier's direct influence is Perret's redesigning of Le Havre after 1945.

It was Le Corbusier who translated the vision of Fourier, Garnier and Godin into modern terms and who represents the zenith of the technocratic utopian tradition. Le Corbusier, Swiss by birth, came to live permanently in Paris in 1916 and by 1922 he was publicizing his *Ville Contemporaine*. This plan together with his later *Ville Radieuse* rank alongside Howard's plans as the most frequently published schemes in the history of urban planning (Figures 2.7 and 2.8). Le Corbusier embraced the technocratic ideology of the large-scale corporations led by the new technical élite,

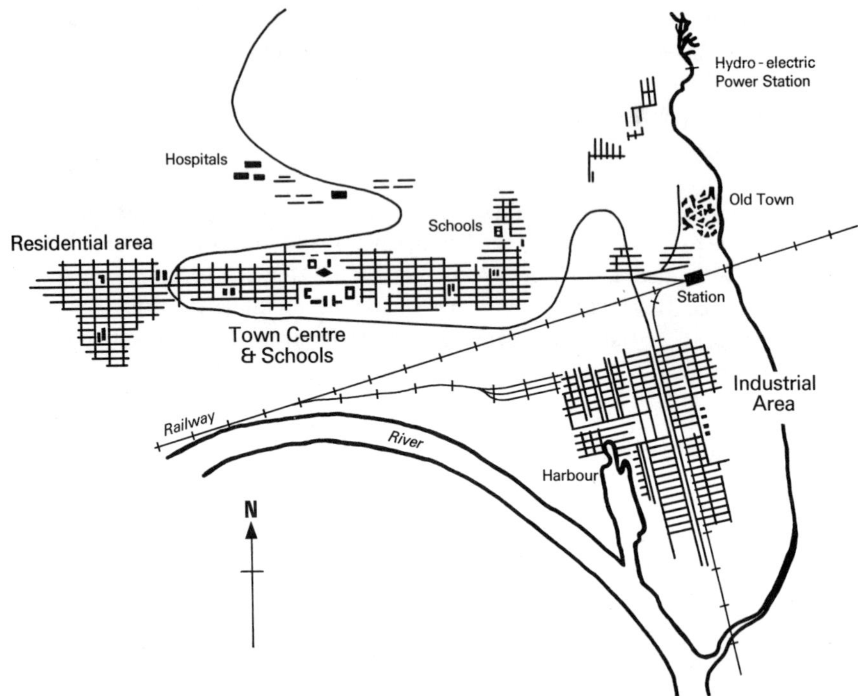

Figure 2.6 Garnier's plan of the *Cité Industrielle*

satisfying the demands of the population for improved living conditions. Thus the élite were made to reside near the city centre in high-rise apartments surrounding the administrative, cultural and entertainment centre while the rest of the population lived in satellite towns on the outskirts. The gridiron city which is characterized by green space with 85 per cent of its surface area devoted to parks, was to be a city of leisure as well as production, the physical embodiment of a social utopia that paid homage to the power of the giant machines that mesmerized Le Corbusier.

In an attempt to give his ideas a focus, Le Corbusier turned to the heart of Paris rather than to the suburban areas which had given birth to the plans of Howard and Sitte. In his *Plan Voisin* he put forward a radical design for the right bank area facing the Île de la Cité. Eighteen skyscrapers would fill the 2 hectares with the headquarters of international corporations, but neither they nor anyone else were interested in this vision that owed as much to the authoritarian antecedents of Paris planning as it did to the need to control the technology of the automobile and steelframed building structures.

Disillusionment with the reception of the *Plan Voisin* pushed Le Corbusier away from capitalism to the syndicalist movement where he began to design a new city for a syndicalist society. *La Ville Radieuse* written in 1933 (Le Corbusier, 1964) was the product of a more coordinated and directed society (Figure 2.8). The city centre is now the residential district which replaces administration with new *unités* housing 2700 residents, each apartment now being allocated according to need rather than position in the status hierarchy. The services of each *unité* like those in the

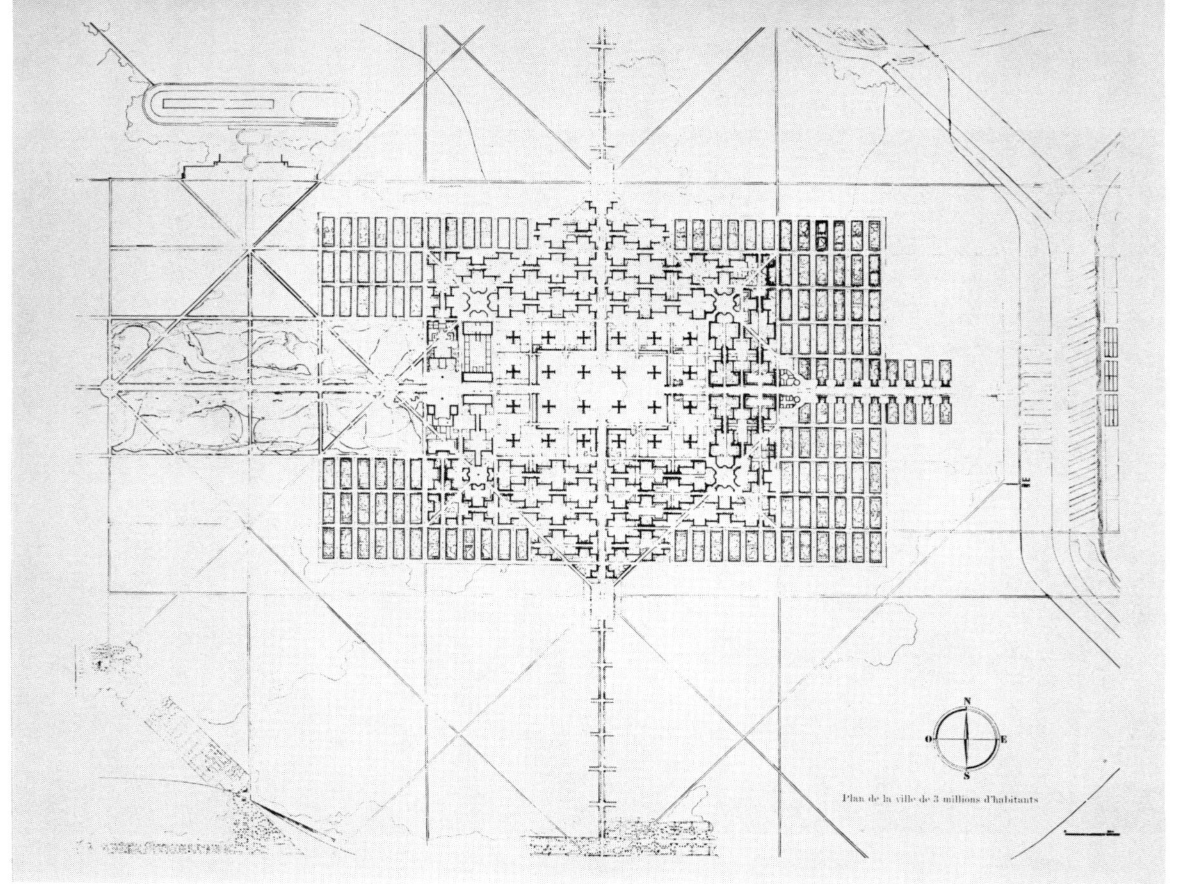

Figure 2.7 Le Corbusier's *La Ville Contemporaine*

Figure 2.8 Le Corbusier's *La Ville Radieuse*

phalanstère were to be in common. Otherwise the emphasis on green space and on accommodating transport remained. *Les unités d'habitation* in Marseilles, Firminy and West Berlin stand as the only memorials to the total idea which many see as having not only influenced a generation of French housing built since 1945 (Vance, 1977) but also the work of architects and planners throughout the world.

While not producing an ideal city the Bauhaus architects Mies van der Rohe and Walter Gropius were also concerned with society and the use of the new designs in concrete, steel and glass to serve society. They were committed in particular to socialism and their ideas had a definite influence on Le Corbusier's design for *unités*. The Bauhaus school designed long north–south oriented residential blocks separated by plentiful open space. These were built between 1927 and 1931 at Dammerstock near Karlsruhe and at Siemenstadt, Berlin to illustrate their theories of density and light. Although he left Germany in the 1930s Gropius did plan the Berlin suburb that bore his name, Gropiusstadt, which embodies many of his ideals that influenced similar urban developments in the 1960s (Chapter 4). Gropius's influence also came to bear on May's urban community built in the garden city tradition at Romerstadt. Sant Elia's *La Nuova Città* (1914) also utilized high-rise buildings in association with concepts of split-level living. At the same time Sartoris (1935) introduced to Italy plans for a belt city incorporating Le Corbusier's ideas.

Sartoris's ideas were not entirely new because the concept of a belt city was a technological solution to the problems of movement that had been discussed in Spain by Soria y Mata in 1882. *Cuidad lineal* could be a link between existing cities, a new urban zone of any length or a ring around an existing city; part of the latter did materialize in a suburb of Madrid. Communication was seen by both Soria y Mata and Cerdá who wrote *Teoria General de Urbanizacion* in 1867 as a formative element of the city, a technocratic solution that Le Corbusier and Sartoris used. However, despite predating Howard and Sitte, the ideas of Soria y Mata were not disseminated beyond Spain until much later.

The tradition of technocratic plans based on various transport technologies has remained as a guiding principle of many plans. Schumacher's plan for Hamburg in 1921 based its fingers of growth on communication lines (Albers, 1977). The MARS (Modern Architects Research Society) plan for London in 1942 made use of an elaborate transport plan to divide post-blitz London into sixteen urban tentacles spreading north and south from a central axis (Figure 2.9). This was not surprising because many of the MARS group were architects and future planners who had embraced the Corbusian tradition. The MARS plan was not unlike the Ruhr plan proposals although on a vaster scale. More recently Ling's plan for Runcorn is an extension of the same tradition married to other principles of new town development. The plans for Greater Copenhagen, Greater Stockholm and Evry (Paris), are other more recent examples where great emphasis has been placed on the impact of transport technologies. The emphasis given to technocratic planning is not that unusual given the fact that the new profession of planning that arose after 1945 had to recruit from pre-existing disciplines that designed our urban areas. Architects and civil engineers thus dominated the postwar burgeoning planning offices and their technocratic vision dominated city developments.

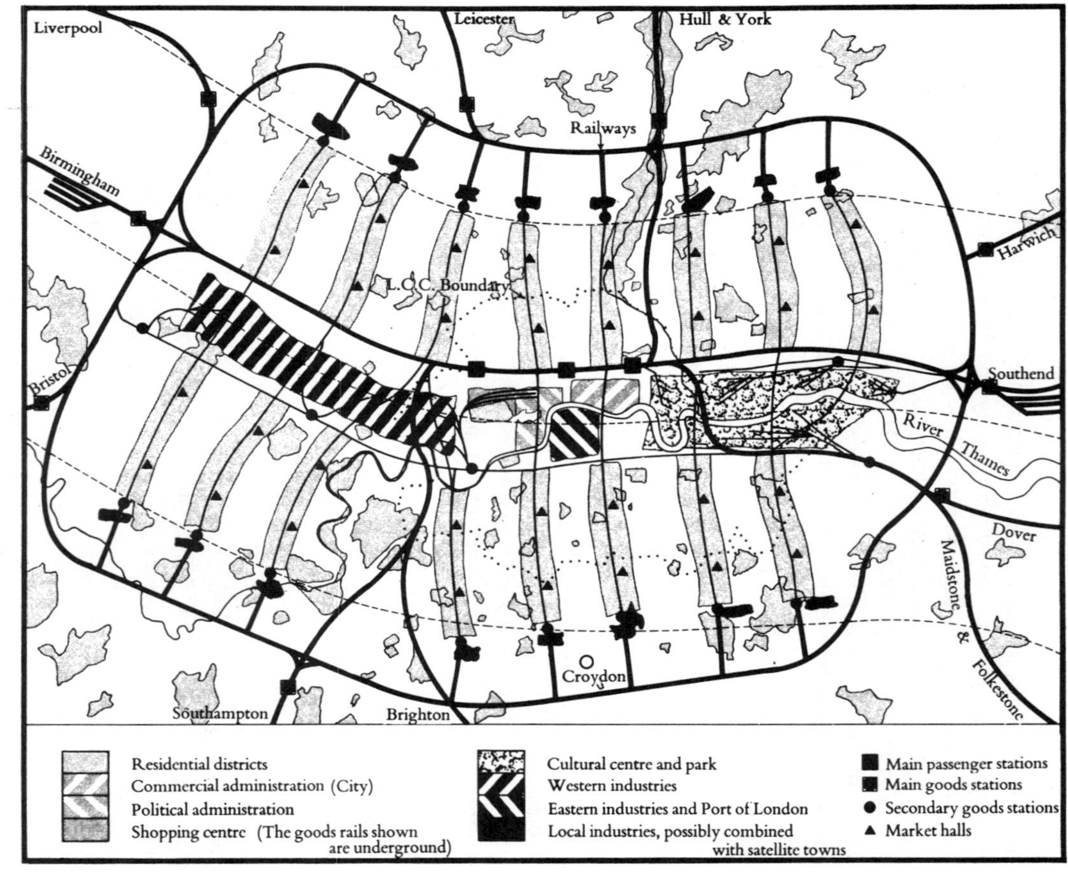

Figure 2.9 The MARS plan for London, 1942 (reproduced by permission of the Architectural Press)

The Tradition of Organic Planning

Organic planning has arisen from a better understanding of our urban past which came from the works of the utopians and romantics. The main emphasis was on the achievement of an intelligible order in cities. Therefore building uses may change harmoniously as they have in the Piazza San Marco in Venice. Parker was aware of organic planning when he designed unused spaces in Wythenshawe in 1927. However, it was left to Geddes to be the tradition's most articulate spokesman. No doubt his biological training had a considerable part to play in his emphasis on the constant reappraisal of needs. He also stressed participation and the need to make the city a living organism in all senses. It was Geddes who developed the term 'Science of Civics' for the purpose of 'making the best of each place in actual and possible fitness and beauty' as he informed the Cities Committee of the Sociological Society in 1919. Geddes (1915) also considered the city within its region in *Cities in Evolution* although it has to be acknowledged that Leonardo da Vinci discussed overspill within a city region context four centuries earlier and Mackinder (1902) had used the concept in *Britain and the British Seas.*

City-region plans rather than city plans are plentiful today. Abercrombie's *Greater London Plan* (1945) and Peter Hall's *London 2000* (1969) besides the official south-east region plans the South-East Study in 1964 and the Strategy for the South East in 1967 and the Strategic Plan for the South East in 1970, are all attempts at organizing the metropolitan growth of London while permitting organic change through the idea of study areas. Hillebrecht's model of *Regionalstadt* (1962) which has been partly realized in the concept of *Grossraum Hannover* and, for a few years *Grossraum Braunschweig* and Boustedt's concepts of *Stadtregionen* (1970) are German derivatives of this tradition. The *Randstad* concept of 1966 and the Greater Stockholm plans are all of the same genre merging the best of the other traditions in a distinctly Dutch or Swedish scheme that permits continuing modification. Continuously monitored structure plans such as the 1974 South Hampshire Structure Plan the Greater Manchester Plan, and the post-Skeffington participation exercises in British planning are developments in the organic tradition. In France the concept of the 'germ' being utilized by the planners of Le Vaudreuil new town and the openness of the plans for the third sector of Marne-la-Vallée are part of the same tradition that has produced flexibility for the future acknowledging the inevitability of social, economic, political and technological developments. In this sense the organic tradition could be seen as the attempt to merge the best of the earlier traditions. It also stems from the recognition of the inevitability and unpredictability of change among the modern planners.

The Socialist Tradition

There is one further tradition that deserves inclusion in this overview and that is the socialist tradition which has arisen from the work of Marx, Engels and their interpreters. It is a distinct tradition in one major sense and that is that neither Marx nor Engels, nor the other socialist philosophers, actually produced plans for cities.

Engels's work on the housing of Manchester's poor and Marx's *Critique of the Gotha Programme* (1968) describe the causes of city problems and prescribe the solutions in terms of a proletarian revolution, their utopian vision. Their vision grew out of utopian thought but they distinguish the 'utopian socialism' of Owen, Fourier and Garnier as 'castles in the air' and dialectically opposed to their 'scientific socialism' (Manuel, 1966).

The Marxists' criticisms of all city developments in West Europe are presented in the form of an analysis of spatial structure and its relationships to the influence of the dominant social structures. The major proponents of this view of the city today look very much to the lead provided by the works of Castells, perhaps the foremost urban political-economist in West Europe. In *Monopolville* he describes the social processes at work in Dunkirk in the 1960s and interprets their impact on the spatial form of the city (Castells and Godard, 1974). Therefore, 'master plans, whatever their scale, have an underlying social and political logic which varies for each plan in exact correspondence with the situation of political hegemony within the institutional apparatus on which the planning agency in question depends' (Castells, 1977 and 1978). To Castells, the city like the state is a tool of the dominant classes and urban space is a material element whose relationship to the dominant class is an important field of study. For Castells the term 'Spatial structure' is a description of the particular way in which the basic elements of social structure are spatially articulated (Pickvance, 1976). However, neither Castells (1972) nor any other of the growing number of planners and social scientists embracing Marxism has moved forward to any view of the city that might result from the elimination of the worst dichotomies that are discussed. Socialist cities do exist within the Italian political framework. Bologna has had a communist municipal government for the past three decades and might be regarded as the closest urban expression of a Marxist ideology given the constraints of Italian government policies. Nevertheless there is still no evidence of Euro-communism or socialism producing a visionary to match Howard, Le Corbusier, Sitte or Geddes. As Pahl (1977) has stated, 'In theory "socialism" and "modern big cities" are incompatible. In practice of course socialists must make do with the aspirations of territorial justice which often lead to further inequalities.'

Similar criticisms of the lack of visionaries can be attributed to the Weberian socialist tradition. The Weberian tradition separates economic and other aspects of society and enables the distinction to be made between the political and economic theories of the city which, in turn, enables the multifaceted phenomena that comprise a city to be disaggregated. Studies that have focused on concepts such as urban managerialism have attempted to look at one major group in urban society and the way in which they structure space (Pahl, 1969: and Williams, 1978).

Figure 2.10 is an attempt to relate the five major planning traditions and integrate the present-day socialist tradition into the same structure. It is by no means definitive but it does serve as an apt summary of the traditions of urban planning. The West European urban tradition has very deep roots within its nations. The traditions which emerge have frequently been reactions to dominant ideologies in various states disseminated by translation and built examples, albeit in imperfect form. These traditions of urban planning and urban thought have been of immense importance in

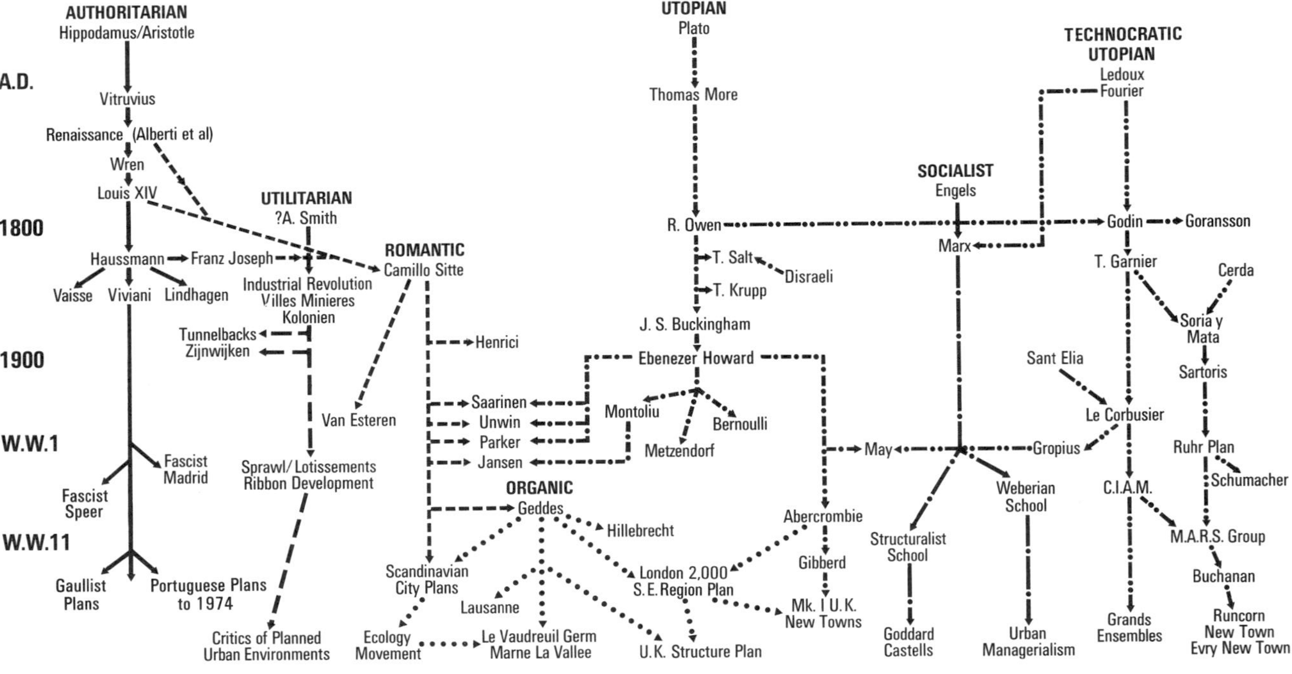

Figure 2.10 The European traditions of urban planning

moulding the form of the West European city that we see in the late twentieth century. One wonders whether the last 20 years of the present century will give birth to such a range of idealists as did the same period a century before. 'Progress is based on dreams which mobilise the mind, cause discussions, start movements and lead to realisations' (Doxiadis, 1968).

CHAPTER 3

Socio-spatial Structure of Cities

A consequence of a distinctive history, national identity and ideology is a distinct social and spatial structure of the city in West Europe. Besides, the study of urban society has many of its origins in West Europe in the work of Tonnies, Weber, Booth, Engels and Marx. Studies of the social patterning of cities have evolved as rapidly as the paradigms in the social sciences so that the descriptions of phenomena based on simple mapping techniques and simple causal relationships, have given way to methodologies which, hopefully, clarify the complexities of spatial variations between and within areas of the city both at a given point in time and through time. Underlying the recent studies of social geography has been the fundamental search for a model of the social and spatial structure of the city in the western world. The result of this quest in West Europe has been a reaffirmation that the city possesses certain distinct social and spatial relationships particularly in the light of comparisons with the cities of North America and Australasia. All too often such studies have been more concerned with perfecting techniques rather than making appropriate generalizations about the social structure of the city. Nevertheless, the outcome has been a move among research workers towards a greater understanding of the subjective nature of the urban environment by its citizens rather than the emphasis on supposed objectivity of the earlier studies. A more contemporary paradigm in the evolution of social area studies has been developed by those who see all social and socio-spatial divisions of the city as the product of the processes of social formation and the interplay of wealth, status and power. Despite the deep underlying differences between the methodologies of basic descriptive analysis, positivist approaches, behavioural studies and structuralism they each draw attention not only to the common elements of the West European and other cities but also to the obvious differences.

Descriptive Studies

(1) Spatial Models of City Structure

The simplest models of spatial structure evident in recent years are those based on the physical form of the city along an imaginary cross-section of the city. The technique has been used by Elkins (1975) and Ashworth (1978) to provide an easily understood picture of the German and Dutch cities respectively (Figure 3.1). Both models are able to emphasize the impact of history on the land use in the relict form of city walls

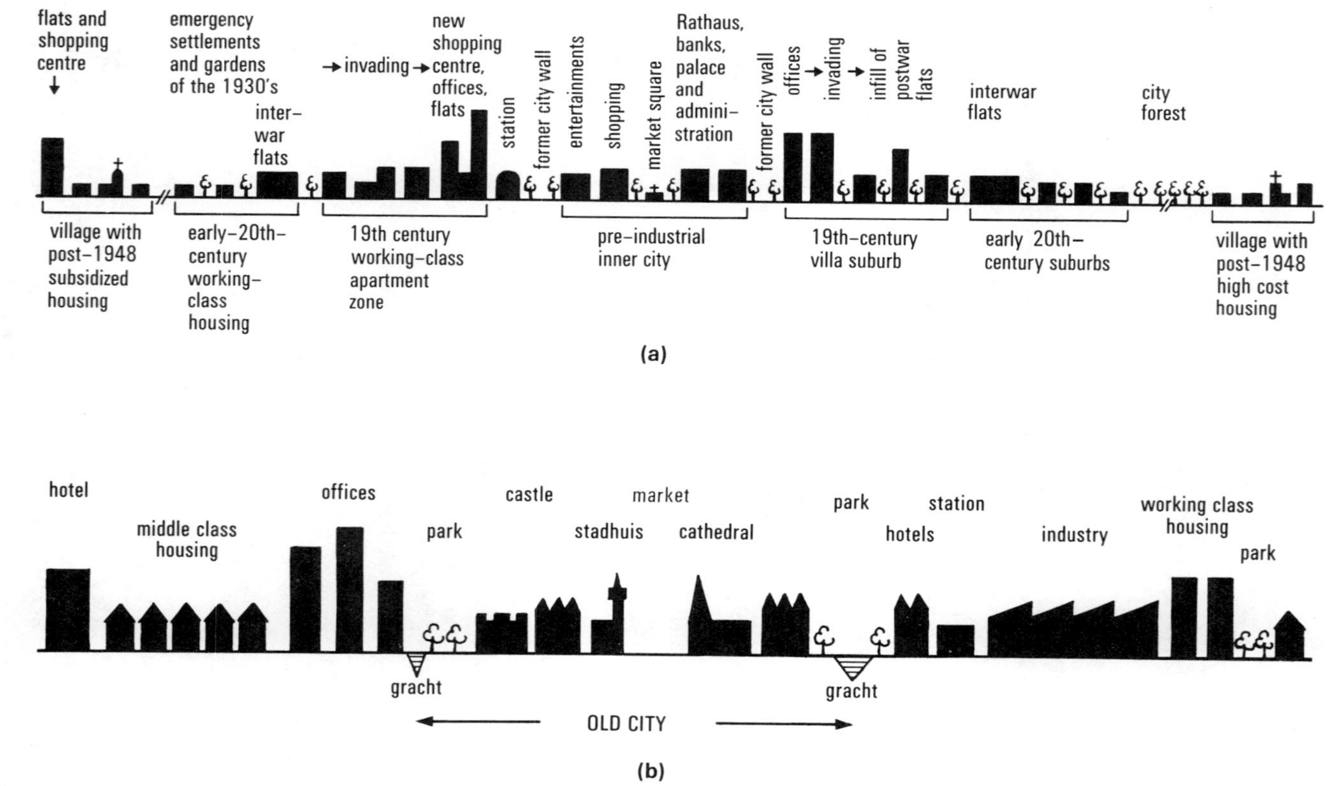

Figure 3.1 Descriptive models of West European cities: (a) Elkins' German city (reproduced from *The Geographical Magazine*, London); (b) Ashworth's Dutch town

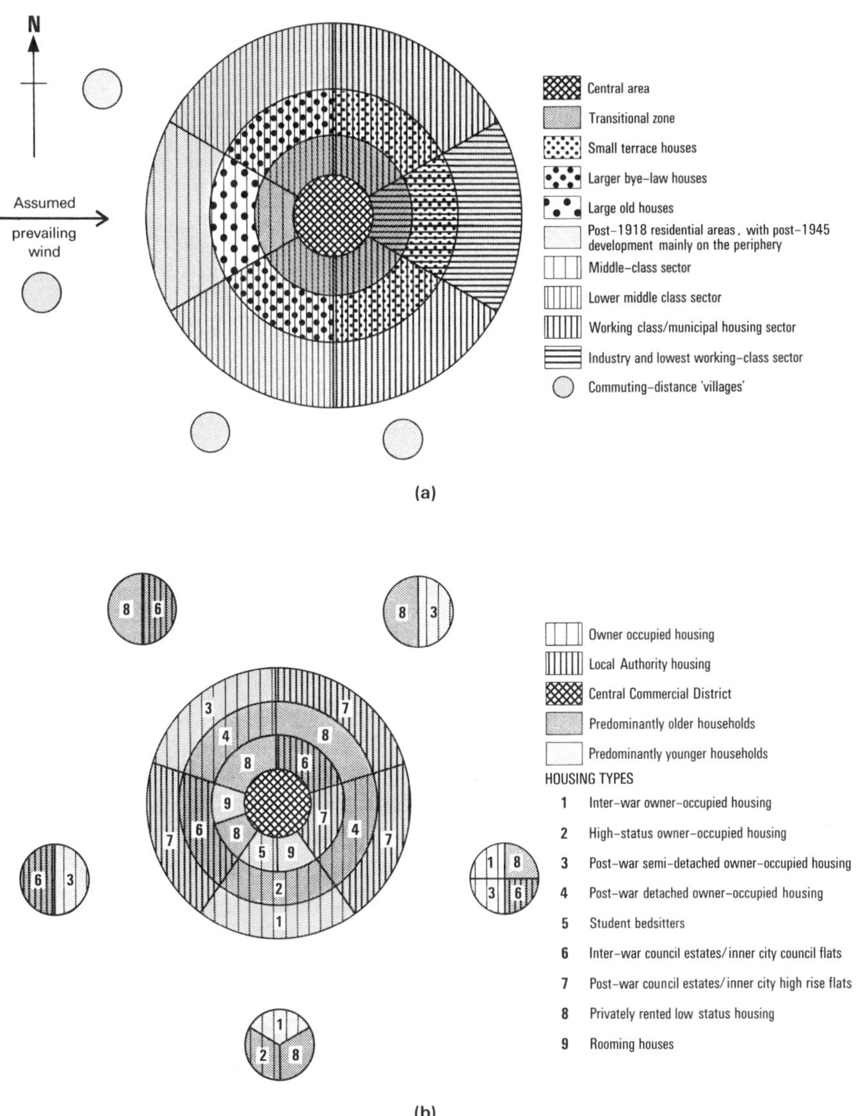

Figure 3.2 Models of the English city: (a) Mann's northern English city; (b) Robson's British city (reproduced by permission of Oxford University Press)

or canals, as well as in some of the unique design features present in the townscape of both cultures.

Others have taken as their point of departure, the work of Burgess and Hoyt and attempted to relate their own formulations, which were the product of more rigorous analysis, to the earlier models. In Great Britain, Mann (1965) produced a model of the northern English city based on a study of three cities. The resulting model resembled a cross between its predecessors containing elements of both the concentric zonation and sectoral pattern (Figure 3.2a). Richardson, Vipond, and Furbey (1975), in a study of housing in Edinburgh, were able to show that the sectoral organization of housing areas is stronger than any concentric zonation, partly as a result of the distinct physical geography of the city but, more notably, as a result of the peculiarly Scottish legal tradition of feuing. An earlier study by Gordon (1971) of the high-status residential areas in the same city over the century from 1855 to 1962 had already noted a factor in the city's socio-spatial structure that is present in many other cities, namely the presence of a relatively permanent high-status area, the Georgian 'new town', close to the city-centre.

Robson (1975), in summarizing social, housing and physical spaces in a British city, also drew attention to the mixed concentric and sectoral form (Figure 3.2b). The model is based on the more detailed quantitative studies that had been undertaken in British cities. These studies had shown how the age of housing was concentrically patterned whereas the socio-economic groups were sectorally organized. In many ways, Robson's model is more developed and tested than the other descriptive models from mainland Europe.

In German-speaking West Europe, similar models were developed at approximately the same time. Boustedt's model of the decentralized city is a very generalized descriptive model which attempts to incorporate the growth trends of German towns into their traditional historic form (Figure 3.3a). He distinguished residential, commercial, service and industrial areas but he did not distinguish between residential areas other than by distance from the city-centre and the ratio between day and night population (Boustedt, 1967). Later (Boustedt, 1975), the same author did attempt to examine the city within its urban region (*Stadtregion*) defining no more than a set of zones around a core city and the relationship between these zones and nearby satellite and commuter towns (Figures 3.3b and 3.3c). In contrast, Lichtenberger's model of the ecological structure of a West European city is based unreservedly on Vienna (Figure 3.3d). Her model, like that of Mann, recognizes the mix of sectors and concentric zones, partly determined, in the case of Vienna, by the course of the Danube and partly by major communications links to the west and south linking the city with the rest of Austria. More importantly, Lichtenberger does attempt to describe the major differences between European and North American cities. First, she stresses the function of the city core as a high-status residential area although there are, in addition, peripheral high-status areas. The old city within the walls maintained its residential function in conjunction with the development of commerce and retailing. Second, the inner city areas are very mixed zones of economic activities and residences with a more concentrated old industrial zone separating the inner city from the suburbs. Finally, the suburban area still contains

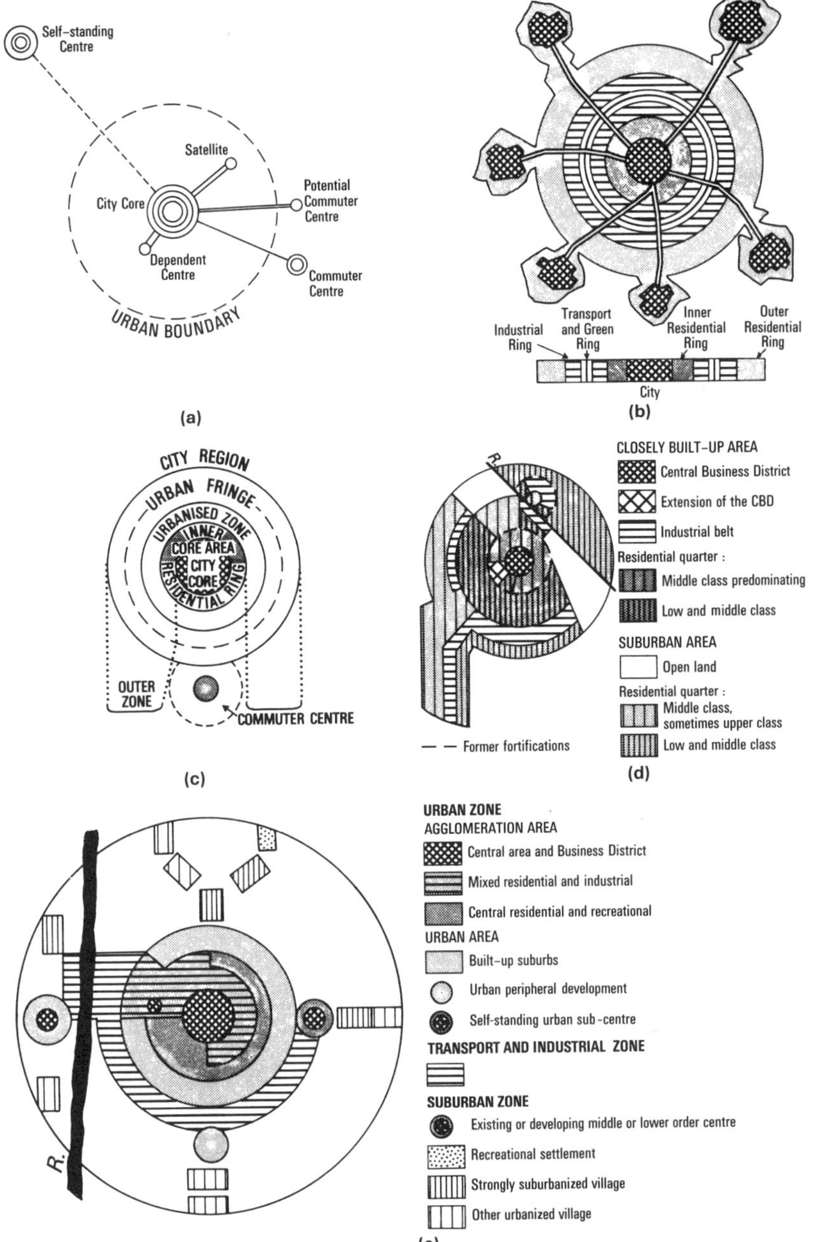

Figure 3.3 (a) Boustedt's decentralized city, 1967 (reproduced by permission of Akademie für Raunforschung und Landesplanung); (b) Boustedt's city-region, 1970; (c) Boustedt's urban region, 1970; (d) Lichtenberger's European city, 1970 (reproduced by permission of Pergamon Press); (e) Nellner's urban agglomeration, 1976

pockets of intensively used agricultural land apart from allotment gardens and weekend houses (Lichtenberger, 1972). In a later work a further divergent trend is noted. The European city had maintained a prosperous city-centre retailing area with an allied growth of suburban superstores in contrast to the peripheral centres and the commercial blight of the central areas of North American cities (Lichtenberger, 1976).

Nellner also preferred to base his model (Figure 3.3e) of an urban agglomeration on empirical studies, Karlsruhe and Bonn-Bad Godesberg (Nellner 1976). Nellner's zones are based on the residential and working population of each zone, the age of buildings, the proportion of rented property, the size of residences and the degree of change in form and functions. While it is possible to question the exceptional nature of the two empirical case studies, Nellner has utilized examples from other cities such as Frankfurt and Kassel to show its applicability to both large and small agglomerations.

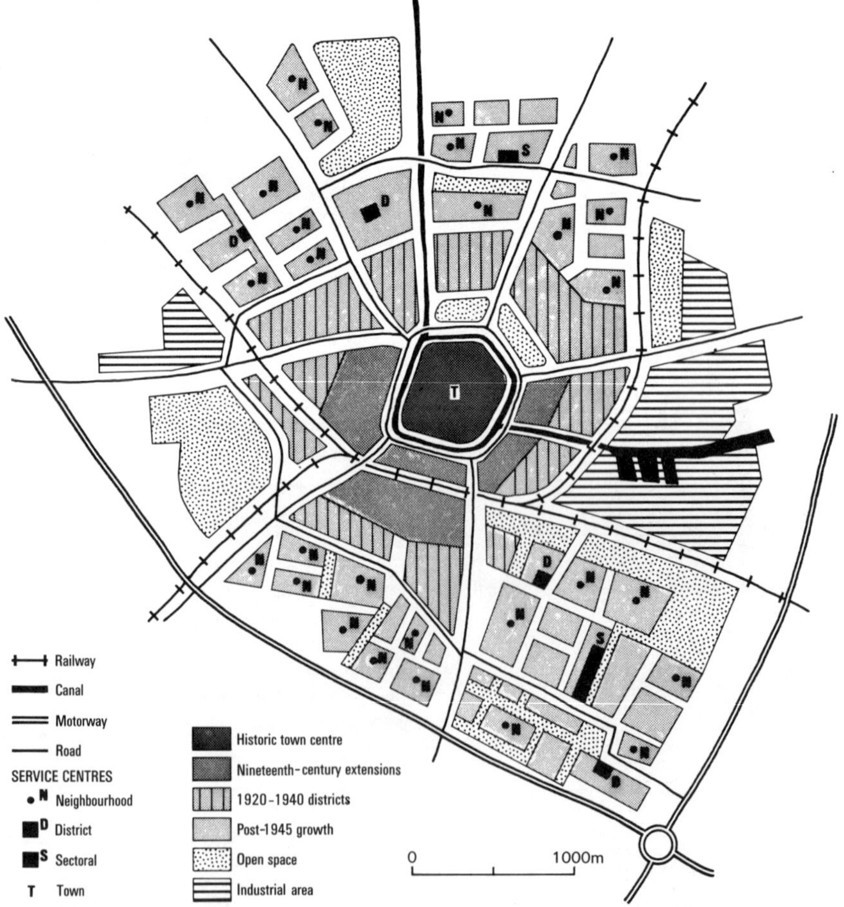

Figure 3.4 Buursink's Dutch town, 1977 (reproduced by permission of Rijksuniversiteit Groningen)

Buursink (1977) has produced a similar model of the structure of the Dutch town which, like the other models discussed so far, discusses the structure in the context of urban growth phases and the distinctively Dutch aspects of urban structure (Figure 3.4). Particular emphasis was placed in his work on the hierarchy of service provision in the postwar extensions but little or no commentary was made on the social composition of the extensions.

(2) Simple Social Patterns

There are numerous examples of the analysis of the social character of a town or city through the cartographic depiction and analysis of a limited number of variables. One of the simplest and most effective depictions of the socio-spatial structure to emerge has been Braun's work on Hamburg (1976 a and b). Braun's social areas of Hamburg for 1961 and 1970 were based on employment data extracted from the census together with some educational, housing and car-ownership data. The thirteen types of social area that emerge from his analysis of the 8410 census areas are described almost entirely in terms of the dominance of particular occupation groups or mixes of groups in an area. His social areas for 1970 are shown in Figure 3.5 which draws attention to several features of the city that more sophisticated

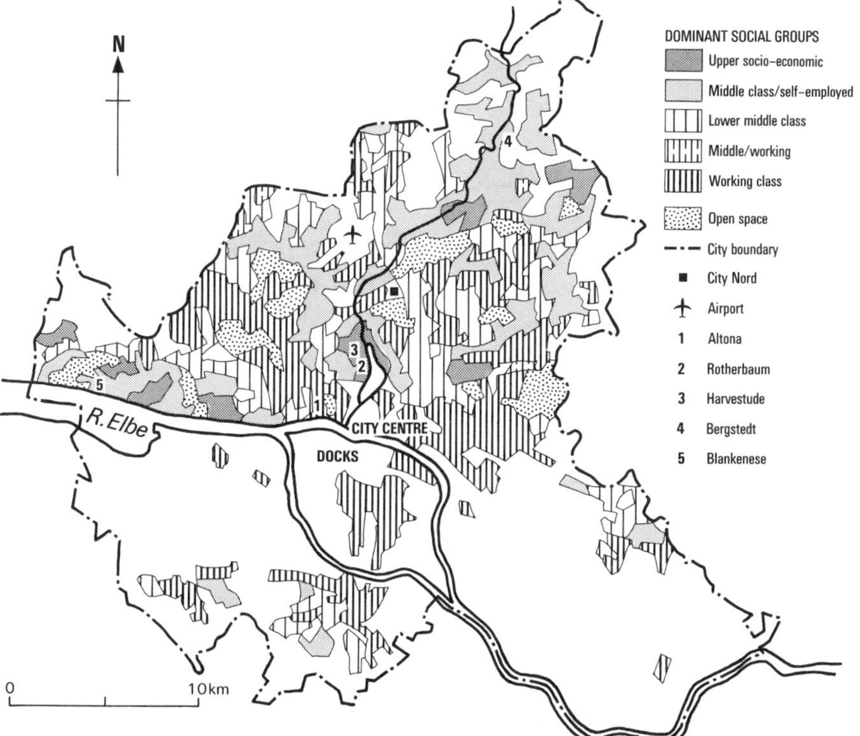

Figure 3.5 Social areas of Hamburg, 1970 (after Braun) (reproduced by permission of Planco)

studies replicate. As in Edinburgh, there are marked high-status zones extending west along the north bank of the Elbe from Altona to Blankenese and north from the city walls through Rotherbaum, Harvestehüde and hence north-east towards Bergstedt. Braun also drew attention to another trend visible in other cities, namely the tendency for the high-status sectors to become increasingly high status over the period 1961 to 1971 whereas in the working-class areas the balance of social groups has remained constant despite population decline. He also notes that the new fringe areas of high population increase have a more balanced socio-economic structure in 1970 than 1961. Niemeyer (1969) also drew similar conclusions to Braun in his study of Brunswick.

A different descriptive method of depicting the socio-economic composition of city districts was used by Gehring (1977) in his study of Luxembourg City (Figure 3.6).

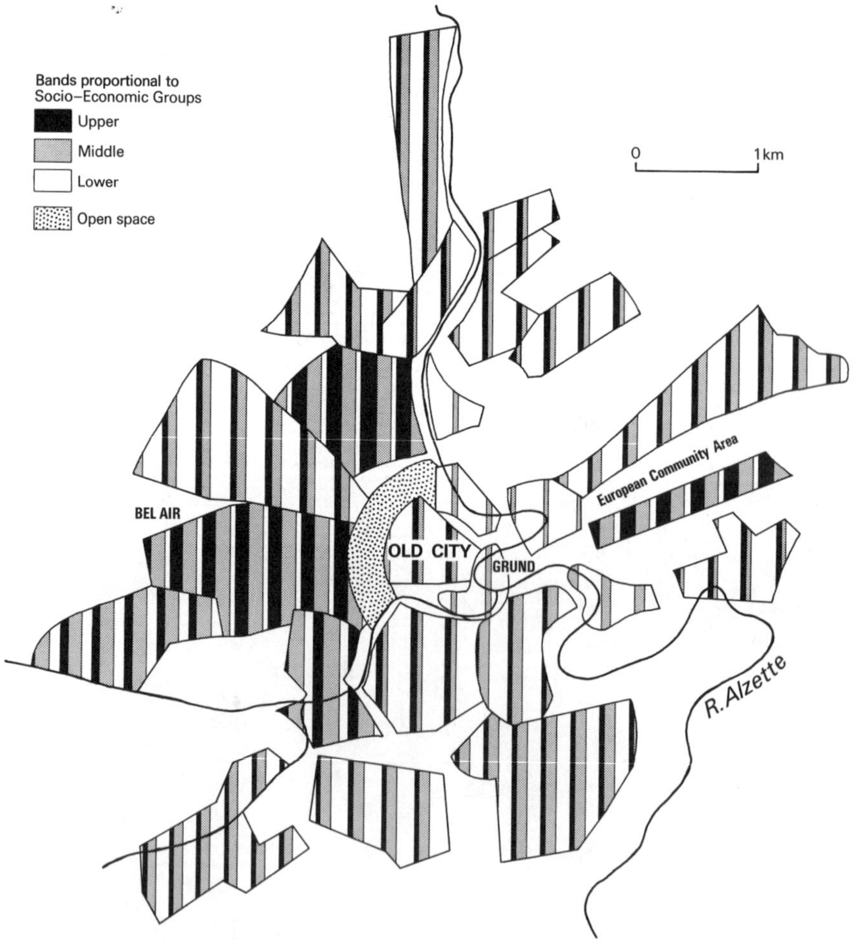

Figure 3.6 Social areas of Luxembourg City (after Gehring) (reproduced by permission of Centre d'Études Géographiques de Metz)

The distinctions between the dominantly upper and middle-class areas to the west of the city epitomized by Bel Air, the socially mixed southern districts and the inner dominantly working-class areas such as Grund, are discernible. The only exception is the dominantly upper-class area of Kirchberg surrounding the European Commission area to the east of the city.

Social Area Analysis and Multivariate Techniques

With the introduction of the more sophisticated methods of analysis from the English-speaking world, the analysis of socio-spatial structure of cities has relied very much on the work that has emanated from North America. What is ironic is that most of the English literature in the field is based almost entirely on non-European studies and the only West European studies are either by Americans or by Britons working on Britain or the New World. However, those studies which have followed the North American positivist methodology as closely as the data constraints permit, have drawn attention to important variations from the North American models besides enabling the researcher to modify existing theory.

One of the earliest studies of social areas by McElrath (1962) attempted to apply Shevky and Bell's principles of social area analysis to Rome. A second study was that by Herbert (1967) of Newcastle-under-Lyme. The deficiencies of the technique and the shortcomings of McElrath's and Herbert's work were discussed in detail by Robson (1969) and are not the subject of investigation here. It is noteworthy that similar French studies are absent mainly due to the lack of suitable French data sets. At the time, there was no data for Rome that would have enabled McElrath to look at Shevky and Bell's third dimension, segregation, and therefore only two of Shevky and Bell's dimensions or combinations of variables, the dimensions of socio-economic rank and urbanization, were compared with contemporary North American studies. Segregation data was not available, presumably because Italian society did not regard ethnic segregation as an important part of society and worthy of census investigation. This in itself suggests that, from the outset, social area studies based on the North American model might have problems in adjusting to European cultural norms. Other notable differences from the North American model were observed in the social areas of Rome. In the American studies, social rank was shown to rise with distance from the city-centre whereas, in Rome, social rank was highest in the central district, a fact that was explained as typical of older European cities where prestige centres on a central plaza. The urbanization dimension was noted as a sectoral phenomenon in Rome unlike the American studies, but no explanation for this difference was offered other than the scale of Italian and North American society.

A second pioneering work was Sweetser's (1965) study of the factorial ecology of Helsinki. Taking as his starting point earlier factorial ecological studies of Boston, Sweetser hypothesized that the three fundamental variables were (a) socioeconomic status, (b) progeniture or young familism, and (c) urbanism. He also hypothesized that a fourth factor related to home ownership would be evident and that ethnicity would fail to appear as a separate dimension despite the presence of a Swedish-speaking minority group comprising 14.5 per cent of the city's population. The resulting study did confirm that socioeconomic status, progeniture and female careerism were three factors that explained 58.9 per cent of the total variance. The third factor, female careerism, was a specific aspect of urban life which identified working women in high-status white-collar occupations. The analysis had already identified a developing feature of West European urbanization that becomes the subject of further analysis among Scandinavian workers in particular. Although Sweetser recognized female careerism as his third factor, it was in effect the fifth ranked, explaining only 7.6 per cent of variance; his hypothesized fourth factor related to home ownership was the third largest, explaining 14.6 per cent of variance (Table 3.1). Despite the inclusion of five of the 42 variables specific to the Swedish minority the ethnic factor did not appear; in contrast to the American studies the minority were found to be more numerous in high-status areas. Although not a factorial ecology, De Lannoy's (1978) study of residential differentiation in Brussels also notes the tendency for the European Economic Community nationals (excluding Italians) and Americans to concentrate in the outer south and south-eastern suburbs such as Ukkel and St Pieters-Woluwe. These are the high social status areas of the city. Sweetser concluded that 'the lesson is plain: variables which are of paramount importance in one urban socio-cultural setting maybe of no consequence in another'. Subsequent studies by West European workers have reinforced this opinion although few English-speaking authorities have been prepared to note this distinction.

The third pioneering study was that of Gittus (1964) who introduced principal components analysis as a method of grouping small area data in contrast to its earlier use by Moser and Scott (1961) for their study of British towns. Her studies of Hampshire and the Merseyside and South-East Lancashire conurbations established the validity of the technique which was developed utilizing more appropriate areal units by later workers.

Some of the West European studies that have used multivariate techniques are listed chronologically in Table 3.1. It is not our intention to review the methodology or to draw attention to the problems of data or size of areal units that are common to all such studies (Johnston, 1978). Nevertheless, there are several common elements in the results of the studies that merit comment. It is very noticeable that, in all the studies that we have cited, the first two factors are generally social rank explaining between 24 per cent and 30 per cent of total variance and urbanization explaining approximately 20 to 29 per cent of total variance. In one study of Amsterdam a second social rank factor is ranked fourth (van Engelsdorp Gastelaars and Beek, 1972). Thus far, the West European studies, with the exception of an interesting study by Friedrichs (1977) of the Hamburg city and region, replicate the North American studies. It is at the level of the third and subsequent factors that the major distinction from other studies can be found. Home ownership, housing, migration and potential mobility, agglomeration of age, building density are descriptions of the third and fourth factors in these studies. Only in Freidrichs's study does segregation appear as a separate factor; it is his fifth factor, explaining 10 per cent and 8 per cent of variance in his analysis of the city and the city region respectively. Friedrichs, like

Sweetser, Hamm (1975) working in Bern and Mischke (1976) working in Pforzheim demoted segregation from the role of an important factor in North American cities to a minor factor in West European cities.

It is possible to suggest several reasons for this intercontinental variations in findings. The first is the cultural factor identified by McElrath and Sweetser and stressed by Robson and most other European studies. A second factor is that the ethnic minorities have not been as large or as easily identifiable in the network of areal units in West European cities because the minorities arrived in significant numbers later than the censuses. While there is some substance to this explanation for the 1960s data, research into the distribution and immigration of foreign workers would suggest that these minorities were present in large enough numbers by 1970 and might have been identifiable in factorial analyses. It is more probable that other factors such as Matti's agglomeration, Schaffer's migration and mobility and Friedrichs's mobility are, in fact, surrogates for the concentration of ethnic minorities because the areas with high scores on those factors are concentrated in the city districts with the largest numbers of foreign-born. On the other hand, some would say that the absorption of immigrant groups, whether Huguenots, Jews, Turks, Poles, Algerians or Indians, are a part of the European urban tradition and that there is evidence that ethnic minorities can and do disperse both naturally and as a result of government policies (Drewe *et al.*, 1978). A final explanation that can be offered is that the results are a direct reflection of the data put into the analysis and that West European censuses are on the whole less concerned with ethnic issues. The evidence suggests that factor analyses have confirmed that there is a West European cultural variant to the social ecology of cities.

Robson (1969) in his study of Sunderland takes up the issue of cultural factors in the explanation of human organization and behaviour. He is in agreement with Jones's (1960) earlier analysis of Belfast which also confirmed that neither concentric zones nor sectoral organization explained the patterns of residential segregation. In the case of Sunderland, the impact of vast areas of local authority housing which had been a part of British housing provision for more than half a century, was most marked. In addition, the effect of planning controls could not be ignored. These particular interventions by local authorities were also shown to have distorted patterns in Exeter (Morgan, 1971). The subsequent principal components analysis of social, demographic, tenurial, household composition and housing condition data identified a first component closely associated with indices of social class, especially high social class areas, which explained 30 per cent of the variability in the data. The sectoral pattern of component scores for the socio-economic component mirrors that of other cities (Figure 3.7a). The two major areas with high component scores are both sectors. The second component was a measure of housing conditions and amenities which both distinguishes between areas of local authority urban renewal and private areas, and between the various peripheral local authority areas by age. The third component identifies those areas of subdivided housing, declining in value, which often house elderly single persons.

Both Friedrichs (1977) and Matti (1972) have undertaken analyses of Hamburg using different areas and selection of variables. Friedrichs's study of the city and its

Table 3.1 Multivariate analyses of West European cities

Authors		Gittus	Gittus	Sweetser	Robson	Herbert	Herbert	Van Engelsdorp Gastelaars and Beek
Date of publication		1964	1964	1965	1969	1970	1970	1972
Census/data date		1951	1951	1960	1961	1961	1961	1960–66
City		Merseyside	Hampshire	Helsinki	Sunderland	Cardiff	Swansea	Amsterdam
Methodology		Principal components analysis	Principal components analysis	Factor analysis	Principal components analysis	Principal components analysis	Principal components analysis	Factor analysis
Number of variables		27	31	42	30	26	26	31
Factor rankings and percentage of total variance	I	Housing conditions 44	Housing conditions 26	Socio-economic status 35.2	Social class 30	Housing conditions 27.4	Housing conditions I 26.8	Social rank I 30.4
	II	31	15	Progeniture 16.1	Housing conditions 29	Housing conditions II 23.5	Housing conditions II 14.5	Housing conditions 20.5
	III	7	11	Home ownership 14.6	Housing 8	Ethnicity/high status 10.7	Family status 8.7	Family stage 12.9
	IV		8	Established familism 13.8			Foreign-born 8.5	Social rank II 5.3
	V		6	Female careerism 7.6				

Table 3.1 Multivariate analyses of West European cities—*continued*

Authors		Schaffer	Matti	Friedrichs	Friedrichs	Schreifer	Vilsteren and Everaers
Date of publication		1971	1972	1977	1977	1977	1977
Census/data date		1961	1966–70	1970	1970	1961 and 1970	1970
City		Penzburg	Hamburg	City of Hamburg	Hamburg Region	Bremen	Arnhem
Methodology		Factor analysis	Factor analysis	Factor analysis	Factor analysis	Factor analysis	Factor analysis
Number of variables		No data	47	16	16	49 (1970) 28 (1961–70)	26
Factor rankings and percentage of total variance	I	Social/ employment status	Traditional social rank 24	Social rank 24	Urbanization 21	Social rank 18	Socio-economic status 31.4
	II	Age of population	Urbanization 20	Urbanization 20	Social rank 20	Family status 13	Family stage 26.4
	III	Migration and mobility potential	Agglomeration 14	Building density 18	Mobility 12	Urbanization 11	Housing 18.4
	IV		Age 6	Mobility 17	Building density 8		
	V			Segregation 10	Segregation 8		

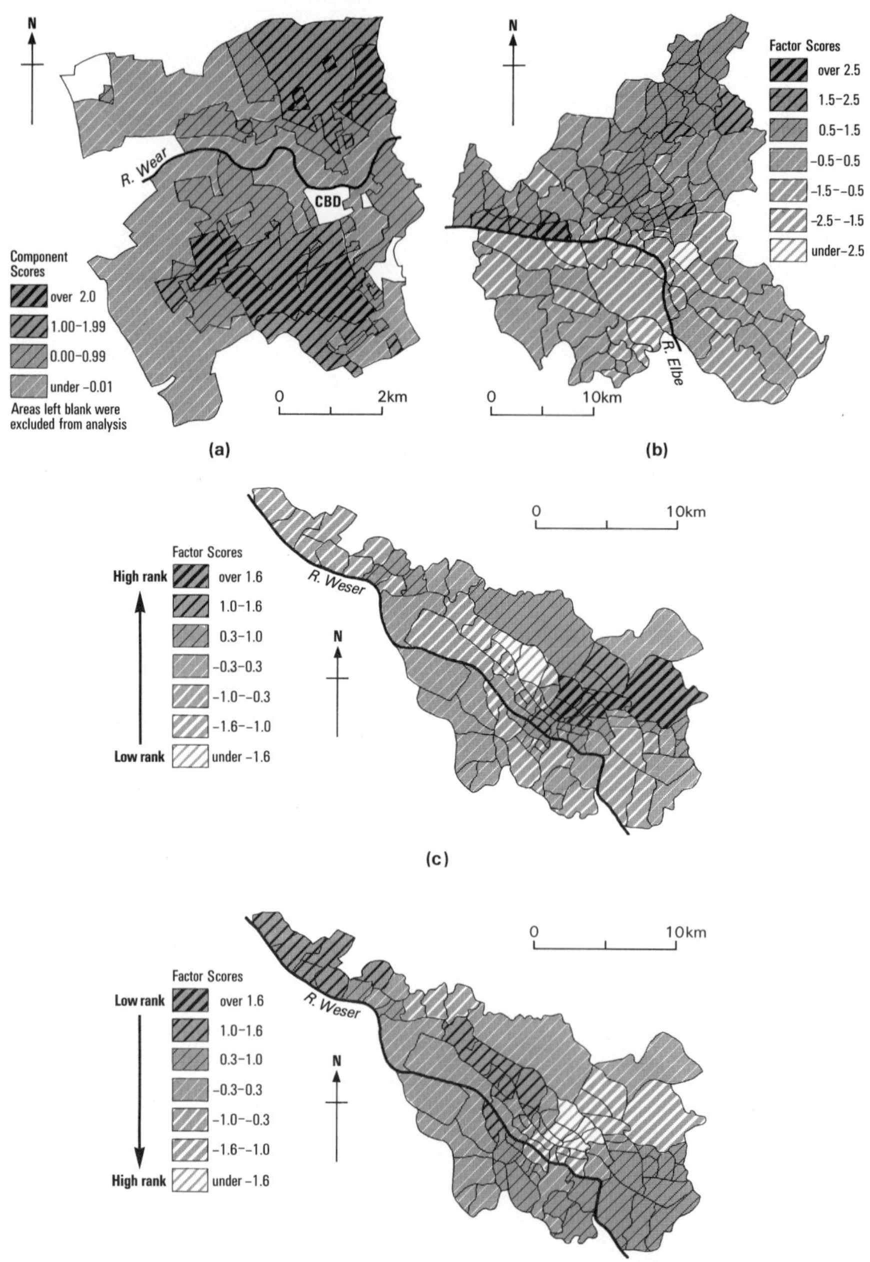

Figure 3.7 Factorial ecologies of cities: (a) Sunderland: component scores (after Robson) (reproduced by permission of Cambridge University Press); (b) Hamburg factor scores: factor I Social Structure (after Matti) (reproduced by permission of Rowohlt Taschenbuch Verlag GmbH; taken from *Stadtanalyse*, originally published in the series rororo studium—copyright ♀ 1977 by Rowohlt Taschenbuch Verlag GmbH, Reinbek bei Hamburg); (c) Bremen (1961) factor scores Factor I socioeconomic status (after Schriefer) (reproduced by permission of Bernd Schriefer, Bremen); (d) Bremen (1970) factor scores: Factor I socioeconomic status (after Schriefer) (reproduced by permission of Bernd Schriefer, Bremen)

region up to 40 km from the central business district used sixteen variables. The results drew attention to differences in the ranking of factors in the city and the region. The first five factors explain 69 per cent of total variance in the region and 83 per cent in the city, thus emphasizing the contrast that exists between the city and region in West Germany. Gittus (1964) also found that the percentage of total variability explained by her components were lower for the more rural area of Hampshire than for Merseyside. In the city (Table 3.1) social rank was the most important factor and the urbanization factor the second, whereas this position was reversed in the region. A similar reversal occurs with the third and fourth-ranked factors, building density and mobility. Matti's 47 variables, while different, were taken from the same census but with the addition of data on electoral behaviour and building structure (Matti, 1972). The first factor in his politico-ecological analysis (Figure 3.7b) was a social structural one that had high scores in the same districts identified by Braun's analyses of social areas for 1961 and 1970 (Figure 3.5). The second factor was highly loaded in favour of social democratic and communist voting, multifamily buildings and the retired, and was taken to be an urbanization dimension. The third factor, 'the agglomeration component', identified the peripheral regions in a similar fashion to Robson's components and could well relate to areas of social housing on the fringes of the city. It would seem from these studies that as a result of the interplay of culture and social history, the outer suburban areas of Sunderland and Hamburg are more similar than are the cities of West Europe and North America.

A further interesting facet to social analysis studies in West Germany has been provided by Schriefer's (1977) study of Bremen. His findings with regard to the 1970 data are tabulated in Table 3.1 and the familiar sectoral pattern of social rank scores has been plotted in Figure 3.7d. As in other studies, it is only the fourth factor, locational character, that contains high positive loadings on foreign-born populations. Schriefer was able to compare his findings in 1970 with those for 1961 although adjustments had to be made for changed areal units and a changed number of variables. He was able to show that in both 1961 and 1970 the ranking of the first four factors had not altered thus suggesting a degree of permanence in the socio-spatial structure of Bremen. The areas of high factor scores for socioeconomic status (Factor 1) for both periods are shown in Figure 3.7c and d. and show a distinct sectoral pattern characteristic of this factor's scores. Over the nine years the total variance explained by the first four factors had declined from 79 per cent in 1961 to 73 per cent in 1970. This is in line with all the studies based on 1970 data whose factors consistently explain less of the total variance than the studies using data from the previous decade.

Both Schriefer and Vilsteren and Everaers (1978) who studied Arnhem in 1976 used Rees' distance grouping procedure in order to categorize the social areas of the city. In Bremen, the distance grouping identified two types of high-status region, the centre and the sector stretching east. The newest residential areas are identified as distinct and two predominantly rural areas are differentiated mainly by the age of buildings (Figure 3.8a). The identical procedure in Arnhem was adopted and mapped at three levels of grouping, the middle of which produced a similar number of categories although the data used differed. The upper-class regions, as in Arnhem and Bremen, are sectors on either side of valued open space (Figure 3.8a and b)

Figure 3.8 Social areas: Distance grouping maps: (a) Arnhem (1970) social areas (after Vilsteren) (reproduced by permission of Katholieke Universiteit Nijmegen); (b) Bremen (1970) social areas (after Schriefer) (reproduced by permission of Bernd Schriefer, Bremen)

whereas the working-class districts are a mixture of districts closest to the Rhine in Arnhem and the Weser in Bremen, and peripheral areas interspersed with middle-class residential areas. This patterning is recurrent throughout West Europe.

Segregation

While most workers have paid attention to the dimensions of differentiation and the patterns of spatial differentiation demonstrated by multivariate techniques, others have turned their attention to the degree to which social groups are segregated. Normally such work has concentrated on the black population but, as we have indicated, ethnic segregation is a relatively minor factor in West Europe. Even in countries where colour of skin is a more obvious differentiating factor there is some evidence that segregation has decreased. Peach (1975) drew attention to the fact that West Indians in Britain were becoming less segregated due to the role of local authority housing in providing for the working class. Jones (1970) has also doubted the use of the term ‘ghetto’ in Britain where segregation indices are very low. However, Peach stressed that, at the same time, polarization or the degree of dominance in the West Indian areas has increased. It should also be noted that segregation is strong *within* the West Indian population, according to their islands of origin. In West Germany the foreign worker populations are dominated by different groups in different cities. In North Rhine–Westphalia, Duisburg and Cologne the Turks are the dominant group, in Bonn and Remscheid it is the Spaniards, in Solingen the Italians, in Wuppertal the Greeks and in Dusseldorf the Italians. Even the local gastronomy has been influenced by these concentrations! On the other hand, Drewe *et al.* (1974) are able to show that the Mediterranean-born foreign workers and the immigrants from Surinam and the Dutch Antilles were concentrated in the older, low-rent housing close to the centre of Rotterdam. Similar concentrations of the foreign-worker populations are also found in many West German cities but there is no evidence to suggest that their degree of segregation is changing with time, mainly because these groups are rarely resident in the city for longer than their employment contract; most return home within three years. They remain clustered often of their own volition rather than by compulsion, because of the strong links which secure them to their core area.

Studies of the degree of segregation between social groups have also taken their lead from North American literature. Gisser (1969) working on Vienna, and Belleville (1962 quoted by Gisser), in his study of Paris *intra-muros* have both drawn attention to the increased segregation at the uppermost and lowest ends of the socioeconomic spectrum. This theme was examined for a range of British towns and cities by Morgan (1975). His analysis showed that the degree of residential differentiation replicated the Viennese and Parisian findings more closely than it did for Chicago and Cleveland on which the study was based. The highest and lowest socioeconomic groups were more segregated, and the indices of segregation in all three European studies were higher for the uppermost socio-economic groups than in the two North American cases. The indices were approximately the same for other groups, with the exception of the lowest where the European cities had lower segregation indices than the North American cities. Therefore, the limited evidence would suggest that residential segregation in West European urban areas is more pronounced for the upper social groups, a fact that is reinforced in the maps showing factor scores for the social rank factor (Figure 3.7) and the social area maps of Braun and Gehring (Figure 3.5 and 6). Morgan (1975) was also able to show that segregation did not increase significantly with city size although the proportion of males in the professional and managerial occupations, which was influenced by the functions of the urban area, did find expression in the degree of segregation. The exceptional case of segregation is that noted by Boal (1970 and 1972) in the rather uneasy political climate of Belfast where the religious-based communities have become increasingly segregated as a response to conflict and the need to find psychological support.

Subjective Analyses

In his work on segregation Morgan (1975) suggested that more attention be paid to the socio-psychological variables that might influence residential segregation in comparative urban areas. Morgan's plea reflected a growing awareness that the statistically complex factorial ecologies did not necessarily explain the decisions made and the relationships seen or perceived by the individual. On the other hand, the areas that had been delineated did form suitable sampling frameworks, in Robson's opinion, for the behavioural and attitudinal research which sought to identify the socio-psychological subjective variables which aid comprehension of the social framework of cities.

There are two levels at which attitudes and perceptions have been studied; at the level of the national urban system comparing the image of towns and at the level of the individual urban area comparing images of districts of a particular city. As we have already seen in Chapter 2, the influence of particular movements on the attitudes to cities and living in cities has been far from even. The Corbusian technocratic influence was very apparent in the post-1945 programmes of municipal socialism where sheer scale and efficiency were, possibly, more important to the architect of Sarcelles, Hulme or Neue Vahr than the minutiae of design or true social well-being. The influence of the garden city movement was strong in early British new towns where the neighbourhood, the meeting of the urban and rural scales of life, came to permeate urban planning. The many early planning schemes were the product of a generation of planners schooled in architecture and engineering who saw themselves as social engineers to the cost of later generations. All these attitudes to towns and cities are just examples of how particular value systems can begin to colour or ultimately discolour our opinion of towns as places in which to live.

Most countries develop a social mythology about towns and cities that is frequently reinforced both directly and indirectly by society often through the media. At the national level, the economic fortunes of regions are reflected in attitudes to a particular place by major industrialists and by the workforce. Hammond (1968) was able to show that the attitude to Durham among Post Office savings bank employees moving to the city was based on a traditional view of the declining north-east of

England. An international company with manufacturing plants outside Portsmouth and at Greenock in Scotland has to invest more in recruitment of employees for the Clydeside plant because of employee resistance based on the traditional British image of the Glasgow region. Enschede was regarded by Dutch civil servants as a location akin to outer Siberia, 'civilization ends at Zwolle', an opinion that would find favour with British civil servants contemplating a move to Glasgow. West German workers and managers will avoid the Ruhr region but prefer the image of Munich as a place in which to live and work (see Chapter 6). In contrast, success in the sporting sphere may counter an otherwise drab image and foster an increase in industrial investment.

It is possible to distinguish the attraction of a town or city for residence and for work. In Zurich, a study undertaken by Iblher (1977) showed that the employer is interested in transport, the area available for a factory or office, the quality of the contact environment and the economic performance of other companies in the city. Transport, however, is the only common consideration for the potential resident. He, or she, is more interested in the availability of recreational activities, housing density, quality and price, education, consumer facilities, social welfare indicators and income levels relative to other cities.

On the whole, national preferences have been reflected in migration patterns to the Mediterranean coast in France, Madrid and Barcelona in Spain, to the south in Sweden, Norway, Finland, Great Britain (Gould and White, 1974) and West Germany, the north of Italy and to *Bandstadt* Switzerland, the urbanized corridor from Geneva to Zurich. There is also a preference for the medium-sized city which has replaced the metropolitan dominance of preferences in previous decades. In a similar fashion, images of the built environment within cities may be formed and indeed may be more powerful than broader regional images. Studies of housing preference have shown how restricted a search for space can become because of the relative importance to the individual of such variables as educational needs, access to work, images of status and the image of the area. The social identity of areas and the address can lead to stigmatization of areas. Damer (1974) recorded the public officials' and private individuals' stigmatization of council estates in Glasgow. Eyles (1968) noted that the desirable Highgate Village area of London was extended spatially by estate agents and by those living on the periphery who pulled the area toward themselves. Labels are given to areas by other purveyors of environmental information such as the local newspaper, radio station and house agent. The acceptance of the labels and images vary with social class, length of residence and residential location. Herlyn (1977) has drawn attention to the relationship between urban parks and the desirable residential areas in West German cities. The better residential environments which are highly rated in preference studies conducted among middle-class groups in Hannover, Bremen, Duisburg and Essen are close to the main urban parks. He shows how this desirability acts like a magnet drawing to it the other social services valued by the middle classes. These areas have more kindergartens, medical facilities and more streets sealed off to through traffic making them safer environments for children. The desirable district, therefore, reinforces its image of desirability.

Milgram and Jodelet (1976) have shown how the stereotyping of west and east Paris continues, with the result that luxury apartments in Belleville (19th *arrondissement*) are more difficult to let than the prized addresses in the 16th and 7th. Respondents saw north and east Paris in the 9th, 10th, 18th and 19th *arrondissements* as more dangerous, and the 18th, 19th and 20th as poorer, while the 16th and 17th were snobbish and rich (Table 3.2).

Milgram and Jodelet were also able to show that there were social-class differences in knowledge that reflected the spatial and social distance of the respondents from those areas that were least familiar to them. Thus, two-thirds of the middle-class residents of south and west Paris knew least about, in rank order, the 20th, 19th, 12th and 18th *arrondissements*, all in the north-east and south-east quadrant. In contrast, between a half and three-fifths of the working-class respondents felt that the 15th, 13th, 17th and 16th *arrondissements* were least known. All but the second-ranked are in the west. In keeping with other findings on social segregation, there is some evidence that the lower socio-economic groups know more of the city than their more highly segregated fellow citizens. Just as Jones (1960) indicated for Belfast, the social values of the population are an invaluable aid to understanding spatial differentiation.

There is much evidence that urban images of West European cities are difficult to form accurately because of their complex street patterns. They frequently undergo some degree of simplification before they are easily conceptualized even by their own residents. Pocock (1976) has demonstrated how irregularities are smoothed in Durham. De Jong (1962) saw the same simplification among Dutch citizens of Amsterdam and The Hague because orientation is difficult with a complex street pattern. A similar tendency was also observed in Milgram and Jodelet's (1976) study where the large meander of the Seine was flattened as an aid to simplifying the structure of Paris. Boyle (1978), working with Sunderland housewives, also observed the propensity to simplify the structure of the town but saw this more as a product of cartographic ability than other workers had suggested.

The study of behavioural patterns has developed considerably over the years partly as a reaction to the objective facts of the census used in multivariate techniques which say little of how people live. One exception to this rule has been the work of Woessner and Bailly (1979) who analysed the images of central Mulhouse with the aid of both principal components analysis and correspondence analysis besides the more traditional methods of analysis. The most important factors explaining the perception of the centre were sex and age and then, in rank order, socioeconomic group, area of residence, length of residence, university training and cultural values. Not only are male/female differences notable but also employed/non-employed which is partly a reflection of male and female roles in society. For men, the centre has parking problems and possesses cinemas and cafes. For the women, the centre is a shopping area and a place they would like to live. Ageing alters the Mulhousians' view of the city-centre particularly in the case of lifelong residents. From a teenage viewpoint of the city centre as marginal to their life, the city centre rises to be a focal point of urban life in middle age only to decline as a focus in old age. With increasing age and length of residence the old town becomes more and more the focus of the town.

Table 3.2 Qualities ascribed to different *arrondissements* of Paris

Qualities	First ranked	per cent ascribing	Second ranked	per cent acribing	Third ranked	per cent ascribing	Fourth ranked	per cent ascribing
Paris of the rich	16	87.6	17	20.6	8	18.3	7	17.0
Paris of the poor	18	38.5	19	31.7	20	29.8	13	11.0
Dangerous Paris	18	38.5	9	31.7	10	29.8	19	11.0
Areas you like best	6	70.6	4	65.1	1	57.8	5	51.4
Areas in which you would refuse to live under any circumstances	18	37.2	19	27.1	10	18.3	8	17.0
Areas you know best	6	73.9	1	61.5	5	58.3	8	57.8
Areas you know least well	20	60.1	13	58.7	19	57.3	18	55.0
Snobbish Paris	16	49.1	6	15.1	8	14.7	17	9.6
'Paris des Bretons'	15	50.0	4	34.9	6	23.4	—	—
Where you would move if you became wealthy	6	33.9	4	31.2	7	24.8	16	21.6
Friendlier, more relaxed atmosphere	6	30.3	5	22.5	4	18.3	7	14.7
Greatest loss of pleasant qualities because of urban renewal	15	43.1	1	14.2	13	13.8	6	10.1

Source: Milgram and Jodelet (1976)

While the areal units from the factorial ecologies provide useful sampling frames they do not explain, as Robson pointed out for Sunderland, why different attitudes and behaviour are present in similar areas. Much emphasis has been placed, in particular, on identifying areas of social malaise and multiple deprivation in cities, indicating their concentration in certain areas of the city (Boal *et al.*, 1974, and Herbert, 1976). Obviously, what is malaise and deprivation is very much socially determined and studies have concentrated on the more obvious manifestations of, for example, criminality, which can reflect a society's concern for property. Thus, studies of vandalism and juvenile delinquency are easier to mount than studies of tax evasion or fraud (Pahl, 1970).

More indication of how people live can be gained from the use of social indicators derived from censuses and surveys which point all too clearly to the areas possessing the worst living conditions. These are in the inner city such as Tower Hamlets, London; Wilhelmsburg, Hamburg; Hochfeld, Duisburg; and Folie-Mercourt, Paris. However, outer city local authority estates can be identified as deprived using the same criteria. The policy result is frequently area-based policies such as the British general improvement areas, housing action areas and community development projects or the inner city partnerships in London, Liverpool, Birmingham, Manchester–Salford and Newcastle–Gateshead, or the West German *Sanierungsgebiet* (renovation areas), or the Dutch *Stadsvernieuwing gebieden* which, many would argue, do not get to the roots of the problems but merely attempt to alleviate the worst symptoms of the disease (Smith, 1979).

Not all the indicators under investigation in West European cities necessarily point to malaise. It is important also to understand the changing demographic structure of the urban population. Population growth has traditionally featured very strongly in urban planning theory and practice since 1945. However, the downturn in the birth rate which began in the years after 1964 has brought in its wake not only changed planning needs, which will be discussed in later chapters, but also changes in the social patterns and behaviour in West European cities. Household composition is altering rapidly as Table 3.3 indicates for West Germany. Both the extended family and the large family have declined as the number of single-person households has risen. Since 1972 over half the West German households contain no children. As fewer children are born so the population 'ages'. The central areas tend to have greater concentrations of older people, frequently living alone in dwellings which they have inhabited for over a decade. Over half the households in West German city-centres are one or two-person households (Herlyn, 1975; and Lob and Wehling, 1977).

The demographic trends in British cities have been shown by Abrams (1978) to be very similar. Single-person households, which numbered 3.5 million in 1970, are predicted to rise to 5.5 million by 1990 of which 75 per cent will be elderly persons. This fact of increasing age is also reflected in the median age of the population which was 24 in 1900, 34 in 1976 and will be 38 by the year 2000.

The changes in birth-rate and household size have important effects on the lifecycle of women in particular. Reduced family size enables women to contemplate a return to paid employment earlier on completion of the family. Likewise, delayed

Table 3.3 Some trends in household composition in West Germany

	1950 per cent	1961	1970	1974
Three- or four-generation households	No data	9.0	No data	4.0
Single-person households	9.0	9.6	12.6	14.1
Percentage of population in households of over five persons	32.0	28.7	27.2	23.9

commencement of childbearing has enabled some couples to increase expenditure early in the lifecycle on important aspects of social status manifestation such as housing. The time that couples have in the middle of the lifecycle without responsibility for children has increased as well. The outcome of all these trends is a general increase in the number of women working, a fact partly determined by new conventional attitudes and partly by economic necessity for many. The new dual-career households make a mockery of socioeconomic ranking data based on the husband's employment and, perhaps, lend weight to demands for new ways of recognizing family socioeconomic status in relation to two careers, one of which might be dormant.

The impact of the changing demographic structure and household structure, when combined with the predictions of changes in the employment structure of societies, will have consequences for the social morphology of cities. The growth of tertiary and quaternary sector employment in the last two decades has produced an increasingly white-collar society with white-collar needs and aspirations. The pressure is for the city authorities to respond to the demands, not only for more space for banking, insurance, local government and other allied office functions (see Chapter 4) but also for space suitable for housing the new office workers. On the whole, the supply of housing for the new bourgeoisie who can be the recipients of high industrial wages, or dual-career families, has lagged behind demand, with the inevitable outcome that the most desirable areas become more socially and spatially segregated. Any impact on cities will also vary between countries and regions within that country. Whether these trends will continue with the changes in employment that are forecast following the microprocessor revolution is not the subject of this analysis, suffice it to say that forecasts indicate a potential swing to personal service and recreation-based activities. One proviso that has to be made is that the demographic and economic changes might not affect the processes of allocation of urban space.

A further important body of behavioural work that has been developed in West Europe, initially serving the distinct cultural needs of European societies, is the group of studies best summed up by the title 'time geography'. The outcome of the empirical work of the Swedish geographers Hägerstrand, Carlstein and Lenntorp has enabled planners to take account of the activity patterns of individuals so that these can be best accomodated within cities by the location of facilities such as day nurseries, banks and libraries, or the routing of public transport and even alternative futures for Swedish society. One aim of the studies is that greater order can be given to the locations of human activity so that all in society may gain the greatest benefits. This aim obviously accords with the dominant Swedish social democratic ideology over several decades. It is a tribute to the Lund team that time geography is used as a policy-making aid by the Swedish government. Similar studies have been undertaken by Dürr (1972) and the SAS Group (1976) in Hamburg, Kutter (1973) in Brunswick, and Klingbeil (1976) in Munich. They all point to the differential life spaces available to citizens based on home location, age, employment, number of children and availability of transport. The analyses of cities that have concentrated on the subjective environment have served to emphasize the role played by attitudes and behaviour in shaping the social morphology of the city. There are attitudes and behaviour patterns in Europe that have enabled the core of most cities to retain a high-status residential area and which have maintained and reinforced the desirability of specific built environments until they become areas of conservation. Studies of malaise have identified problem environments possibly in too deterministic a fashion although one must also be wary of interpreting other demographic and social indicators in a similar fashion. With many of these studies it is probably too early to identify the specifically European patterns of behaviour, although there must be European processes that give rise to the distinctive social patterns that were outlined earlier in the chapter.

'Radical' Studies

The dissatisfaction with both the positivist approaches of multivariate analysis and the behavioural approaches stemmed partly from the fact that neither approach offered any all-encompassing explanation for the socio-spatial framework of cities. This explanation, as indicated in the two previous chapters, has been provided in particular by the radical analyses of social processes within cities. The city cannot be analysed in the view of the structuralists apart from the web of structural interests which determine it. It might not be solely the structure of a given society at one point in time but rather the impact of a series of ideologies which have each created their own city. Thus, in its built form, the city becomes a palimpsest of past ideologies as Lichtenberger (1970) indicates in her studies.

Perhaps the most important modern exponent of the structuralist approach has been Castells and in his analysis with Godard of Dunkirk (Castells and Godard, 1974) he has attempted to show how the particular approach offers an explanation for the complex processes of spatial segregation. Structuralism has a particularly strong tradition in France which dates back to Lévi-Strauss. Castells' main theoretical stance was outlined in his earlier work *La Question Urbaine* (1972): that a society and the social forms of that society such as space are the product of the actions of individuals whose behaviour is determined by the individual's location within the structure of society and by the individual's economic power. The social-class conflicts that are the consequence of the structure of capitalist society are expressed through and in urban planning and urban social movements such as the protest movements opposing urban renewal in Paris (Castells, 1978) and those opposing motorways in Barcelona (Borja, 1978).

For his major empirical analysis (Castells and Godard, 1974) the city of Dunkirk was selected because the city was undergoing rapid expansion following the establishment of the USINOR steel plant, an enlarged port, oil refineries and shipyards. The new economy of the town produced advantages for industrial development, for the development of the centre and its office and retail function allied to the growth of a residential area for the managers, and the development of a new working-class housing area related to redevelopment of older housing areas and rural housing. Besides these groups, there is a small local middle class who are trying to manage the local community against the growing power of the former three social groups. These are represented politically by the Gaullists and apolitical groups in control of the city, the social democratic group controlling the *département* and the socialist communist union with its power base in the working-class areas. Not only are these groups socially and politically separate but they are also spatially segregated (Figure 3.9). Migration patterns are reinforcing segregation, as we have seen in other cities; 80 per cent of residential movement is to areas of similar social status and between 32 and 37 per cent of movement is within the same *commune*. High status has become concentrated by the sea while the rest of the housing is spread through the city with relatively weak segregation.

Castells goes on to illustrate how the varied social interests struggle for power and how the ideologies of each group find expression in the townscape. The official planning documents become tools of the struggle used by the dominant groups to aid continuing control. Infrastructural improvements are seen as ways by which it is hoped that the town will approve of the national proposals for new urban areas. The establishment of the *Maison de la Culture* is seen as an example of the bribery of the middle classes. The development plans are instruments of social control and, as such, the *Livre Blanc* is seen as the product of the commercial middle classes of the town and the big industrial managers of the port because it argues for a town centred on the old core and the new port-industrial region. The social conflicts in Dunkirk can be crystallized into four groups:

(1) opposition between the old and the new;
(2) opposition between the middle classes and workers;
(3) opposition between Dunkirk/Flemish/port and the suburban/foreign/industrial zones; and
(4) opposition between the town and the country—a dichotomy that has had no substance in England and Wales (Pahl, 1970).

In diagrammatic form (Table 3.4), these conflicts explain almost completely the form of the built-up areas of the city especially when they occur in combination. The combinations of conflicts are the basis of four ideologies. First, the ideology of consumerism which is characteristic of the dominant middle classes. This is the ideology of dominance of new over old, middle class over workers, the immigrant over the local and the town over the country. Second, is the family ideology of the

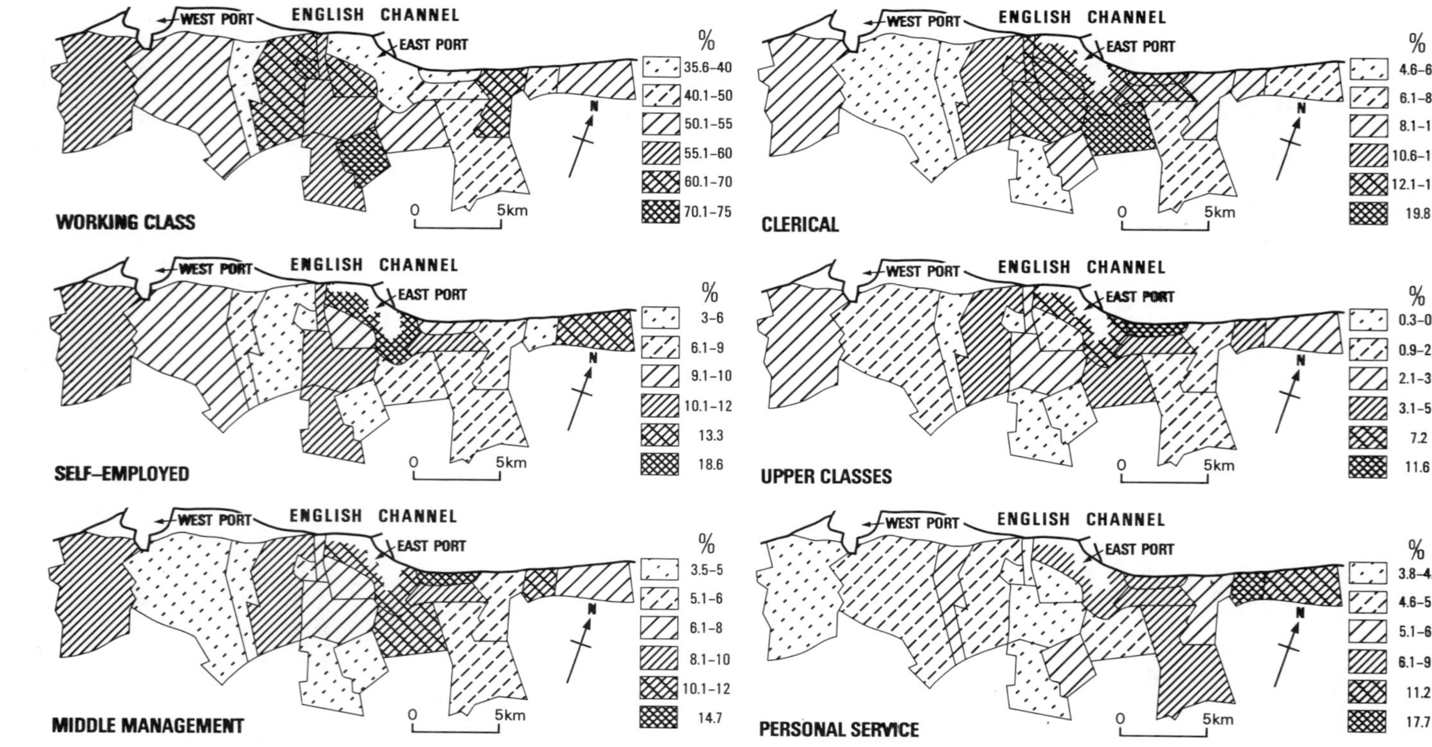

Figure 3.9 Social areas of Dunkirk (after Castells) (reproduced by permission of Mouton, Paris)

Table 3.4 Urban conflicts and their spatial expressions

		New developments		Old districts	
		Middle class	Workers	Middle class	Workers
Country	Local Fleming/Dunkirk	? Lacking substantiation (existing in places)	HLM, Reconstructed Dunkirk (canal side)	Centre of town, Malo les Bains	Docker *quartiers*, port, St Pol
	Newcomers	Residential area Malo les Bains	New areas and industrial areas	? Lacking substantiation (existing in places)	Shanty towns, hovels and chalets
Town	Dunkirk			Old rural towns and large landed properties to the east of town	Villages
	Newcomers	Suburban semi-rural area	Single-person homes, caravans		Rehabilitation of rural towns for immigrants

Source: (Castells and Godard, 1974)

petit-bourgeoisie where old dominates new, middle class the worker, the local the immigrant, and the country the town. In the third ideological type, the basis is that of the traditional community in which old dominates new, worker dominates middle class, local dominates the immigrant and town dominates the country. Finally, there is the ideology of class conflict where the new and the worker are opposed to the old and the middle class, while the newcomer and the town are opposed by the local and the rural interests. Each ideology dominates in particular districts of Dunkirk; consumerism is especially strong in the residential zone of Malo les Bains; familism dominates the rural towns and the older suburban sprawl of the interwar and postwar period; the traditional community ideology is strongest in the *quartiers* around the port; the class conflict produces opposition between the new residential areas and the centre of Dunkirk.

In order to obtain clarity from the variety of ideologies and conflicts that are present in the city, the planning process is utilized not as the product of the dominant ideology, consumerism, but as the outcome of a political balancing act in the interests of the dominant ideology. The *schéma d'aménagement* is seen as a *scenario de compromis*, the product of a conciliatory effort by the state that attempts to retain the decisions of the dominant group so long as the various social groups or movements can coexist. In this way the planning process becomes a part of the urban political process, part of the way in which national ideology is translated into local urban development and by which the locally dominant ideology responds to the pressures from other ideologies. The conciliatory efforts and responses, however, are regarded as only involving those options or areas of the plan where they do not involve any fundamental contradiction of the dominant ideology. The neutrality of the plan, whether in a social or technical sense, is seen as a part of the method by which the dominant ideology is able to control the planning process.

At the level of the individual city the structuralist theories offer a new, more universal theory of socio-spatial patterns although it is notable that the work relies on simple percentages for relatively large areas in contrast to the small area data of the multivariate techniques. The work can also be criticized on the grounds that it is rather retrospective in its view and cannot be utilized in a more predictive manner than the mere extrapolation of continuing political attitudes. *Monopolville* remains the sole study which examines the whole urban system. Other studies including several by Castells himself (1973 and 1978), using the same theoretical position, have tended to focus on particular policies where the conflicts are reduced more easily to one or two dichotomous situations and a few areas of the city. Hence, there has been a concentration on the urban protest movements by Borja, Pickvance and Lojkine (Harloe 1977).

Castells (1973) has also taken this more restricted empirical material in an analysis of urban renewal and urban conflict in Paris. Urban renewal is seen as accentuating residential segregation and, in particular, the city of Paris is becoming a preserve of the higher social strata. This has been linked to Paris' growth as a tertiary centre (Chapter 4). Centrality has become the mainspring of change, so much so that the new transport lines are built to develop the central location. At the same time, new commercial centres are being developed in the areas of renewal to aid the ideology of consumerism in its dominance over the city. Renewal is a means by which the working-class political hold on France's capital city is broken by the increasingly middle-class inhabitants and voters. By handing over areas to private development the authorities are, in Castells' opinion, creating the conditions in which the capitalist system can continue. Thus, Algerian areas and those of the lowest social strata are subject to renewal whereas the areas of most insalubrious dwellings are ignored. By reference to several renamed areas Castells illustrates the effect on the city's social geography. In one *quartier* the removal of insalubrious dwellings was soon replaced by an 'urban reconquest' conservation and renewal programme in an area formerly housing ethnic minorities, immigrants and the working class. Where social housing was promised the number of homes built was not enough to rehouse the pre-existing households. Protest movements were galvanized into action by the political left. Political and physical battles were lost, though, more importantly for the researcher, the theoretical stance of the Marxist was strengthened by the evidence collected showing the dominance of consumerism, centrality and the support of the organs of the state (Castells, 1978). Private affluence and public poverty are part of the same basic problem, the class struggle.

A further perspective on the socio-spatial organization of cities comes from the neo-Weberian approach. The emphasis and central concern shifts away from the holistic view of the economic and social system to the analysis of power within the social system. The emphasis is placed on both spatial and social constraints on access to urban resources that highlight, in particular, the role of bureaucracies, the urban managers and others who give access to life chances such as the mortgage lenders (Ford, 1975; and Williams, 1976 and 1978). On the whole, the main examples of this work like that of the neo-Marxists have not been developed in the context of a whole European city but rather elements of the city. Where urban conflicts occur the neo-Weberian sees them as being independent from other social conflicts and able to be identified by the researcher as the degree of access to housing or housing class. Therefore, works such as Rex and Moore's study of Sparkbrook, Birmingham, have concentrated on urban managerialism and the conflict between housing classes rather than on those who control the city bureaucrat, or the origins of conflicts in the search for housing (Rex and Moore, 1967). Damer (1974) also looked at the way local authority managers helped to create Wine Alley, while others have looked at community action groups, residents' associations and their basis within housing classes (Dennis, 1972).

Both of the radical perspectives do help to exemplify the basic premise of this book, that the West European city is distinct. Although both the theories of the Marxists and the neo-Weberians begin from the premise that the socio-spatial structure of cities is the product of a particular mode of production and the variety of attitudes and patterns of behaviour among those who operate the capitalist system, both explanations rely, at least as far as the empirical evidence suggests, on the need to introduce explanations of the local structure of society. Castells, therefore, relies very heavily on the role of the multiplicity of planning and development agencies that are peculiarly French in their operation, powers and interactions with other agencies at work in the built environment. To understand the empirical evidence demands an understanding of France. To understand Labyrinth Stadt, as the authors indicate in their material, it becomes essential to understand the West German political and economic system (Andritsky *et al.*, 1975). To understand the evidence of urban managerialism or the property machine it is essential to have a knowledge of the political and economic system of Great Britain. There are many who might agree with Pfeiffer's (1973) view:

> It is possible that Marxist theory satisfies the psychological need for a general simple theory of our society but it does not help us solve urban change. It delivers no criteria about how to handle a complex system of homes and hospitals, streets and shopping centres, sewers and subways for different groups with different interests on how to balance the old and new parts of a city.

Castells (1978) is also quick to point out that 'Marxist theory ... has no tradition of the treatment of an urban problem'. As yet it would seem that the holistic perspective provides a greater understanding, but that it depends on the descriptions of systems which are distinct as a result of national histories, and the nation's own variations of its dominant ideology. In addition, as the Dunkirk study has shown, cities can still have distinct ideologies such as the local 'Flemish' one which are almost unique; the holistic perspective still has to take into account the uniqueness of a city's or a region's own history and culture. The time dimension and evolution are undervalued. It is this continual interplay of the main currents of history, national and/or local identity and ideology that the structuralists cannot as yet obscure.

No matter whether one adopts the stance of description, positivism, reductionism or structuralism, distinct elements in the socio-spatial structure of West European cities are in evidence. Perhaps from the overwhelmingly Anglo-American view of the city, too much emphasis has been placed on the value of studies emanating from North America. It is only in recent years, with the translation of the works of Castells, that more English-speaking academics have come to recognize that West European social scientists have been aware of the socio-spatial processes at work in the city. The observations of these workers have suggested that socially the city in West Europe is a distinct entity, the product of the variety of cultural histories.

Part II

CHAPTER 4

Policies in the Tertiary Sector

The economic structure of the cities of West Europe has been under considerable pressure for change during the last 20 years. The growing proportion of the employed population working in the service sector as opposed to the primary sector and manufacturing industry has brought new demands for urban land-uses on a scale hitherto unknown. The office has become more than an appendage of the factory units as many office functions no longer need contiguity with the manufacturing process, requiring instead the benefits of externalities offered by office clusters. The growth of activity in what may be described in a general sense as the finance sector is but one of the new demands which has nurtured the massive expansion of demand for office space, and in its turn has done much to provide the new building to satisfy this demand. The major difference between North American and West European cities and especially their central areas in this respect, is that the latter have had to change or adapt on a much larger scale to cater for this demand, altering in the process land-use patterns which had survived for perhaps two centuries or even longer. The manner in which cities have responded to these demands has varied greatly.

Paralleling what has been termed the 'office boom' has come a revolution in retailing, creating new demands for larger-scale retailing facilities. A gradual change towards retailing from outlets of an increasingly large scale has rendered obsolete many small-scale retailing units in an economic and a physical sense. A part of this change has potentially involved the transfer of retailing away from its traditional focus of the city-centre, towards edge-of-town or out-of-town locations. Once again, however, the variation within Europe in the way in which retailing has been transformed is dramatic and the individual responses of planning authorities in various countries has varied from almost total *laissez-faire* to a rigid control which has kept the decentralization of retailing to a minimum. This chapter concentrates particularly on changes in two important areas of urban activity within the tertiary sector, those of retailing and office functions. Initially, however, it is revealing to examine the growth of the tertiary sector in the much broader sense, including all urban service employment.

The Growth of the Tertiary Sector

The rise of the tertiary or service sector in national economies may be examined through an analysis of the national employment structures. While not every part of the increase in this sector is necessarily reflected in demand for new urban premises, a significant proportion has had this effect and the scale of the increases in some cases is very important. The relative shift from industrial employment to the service sectors has magnified the new space demands within the city itself, since the employment focus of the service sector is the central city. While industrial employment has become increasingly peripheral, there has been rather less suburbanization of other functions, the reasons for which are discussed elsewhere in this chapter.

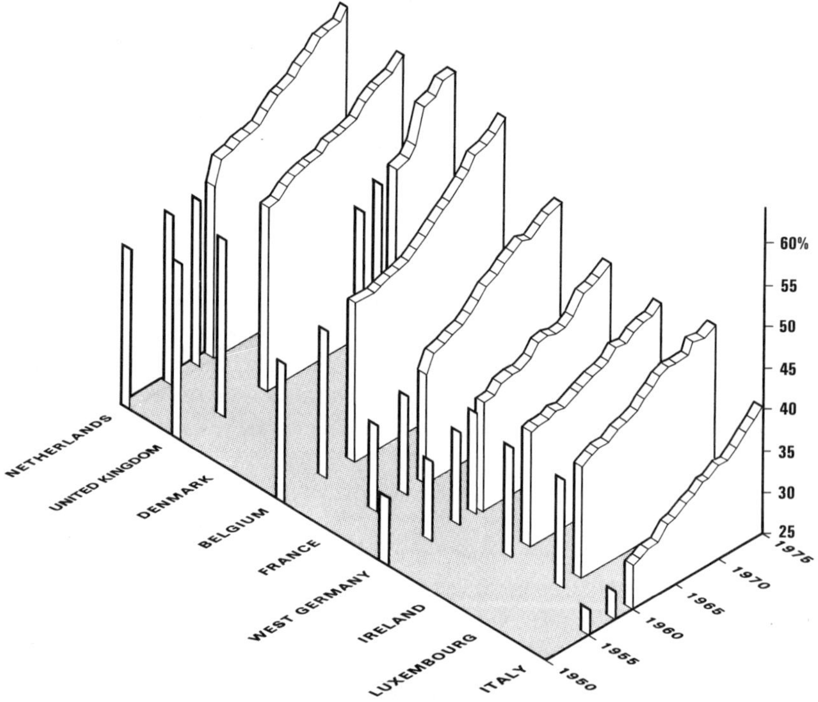

Figure 4.1 Service sector activity as a percentage of total employment in selected countries of West Europe 1950–75 (Source: Eurostat: *Regional Statistics*, 1976)

The general pattern of increases is shown in Figure 4.1, as far as the availability of data allows. By 1960, at least three European countries, the Netherlands, Belgium and the United Kingdom, were approaching a position where nearly half of the employed population were in the service sector. By the end of the study period, all except Italy had more than 45 per cent of their workforce in services. The leading countries of the Netherlands and Denmark were approaching the position where six out of ten of their workers were active in this sector.

If the analysis is shifted to just one component of the service sector, that of finance and insurance, then the increasing demands on space in the urban area are again emphasized. The number of persons employed in these areas rose dramatically in most countries of West Europe during the 1960s and 1970s. The actual number of workers in this sector for the five countries of West Europe for which these separate statistics are available amply illustrates this trend, as shown in Table 4.1.

Table 4.1 Persons employed in banking, finance and insurance and the percentage of total employment in these sectors, in selected countries of West Europe (1961–75)

		1961	1970	1975	Increase 1961–75 (per cent)
Belgium		64 000	93 000	189 000	
	per cent total employment	2.47	3.13	6.07	195.0
United Kingdom		803 000 (1960)	1 129 000	1 298 000	
	per cent total employment	3.67	5.03	5.72	61.6
Ireland		16 000	22 000	26 000	
	per cent total employment	2.50	3.07	3.54	62.5
West Germany		667 000	933 000	1 120 000	
	per cent total employment	3.27	4.29	5.37	67.9
France		458 000 (1962)	893 000	1 096 000	
	per cent total employment	3.72	5.63	6.52	139.3
Netherlands		No data	230 000	266 000	
	per cent total employment		6.02	6.94	—

Source: Eurostat: *Regional Statistics* (1976)

In some instances, the increase in employment in this sector was quite exceptional. For example, in France it entailed an additional half-a-million jobs between 1962 and 1975, comprising an increase of the order of 140 per cent. In Belgium the rise was even greater, with almost a threefold increase in this sector from 1961–75. It is worth noting at this stage that in one year alone 1972–73, the number almost doubled, from 101 000 to 180 000. Office floor space, an almost exclusively urban phenomenon, has therefore been in ever-increasing demand. The location of the supply of the new offices has varied between the centre of the major cities, to less traditional out-of-town locations. Offices have shown a distinct tendency to form agglomerations both in terms of concentrations in particular cities and in terms of the formation of office quarters in individual cities. In each case, the external economics obtained are obviously perceived as being very important, although the necessity to maintain such patterns has been increasingly questioned.

The Supply of New Floor Space

While the demand from the tertiary sector for new floor space in urban areas has undoubtedly been dramatic, its supply has been equally forthcoming. Indeed, perhaps somewhat contentiously, the property 'boom' of the postwar period, variously timed in different parts of Europe, has often produced an oversupply, particularly of office floor space. The major periods of activity in the property sectors were in the 1950s and 1960s in the United Kingdom, but rather later in other countries such as Germany, Belgium and France, where much major activity began after 1965.

It should be emphasized that the methods of financing new urban developments do vary within Europe. Nevertheless, it has been increasingly apparent that the large-scale financing of offices during the last two decades has followed a British pattern. Indeed, throughout Europe, British property companies themselves have been actively promoting new developments. The major characteristics of this pattern has been for new buildings to be financed as a speculative investment to be leased to potential tenants.

The reason for the spectacular rise in the importance of the property company as an agent of urban change has been well documented by Goodall (1972). Briefly, however, the process may be summarized by pointing to the massive flow of funds available for property investment in the postwar period via insurance companies and pension funds. Further, the restrictions on the increasing of capital in postwar Britain could be circumvented by the so-called leaseback transaction. This enabled a company to sell its interest in a property, but to lease it back from the purchaser. In the process, the company raised much-needed capital and the purchaser, often an insurance company, had found in property a secure investment for part of its funds. Property companies themselves were often funded by insurance companies or pension funds. By 1960, however, the insurance companies were seeking for themselves a greater participation in the operations of the property companies which they financed. All of this activity meant that property, seen as an investment with a very high return, in comparison with other investment and the added advantage of being at that time virtually inflation-proof, was being actively developed.

Before the British form of property development could be accepted in Europe, however, certain traditional attitudes had to be changed. For instance, in France offices were normally financed by the owner and eventual occupier despite the very high costs involved. There was no established tradition of speculative office development prior to British involvement in the French property market. Indeed, in the mid-1960s, 80 per cent of new office space was for owner-occupancy. The situation changed rapidly in the 1970s, however, as British companies turned their attention to property development in Europe, and the balance in new office provision was reversed so that approximately 80 per cent of new office space was built speculatively. In much of Europe from the late 1960s onwards, British property companies became very active as promoters of new urban development. Their somewhat voracious methods were not always welcomed. In some cases, and notably in the case of Brussels, they were totally insensitive to the pre-existing urban fabric. In this case, controls were imposed somewhat belatedly to prevent further transformation of sensitive parts of the city.

Locational Problems

The impact of the new demands for space by the entire tertiary sector were felt initially by the central areas of European cities. More recently such demand has spread to the periphery in the form of out-of-town retailing movements and a growing demand for suburban office parks. In the central area, however, major changes have had to take place, as obsolete office space has been cleared.

War damage enabled local authorities in many cities to completely replan their central areas. For instance, Cologne lost 75 per cent of its central area buildings, while in Britain, Southampton, Coventry and Plymouth lost well over half of the retailing space in their central areas. The opportunity to replan was grasped firmly by some cities to plan a city-centre for the second half of the twentieth century. The example of Coventry is a good one, although some 20 years after completion, the new shopping centre, built as an open-air pedestrian precinct, looks somewhat dated. A detailed description of Coventry's restructuring has been provided by Davies (1977).

The redevelopment process pursued in the postwar period affected other land-uses in the city. Small-scale industry, for instance, was frequently displaced without any compensating development elsewhere. Medium and large-scale industry has often moved towards the suburbs of major cities, creating suburban concentrations of industry and leaving behind areas for redevelopment, partly used for new construction for the tertiary sector.

The increase in the role of pan-European and other international organizations during the postwar period has brought about the concentration of the administration of many such organizations in a few selected cities. As Figure 4.2 shows, foremost among these are Paris, London, Geneva and Brussels. Others, however, also have substantial numbers of such functions and some cities are consciously promoting their image as a site for international meetings and headquarters locations. Both Vienna and Helsinki hosted important international conferences during the 1970s, culminating in the SALT II signing in Vienna in June 1979, one international gathering which was an important new function for the city and part of this consciously promoted image. OPEC (Organization of Petroleum Exporting Countries) has had its headquarters in Vienna since the mid-1960s when it moved from Geneva. More significant in numerical terms was the opening of the 'United Nations City' in Vienna in 1979 making it the third United Nations city in the world after Geneva and New York. The development is capable of housing 4600 international civil servants and was financed by the Austrian state (65 per cent) and the municipality of Vienna (35 per cent). It is leased to the United Nations for a purely symbolic rent for a 99-year period (Burtenshaw 1981; and Lendrai, 1979). This clearly indicates that the city is willing to pay for its new role, presumably in the expectation of other benefits to be gained in the long term through multiplier effects in the local economy as well as less tangible benefits to national status. It may also be noted that it has been shown that visitors to conferences in Vienna spend 50 per cent more on average than those on vacation and that the hotel trade has a vested interest in encouraging its international role. Plainly, all these functions have brought with them increased demand for office space in these cities, which is a significant factor in their economic structure.

Brussels illustrates many of these characteristics very well. In this case, we can see

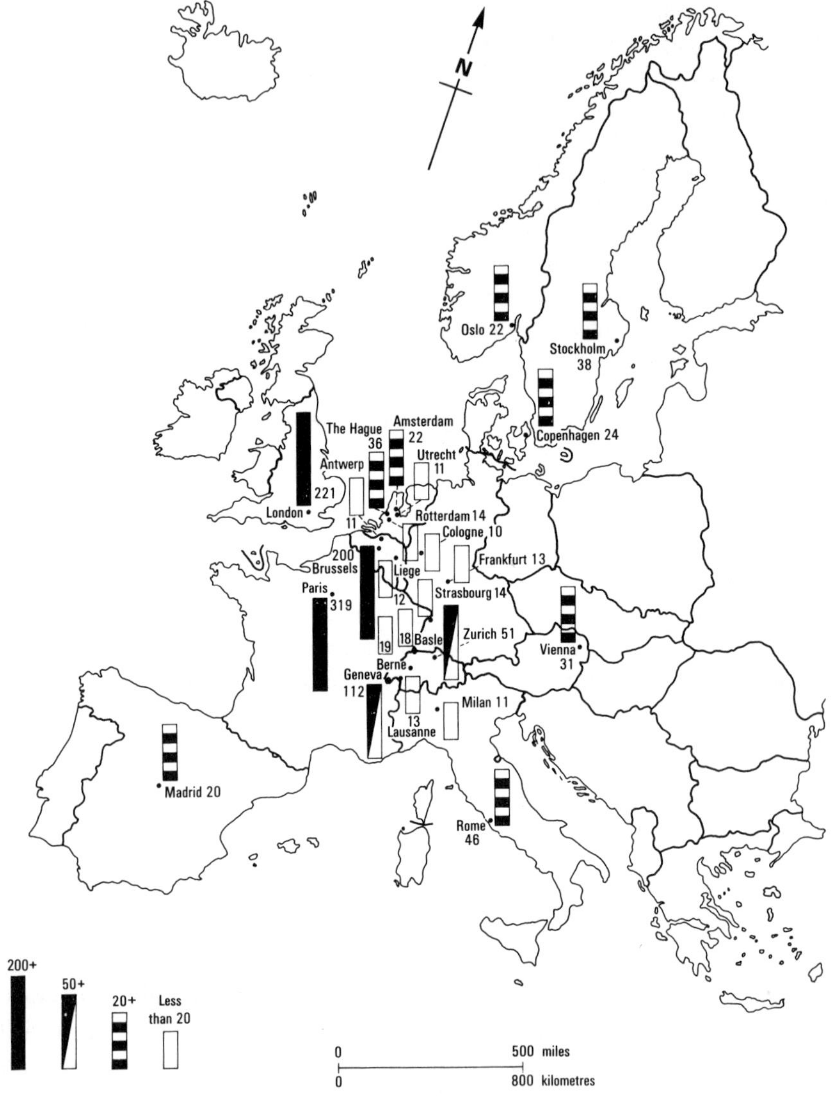

Figure 4.2 The location of the headquarters of international organizations in West European cities, 1977 (Source: *Yearbook of International Organizations*)

that the role of a capital city imposes special demands for working and living space on the city, and when the city fulfils the function of international as well as national capital these demands can be intense. Brussels, for example, is the location of 48 per cent of all Belgian employment in finance and 24 per cent of all Belgian office employment. In addition it is the headquarters of the European Economic Community, Euratom and, since 1968, NATO. Some 80 000 employees work for the 2800 foreign firms located in the city, including 8000 for the European Economic

Community alone. Developments to accommodate these functions have occurred both in the traditional central area but have also, of necessity, spilled over into the *Schumannplein* (EEC), the 'Manhattan' complex around the Nord station (van Hecke, 1977).

It is interesting to note that Bonn, the first German city, occupies only twentieth place in this European league table, and that the largest German cities have had to cater in only a very minor way for the demand from these international functions. The lack of a dominant, if not primate, capital city partly explains this, but reference must also be made to the relatively late rise in importance of West Germany while other cities such as Paris and Geneva, the latter in traditionally neutral Switzerland, had already gained a foothold in the establishment of such organizations.

The Control and Direction of Office Development

The office was not fully recognized as a major urban function requiring specific direction and control until the 1960s. Even then, there was a wide variation in attitudes towards potential office development, from a permissive *laissez-faire* policy such as that prevailing in Brussels to comparative restraint, of which the most notable example is London. Between the two has been a broad spectrum of policy solutions.

The policies may be divided into two groups. On the one hand there are those policies which have favoured deconcentration to subsidiary centres at some considerable distance from the central city while control has been simultaneously exercised to a greater or lesser degree in the central city itself. This policy may indeed be seen on a national as much as a metropolitan scale. In contrast have been policies to encourage office concentration in locations other than the centre of the city, but often in a suburban rather than a more distant location. In practice, in most cities where office control policies have been found necessary, they have oscillated between elements of each of these two broad policies, but in the final analysis one can usually point to a marked emphasis in either one or the other direction.

There is a distinction between countries with an active national policy for office location and those with no planning at this level. In the case of the United Kingdom, in 1964, as a control measure, an office development permit system was introduced and survived until 1979. Central government concern at this level was further underlined by the proposals of the Hardman Report (1973) on the dispersal of civil servants from London to the provinces. Similarly, the Swedish government has taken steps to control its own office development and has moved jobs to provincial locations from Stockholm. In other countries, however, notably West Germany, no such national policy exists within which to fit a local plan for a particular urban centre, although in the case of West Germany, the absence of such a policy is largely explained by the federal structure of that country. The contrasts in office location policies currently in operation in West Europe are made particularly obvious through a comparison of West Germany, and the cities of London and Paris. Although this approach may be seen as being somewhat selective, the detailed comparison is valuable in highlighting the essentially different policies involved.

At the scale of the medium-sized city, it would be true to say that German planners have been the most positive in offering solutions to the demand for office space which they experienced during the 1960s and 1970s. At a local level, a close examination of German cities exhibits five major responses to the demand for office space in the city.

The five responses are: (a) inner ring-road developments, often closely linked to the central area; (b) overspill from the centre into desirable residential area; (c) the establishment of inner suburban nodes of office development; and similarly (d) nodes in the outer suburbs. Finally there is (e) the use of major transport interchanges as office locations, frequently linked to the establishment of entirely new office parks.

The first response represented an early attempt at a solution to the office problem and can be identified in Cologne and in Hamburg. Overspill into desirable residential districts has been evident in both Hamburg and Frankfurt. In the latter case, such growth into the city's Westend area met with considerable opposition. In Hamburg, the Harvestehude and Rotherbaum districts, to the north of the city (originally developed in the nineteenth century along the shores of the Alster lake) have provided other classic examples of this style of overspill development. A more restrictive policy is now operated in this area to prevent its further transformation into a totally office-dominated quarter. There can be little doubt that, in social terms, such office growth can be very damaging in its disruption of well-established urban communities. For instance, the Westend district of Frankfurt lost 6729 persons between 1961 and 1970, or a loss of 22 per cent of its population. In their place 17 per cent of Frankfurt's office space is now in this quarter, compared to 31 per cent in the centre itself. Restraining policies have been introduced, but at what is now agreed to be a somewhat late stage in this process of urban change.

The establishment of specific nodes of development has been a part of a more coordinated planning policy, which in German cities has taken the form of comprehensive structure plans. Where inner suburban schemes have been tried they have been conceived not solely as an office project, but as part of a wider scheme to revitalize the inner suburb and enable it to share the advantages of the outer, often more affluent suburb. In this sense, they have their parallels in Paris where the establishment of new *centres restructurateurs* in the suburbs such as that at Créteil, in the south-east of the city, have included a large element of office employment, often in the public sector. A German example can be found in Hamburg, where the Hamburgerstrasse development, while situated on one of the eight designated axes of growth for the city is in an inner suburban area, relatively deprived of modern facilities. The development, in common with others like it, includes a retail centre and other services as well as a residential component.

Outer suburban nodes have been planned, but are rather less frequent. At Laatzen, in southern Hanover, office development has been permitted associated with a new covered suburban shopping centre. Similarly, to the east of the same city an office development has been permitted at Röderbruck. Such solutions have obvious disadvantages, not least that of limited levels of accessibility by public transport since, as in the case of Laatzen, they are sited at the termini of public transport routes to the central city.

In a European context, the most distinctive planning contribution to the problem of the office has been the office park. Such suburban, 'greenfield' locations are commonplace in North America and can now be found in cities in West Europe. Distinctively in Germany, however, they are found around much smaller cities than elsewhere, although there are British examples of greenfield single-enterprise locations such as the Vehicle Licensing Office in Swansea and the IBM polder in Portsmouth.

The development of Hamburg City Nord is a large-scale example of this style of office concentration and is examined below in more detail in a comparison with La Défense, a new suburban development to the west of Paris. Other examples include Bürostadt Niederrad, midway between Frankfurt and the city's international airport. Such locations are by now classical locations for office parks in both North America and Europe. In fact, this development, whose location is shown in Figure 4.3, has not met with local success and the city planners have shown that 77 per cent of the firms in the city saw no advantage to moving to Niederrad and 57 per cent found that it had severe restraints, particularly in terms of problems of staff recruitment. The fact that it is in a relatively poor part of the city may partially explain some of these problems. Additionally, its position in relation to the public transport system is not particularly good, despite being close the the airport, and in a European context perhaps more than that of North America, this is still a major location requirement.

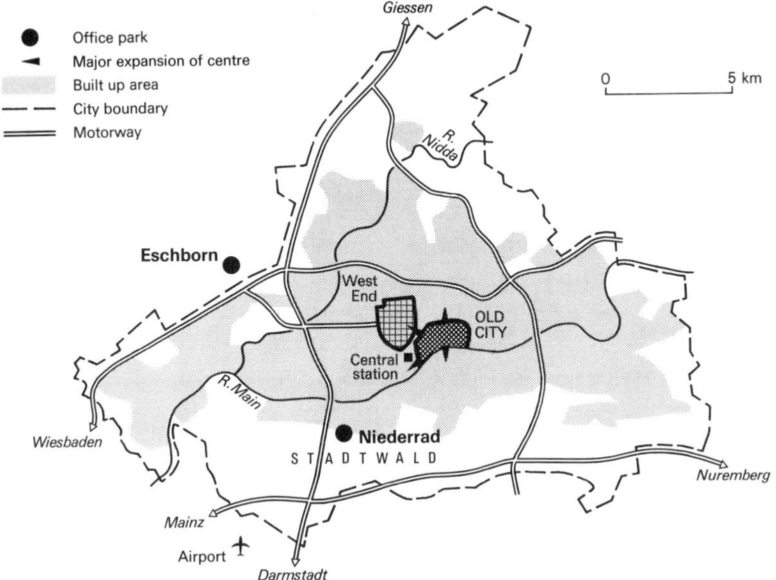

Figure 4.3 The location of major office developments around Frankfurt

The various policies adopted in Germany and elsewhere may be summarized diagrammatically and are shown in Figure 4.4. From the description of the German policies given above, it will be apparent that some though not all of these policies

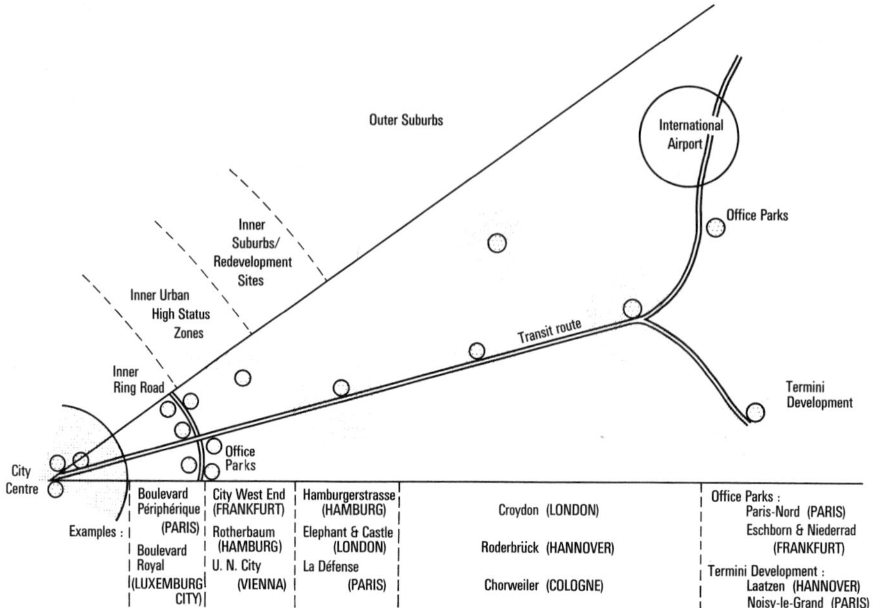

Figure 4.4 Spectrum of office locations in West European cities

included in Figure 4.4 can be identified in German cities. The notable exception is the long-distance decentralization solution. This policy has been attempted in Britain on a large scale both in the public and private sector: it is true, however, that here as elsewhere, such as Sweden, the long-distance decentralization of offices is particularly important for offices in the public sector forming part of a broader government regional aid policy.

While medium-sized German cities provide a variety of approaches to the problems of office location, it is the major capital cities of other countries in Europe such as London, Paris, Vienna and Brussels which have had to face even greater problems associated with large-scale demand and supply of office space.

The special pressures for new office space in Brussels led to the so-called 'Manhattan plan' for the Noordwijk district. Here the 1967 development plan laid out an office complex covering 53 hectares which provided office accommodation for 75 000 workers in around 1 million square metres in 40 tower blocks up to 160 metres in height, together with 15 000 parking spaces and 5000 000 square metres of shops. The scale of this development compares with La Défense or Croydon, but it is located much closer to the traditional central business district than either the Parisian or London cases (van Hecke, 1977).

In London, the history of office development policy illustrates the growing awareness of the importance of office development since 1945. In the period immediately after the war, there was little apparent concern about offices other than a desire to reconstruct those lost through wartime destruction. The County of London *Development Plan* in 1951 acknowledged the fact that there was some congestion, but nevertheless increased the area zoned for offices from 322 to 374 hectares. However, the theme of deconcentration was already apparent as indeed it had been as early as Abercrombie's Plan for Greater London in 1943. This theme was embodied in the plan eventually approved in 1955. Active moves towards decentralization took place on a limited scale, although the fact that administrative control was divided between the former London County Council (LCC) and the surrounding counties, prior to the creation of the wider Greater London Council (GLC) in 1964, made coordination difficult. Increasing commuting problems, brought about by an increase in office floor space from 7.7 million square metres in the central area in 1948 to 11.5 million square metres in 1962 (Daniels, 1975), emphasized further the need for major policy changes.

During the 1950s offices were developed at a rapid rate in London, successfully competing against other land-uses. By the early 1960s there was an increasing call for greater decentralization and for offices to move to various towns and suburban centres outside London in the period after 1956, a trend already encouraged by some county councils such as Middlesex and Essex. But such moves were not without their own locally generated problems, and by 1964 most counties had reversed their policies. By that time, firms were being attracted to the peripheral areas not only from the LCC area but from elsewhere in the United Kingdom. Thus these deconcentrations outside London were not necessarily helping directly the problems presented by London itself. A major exception to the policy reversal of 1964, however, was Croydon, which continued to pursue an active policy of office development.

The Croydon Corporation Act passed in 1956 was the first instrument designed to encourage major office expansion in a medium-sized suburban centre. The local authority, eager to attract new offices, initiated the act to enable the purchase of one hectare of land in the central area of the town. There was no doubt a fair measure of civic pride as well as financial incentive as the motivating force behind this action. This area and adjoining land, the local authority leased to private developers, resulting in 19 000 square metres of offices and only 150 square metres of shops (Daniels, 1975). Fortuitously, this action by Croydon coincided with a general adoption of a deconcentration policy, resulting in the allocation of a further 18 hectares by the local authority for decentralizing offices. In fact, development has spilled over the limits of this area and new office space has been provided in excess of 600 000 square metres, in which nearly 30 000 workers are employed. The success of Croydon has been dramatic in concentrating the dispersion of office functions in such large-scale development.

The importance attached to the decentralization policy was underlined in 1963 by the publication by the British government of a White Paper on London's office problems, including the recommendation to establish the Location of Offices Bureau (LOB) with a role to encourage decentralization and to supply intending companies with information on potential moves. The White Paper looked towards suburban office centres as well as those further afield.

While the 1963 White Paper produced broad strategies, a White Paper in the following year introduced a major planning control. It was embodied in the Control of Offices and Industrial Development Act 1965, and took the form of a system of Office Development Permits (ODP) for new office buildings and for conversions from other uses. The ODP system was applied retrospectively from November 1964 to all new buildings for which permission was sought. The ODP system has since been applied more generally than its original area of operation of the London metropolitan region, within which all office space of more than 300 square metres required an ODP prior to development, though by the 1970s this was raised to 1000 square metres.

While there is a broad policy favouring decentralization on a national scale and to a degree on a metropolitan scale, recent policy changes have been important in emphasizing the problems inherent in continually encouraging a dispersal of office functions. The exodus of many office workers to locations outside the capital has left many inner London boroughs which have never been important locations for offices, without the means of achieving a balanced employment structure. This stimulated central government action in 1977 in redefining the role of LOB to include the attraction of jobs to the inner city, although the LOB did not survive to actively carry out this role. This refocusing of interest on this area is part of a more general reappraisal of priorities in urban planning evident in the last few years, culminating in a major policy statement in 1976, which is discussed further in its more general context in Chapter 11. In 1979 the LOB and ODP policy were abandoned in the return to a free market economy but it will take several years for this policy to have any effect on office developments in London.

The situation in Paris has certain parallels to that of London, but also some important differences. On a national scale, the designation of eight *métropoles d'équilibre* in 1965, fostered the concept of deconcentration from the capital. The impact on the office sector has, however, been minimal and indeed only Lyons can be seen as offering any viable alternative to Paris as an office centre, with a limited concentration of financial and regional functions.

In Paris itself, a major part of the office location policy revolves around the successful completion of La Défense, the major suburban node to the west of the city, outside the boundaries of the former *ville*, (since 1965, the *département de Paris*). The regional plan for Paris, discussed in Chapter 11, suggests that offices should be encouraged in a number of new growth nodes, both in the inner suburb and in the new towns. There has been a general and marked trend of office development moving towards the west of the city. The east–west imbalance of the central city itself can be illustrated by the fact that, while population is approximately equally divided either side of a central north–south dividing line, job growth to the west in the period 1962–68 was much more significant than the east, the share being 68 per cent and 32 per cent respectively.

A further problem has been that of preserving the centre itself from the demands of the office developer. Only one major 'skyscraper' breaks the skyline of the city—that of the Tour Maine-Montparnasse. This massive development (14 hectares) has been the subject of much criticism, on both planning and aesthetic grounds, and contrasts starkly with the policy epitomized by the development of La Défense to the west of the city. The Tour Maine-Montparnasse is now a dominant and somewhat intrusive landmark in southern Paris but it has also brought about a very high concentration of office workers (20 000 are employed in the building), in an already congested area.

The policy in Paris has therefore been to favour office development in certain parts of the city and to discriminate against such development elsewhere. In 1974, the government introduced an annual 'ceiling' of office development of 900 000 square metres per annum of which 20 per cent was to be in the five new towns, while only 70 000 square metres was permitted in the *département de Paris* itself.

The major instruments of control lie in the granting of planning consents (*agréments*), which are required for any building in excess of 1000 square metres, and in a taxation system levied on new building which is locationally selective. In a general sense, the *agrément* system is operated to favour the hitherto less-favoured eastern sectors at the expense of the west, although it also discriminates in favour of the new towns of Paris, its new suburban growth poles, whereas with certain exceptions it works against Paris and its western *département* of Hauts-de-Seine. The exceptions lie in the eastern part of the Paris *départements*, especially the Bercy–Gare de Lyons zone which is being developed as an office quarter away from the more traditional western concentrations within the old *ville*. The building development tax (*redevance*) is similarly selective, as Figure 4.5 indicates. Zone 1 covers the western part of the *département* of Paris, and the western *département* of Hauts-de-Seine. The second level of tax applies in Zone 2 to the west and south-west of Zone 1, again discriminating against the suburban areas which had proved most attractive in the 1960s and early 1970s. Zone 3 covers most of the rest of the continuously built-up urban area. There are, however, a large number of nodes within the generalized zones, especially in the case of the city, where office development is to be encouraged. In central Paris, two such areas, the controversial Les Halles site and the Bercy–Gare de Lyons site in the eastern part of the centre are similarly designated as exceptions to the area surrounding them. The tax was originally introduced in 1960 as a uniform tax on development, but it was altered in 1971 to be imposed differentially within the Paris regions, favouring the eastern and peripheral areas and penalizing the western and central areas. While it could be argued that the tax, levied only once, on completion of the building, and not on an annual basis is hardly punitive in the context of total construction costs, it may persuade some developers to move into an area of low tax compared with the highly taxed western sector. It could be further argued, however, that land costs, themselves a reflection of differential demand, could carry out this task with equal effect.

However, Paris has demonstrated the urgent need for such measures in the face of growing employment in the tertiary sector.

Table 4.2 clearly shows that the continuing growth of the service sector has necessitated some degree of control particularly since the previous growth has been channelled in only one major direction.

Paris and its immediate ring of *départements* of Hauts-de-Seine, Seine–St-Denis and Val-de-Marne have also been losing industrial jobs at a rate of 15 000 per year in this period, representing an employment redistribution which has exacerbated the office location problem. Clearly, therefore, a detailed strong policy has been required.

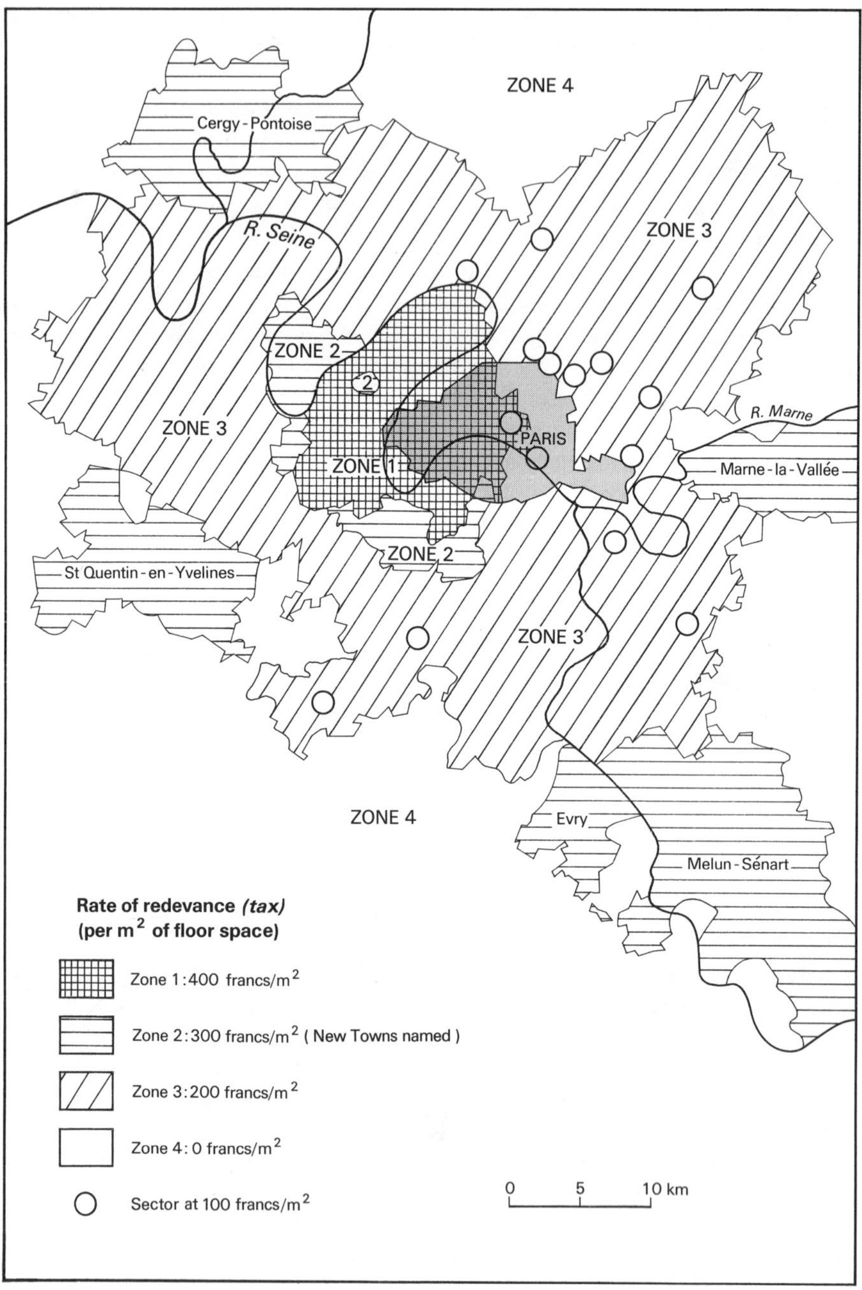

Figure 4.5 Office development tax zones in the Paris region

Table 4.2 Changes of employment in the Paris region (Île de France) by employment sector (1968–75)

	1968	1975	1968–75 (per cent change)
Primary	52 356	39 575	− 24
Construction and public transport	367 912	367 900	—
Industry	1 399 392	1 356 060	− 3
Commerce and services	2 451 900	2 838 025	+ 16
Total	4 271 560	4 601 560	+ 8

Source: l'Institut d'Aménagement et d'urbanisme de la Région de l'Île de France

A part of this policy has been the development of La Défense, paralleling the similar development of City Nord in Hamburg. It would be tempting to add Croydon to the comparison, but that represented office development, albeit spectacular, in an existing centre. Both La Défense and City Nord are new suburban centres, offering much more than merely office functions. Figure 4.6 shows each centre in detail.

La Dèfense, with a planned office floor space of 1.55 million square metres, is a high density concentration of tower blocks. Part of a much larger scheme of urban rehabilitation, including the suburb of Nanterre, it includes 6820 apartments in its plans. Its transport system is such that it could be carried out only on a completely cleared site, with multi-level transport systems affording links to the SNCF, the express metro (RER), bus services and major road routes. On completion it is intended that approximately 110 000 people will work there, with a further 20 000 residents. It is not without its developmental problems such as that of vacant office floor space during the economic recession of the 1970s. Furthermore, it is unlikely that its regional shopping centre of 120 000 square metres will open on schedule, since the major retailers involved are seeking its postponement and one has withdrawn from the scheme. This problem has, however, little to do with the viability of La Défense as such, but is rather more a reflection on the general problems of retailing planning in the city as a whole, which are further discussed below.

Hamburg's City Nord is an essentially similar though somewhat smaller concept. It is different in physical appearance, however, since it has lower-rise office blocks than La Défense. It occupies a 95.1 hectare site, with a planned total of 638 000 square metres of offices, 20 000 square metres of shops and 50 000 square metres of residential space. It has a central area of shops, restaurants and hotels and it is intended that its planned workforce will be in the order of 32 000. In both La Défense and City Nord, the plan exists to create a concentration of office activity sufficient to attract the city-centre office to a suburban location. In the case of City Nord, it has had some success, with for instance the oil company BP AG leaving behind 22 000 square metres in nine locations in the city-centre of Hamburg to take up 31 000 square metres in City Nord and, similarly, Esso moving from 33 000 square metres in eighteen different locations to 36 000 square metres in the new development. La Défense has had a similar success with the presence of major

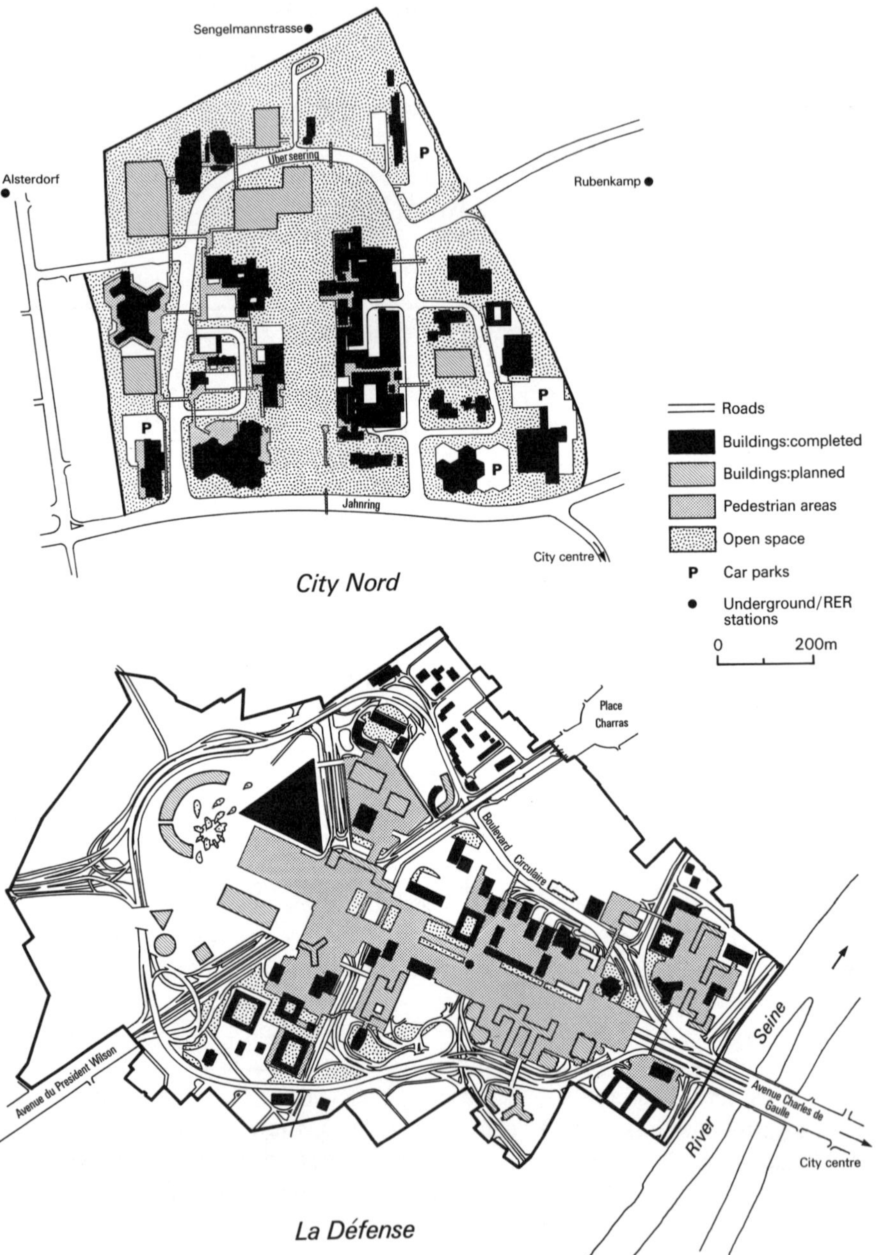

Figure 4.6 Planned suburban office centres in Hamburg (City Nord) and Paris (La Défense)

multinational concerns such as IBM, Dunlop, Esso and Rank-Xerox, together with major domestic office users such as Electricité de France (EDF) and the major bank, Crédit Lyonnais.

While in Britain, France and Germany office development has come under increasing control, in Belgium, and particularly in its capital, Brussels, there has been far less restraint. Office development began on a large scale in 1971, mainly financed by overseas finance. British property companies were foremost in this process and the effect has been a virtual transformation of l'Avenue des Arts, with modern speculatively built office blocks changing its skyline. The problems of oversupply have been very evident in Brussels, with vacant office space being the subject of much public criticism. Brussels and its recent experience emphasizes further the need for strong policies towards the control of office development.

The office has been recognized now as a major urban function, but it has taken time to evolve effective means of control and even now the degree of effectiveness is difficult to assess. But in itself the recognition of the office as the major twentieth-century employer, and as such a vital component in urban and regional planning, is important. This theme will be followed further in the analysis of major city plans in Chapter 11.

Control and Development in the Retail Sector

In the field of retailing, there has been considerable variation in the extent to which European urban centres have responded to recent changes and innovations in this sector of the economy. One reason for this is the wide variation in the structure of the retail trade itself. At one extreme, in Italy, the continuing dominance of the independent retailer has hindered innovation in the form of large scale, edge-of-town, or out-of-town retailing. Such innovation requires capital availability which has usually been the preserve of large retailing organizations, or property companies. The latter are unlikely to be involved when there is little demand for new retailing premises since the retailers are small in scale, operating from only one location. At the other end of the scale, in the United Kingdom a considerable dominance of the retail trade by a relatively small number of retailers ensures a competitiveness often involving large-scale innovation, backed by considerable capital formation. Figure 4.7 illustrates the variation across the European Economic Community at the present time in the structure of the retail trade.

A second reason lies in the variation in control of the retail sector. In some cases, new retailing units have been built with practically no control. For instance, new hypermarket development in both Germany and France was originally subject to little control. Only later did planning authorities seek to direct this form of retailing. On the other hand, in the United Kingdom the new retailing typified by the hypermarket has been the subject of the most careful control from the outset and that control continues unabated, severely restricting the number of true hypermarkets which have been built in the United Kingdom.

Three major retailing developments can be distinguished in the West European city, each bringing with it a consequential series of responses in the commercial structure

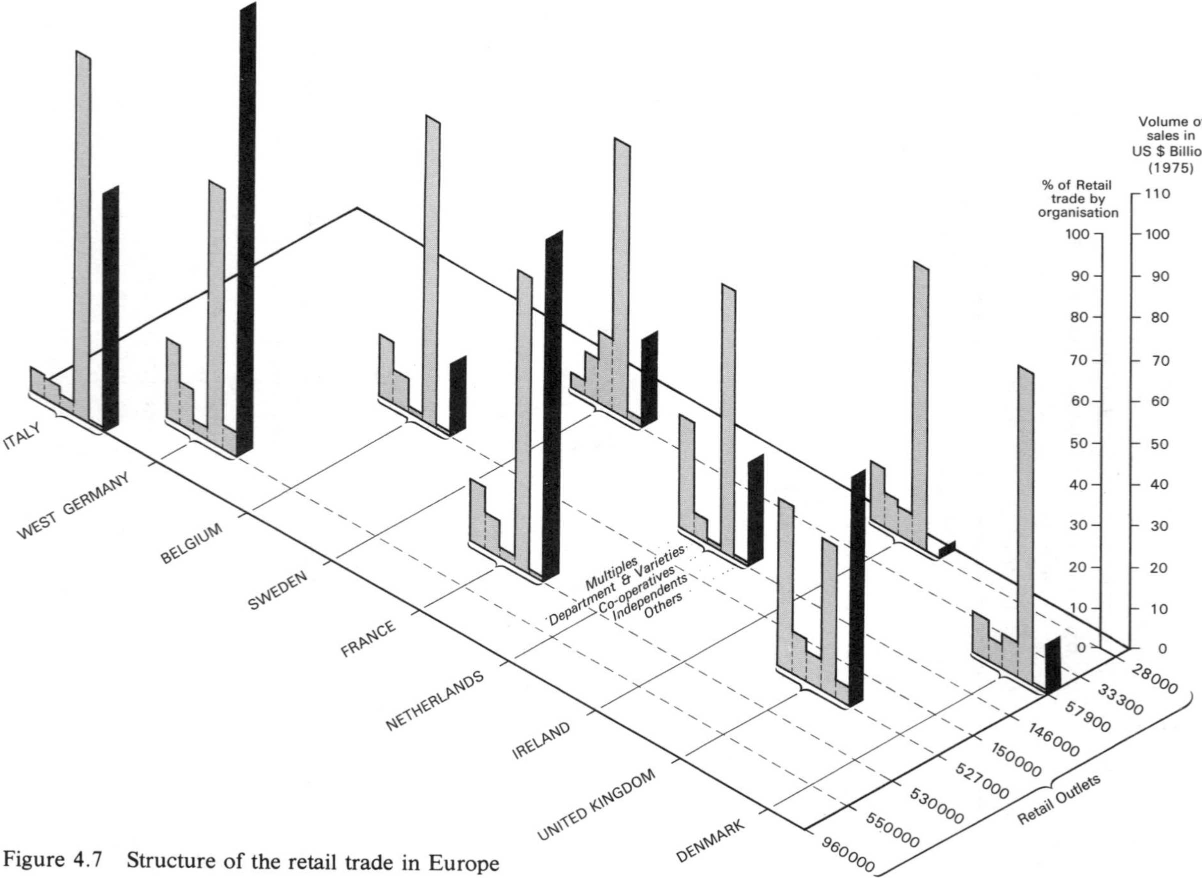

Figure 4.7 Structure of the retail trade in Europe

of the city. Firstly, there is the development of hypermarkets and superstores, often, but not always, in an edge-of-town or out-of-town location. There are problems of defining a hypermarket, but a useful definition has been put forward by MPC and Associates Limited (MPC, 1974). They defined a hypermarket on an initial count as (a) a store with a selling area of at least 2500 square metres (25 000 square feet) on one level, specializing in food but with a wide range of other convenience goods; (b) it adopts self-service methods with at least fifteen checkouts; (c) usually 3 to 6 km (2 to 4 miles) from the town centre; and (d) its car parking area, adjacent to the store, is in excess of three times its selling area. In fact other developments not fulfilling each of these criteria have been built, often termed superstores, sometimes smaller than a hypermarket, but more importantly varying somewhat in their retailing methods.

A second development has been the introduction of the regional shopping centre, similar to North American shopping 'malls'. Such centres situated outside established cities contain at least two department stores and around a hundred other shops together with other associated facilities. Car parking is provided on a large scale. The regional centre is planned to serve a much wider area and a larger population than the other 'out-of-town' facilities defined above. An intermediate stage of this type of development can be identified in West Germany where Ruhrpark outside Bochum and the Main–Taunus Centrum near Frankfurt were each developed as major regional centres, but with open malls rather than the fully enclosed centres currently being developed. The third development has been the redevelopment of the city-centre with major new retailing facilities, either in a pedestrianized precinct or in covered malls. In the recent past, many of these have been on the scale of the out-of-town regional shopping centre. The impact of these three changes in retailing is very varied in Europe and each is now examined in turn to illustrate this variation and to point to the consequential changes in the city's retailing structure.

Hypermarkets in Europe showed a very uneven pattern of distribution during their period of development, as Table 4.3 shows.

Table 4.3 Hypermarkets in Europe (1974)

	1974
Austria	9
Belgium	46
Denmark	2
France	212
Italy	3
Netherlands	7
Sweden	22
West Germany	406
United Kingdom (superstores)	56

Source: MPC and Associates Limited (1974)

The widespread diffusion of the hypermarket in the French, Belgian and German city contrasts sharply with the situation in Britain. Studies of the French hypermarket have suggested that its impact on pre-existing retailing within the town has not been as great as at first feared. However, it is this fear which has held back the development of hypermarkets in the United Kingdom. Belgium, however, has shown far less reluctance and has generally welcomed new forms of retailing more quickly than many of its neighbours. The first supermarket was opened in 1958 and the first hypermarket as early as 1961. The pattern of location has thus had both the time to develop, and a general absence of planning restraints designed to preserve the existing locations.

The contrast between the concentration of the department stores in the large cities, Brussels alone having 39 of the total 119, and the dispersal of the hypermarkets, the Brussels region having only twelve of the total 75, is clear. Similarly, the location within the city-region (Table 4.4) shows a marked contrast. The department stores occupy high rent sites in the city-centres, including nine within central Brussels and six in central Antwerp, while the supermarkets are more widely dispersed in both central and suburban locations. The hypermarkets, typically, have selected low-cost peripheral sites, with access to the main road network, such as ten on the periphery of the Brussels region and five around Antwerp (Merenne-Schoumaker, 1970; Spork, 1972; and Vlassenbroeck, 1975).

Table 4.4 Location of stores, supermarkets and hypermarkets in the Brussels region (1975)

Location	Department store	Shop type, 1975 per cent Supermarket	Hypermarket
City-centre	71	57	4
Semiperipheral	26	35	8
City-periphery	3	8	88
Total Number	119	721	75

Source: van Hecke, 1977

In Britain, however, more resistance has been present. In 1972, British local planning authorities were requested to inform central government of any large-scale retailing proposals of over 5000 square metres, outside existing city, town or district centres. By so doing, it effectively removed this particular form of land-use from local control (Department of the Environment, 1972). The concern of central government essentially hinged around the possible problems for existing areas, the transport implications for large scale out-of-town developments and the feeling that not all members of the community could share equally in the use of this new form of retailing. There was, therefore, a desire to ensure the continuing prosperity of the existing retail centres. It was felt particularly than the non-car owner would be disadvantaged by a lack of access to hypermarkets unless close attention was paid to public transport facilities. This policy by central government ensured a very slow diffusion of hypermarkets in Britain. The first was opened in Caerphilly in South Wales in 1972, but was rather small by standards of continental Europe, with a selling area of only 5500 square metres.

Meanwhile, elsewhere in the United Kingdom, and especially in many towns in northern England, superstores were being widely developed. These have been defined, once more by MPC and Associates Limited (1974), as having a selling area between 2000 and 4000 square metres, with a more limited range of non-food items than a hypermarket. Its method of merchandising can be somewhat crude with goods sold direct from their cartons stacked in specially designed caging rather than displayed on shelves. The number of checkouts varies between ten and twenty whilst the car-parking area is between one and three times that of the selling space. Superstores, so defined, became very popular, particularly where sites could be easily found within or on the edge of industrial cities. Often an inner city site could be found for such a store, while the local authority was pleased to see a new commercial use in a declining area. It was noticeable that there was a considerable delay before the introduction of superstores in cities in southern Britain, where sites in these less industrialized urban centres, were more difficult to obtain. A market leader in this field is ASDA (Associated Dairies), whose stores are shown in Figure 4.8 together with true hypermarkets developed by Carrefour, a leader in this field in Europe.

The hypermarket, however, was restricted everywhere. Central government did allow a development at Chandler's Ford in South Hampshire, which opened in 1977. Its progress was to be closely monitored particularly in terms of its impact on surrounding retailers. The impact study demonstrated that although some local shops had been affected, its influence had been spread very widely and was not felt by any one particular centre (Wood, 1976).

The scale of hypermarkets has increased in the United Kingdom from these early innovations of around 6000 square metres. The hypermarket at Patchway, near Bristol, opened in 1978 and operated by Carrefour, as are those at Caerphilly and Chandler's Ford, is 9000 square metres in extent. It is interesting to note that the hypermarket, during this period of close control in the United Kingdom, has been adopted for a variety of purposes. For instance, Carrefour also operate a hypermarket within the shopping centre of Telford new town in Shropshire, situated, somewhat surprisingly, alongside a more conventional supermarket. The period of control in Britain meant that the hypermarket has been adopted only very selectively and will continue to be restricted.

In December 1977, the British government's Department of the Environment (DOE) issued a further report on hypermarkets (Department of the Environment, 1977). It noted that the larger food stores already permitted had had little impact on the independent food retailer within 15 minutes' drive time of the new developments. They had had rather more impact on multiple food retailers' and cooperative stores' supermarkets, where there had been an average fall in turnover of 20 per cent for such stores within the catchment of hypermarkets, compared to an average fall of around 3 per cent. In general, the larger the supermarket, the greater had been its impact. The development control policy note issued in 1977 highlighted the major planning issues once again.

At this time, the DOE was stressing the importance of access for both pedestrians and public transport as well as for the motorist and saw particular merit in accommodating new stores within existing urban areas. This location was seen as being particularly advantageous if it was within an expanding or developing town

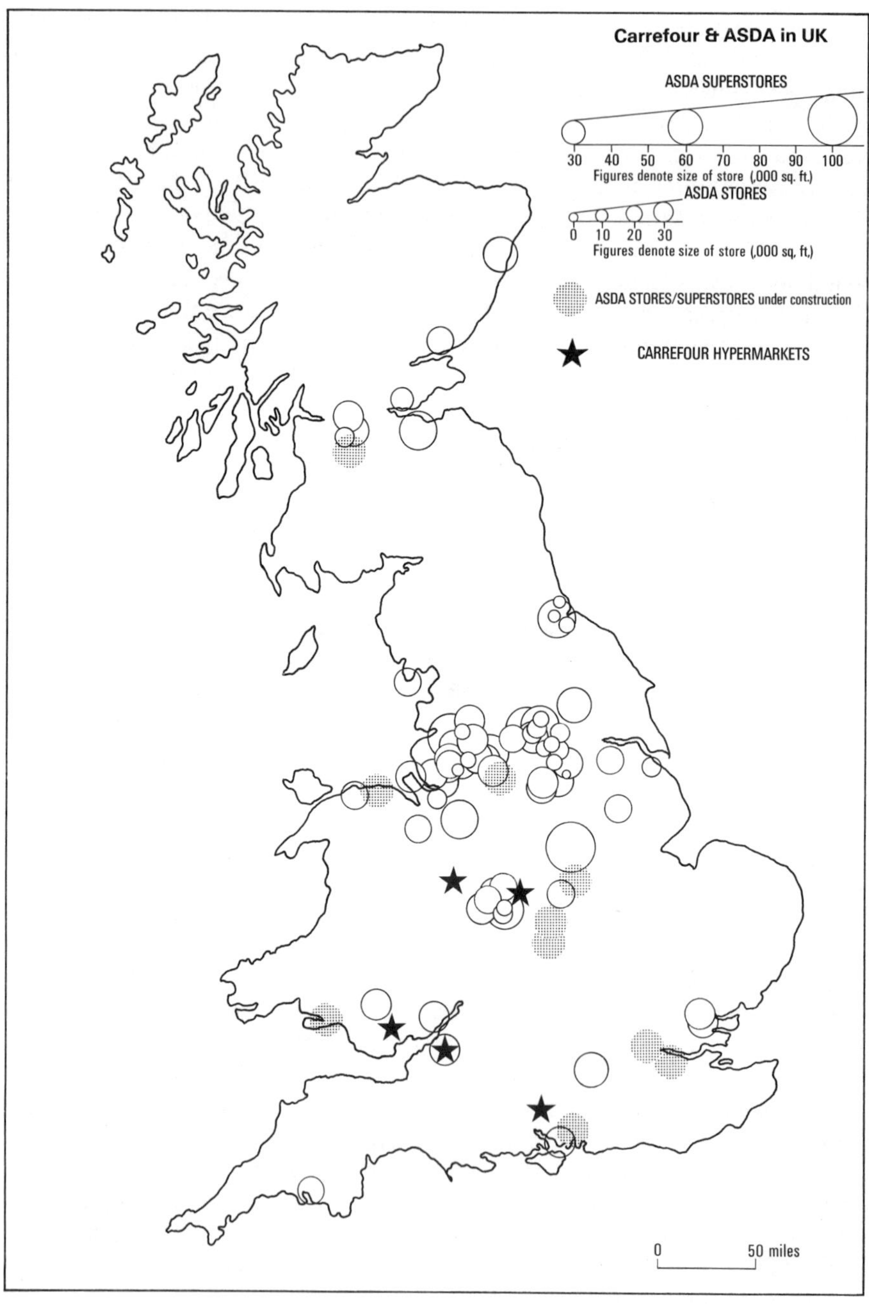

Figure 4.8 Distribution of ASDA superstores and Carrefour hypermarkets in the United Kingdom, 1978

centre, or if the new retailing development could act as the nucleus for a district centre. The hypermarket 'issue' was also seen as part of a wider debate on the fate of the inner city. Indeed, in October 1978 the Greater London Council, in a policy statement, pointed to the acceptability of such new forms of retailing in the inner parts of the capital. This may be seen as part of the continuing direction policy in the United Kingdom, which still appears sharply contrasted to much of the rest of Europe.

In a number of European centres, the second major development, the regional shopping centre, has been adopted. Nowhere, however, has it been as widely adopted as in the Paris region. The regional shopping centre represented an American concept introduced into the European city. In Paris, one of the first to open was Parly Deux in 1969. The promoting company sought to demonstrate that it was possible to provide a standard of retailing equal to that of the central city. Accordingly, Parly Deux was built to very high standards and fitted well into the affluent suburb of Le Chesnay near Versailles in south-west Paris. Comparatively speaking, Parly Deux was not a large centre. Indeed, its 55 000 square metres is small compared with many of its successors. Its arrangement of retailing and other facilities is, however, typical, with two major department stores sited at either end of a covered shopping mall, which contains some 107 additional shops, together with restaurants and cinemas. In 1970, Parly Deux had a turnover of 288 million francs, in 1971, 387 million francs, and by 1972 420.85 million francs (Groupe Balkany, undated). Encouraged by this success, the same promoting company built other centres in the Paris region with Vélizy Deux (75 000 square metres) opening for trading in 1972, Rosny Deux (83 000 square metres) in 1973, and Evry Deux (71 000 square metres) in 1975. These, together with other similar centres, formed a complete network of such centres around Paris, as shown in Figure 4.9.

The *centre commercial régional* was not, however, without its problems. On the credit side, they did much to give to the suburbs a much-needed structure and as such fitted into the *Schéma Directeur* or regional plan, originally published in 1965. A number of the centres were situated either in the new towns or in new suburban growth poles, as indicated in Figure 4.9.

The centres were planned, however, in a very short period of time, with the possibility that true levels of demand had not been accurately ascertained. It is certainly true that elsewhere on a world scale where such centres have been built, such as in the corridor stretching northwards from Chicago to Milwaukee, where 25 regional centres have been built, there has been an overprovision of shopping of this type. In these circumstances, the more marginal sites may be somewhat exposed in economic terms. In any event, at least one of the regional centres, Créteil Soleil, has had problems, and a further one at La Défense is currently being delayed. It should be pointed out that the relative weakness of the major French retailers compared to similar concerns elsewhere, made Créteil somewhat vulnerable. The centre had a branch of *Printemps*, which suffered major losses in 1975 and 1976. It countered by closure of branches, including in 1976 the furniture and domestic appliance sections of its store at Créteil, to be followed in October 1977 by its complete closure. This action shifted the focus of attention to the planned centre at La Défense, one of the

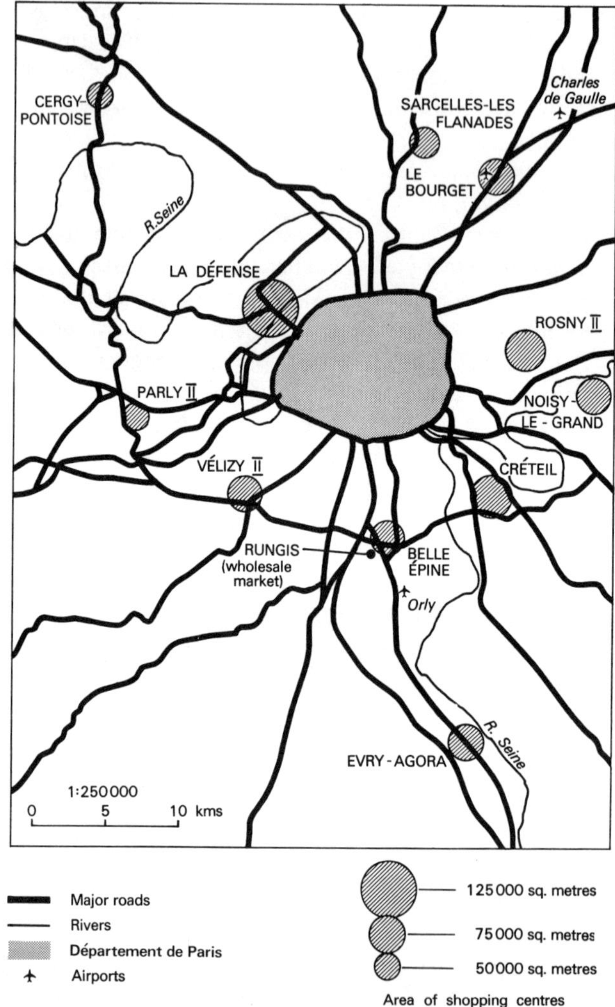

Figure 4.9 Regional shopping centres in the Paris region, 1978

largest of the *centres commerciaux*. Both *Printemps* and the other 'anchor store', *La Samaritaine*, sought to postpone the opening of this centre by three years, claiming that the 'climate' was not right for such a new development and that La Défense was running behind schedule. Whatever the eventual outcome, the setbacks and uncertainties have demonstrated that the regional shopping centre has not met with unqualified success where it has been adopted on the scale attempted in Paris.

Elsewhere the concept of the regional shopping centre has not been widely adopted. In the United Kingdom, the problems associated with land acquisition and the obtaining of planning permissions have limited development to just one centre, Brent Cross in north-west London. This project was initiated in 1956, with planning permission being granted in 1972, and opened for trading in March 1976. Unlike

Paris, suburban London is extremely well served by a hierarchy of important suburban centres such as Richmond, Kingston-upon-Thames and Croydon. There was, however, a noticeable sector in the north-west of the city into which a major regional centre could fit and draw its trade from further out along the same sector. The strategic location of Brent Cross at the junction of the M1 motorway, the A41 and the North Circular Road is a major factor in its success.

While many of the regional shopping centres described above are in the existing built-up area, they are not a part of an existing central city. The redevelopment of a part of a city-centre, or the addition of a major retailing development adjacent to it is the third retailing development which may be identified. In this case, the examples are by no means confined to Britain and France, since the destruction of the 1939–45 war gave to many the opportunity to replan the retailing centres. In others, such as Stockholm, there has been a deliberate policy to redevelop the pre-existing central zone to produce a retailing centre which offers more modern retailing premises in traffic-free surroundings.

The initial developments in city-centres during the postwar period were often open-air pedestrian precincts. By the 1970s, however, the new shopping centres were generally covered shopping areas. Some were on a very large scale, dominating the pre-existing retailing, such as the Hoog Catherijne Centre in Utrecht, or the Eldon Square development in Newcastle upon Tyne. Others attempted an integration of residential functions and retailing, such as the limited integration in Nottingham with its Victoria Centre, or the more general integration with a range of urban functions, including offices, such as La Part Dieu in Lyons.

There are problems attached to the building of major new covered centres which may dominate the retailing of a city simply by nature of their size. In their impact study of the Eldon Square development in Newcastle, Bennison and Davies (1977) analysed the movement of retailers from elsewhere in the city (illustrated in Figure 4.10). In general terms, the development of Eldon Square, although in itself tremendously successful for the retailers in it, has led to the shift northwards of the centre of gravity of the retailing, leading to the considerable decrease in the importance of some of the southern zones of the city-centre. The distribution of vacant retail units shown in Figure 4.10 further emphasizes this. On the other hand, some similar developments are able to bring new retailing to a centre without having such adverse effects. The lack of such problems may well be a reflection of the increase in size of the centre, with the larger centres well able to sustain a major addition. One such example may well be the Arndale Centre in Manchester, consisting of 200 shop units, eight major stores, a multistorey car park for 1800 cars and 20 000 square metres of office space. In total, lettable area is in excess of 100 000 square metres making it one of the largest covered shopping centres in Europe. The signs as yet, however, indicate that Manchester is sufficiently large to withstand the new addition without excessive loss of trade elsewhere. In the case of Newcastle, however, 40 000 square metres of retailing in the Eldon Square centre was a very major addition to the retailing space of the city, and quite sufficient to change the whole balance of the centre.

Rivalling these British developments in size, is La Part Dieu development in

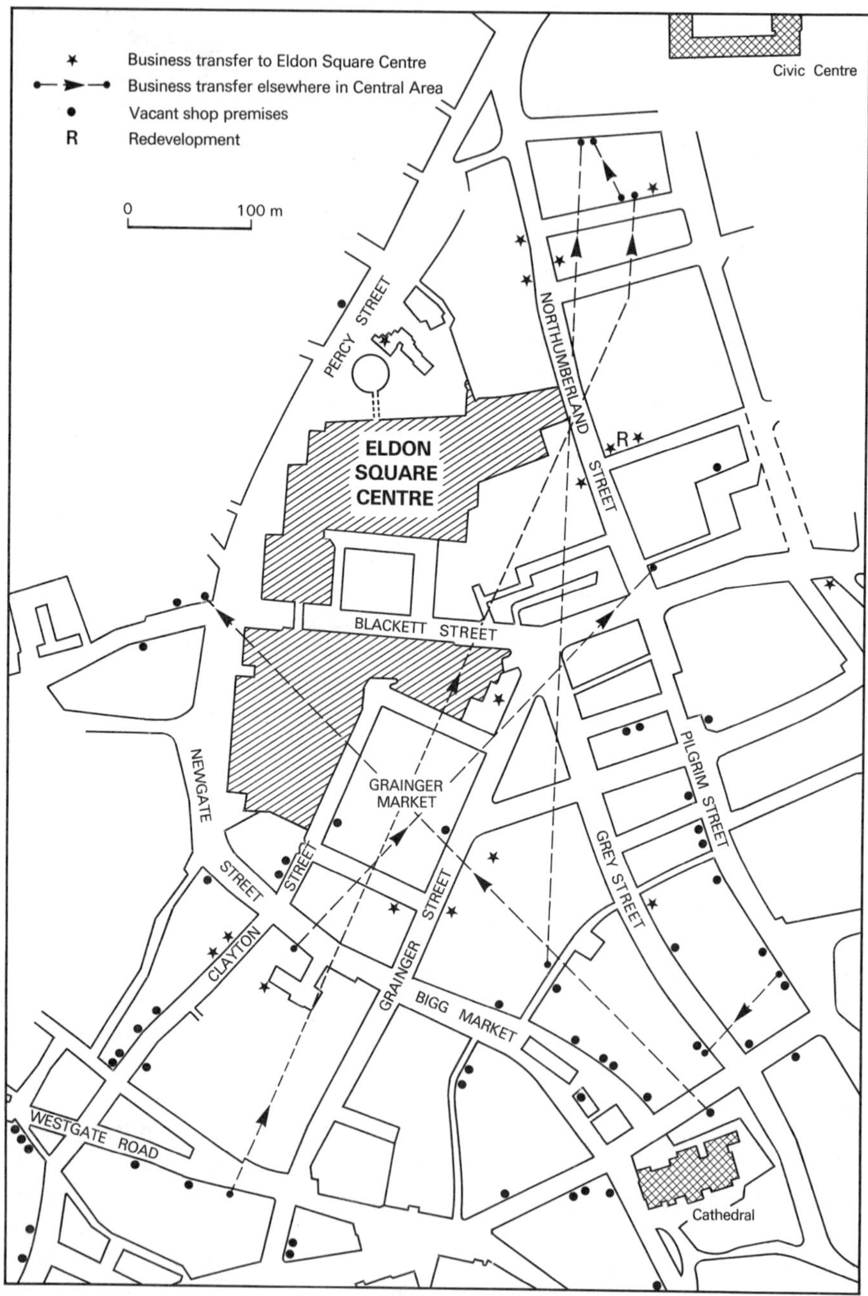

Figure 4.10 Transfer of businesses within the central area of Newcastle upon Tyne 1976–77 and vacant shop premises, 1977 (after Bennison and Davies, 1977) (reproduced by permission of Retailing and Planning Associates)

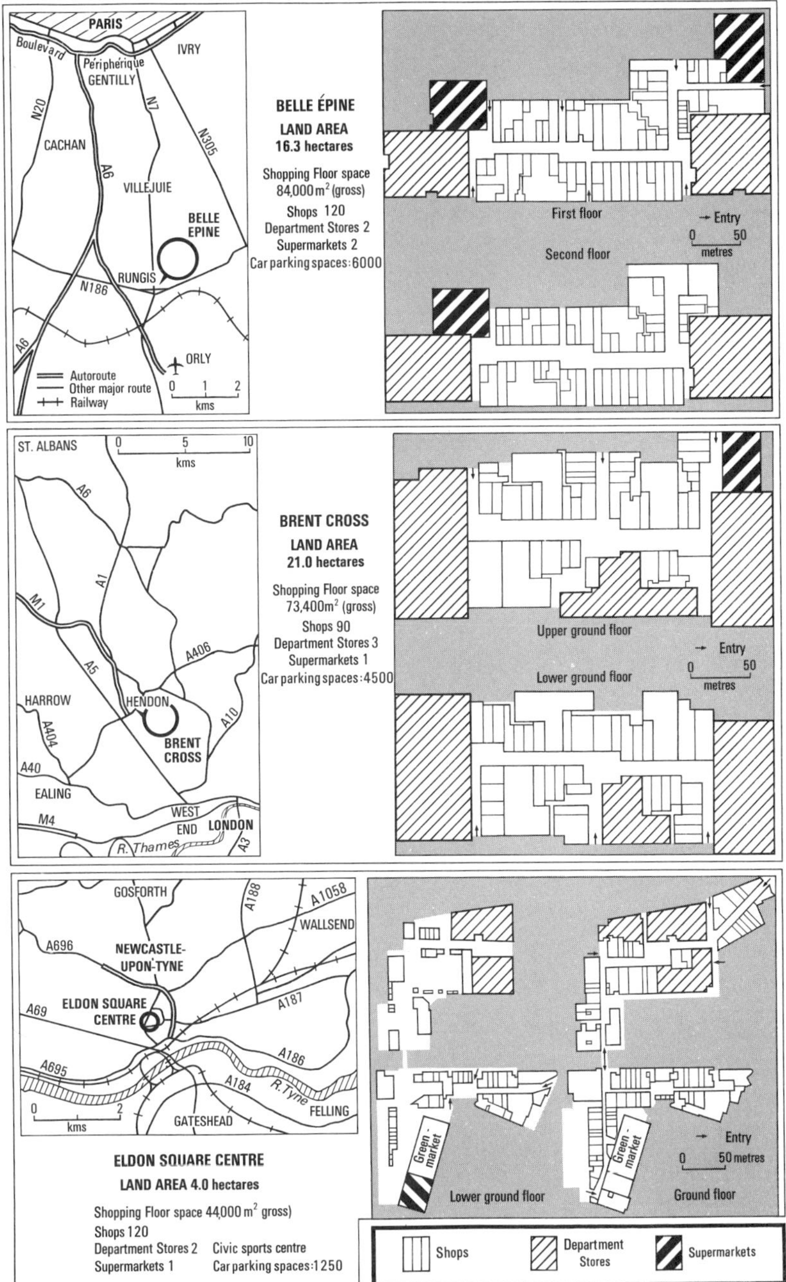

Figure 4.11 Regional shopping centres—the alternative approaches: (a) Belle Épine (Paris); (b) Brent Cross (London); (c) Eldon Square (Newcastle upon Tyne)

Lyons, with its retailing component totalling 110 000 square metres, with two department stores, three other major stores and 250 shops. It differs, however, with its greater commitment to office development with 450 000 square metres of office space.

Figure 4.11 illustrates three of the major centres discussed above to demonstrate their major differences. Each one may be seen as a new regional shopping centre, but they vary in their location from the outer suburban (Belle Épine, Paris), the inner suburban (Brent Cross, London) and the central city (Eldon Square, Newcastle upon Tyne).

The last 20 years has seen rapid changes in the retail sector. While it is tempting to suggest that those cities which redeveloped at a relatively early stage in the period missed the opportunities afforded for the construction of climatically controlled covered malls, this may not be supported by the facts of the situation. The fitting of major new centres into pre-existing shopping centres involves a delicate adjustment process and there is in Europe no consistent evidence to show that it is easily achieved, although it is by no means impossible. In a similar fashion, the out-of-town shopping mall has been shown to present problems unless it is very carefully controlled.

Changes in Wholesaling

It is not only in the office and retail sectors of tertiary activity that major changes have taken place. For instance, wholesaling has become more dispersed as sites have been selected offering less congestion than the central city and greater accessibility to and from the major road network. In both London and Paris the major food wholesale markets of Covent Garden and Les Halles respectively had by the 1960s become anachronistic in terms of their central city location. The moves to Nine Elms (London) and Rungis (Paris) have partially solved these problems, particularly in the case of Rungis which now occupies a strategic site close to Orly Airport and alongside the main autoroute south of Paris. Rungis has not fulfilled its original aim, however, of becoming more than a wholesale centre with major commercial and recreational facilities. It is situated close to Belle Épine, a regional shopping centre, but its offices are closely tied to the market function and its projected recreational and entertainment facilities could not face competition from the traditional attractions of central Paris. A further example of dispersal in the wholesaling sector is at Saarbrücken, where a regional wholesale centre is proposed to replace existing wholesaling functions both in Saarbrücken itself and in several cities of the eastern part of the Lorraine. Further movement of this particular function from established inner city locations would seem likely as wholesaling seeks the accessibility offered by new outer locations.

Patterns and Prospects in the Tertiary Sector

The pressures for change in the city have been very great indeed. Few city councils would opt for dispersion on a scale which could destroy the product of several centuries. Downtown decay would be a blight on the West European city which would be a betrayal of the strong tradition of European urbanism. More at issue is the degree of control and direction which combine to form a coherent planning policy. The safe approach of Britain to retailing developments in the general protection of its existing urban centres is a sharp contrast to anarchic planning of central Brussels or the relatively free dispersal of retailing into hypermarkets and regional shopping centres in France. It may be safely concluded that control policies are needed for office development from a number of points of view. Unrestricted speculative office development is socially and aesthetically unjustified, particularly when it displaces residences or even diminishes the quality of life for remaining city residents. A planning policy which uses the very powerful force of office growth to promote development where it is required, breathing new life into otherwise stagnating parts of the city, must meet with general approval. The Hamburgerstrasse development cited here is a good example of such a policy at work.

Strict control may not be the sensible long-term policy in all spheres of tertiary activity. Already in the case of the inner areas of London, problems have emerged as control measures have pushed economic activity well beyond the reach of these areas into outer metropolitan centres. Similarly, in the field of retailing, a middle course is to be preferred to one of complete control. The economic arguments in favour of out-of-town food retailing are very strong and there are signs that more European countries have now accepted the inevitability of this form of retailing. Naturally safeguards have to be included to protect those who have to rely on public transport for their journeys to shop but this problem is by no means insuperable as the diversion of bus routes into the Ruhr Centrum, Mülheim and Brent Cross have shown, given the political will and community involvement in decision-making. The movement of some functions such as food wholesaling would appear to be desirable from all points of view, since it ensures quicker turn round in the market as well as a more economic operation in general.

A serious area of doubt, however, must be in the area of regional shopping centres. This may be one area where close control at a high level is of vital importance. These centres render city-centre retailing at best unbalanced and at worst economically non-viable. Only in the largest can there be any real element of choice for the consumer. There are dangers in overprovision of regional centres, as demonstrated already by Paris. Fundamentally, however, they do create a uniformity of retailing which makes it difficult to distinguish the location of such centres anywhere in the western world. They lack the distinctiveness of the traditional centre of the European city, reflecting its growth and its heritage. Environmentally intrusive on their exterior with their huge car-parking lots and often bulky, drab architecture, inwardly they are environmentally sterile. They are not the true inheritance of the city in West Europe, where careful treatment of the existing city-centre can yield vastly superior results as many cities have shown.

CHAPTER 5

Urban Transport Planning

Some of the earliest known European planning legislation was concerned with solving the urban transport problem, when in the first century A.D. wheeled vehicles were prohibited in the city of Rome during the hours of daylight. The nature of the problem and the difficulties inherent in most situations stem, at their simplest, from a dilemma that is as old as urban civilization itself. Cities are established and grow because agglomeration offers a reduction in the costs of transport. But the concentration of people into a small area gives rise to congestion and increased transport costs. If urban governments react by doing nothing, then the increasing congestion inhibits the accessibility that is the city's *raison d'être*, whereas if they act to regulate the use of transport they raise its costs with the same potential effect.

It is possible to view the task of the urban transport planner as simply to reshape the city to accommodate the changing demands of transport upon it, so as to maximize the efficiency of movement. The context within which such planners worked in the major conurbations of Europe was composed of a 'large, rapidly changing urban area, a central concern for rising car ownership; an expectation of large investment funds for new and modified infrastructure, a belief that society should cater for all of the demand for mobility which was anticipated by a future date' (Moseley, 1979).

Two difficulties were always inherent in such an approach. First, future demands were predicted on the basis of current transport provision for a limited group of transport users, and the supply and demand for transport facilities are in practice related, not independent variables. Secondly, the function of transport is not only to satisfy demands for movement. It is a land-use in its own right, occupying as much as 30 per cent of the land area of cities. It is a major determinant of the physical structure of cities and both a creator and a reflection of the values and lifestyles of citizens: 'In defining the functions of transport, one is drawn back to the question of what sort of city one wants' (Thomson, 1977). The Economic Commission for Europe (1973) identified from among many three families of models that illustrated the differing aims of transport planning in European cities. Apart from the 'economic priority models' where the purpose of transport is to maximize the efficiency of the city's economic functions, there are 'welfare priority models', which stress the accessibility of citizens to the services of the city, and 'environmental priority models', where undesirable impacts on the urban environment are minimized.

The potential value of an international comparative approach where common solutions to common problems can be designed has long been apparent. The

Economic Commission for Europe called in 1974 for a definition of 'those problems which are of equal concern to all cities and states which require for their solution the closest kind of cooperation, joint research and the exchange of data and experience'. Such international forums have aided the diffusion of ideas on this topic across international boundaries more rapidly than in most of the aspects of planning discussed in this section. Distinctive national policies are less easily discerned. In continental terms, however, the distinctive history of the European city, the importance of its relict building forms, and the attitudes of Europeans towards accessibility, renders the experience of North American or Australian cities less relevant. If the West European city has distinct planning goals, as a central theme of this book asserts, then transport planning, as a major instrument of attaining these goals, will be distinctly West European.

The variety of proposed solutions makes a rigid classification of examples difficult, as there are few cities that have not, at some time or other, considered some application of most of the planning and management ideas discussed. Throughout West Europe, a common appreciation of the nature of the problem and a common determination that a solution must be found have not led to any consensus on either the goals to be achieved or the methods of attaining them. There is, however, a common sense of urgency that pervades the plans of city after city regardless of size or national identity, that was dramatically expressed by the Parisian planners in 1972. 'We are faced with two alternatives; either the traffic problem will be resolved in the future, or the economic, social and cultural life of the region already becoming day by day more sluggish will become completely paralysed' (Préfecture de la Région Parisienne, 1972).

The Demand for Transport in Cities

The typical journey taken within the urban region is short. A survey taken in London revealed an average journey length of only 1.5 km (Greater London Council, 1966), and similar work more recently in other West European cities has demonstrated a similar pattern. To this characteristic must be added two other peculiarities, the wide variety of origins and destinations that produces a complex and dispersed network of flows throughout the city, and a distinctive and extreme peaking of demand over time which produces regular daily and weekly rhythms.

The main exceptions to the dispersed pattern of the demand are the through traffic that results from the traditional function of cities as route centres and the long and medium-distance commuter flows that typically result in high density flows along narrow radial routes. In London, for example, 1.5 million people are transported from the suburbs into a few square kilometres of the inner city, within 1.5 hours on each weekday morning. The concentration of attention of these remarkably concentrated and regular commuter flows from the suburbs should not conceal the even more numerous, but less dramatically concentrated, flows that criss-cross the city. Goods' deliveries, for example, account for around 30 per cent of all vehicles on city streets (Organization for Economic Corporation and Development, 1974). The journey to work rarely accounts for more than 35 per cent of transport demand, and many of these trips are both short and not radial to the city centre. Even in London, which has the tradition of long-distance commuting described above, about a quarter of all journeys to work are by foot or bicycle (Blake, 1974) and the proportions for smaller towns is likely to be even higher. Similarly, journeys to shops, schools, leisure and those made in the course of business are less likely to conform to the characteristics of the commuter journey.

The requirement is therefore for a transport mode capable of handling economically a large number of short journeys over a wide variety of routes, with a capacity to accommodate a short but intense peaking of demand. Neither speed nor comfort are high-priority attributes. As yet no single transport system has been devised that possesses all these characteristics. Where flows of sufficient magnitude and regularity exist rapid transit systems of one kind or another satisfy the requirement for high capacity, but for the majority of intraurban journeys the flexibility of routing, and instant availability of the internal combustion-engined car, taxi, van or lorry have proved ideal.

This response of urban travellers to their transport needs has created another problem which the solutions described in the rest of this chapter are designed to solve. The motor vehicle, especially when used by an owner-driver has a number of fundamental disadvantages as a means of urban transport. Above all it is profligate in its use of space both when in use, and also for the 98 per cent of its existence when it is stationary. In Central London, for example, 800 000 cars are parked for periods of 8 hours or more each weekday. Consequently either existing transport routes become congested or large tracts of scarce urban land are used to ensure its continued circulation and parking. Most European cities devote between 10 and 20 per cent of their overall land area to accommodating the car. In Cologne, for example, road and parking space took up twice the area of the city's parks and almost half as much land as was devoted to buildings of all types. This disadvantage could be ignored when only small numbers of motorcars were in use and it is the rapid postwar increase in the number of cars used for intraurban journeys that has created the problem. The growth of cities in population and extent, the substantial increase in the real disposable income of citizens, and the desire of citizens for more space in lower-density residential areas as described in Chapter 6, have all both increased the demand for transport, and made it more likely that the private car would satisfy that demand.

The benefits of the motorcar to the owner were obvious, the costs incurred by the city as a whole were usually less tangible or measurable. There has, however, been a growing awareness of the costs of congestion, accidents, physical damage and visual intrusion into the environment that can be debited to the car when used in large numbers. Similarly, consumer choice between the use of private and public transport was increasingly distorted. For any particular journey the extra costs to the individual of using a car are small, and have either already been incurred, or will be borne by the public authorities. Increasing car use eroded the competitive position of alternative public transport as declining passenger revenues led to increased costs, and a pruning of routes and services. Certainly by the mid-1960s there were attempts to draw up a cost–benefit account of the car in many cities in Europe, and, although the detailed economics often remained obscure, there was a growing feeling that a problem of new and substantial dimensions had been unwittingly created and that solutions must be sought.

The Range of Possible Solutions

Few towns, and none of the major European conurbations, have committed themselves to a single transport system. It is not therefore realistic to talk of 'motorcar cities', 'bus-cities' or even 'pedestrian-cities'. It is possible, however, to arrange European cities along a spectrum which ranges from private to public transport according to the dominant 'mix' of the policies selected. Almost all cities have endeavoured to maintain and enhance some public transport while also making some effort to accommodate the motorcar. At the extremes a complete dependence on public transport can be found only in small specified areas of a few examples, while the most complete attempt to give free rein to the motorcar is the 1943 plan of the MARS (Modern Architects Research Society) group which redesigned London around a series of arterial roads—a plan that existed only on paper (Chapter 2 and Figure 2.9). A similar plan for a grid of motorways was proposed for Berlin in the 1946 *Kollektiv Plan*.

Such a private–public spectrum of transport strategies can be related to another spectrum of morphological archetypes. These range from a 'weak-centred city' at one extreme, where most jobs are dispersed throughout the city, to a 'strong-centred city' where employment, and also other less well-documented motives for travel such as shopping and entertainment, are strongly centralized. Thomson (1977) has gone so far as to try to calibrate such a spectrum suggesting that 120 000 city-centre jobs is the maximum capable of being served in a motorized 'weak-centred' city, while at the other extreme high-density public transport can support well over a million city-centre jobs in 'strong-centres' such as London and Paris. Such a comparison of morphological and transport archetypes begs the question whether the transport policies were devised as the only possible response to the existing urban structure, or whether favoured transport strategies are being used as an instrument for the creation of a desired urban form. Certainly some of the best examples of the 'weak-centred' city in Europe are 'new towns'. In Milton Keynes, for example, decentralization of functions was seen as a goal to be achieved through motorcar accessibility to all parts of the town (see Chapter 13). In Copenhagen, on the other hand (Thomson, 1977), residential suburbanization and the decentralization of employment which has left only about 250 000 jobs in the inner city, had occurred without a strong central design, and the task of the transport planners has been to try to serve what they regard as an undesirable morphology. At the other morphological extreme the 'strong-centred' cities, of which the biggest examples are London, Paris and Madrid, have responded by developing high-density transport systems to serve the structure that has evolved, while also endeavouring to decentralize functions which in turn will create new transport requirements (Table 5.1).

'A large city is mechanically different from a small city, just as a horse is mechanically different from a dog' (Thomson, 1977). The size of the city, in both

Table 5.1 Transport characteristics of some European cities

	City-centre jobs per km^2 of city area	City-centre jobs as per cent of total	km Urban railway	km Urban motorway
London	44	16	962	54
Paris	44	18	464	96
Hamburg	46	9	274	30
Stockholm	13	9	340	174
Manchester	54	—	—	—
Copenhagen	18	9	125	45
Vienna	—	8	58	6
Athens	26	9	26	0

Source: after Thomson, 1977

population and physical extent, is the most important determinant of the chosen point on the spectrum of solutions. Size not only increases the intensity of the problem but also alters its nature. Small towns will satisfy a large proportion of their transport demand by walking and cycling, and the use of the motorcar poses few problems. As size increases the flows become large enough to support bus services. The conference of European Ministers of Transport in 1972 recognized a critical settlement size of from 100 000 to 150 000 inhabitants, as being sufficient to support a viable intraurban bus system, and sufficient for car-use to be discouraged by restraints. Surface and underground railways generally need populations of over a million to provide flows of sufficient density to justify their construction, although the development of tram and 'mini-metro' systems may prove viable in cities with fewer inhabitants as in a number of West German cities. Such a simple classification of model choice by population size seems to be borne out empirically although the calibration of the model varies widely from country to country, and many other variables will intervene to distort the pattern (Table 5.2).

The physical setting will exacerbate particular problems and favour particular solutions. River crossings concentrate traffic in flows and encourage high-density solutions. Rotterdam, for example, would have difficulty justifying the costs of metro construction on population size alone. The first two bridges were built across the Nieuwe Maas in 1878. The development of the city's southern suburbs increased the demand for trans-Maas traffic and the Maas tunnel was opened in 1942. Further expansion of the southern suburbs and increasing car ownership caused traffic through the tunnel to increase from 8 million vehicles in 1950 to 24 million by 1962. Predictions of transport demand prophesied further growth and the new Brienenoord bridge and Benelux tunnel were both used to capacity almost immediately they were built. The alternatives therefore were either to build a further five or six bridges or road tunnels by the end of the century or to install a short metro line under the river which alone could carry 30 000 passengers an hour. The Rotterdam river-crossing problem finds an echo in many other cities. In Stockholm surface railways provide the inter-island links and in both London and Paris the underground systems carry a high proportion of the river-crossing traffic. Coastal and lakeside sites, such as Geneva and Zurich, and 'offshore' island sites such as

Table 5.2 Public transport use in Dutch[a] and Italian[b] cities

	Pop (000)	Bus/tram passengers (million)	Trips per hour
Amsterdam	751	178	237
Rotterdam	615	150	244*
The Hague	479	100	209
Utrecht	251	41	163
Groningen	163	12	74
Nijmegen	148	11	74
Maastricht	111	12	108
Milan	1 723	475	276†
Turin	1 199	225	188
Genoa	804	212	264
Bologna	490	158	322
Florence	465	112	241
Verona	271	33	122
Padua	240	33	138
Modena	178	44	247

* Not including metro passengers
† 643 if metro passengers are included
Sources: [a] Rijksplanologische Dienst. (RPD) (1976); [b]Città di Torino (1976)

Portsmouth, similarly distort the simple relationship between population size and traffic intensity. The tendency of political boundaries to run along rivers is a further complication that may hinder the development of an effective policy for handling the cross-river flows, as for example in Mainz where the river constitutes the *Land* boundary. The extreme case is perhaps found in Venice where the single causeway between the mainland and historic lagoon city could not begin to handle the traffic that would normally be generated by a city-centre. Instead its inadequacy provides the opportunity for the complete exclusion of the motorcar and its replacement by the public transport of the *vaporetti* (the water taxi) and the gondola.

Transport policies have to be imposed upon an existing city with a given morphology and transport infrastructure. The presence of a valued historical legacy has often, in practice, favoured the adoption of policies of motorcar restraint and the encouragement of forms of transport considered to be less environmentally damaging. Similarly, the survival of transport installations, such as city-centre railway stations, engineering works and rights of way, may render viable transport systems whose construction would not now be justified. Again, in practice, it has often been public transport, especially railways and trams, that have been favoured by such inertia.

The social character of a town, in terms of age, income and class should be a determinant of the mix of transport policies adopted and even the viability of different forms of transport in particular districts of the city. This is, however, difficult to demonstrate empirically. A greater-than-average reliance on public bus transport, and a greater profitability of bus undertakings, can be found, for example, in Bournemouth and Bradford, and this can be related to the elderly age structure of the former and the social class of the latter, but quite contradictory examples can be easily produced. Logically these social variables should favour the adoption of public transport solutions but the profitability of undertakings clearly depends on many other factors.

Attitudes towards transport, and particularly towards the use of transport planning to attain other desired planning objectives, clearly depend on the overall ideology of the city's administrators. Transport policies in practice evolve as a balance between the economic and welfare motives, and between the various lobbies that influence the decision-makers at national and local level. Nationally the 'car lobby' has been influential in the countries of West Europe with important motor vehicle industries. In West Germany, for example, a little less than a fifth of the labour force find work in this important export industry and its offshoots, while in Britain and France the government itself has a large direct investment in the manufacture of motorcars.

At a local level it is to be expected that a leftwing city government as in Bologna would operate rigorous car restraint policies and partially free public transport, while a rightwing city government as in Milan has traditionally favoured new road construction. In most cities elements of both change and stability are present. Changes in political control may be a result or an effect of change in transport policy. There is little doubt that public opposition to the London Ringway proposals were a major cause of the Labour victory in the 1973 GLC elections, and the regular swing of the political pendulum in cities such as Nottingham is reflected in equally regular changes in transport management strategies. There is, however, a built-in stability on the professional side to counter political change. Planners, and transport managers possess the innate conservatism that afflicts professions with a lengthy training and hierarchical structure. Many of the struggles over transport policy that occurred in the town halls of Europe in the 1970s were essentially between transport specialists implementing a received conventional wisdom, and the spokesmen of an articulate public opinion which had shifted radically against attempts to accommodate growing motorcar use. The opportunities for the expression of such dissent varied with the national planning laws and customs but was apparent earlier in British, Scandinavian and Netherlands towns, and generally appeared only towards the end of the decade in French and Italian towns.

Finally, the choice of solution cannot be determined by reference to the individual city alone. Regional, national and even international demand for movement imposes further constraints on the range of choices available. Cities act as ports, airports and even international road entry points. Geneva, for example, is under considerable pressure to construct a costly new urban motorway link either tunnelling under the Lake or through the southern suburbs of the city, in response to the demands of traffic on the E2 and E15 routes, most of which is neither originating nor terminating in the city, or in many cases even in the country, whereas the city-canton has the highest population density of all the Swiss cities and has little land to spare for such projects (Chapter 12) (République et Canton de Genève, 1977).

It is apparent that many of these constraints on the choice of transport policy are more effective in the cities of West Europe than in the rest of the western world. In particular the existing heritage of the built environment is more plentiful and more valued, which in turn reflects different values in the choice of residential amenity and lifestyle. There is also a longer established welfare tradition and a public acceptance of restraints on motorcar use that has developed in response to a quite different experience of the availability of space. While 'motorization', and the accompanying 'suburbanization' of industry, retailing and residence on the North American pattern can be seen as a possible European future, it is only one among a number of alternative strategies open to the West European city.

Solutions: Planning for Private Transport

(1) Policies of Accommodation

The steady increase in the popularity of the motorcar for intraurban travel in the last 20 years is well documented and the advantages to the individual of opting for the car in preference to public transport have been adequately stated (Meyer *et al.*, 1965). It is not really surprising that the initial response of planners to this growth in public demand was to endeavour to accommodate the demand by providing road and parking facilities that would enable its advantages to be realized. The benefits to the user were apparent from the first, the costs to a wider society only became apparent when the number of cars in use increased beyond a certain level. By the time that threshold had been reached, a substantial portion of citizens had invested in cars, many others aspired to do so, and their rights to use them could only be denied with difficulty and at some political risk in a democratic society.

By the end of the 1960s cities such as Munich, Birmingham and Turin had built complete systems of ringways and radial routes of motorway standard, with considerable governmental assistance. The influential *Traffic in Towns* Buchanan report (Ministry of Transport, 1963) was interpreted by some as a warning of the costs of adapting old cities to the new transport demands but many practising planners saw it rather as propounding the development of 'transport corridors' which would remove traffic from interstitial neighbourhoods, and justify the building of high-quality urban motorways. Buchanan himself at a GLC enquiry in 1971 commented that 'the failure to provide an adequate road network was producing devastating environmental results besides congestion'.

Parisian experience has been regarded initially as an archetype to be imitated, and less than a decade later as a warning to be heeded. Paris, in common with many other cities, responded to the growth in car ownership by an expensive attempt to accommodate it. The PADOG plan of 1962 and the *Schéma Directeur* of 1965 both included an extensive new motorway-standard road-building programme. Some 800 km of new expressway were planned (Figure 5.1) which included two-and-a-half ringroads. These were the *Boulevard Périphérique* at about 5 kilometres from the city-centre just beyond the walls of the *ville de Paris* and the Outer Ring (the *ARISO*) which linked the suburbs of Versailles, Orly and St Denis, at about 10 kilometres from the centre, with a third ring beyond these, the *Rocade de Banlieu* which was proposed only in its southern segment. The flow of traffic through the inner city was to be maintained by instituting the most extensive one-way circulation system in Europe, and by building a new west-to-east expressway through the centre including tunnelling underneath the Place de la Concorde and the Louvre. A parallel east-to-west expressway along the *quais* of the left bank was also proposed. In addition the eight major radial routes that linked Paris to the provincial cities of France were to be completed to motorway standard and linked to the *Boulevard Périphérique*. Although there was to be a simultaneous substantial investment in new public transport facilities, there was no formal policy of restraint on car-use and even proposals to restrict parking, such as meters in the inner city, were rejected on four occasions during the 1960s.

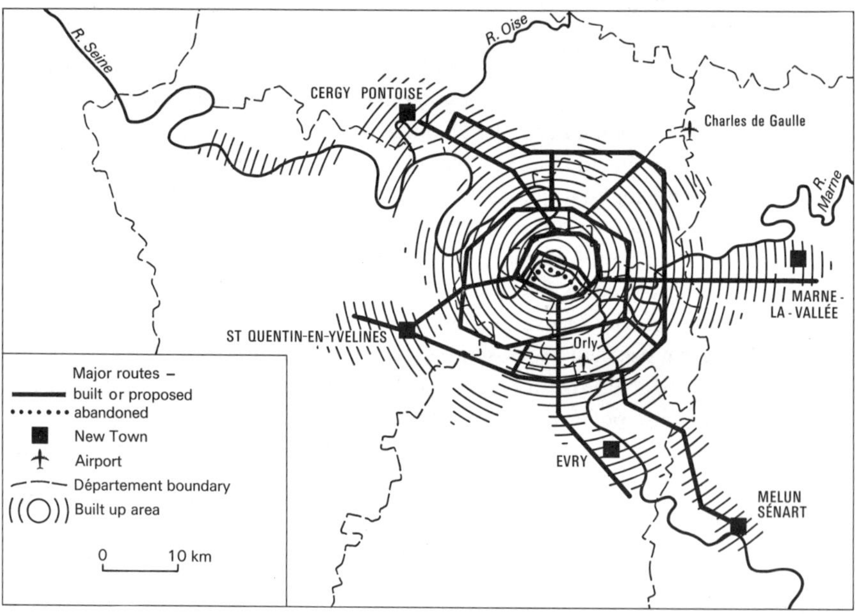

Figure 5.1 Major road planning proposals for the Paris region (reproduced by permission of I.A.U.R.I.F.)

A distinct shift in emphasis can be noted in the first few years of the 1970s, reflecting changes in public opinion, in the conventional wisdom of planners (Chapter 11), and in the presidency of the Republic. The *Boulevard Périphérique* has proved inadequate and dangerous. The left bank motorway proposals were amended in 1971 and abandoned altogether in 1974. Even parking controls became more acceptable and were slowly introduced, and enforced, after 1974.

London in the 1960s had a tradition of public transport use, especially for the journey to work, and an interwar and postwar history of very little major road construction. The feeling in the GLC was that the city had fallen behind its continental counterparts in improving the mobility of its citizens and a major road-building programme was long overdue. Figures on the length of urban motorway available for each million inhabitants, which was 40 kilometres in Paris and well over 100 kilometres in many North American cities, were used to publicize the point. The result was the London Ringway plan (Figure 5.2) which proposed no fewer than four complete circular routes around the city, totalling almost 600 kilometres, at various radii from the city centre. Neither the plans, nor the roads themselves, were completely original, since successive London plans, including Abercrombie's 1945 plan, had included some ringroad proposals and the new scheme would incorporate the incomplete results of previous plans, such as the North Circular Road built in the 1930s. The scale of the enterprise and the determination of the council to implement it were, however, original and provided a radical solution to the problem of filtering the traffic from nine radial motorways built since 1959 into the city. Road space would be provided for an additional annual 74 million vehicle-kilometres, compared with an existing 34 million vehicle-kilometres.

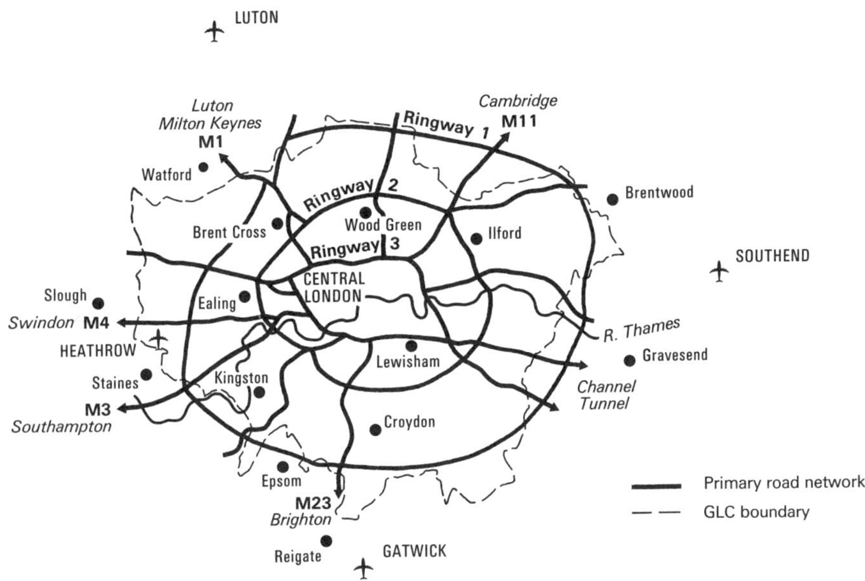

Figure 5.2 London's Ringway proposals

Opposition was slow to develop and focused on the cost of the project in terms of both construction cost, estimated at £2500 million in 1972, and the loss of existing housing, variously estimated at between 3000 and 6000 units. Opposition had grown by 1971 when two-thirds of all public objections at the Greater London Development Plan enquiry concerned the transport proposals, and the council modified the scheme by halving its cost, and downgrading the road standards proposed. A combination of local protestors whose homes were threatened with demolition, and a more general shift in public opinion towards public transport as part of a more diffuse but popular conservation ethic, made opposition to the ringways a major plank in the Labour party challenge to the Conservative-controlled GLC in the 1973 election. This policy, together with a general national swing in Labour's favour, swept to power a party inextricably committed to cancelling the road plan and producing a transport policy that favoured public transport. Although this political change parallels the shift in Parisian policies from those of Pompidou to those of d'Estaing, it was more abrupt and public, and even a reversion to Conservative control could not resurrect either the ringway plan or the spirit in which it was conceived.

The accommodating policies of London and Paris were initiated in a large number of smaller towns, some of which such as Munich built complete ring and radial urban motorway networks. Similarly the *volte-face* of the early 1970s percolated through to the provincial towns during the course of the decade. By its close, planners in cities throughout Europe, with perhaps the notable exception of Athens, had accepted the view that, 'no amount of ingenious juggling by engineers and architects is capable of adapting long established centres to accommodate large flows of traffic and vast highways, except over a period and at a cost that makes it an irrelevancy' (Bendixson, 1974).

(2) Policies of Restraint

Various methods of restraining car and lorry use and making the costs of their use payable by the user have been canvassed, including differential road pricing by time or space, or even a policy of non-action so that the resulting congestion discourages continued use. The most common policy, however, has been to physically prevent car access to limited areas and the dedication of these areas to pedestrian use. A recent report of the OECD (Organization for Economic Cooperation and Development, 1974) revealed that the cities of Europe were experiencing a 'creeping pedestrianization' of their central areas, and that a wide variety of approaches had been adopted. An alternative to the complete exclusion of vehicles is to exclude only certain categories and to allow buses, as in Hannover and Bremen, or taxis or delivery vehicles, or to permit vehicles only at certain times such as before 10.00 am in Innsbruck and most West German cities. Spatially, selective prohibitions of this sort impose costs on existing businesses and residents which often restricts the size of area selected. Pedestrianized areas as large as in Munich or Copenhagen are exceptional. A ring-and-loop traffic system, as in Norwich, the city which pioneered pedestrianization in the United Kingdom in 1962, improves vehicle access to the city-centre while preventing through traffic movements (Figure 5.3), a scheme that has been widely imitated.

One of the most radical experiments in restraint policy occurred in Nottingham where previous attempts at accommodation through major road-building were reversed in 1972, and a strategy based on imposing time-penalties on drivers was instituted. All routes into the city-centre were controlled by traffic signals that imposed lengthy delays at peak times, although buses were routed quickly through this 'collar'. Opposition by the car-using public and the failure of even these draconian measures to increase markedly the use of buses which were offered as an alternative, led to the abandonment of the strategy when the Conservative party won control of the city council in 1976. The idea cannot be counted a complete failure in that modified versions of such 'collar' policies have been applied in other towns, including Leicester and Southampton.

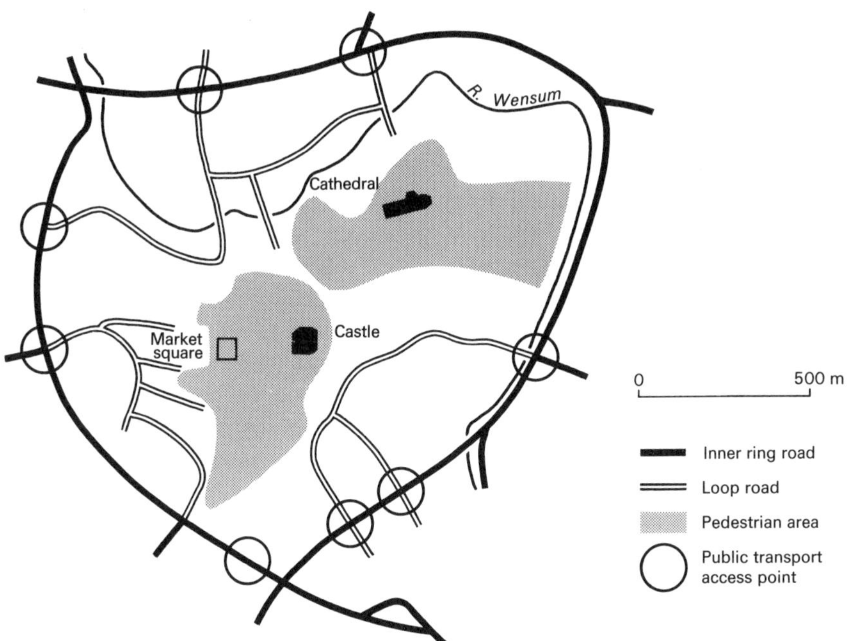

Figure 5.3 Norwich ring-loop traffic management scheme (reproduced by permission of Norwich City Council)

Restraints on the parking of cars can be as effective as those on their movement, and simultaneously increase the amount of road space available for circulation. London introduced parking meters as early as 1958, and halved the amount of onstreet parking available between 1961 and 1971. Other major cities were much slower to follow this lead with parking in Paris and Vienna still being largely uncontrolled. Parking policies can be more than a simple restraint on car use. They can, through different pricing strategies, be a subtle instrument differentiating between types of user, such as short-stay shoppers and long-stay commuters, different districts of the city, and even combined with public transport in park-and-ride schemes. Oxford and Nottingham, among other examples, run park-and-ride schemes for Christmas shoppers, and Southampton for football spectators. Local authorities have found it relatively easy, once the political will is present, to control on-street parking, but much harder to control the availability of off-street parking, much of which is provided by private concerns for their employees, or customers. With as much as half of the parking spaces in the central city being outside the direct control of the local authority, parking restraint strategies are rendered both less effective and socially discriminating. In Central London, for example, there were 51 000 private non-residential parking spaces in 1974 compared with only 23 000 public off-street places (Netter, 1977). Only a few years ago local authorities encouraged the provision of private parking, and now cities in Britain, the Netherlands and Scandinavia are seeking ways of taxing such spaces, or closely controlling them at the stage of planning consent.

(3) *Policies for Alternative Private Transport*

The dominance of the owner-driven motorcar as a method of private transport has led planners to underestimate the importance of other forms of private transport and, with the exception of a handful of cities, neglect their potential. Travel by foot, for example, is an essential part of every journey, but until recently little provision for, or encouragement of walking was made. Even in a city as large as London around 17 per cent of all journeys to work were undertaken on foot. This percentage is not far short of the number travelling by train, and appears to be growing slowly.

Pedestrianization can be viewed not only as an instrument of traffic control but more positively as a long overdue provision for an alternative mode of transport. The pedestrianization of London Street, Norwich, Strøget, Copenhagen, or Lijnbaan, Rotterdam, in the early 1960s, was followed by the creation of complete networks of pedestrian routes in Bremen, Essen and Munich between 1965 and 1967. Such thinking can be taken further with the weatherproofing of routes such as Exhibition Road in London's South Kensington and from the station to Kropke in Hannover, and even the introduction of pedestrian conveyors where the density of the traffic justifies the investment, such as for example at Gothenburg station in Denmark and the Bank in the City of London. The limits of such policies are the costs they impose on other traffic, and the short journey length attempted on foot, which in practice are between 1 and 1.5 kilometres (Cottle, 1973).

The bicycle provides cheap, pollution-free transport, at a speed not far short of the average for inner urban journeys. The decline in its use as a means of transport rather than a sport can be attributed to an intrinsic lack of comfort and to its increasing vulnerability to other traffic. The latter can be reduced by a separate routing system which should lead to an increase in bicycle use with consequent savings in road space. The provision of segregated bicycle or motor-cycle routes was relatively easy in new towns such as Stevenage or Zoetermeer, or in new housing developments such as Stockholm's Västeras. The imposition of a bicycle priority system on an existing town has proved more difficult with attempts at Cambridge, Peterborough and Portsmouth making use of a mixture of existing and new roads. In the last case the opposition of residents and shopkeepers to restrictions on motorcar access successfully caused the abandonment of the scheme. Nevertheless, in both Cambridge and Peterborough more than a fifth of all work trips are taken by bicycle.

Hired cars and taxis combine some of the flexibility of the privately owned car, with many of the space-saving attributes of public transport. A relatively small fleet can handle a large volume of traffic. London's 10 000 taxis, for example, carry between 30 and 40 per cent of all the West End's passenger traffic (Bendixson, 1974). Licensing anomalies often restrict their availability, most notably in Paris, planners have been slow to recognize taxis as a 'public automobile service', and cost precludes their use by many. Nevertheless, privileged use of road space alongside buses, as in London's Oxford Street or the Parisian bus lane system, and the experimental development of communal taxis, or 'dial-a-ride' schemes, as in Gothenburg, Amsterdam or Montpellier, are an indication of an increasing recognition.

Solutions: Planning for Public Transport

Planning solutions that rely on public transport playing a major role were motivated by three main concerns. It was evident in cities throughout Europe in the 1960s that public transport operations were in increasing financial difficulty. The cycle of declining patronage and contraction of services threatened their continued operation and posed the stark choice between intervention or ultimate extinction. In the three largest cities of the Netherlands, for instance, the financial deficit on municipal transport undertakings increased from Fl25 million in 1961 to Fl450 million in 1973. The steady 4 per cent annual decline in passenger numbers on London Transport undertakings throughout the 1960s and early 1970s, was around the average for major conurbations in West Europe. Secondly, the costs of alternative policies brought together taxpayers, residents whose homes were threatened by road proposals and, latterly, energy conservationists, into a powerful public transport lobby. Thirdly, and least effective, was an equity argument that appealed on behalf of those destined always to be 'captive to public transport' by virtue of age, infirmity or poverty, despite its deterioration. The welfare argument prepared the way for operational subsidies while the economic argument sanctioned capital investments at least as great as those demanded by private transport. As a result there occurred a renaissance of interest in public transport and in many cities some transport systems received their first new investment since they had been built in the nineteenth century.

The range of solutions applied across the continent is wide, and even within individual cities different forms of public transport were built, often in a confusion of complementarity and competition. It is useful, however, to distinguish between railway and bus systems. The former are characterized by their use of a fixed and exclusive right of way, which is costly to acquire but confers benefits of speed and high capacity. The cities that make a proportionally high use of urban railways, especially for long-distance radial commuter journeys, such as London or, on a smaller scale, Liège, Liverpool or Hannover, use in almost every case an historical endowment of routes that would be prohibitively expensive to construct today. Most transport policies have confined themselves to encouraging the use of these facilities and extending their scope, rather than building new lines. Among the exceptions to this is Liverpool where a 3.2 kilometre loop line and a 1.9 kilometre link between existing termini have essentially tidied up the Victorian heritage (Halsall, 1978). Although examples of completely new rail systems are rare, the few that have been built are spectacular. The new town of Zoetermeer, near The Hague, includes a purpose-built commuter railway system with six new stations in the residential districts of the town, and a frequent service known as 'the sprinter' into the city. In Paris, the Réseau Express Régional (RER) which will provide two cross-city routes was proposed as an integral part of decentralization policies (Chapter 11), and link the outer suburbs with the metro lines of the inner city. But like all transport investments, the RER benefits some groups more than others and in this case it is the long-distance commuting office worker who gains most.

Surface railways were built to carry dense regular flows over the relatively long suburb–city line haul, and metros or subways were designed mainly as inner city distributors, although the larger systems, notably those of London and more recently Paris, have extended lines into the suburbs. Given the very high cost of metro construction, and the high volume of traffic needed to justify their use, it is remarkable that after more than 50 years when little was invested no less than eleven West European cities are building new underground systems and some of the fifteen existing systems are being extended. London's Victoria and Jubilee lines and the extension of lines 3, 8 and 13 in Paris, have improved the cover and connectivity of the largest and busiest networks. Antiquated systems such as in Glasgow have been extensively modernized (Acton, 1979). A number of cities, including Hannover, Cologne, Essen, Antwerp and Brussels have built underground sections to their tramways which in the last city has been converted into a fully fledged metro. But more remarkable has been the building of new metros in cities previously considered too small to support such high-capacity transport. The case of Rotterdam is explicable in terms of the Maas crossing, but more recent developments in Amsterdam, Marseilles and Seville owe more to faith than accurate appraisals of their economic viability. In Lyons, the new metro which many saw as a 'white elephant' now carries 120,000 passengers a day, over 30 per cent of whom did not use public transport previously. The metro has become the spearhead of a campaign to support public transport.

Trams offer lower construction costs and greater flexibility in responding to changes in demand, and can sustain either the speed advantages of exclusive track or the convenience of circulation on the public road. There are a wide variety of light street railway systems running on, above, and occasionally under, the surface. Some, such as the Copenhagen *S-bane* or the *S-bahnen* in Berlin and Hamburg, are little different from suburban railways serving long-distance radial flows, while others such as the trams of Brussels or Rotterdam are short-stage distributors akin to high-capacity buses. As with underground railways, light street railways have returned to favour with transport planners after a generation which rejected them as slow and congestion-creating. Unfortunately in many cities, notably in Britain, the renaissance of interest occurred too late, and trams remain only as seaside novelties. High capacities, a frugal use of manpower and a realization of the potential offered by reserved track sections has considerably extended the role of tram systems in cities with existing networks, such as Amsterdam, Oslo and Vienna. A number of new networks are planned including both 'supertram' systems, as in Tyne and Wear where similarity to a conventional railway has led to disputes about who should operate it, and 'minitram' systems, such as has been proposed in Sheffield and the London borough of Croydon (Milne, 1974), which are little more than reserved track bus systems.

Buses have carried the majority of public transport passengers in cities for two generations. In small and medium-sized towns they are generally the only public transport available, and in the major conurbations they act as collectors and distributors for rapid transit and handle the bulk of short journeys. Despite their operational flexibility and absence of costly fixed investment in track, a decline in the numbers of passengers carried has been evident over the last 10 to 20 years in almost every city in West Europe (Heggie and Bailey, 1977). This decline has caused concern among planners and politicians, who regard a viable bus system as a necessity for the carless residuum of citizens, and an essential prerequisite for the success of car-restraint policies.

The strategies that attempt to stem the loss of passengers are of two types. There are those that tilt the balance of financial advantage in favour of buses, and almost all local authorities subsidize their bus undertakings through tax concessions, investment grants or operational subsidies. In a few cases, this policy has gone further and buses have been operated as a free welfare service rather than a trading enterprise. Both the complete but shortlived Rome experiment with free buses (Tumiati, 1972) and the longer-term but more restricted experiment in Bologna (Kupka, 1976) did increase the use of buses but only marginally at the expense of the motorcar. Few cities have been tempted to imitate these examples. If buses are to offer an alternative to the car, and not just a safety net for the carless, then speed, reliability and convenience appear to be more important than fare levels. The bus-only lane, taken to its logical extreme in the exclusive bus roads of the new towns of Runcorn and Evry, is a low-cost, effective strategy that has been applied throughout the continent in various forms. Combined with better publicity and new timetabling such bus priority schemes have stemmed and in some cases marginally reversed the decline in bus passengers in cities as varied as Southampton, Gothenburg, Turin, Reading and Breda.

Solutions: Planning for Integration

If the 1960s can be characterized as the period when planners began in city after city to plan for improved public transport, then the 1970s can be typified by the drive for integration, in both the physical sense of interchange between different transport modes, and in the administrative sense of the creation of coordinating transport authorities.

The largely piecemeal growth of public transport facilities and the policies for their support left a legacy of confused ownership and management. Competition between similar modes under different management, or between different modes under the same management, weakened the financial position of the undertakings and generally added little to the convenience of the customer.

A realization that almost all journeys were multimodal, and that different modes could specialize in separate parts of the journey led to more attention being devoted to transport interchanges. At its simplest this involved the siting together of bus, train, tram and taxi facilities most usually at the railway station whose location was regarded as fixed, although at Bochum it too was moved to a more convenient site. New central interchanges were the major landscape manifestation of integration which could imply more far-reaching transport strategies. In Amsterdam, for example, buses are used as collectors in the less densely peopled suburbs, feeding tram routes that handle the denser inner city flows. Similarly in Paris, the RER and SNCF railway lines handle the longer-distance traffic, linking with the metro and bus network for distribution within the inner city.

The flexibility of the private car can also be combined with the high speed and capacity of rapid transit in various ways. Park-and-ride facilities have been provided outside the inner city as an integrated part of car restraint policies, and subsidized parking encourages a change of transport to railway, metro, tram or bus services. In Copenhagen, for example, car-restraint policies in the inner city are combined with generous parking provision at the suburban *S-bane* stations. The Dutch propose to reduce the amount of public parking available in the three largest cities to a standard of 30 places per hectare and to concentrate almost all of this at the suburban rail and metro termini (Rijksplanologische Dienst., 1976). In Paris where restrictions on parking have been traditionally lax, and with a consequently large-scale disregard of parking regulations a two-tier hierarchy of park-and-ride facilities is planned. Around 15 000 free places will be sited at the outer surburban railway stations, and a further 13 000 chargeable places will be available for those who prefer to drive into the inner suburban stations.

The problems of integrated transport management have generally proved to be more intractable. The earliest case was the *Berliner Verkehrs Betriebe* founded after the creation of Greater Berlin in the 1920s. Today it is among the largest local transport organizations in West Germany. The creation in 1965 of a *Verkehrsverband* in Hamburg, charged with the future planning and current management of all transport within the Greater Hamburg city-region has been hailed as 'the outstanding institutional innovation of our time in the field' (Thomson, 1977). Its success in increasing the use of public transport while lowering the costs caused by duplication is impressive, but attempts by other cities to imitate this have had a mixed response. Hannover has had a unified fare and timetabling structure for trains, trams and buses since 1962, without slowing down significantly the drift away from public transport. Other West German cities, of which the largest is Munich, have successfully integrated operational aspects of urban public transport, including the use of common tickets.

Integration beyond this level has proved much more difficult. Different transport organizations have different cost structures, functions and operational traditions. In practice there is often a sharp difference in approach between railway companies, whose suburban operations are only a small part of a national network and tram and bus undertakings that operate only in the city. Even in smaller towns there is a marked distinction between the structure of fares, timetables and cross-subsidies of municipal companies and the subsidiaries of national companies.

In Britain the 1968 Transport Act tried to focus on 'the totality of transport' and established coordinating Passenger Transport Authorities, which at their best, as for example in the SELNEC region (south-east Lancashire and north-east Cheshire, centred on Manchester) produced coherent management strategies, but could equally become no more than a forum for the exchange of information. It has been argued that the fragmentation of political control between different local authorities, and in particular the political separation of cities from their outer suburbs, made transport planning for the city-region difficult. British cities, even after the 1974 reorganization of local government, suffered from a division of responsibility between county and borough authorities. In Paris the RATP cooperates with, but does not control, the

SNCF's suburban rail services. In practice few of the large European conurbations have followed the advice of the Economic Commission for Europe (1973) and integrated their urban transport at all three levels of services and fares, management policy and long-term strategic planning. In Stockholm the SL, or Greater Stockholm Urban Transport Authority, was established in 1967, to move towards this ideal, and now operates bus, tram and underground railway systems, both within the city and the surrounding 'county'. In addition the state railways operate the commuter rail lines under contract to SL (Poole, 1976). Among the primate cities Copenhagen has proceeded furthest, as a result perhaps of the existence of a Greater Copenhagen Regional Planning Council that brings political responsibility to the regional level, and the existence of an efficient public transport system as a necessary prerequisite for the success of the city-region plan as a whole.

The Future

The increasing use of the private car and its freight-carrying equivalents, has encouraged the suburbanization of people, jobs and services already initiated by the train, tram and bus. A style of urban living centred around the two-storey family house with garden and garage has been attained by many, and is desired by many more (Rijksplanologische Dienst., 1976). The movement demands occasioned by such a way of life can be adequately met only by private transport. Serious attempts to restrain car use are therefore an assault upon the valued achievements or aspirations of citizens. In addition few planners have had the opportunity to plan upon a *tabula rasa*, but must work with a legacy of transport facilities, companies, demands and habits. Overshadowing their efforts has been the cloud of the predicted future growth in car use, and the spectre of the American example which has been regarded as the harbinger of the fate of the European city. Small wonder, therefore, that conclusions have often been gloomy and many transport plans are seen as short-term palliatives that only delay the approach of armageddon, which is imagined to be either the thrombosis of the cities' transport arteries through increased demand, or alternatively the rebuilding of the European city in the style of Detroit or Los Angeles.

Radical solutions designed to stave off these advancing spectres have generally relied either on new technology or the creation of new urban structures. New mixed-mode vehicles, guidance, routing and propulsion systems have been announced at regular intervals (Richards, 1966), but these generally contribute little to solving the social, economic and political aspects of the problem. Much simpler technological innovations have often been more effective, such as for example the 'flexibus' that eases services in the cramped inner city, or automated ticket issuing and cancelling machines that economize on labour cost. 'Until a new approach is designed for the analysis of cities, to discuss how well they meet human needs, rather than how well they function as machines, there will be no reliable way of assessing the adequacy of these transport systems or the best way of improving them' (Thomson, 1977). Similarly attempts to destructure the city to create patterns of demand more easily served by public transport (Heeger, 1977) is having only marginal success. 'Cautious incrementalism' (O'Sullivan, 1978) using on the whole existing technologies, and causing only those adjustments in lifestyle acceptable to the majority of the citizens of democratic cities, is the pattern for the future as for the present. While spectacular success is unlikely, equally those prophets who foresee the collapse of Western urban civilization beneath the unsolved urban transport problem are still likely to be confounded.

CHAPTER 6

Housing

'Residential patterns largely expose the cultural values that people hold, the consumption profile they strive for, their views of themselves and the ways in which they judge others' (Daun, 1976). To the Swedish ethnologist Åke Daun, housing policy, more than any other policy for the built environment in the cities of West Europe, is a mirror of the society that builds the housing. The results of successive attempts by societies to solve the need for shelter, and the mismatch between past provision and present-day needs and wants, constitute much of what is defined loosely as 'the housing problem'. Housing policies in all the countries of West Europe are formulated at a national level because each society perceives the problem as a national one. Therefore, in implementing housing policies, governments have translated ideology and social values into bricks and mortar with the assistance of city governments who have planned for residential developments within the guidelines of national policy. It was the theme of the first part of this book that history, nation and ideology were fundamental determinants of the European urban tradition and all three are undoubtedly strongly represented in this consideration of housing. In addition the influence of the tradition of European urban visionaries is very apparent, particularly in the built form of the residential schemes that will be examined.

Policy Determinants in European Urban History

Until the nineteenth century the provision of housing in cities was slow. The accretions of housing around the periphery of towns or the reconstructions within the urban area were constructed relatively slowly and, only in exceptional circumstances, did large-scale rebuilding or large extensions to the built-up area occur. One such case was the rapid spread of London beyond the limits of the walls in the years following the Great Fire in 1666, and another was Gävle (in Sweden) after the fire in 1888. In many cities in central Europe the *Altstadt* (the historic city centre) was still a recognizable residential area until the twentieth century and has remained so despite the growth in non-residential uses.

With industrialization, a marked change took place in the provision of housing. Housing was no longer a part of the shelter provided by a feudal society but an integral part of the entrepreneurial philosophy underpinning industrialization. To the industrialist, anxious to profit from new technologies, housing for workers was essential but the costs of this provision were to be kept as low as possible. The concept of housing markets with economic rents was introduced into housing in order that the industrialist/developer could gain as much profit as possible from the workers' shelter as from their labour (Vance, 1977). The result of entrepreneurial initiatives was what Vance termed the 'generalization' of the housing stock in the new industrial centres of Europe. Vast areas of housing almost identical in both outward appearance and internal provision, grew around the mills and mines of the Ruhrgebiet, the Nord coalfield, the South Wales valleys and the Borinage.

Bochum in the Ruhrgebiet was developed as a coalmining centre by several mine-owners who each built their distinctive 'colonies' adjacent to the 30 or more mines scattered through the city territory, such as the colony attached to the Robert Muser mine at Werne (Thomas and Tuppen, 1977). Colonies were also attached to other industrial sites such as the Krupp foundry. In the Emscher zone of the Ruhrgebiet, the settlements that sprung up were almost entirely residential colonies for the large mines and visitors to Duisburg-Hamborn, Bottrop, Buer, Herne and Castrop-Rauxel cannot but be struck by the generalized building forms.

Similar vast relatively uniform extensions to the built-up area occurred in northern France. The built-up area of Lille expanded fivefold in the period 1850–1919 while neighbouring Roubaix and Tourcoing merged into one another tripling their surface area between 1830 and 1880 and engulfing other villages. The new factories of firms such as Agache and Kuhlmann each had a surrounding *quartier ouvrier* or *cité* with its monotonous housing so that tentacles of uniform, insalubrious housing extended out from the towns. By 1900 one-third of the population of Roubaix–Tourcoing were living in uniform cramped workers' settlements (Notes et Études Documentaire, 1976). Industrial growth had brought with it the generalization of housing which became a continuing tradition. However, the moral responsibility that society possessed for the worst evils of the new housing was already being stressed by Dickens, Engels, Ruskin and Zola. The pressure for society to take responsibility for shelter had begun to force governments into action.

Thus by the turn of the century the foundations for public involvement in housing provision had been laid. The protective legislation which originated in the form of the Health Acts in Britain spread to other countries. The philanthropists such as Owen, Salt, Buckingham, and the new housing trusts such as the Guinness Trust, showed the value of improved standards, lower densities and non-profit-making philosophy (Chapter 2). The cooperative housing movement was founded in 1869 in Denmark, 1870 in Sweden and 1889 in Germany as an alternative means of providing housing, thus establishing another strong tradition in European house-building.

The problems faced by European society in the wake of the First World War inevitably resulted in policy changes which affected housing provision. The concept of the community as a provider of modern housing, which was a part of the British tradition of providing shelter expressed since the seventeenth century in the form of almshousing (and even earlier in the European monastic traditions) was strengthened after the war with increasing local authority provision of homes for rent. Rent controls were introduced in the private sector in many countries in the wake of the depression and have come to form an essential part of policies. In

Germany the trade unions' involvement in house-building began in the period 1922–26 with the founding in Hamburg of a labour building association to cater for housing need, an advisory house-building group (*DEWOG*) and a city and trade unions combine for house building (*GEKABE*), the forerunner of *Neue Heimat* which is a trade unions-backed housing authority (Fuerst, 1974).

By the end of the Second World War the historical precedents for present policies had been laid in the majority of countries. However, the destruction wrought on cities throughout Europe by military activity (including destruction in Spain during the Civil War) forced the authorities to devise policies which catered for the enormous shortages of housing. The Netherlands were short of 300 000 units in 1950 (Smith, 1973). In West Germany various *Länder* passed reconstruction laws which were implemented by the cities in rapidly rebuilding housing with some success in Hannover and Kiel, but ignored in Cologne by the city planning director with unfortunate consequences for the pace of reconstruction (Green, 1959; 1964). In contrast, in Britain all initial investment in housing was channelled into the local authority sector for almost a decade. The most severe shortages (4 million to 5.5 million units) were found in the German cities where up to 60 per cent of dwellings were destroyed or damaged in, for example, Berlin, Hamburg, Hannover and Essen. Many felt that it was easier to rebuild on new sites than to clear the rubble (Blacksell, 1968). Two-and-a-quarter million homes had been destroyed in the new West Germany, and in Italy more than 1 million dwellings were damaged.

Most countries had frozen rents before or during the war; Sweden, for example, did so in 1942. Building costs were escalating so that the economic rents for new dwellings outstripped those for older dwellings of a comparable type. To ensure that dwellings became available for the lower-income groups, governments were forced to subsidize social housing. These subsidies were increased as land and building costs moved steadily upwards. Obviously there are various forms of subsidy of which the six most important are: (a) non-repayable grants (Republic of Ireland, Luxembourg); (b) loans at privileged conditions of interest and/or amortization (France); (c) interest subsidies (Denmark, Belgium, West Germany); (d) annual subsidies that are based on the difference between economic and actual rents (Netherlands); (e) tax reliefs (United Kingdom); and (f) individual subsidies (West Germany) (Theunissen, 1974). Although examples are given above in parentheses these are not exclusively the subsidy used in each country. These policies have grown from the problem of providing for shortages both as a result of the war and as a result of demographic and social changes that occurred at the same time in the period between 1945 and 1960.

Social Determinants of Policies

There is a series of important demographic trends which have influenced housing policies. Much of postwar policy has been influenced by the rising birth-rate in the first fifteen years after the war. Household formation was also expected to grow, with the result that the future task for most cities was one of accommodating increased numbers on a diminishing land area. The policy outcome was to concentrate both on adding to the housing stock on the periphery and also the renewal of the stock in the centre, two policies governed as much by the cost-benefit yardsticks of the economists as by the fulfilment of political targets. However, trends in fertility have altered since the mid-1960s with several countries reaching (West Germany, Switzerland) or approaching (Britain) 'zero population growth'. Inevitably changes in policy resulted. In countries where housing supply matches demand, more steps are being taken to improve the older housing stock including, in the case of Hamburg, the poorer dwellings built in the immediate postwar period.

The structure of the West European population is altering with smaller families enabling women to contemplate returning to work sooner than previously, providing additional disposable income. The resulting trends can be demands for improved space standards in the home either for their own sake or to accommodate a wider range of labour-saving domestic equipment. The most recent trends in the birth-rate suggest that society will in general become older. Combined with increases in longevity and the retention of unitary family dwellings, partly reinforced by welfare state provision and the role of life insurance in providing in particular for widows, the number of single-person households is rising and household formation is unlikely to decelerate at the same rate as the birth-rate.

Little attention has been paid to the elderly sector of the population but studies emerging in Britain, France and West Germany point to the growing trends of retirement migration which affect certain city-regions more than others. Studies have noted the specific urban destinations for migrants aged over 65 years (Cribier, 1970; Koch, 1976; and Law and Warnes, 1973). In France, Nice and other cities of the Côte d'Azur, the new resorts of the Languedoc coast such as La Grand Motte, and the Atlantic resorts of Biarritz and Royan are focal points of retirement migration as is the rural fringe of almost all cities. In Germany, Koch (1976) notes a similar southward drift to the small towns of the alpine region, south and east of Munich, besides a flight to the urban fringes of Rhine–Main, Hannover and Hamburg. The small town is seen as most preferred by 55 per cent of those in the age groups 50–65 years and over 65 years; on the other hand, a higher proportion of this age group than any except 25–34 years also prefer living in the city.

Migration, as we have noted above, is an important variable in calculating the level of housing provision at a city level. Large-scale migrations in central Europe put extreme pressure on authorities in West Germany and Austria in the postwar period. In Sweden between 1940 and 1970 the proportion living in urban areas rose from 55 to 80 per cent. This represented the provision of housing for an extra three million people in the towns and cities. For instance, the urban population of the Republic of Ireland rose from 32 per cent in 1921 to 43 per cent in 1961, and that of Finland from 14 per cent in 1920 to 56 per cent in 1960. In Spain, King (1971) has shown how the authorities there underestimated requirements caused by internal migration which provided a shortfall of approximately 850 000 dwellings in urban areas during the 1960s. Studies in the region of the Middle Rhine Highlands including the cities of Cologne, Trier, Aachen, Koblenz and Siegen have also shown the selectivity of migration (Gatzweiler, 1975). Cologne, Bonn and the Rhine–Main cities (Frankfurt, Wiesbaden, Offenbach) are magnets for the 21–34 year age group, whereas only Bonn continues to be an urban magnet for the older age groups.

Within cities the migration currents are far from even, despite the general levelling of the urban-density gradients resulting from the decentralization of people. The pressure of migration on eastern Lyons is greater than on the west, while migration to the eastern suburbs of Düsseldorf and to south-east Geneva is stronger than in other directions.

Perhaps these migration flows do no more than reflect the changing social norms in West European countries. Obviously the variations in per capita income and cost of living indices between countries and between cities affect these norms. In absolute terms the relative per capita income of the Swiss in 1967 was three times that of the Spanish and 50 per cent higher than that of the British. Obviously such variations in income, if not eroded by increased living costs, will explain international variations in interior space norms and housing types. An illustration of various space norms can be seen in Table 6.1:

Table 6.1 Area of residential land per person in select areas (in square metres)

Marseilles (France)	67.0
Switzerland	67.0–171.0
Cumbernauld (Scotland)	47.0
English/Welsh new towns	153.2
English major industrial towns	116.0
English towns over 10 000 population	94.0

Source: after United Nations, 1973

Other cultural and historical determinants of housing density must not be ignored although here the evidence is more suspect. The French tradition of high urban densities, epitomized in the work of Le Corbusier (Chapter 2) has been maintained, as will be examined later, in the concept of the *Grands Ensembles.* In Scandinavia the ideas of Sitte have been adopted and Gropius's influence on German housing is also very strong. Similarly, the low-density anti-urban preference of British citizens is enshrined in most housing schemes in England and Wales, although not in Scotland, as Table 6.1 illustrates for the new town of Cumbernauld.

Aspirations for specific types of housing are important. At a local level perceptions of housing need, quality and desirability reflect current social trends and indicate potential patterns of demand; while at a national level, perceptions concerning the housing stock and environment of a city can and do influence the rate of urban growth in different cities.

Wilmott and Young (1973) in a survey of London families showed that 50 per cent wanted a larger home, and only 22 per cent a smaller one, and many in this latter group were elderly. Of those who had gardens, 44 per cent wanted larger gardens and 35 per cent the same size. The implications for the space demands of households are very clear in this case. These figures confirm the overall pattern of demand in the United Kingdom which is for detached or semi-detached housing, with only a small minority in favour of flats or apartments; only 1 per cent in a 1960s survey wished to live in high-rise flats and only a further 11 per cent in low-rise flats.

Racine and Creutz (1975) also have evidence to show that 68 per cent of French people want to live in a private house at a density of 20 to 25 houses per hectare, yet this density is rarely favoured in land-use plans. The authorities, governed by a philosophy of combating shortages, have yet to respond completely to these new values. Swedish authorities have also noted the fact that the numbers of houses in cities such as Stockholm rose rapidly while the population stagnated, a reflection of improved space expectations; housing production has changed to accommodate the changed tastes of the Swedish. In the 1960s, 70 per cent of dwellings constructed were apartments, whereas in 1977 70 per cent were houses (Wohlin, 1977).

Table 6.2 Preferred settlement type and household composition in the Netherlands

Preferred population size of city/town	National	Single persons	Household composition: Households with children: Less than 4 years	Over 4 and under 4 years	All 5–10 years	5–10 years and over 10 years	Only over 10 years	Unmarried and married, without children, aged 40 and over
	per cent							
>256 000	14	17	12	10	8	10	13	20
64 000–256 000	19	17	17	21	23	22	19	18
16 000–64 000	18	20	17	18	18	17	17	18
4000–16 000	24	21	23	25	28	27	29	22
<4000	25	25	31	26	23	24	22	22
	100	100	100	100	100	100	100	100

Another study originating from the Netherlands has attempted to relate the most desired settlement type to household size (Table 6.2). The desirability of a particular town size depends on the stage in the life cycle of the individual, although the urban village and village are generally the most popular locations. However, city life in the smaller urban agglomerations of 64 000 to 256 000 is desirable for a significant proportion of the families with small children. A similar survey comparing income groups and preferred cities did show that the lower socio-economic groups preferred the large cities, whereas the higher social groups preferred the middle-sized centres or the villages. Otherwise almost a half of the middle socio-economic groups preferred to live in settlements with under 16 000 inhabitants.

A further Dutch study relating desired residence to present residence, at the simplest level, indicates that people are happiest with a similar-sized settlement to the one in which they already live. City residents would opt for village life as would those in the large towns. The newly built areas within the urban area are preferred to residence either in the city/town centre or on the periphery. In a country with an overall population density as high as that of the Netherlands, the implications of fulfilling such a set of preferences is serious and can be used both to call into question existing policies for housing and to justify policies that could result in altered preferences favouring the *status quo*.

Studies of the attractions of German cities to the employees of 4000 firms by Monheim (1972) also drew attention to the variable perceptions of a sample population of office managers. Respondents were asked in which city they would like to live. The results shown in Figure 6.1a indicate that 31 per cent wanted to live in Munich and 20 per cent in Hamburg. Only one in five wanted to live in non-metropolitan regions. Why over half those who chose Hamburg already lived there is not explained. This contrasts with Munich where 70 per cent of the choices came

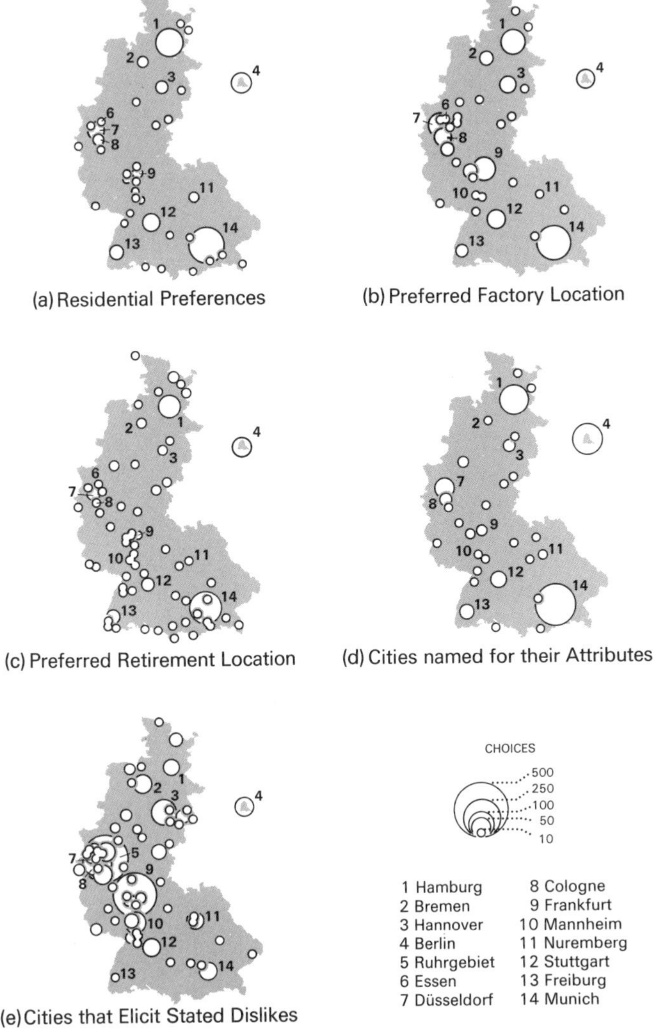

Figure 6.1 City preferences in West Germany (after Monheim)

from outside of the city. Munich's role as the most desirable place of residence has grown since 1964 when it displaced West Berlin, and it is also the most preferred location for industrial plant followed by Düsseldorf and Hamburg (Figure 6.1b), and the most preferred location for retirement (Figure 6.1c) despite the selection of more non-metropolitan centres in Bavaria. Munich elicited more sympathetic statements in all places of survey except Hamburg (Figure 6.1d) and was named almost twice as frequently as Hamburg and five times as frequently as Cologne. The implications for housing provision in and around Munich are obvious and Munich's policies to date have catered for one of the most rapidly growing populations in West Germany. On the other hand the cities of the Ruhr which received 22 per cent of the derogatory statements (Figure 6.1e) must obviously regard the nineteenth-century built environment as a liability. While there might be pressure to replace the outmoded housing stock there is not the pressure to find new housing areas.

Housing policy endeavours to accommodate known preferences, given the ability of the individual urban centres to respond to them. On the other hand opinions are given to the policy-makers which they can either follow or, as in the case of the Netherlands, counteract. The more direct social indicators derived from traditional demographic predictions and migration are still accepted by policy-makers and must be seen as a foundation for present policies together with the experience gained from the examination of urban history.

Housing Policies in European Countries

Data sources in the field of housing are extremely variable even between works published in the same year in the same country! There is also the problem of comparing definitions such as 'social housing' in different countries. The basic data on housing provision and quality is given in Table 6.3 and 6.4 where every attempt has been made to use comparable data.

Comparisons of housing provision in these countries are beset by the problems of comparability of data both in definition and time. For this reason United Nations and European Community sources have been used rather than national data sources. France and Belgium have more houses per head of population but in the former these are frequently in rural or recreational areas used as second homes by the urban population. In terms of persons per dwelling there is a marked north–south gradient which ranges from the low densities of Sweden and Denmark to the high densities of the Iberian peninsular. Densities per room show a similar gradation with the notable exceptions of Finland and Ireland. The figures for completed dwellings do distinguish between the affluent and poorer nations although no account is taken of the proportion of building improvement and refurbishing.

Of the traditional measures of quality used by the United Nations the available data illustrates a marked north–south gradient through the continent in provision of interior piped water, toilet facilities and electric lighting. The only exceptions to this picture are Ireland and Finland. The highest proportion of high-density living in towns (two persons and more per room) is found in Finland, followed by Italy, Portugal, Spain and France. In every other country less than 10 per cent (0.8 per cent

Table 6.3 Housing in West Europe in the 1970s

Countries	Population (millions)	Dwelling stock (millions)	Persons per dwelling	Persons per room (per cent)	Owner occupied (per cent)	Public rented (per cent)	Dwellings completed per year (1000)	Dwellings completed per 1000 inhabitants (1972–76)	Housing construction (per cent of GNP)
Austria	7.4	2.471	3.00	0.9	48		50.0	6.8	
Belgium	9.8	3.9	2.4	0.6	59	5	76.9	8.4	5.7
Denmark	5.1	2.0	2.5	0.8	52	18	39.0	7.0	4.8
Finland	4.712	1.315	3.30	1.3	61		40.0	8.6	
France	52.9	21.5	2.4	0.9	50	50*	575.5	10.0	6.9
West Germany	61.5	24.0	2.6	0.7	39	18	371.1	7.2	5.4
Republic of Ireland	3.2	0.8	3.8	0.9	75	25*	23.0	8.6	3.8
Italy	56.2	18.6	3.0	1.0	56	44*	178.7	3.8	7.0
Luxembourg	0.4	0.1	2.8	0.6	59	2	3.3	7.0	9.0
Netherlands	13.8	4.5	3.1	0.7	40	35	106.8	8.8	5.3
Norway	3.9	1.139	3.10	0.8	53		35.0	11.2	
Portugal	9.6	2.233	3.90	1.1	51		35.0	3.7	
Spain	33.2	7.567	4.00	1.0	46		260.0	9.6	
Sweden	8.0		2.70	0.8	36		103.0	13.0	
Switzerland	6.281	1.6	3.30	0.7	34		66.0	11.6	
United Kingdom	56.0	20.6	2.7	0.6	54	33	324.1	5.7	2.9

* = all rented

Sources: Statistical Office of the European Communities, Luxembourg, Annual Bulletin of Housing and Building Statistics for Europe of the Economic Commission for Europe of the United Nations, Geneva, Nationwide Building Society

Table 6.4 Housing quality in West Europe (latest figures available)

Countries	Percentage lacking interior piped water	any toilet	electric lighting	per cent pre-1945 houses	per cent 2 + persons per room in urban areas	per cent <1 person per room in urban areas
Austria	14.7	30.3	—		6.1*	44.0*
Belgium	12.9	0.1	0.4	55	7.2	57.1
Denmark	3.3	12.0	—	46	5.7	46.8
Finland	52.9	—	11.4		32.5	20.5
France	2.8	45.2	0.2	52	13.0	40.4
West Germany	1.0	—	1.0	42	2.7*	53.3*
Republic of Ireland	28.2	29.2	17.0		11.7	52.1
Italy	13.9	10.5	4.1	42	31.6*	28.3*
Luxembourg	6.5	0.5	0.5	52	5.0	58.7
Netherlands	1.0	0.1	1.9	39	2.1	94.6
Norway	7.2	0	—		4.6	91.5
Portugal	71.1	—	59.5		25.3	38.0
Spain	55.0	33.9	10.7		20.0	77.8†
Sweden	5.7	0.3	—		4.8	48.1
Switzerland	3.9	0.3	—		1.4*	71.6*
United Kingdom	1.3	11.4	—	54	0.8*	85.0*

* both urban and rural areas
† less than five per room
Sources: Statistical Office of the European Communities, Luxembourg, Annual Bulletin of Housing and Building Statistics for Europe of the Economic Commission for Europe of the United Nations, Geneva, Nationwide Building Society.

in the United Kingdom) live in overcrowded conditions. The converse, that is those living at densities of less than one per room, is a more complex pattern which distinguishes the countries of low-density dwelling—Netherlands, Norway, Switzerland and United Kingdom—from the majority, where half the population is living at low densities. The proportion of owner-occupation is highest in Ireland, Belgium and Finland and lowest in those countries with the greatest breadth of choice of housing markets—West Germany, Netherlands, Sweden and Switzerland.

Case Studies of National Policies

(1) Sweden

Swedish policy priorities were laid down between 1945–48 as follows: (a) the abolition of crowded living conditions and raising the space standards; (b) improving equipment standards; and (c) overcoming the general housing shortage. The reasonable cost of residence for a family was suggested as 20 per cent of the average wage of a factory worker. It was also decided to involve local authorities in the planning, construction and management of housing in order to reduce the role of the speculator. Since 1967 use values are employed in assessments of housing need rather than market or scarcity values. In this way national ideology has governed policy outcomes (Headey, 1978). Central government loans for construction plus subsidies to families with children to help with living costs were approved; over 1.3 million households received housing allowances in 1975. The loan system was amended to enable the system to adjust more easily to inflation but this has given way since 1974 to a system of guaranteed interest rates but with differential guarantees in order to neutralize the gains that might have accrued from tax allowances to home-owners. In 1975, 85 per cent of new housing was financed by state housing loans (Ministry of Housing and Physical Planning, 1976).

Support for urban renewal has increased since the 1950s and from 1973 it has been possible for local authorities and tenants to apply for aid for modernization and to be consulted during the process. It is estimated that between 20 000 and 30 000 houses need to be modernized or combined each year. Legislation on expropriation (passed in 1967) has severely limited the gains that could be made by landowners. This enables land purchase legislation to be kept in line with the policy that housing shall not be a source of profit-making revenue (Bengtson, 1974). Since 1975 developers must acquire land through the municipality which receives special loans to aid the acquisition of land. The municipality must also introduce five-year rolling plans for housing. Most housing is built by cooperatives or non-profit-making corporations governed in part by local authority appointees and in part by independent members. The housing corporations are therefore an instrument of local authority provision and have built 45 per cent of the housing completed since 1945. The municipally controlled corporations are responsible for 74 per cent of flat developments, whereas single-family homes are dominated (97 per cent in 1975) by private investors, half of whom are individuals building a single house. Housing allowances which are means-tested come from the state and the municipality. In the rented sector there was control from 1942 until 1975 when utilization-value rent (a rent determined on the quality and location of the dwelling) was phased in. Rents have to be comparable with municipal housing which is a cost-price rent. There are also direct rent allowances for low-income families, pensioners and the handicapped (Wohlin, 1977).

(2) Denmark

Danish policies are not unlike those of Sweden. The tradition of non-profit-making housing authorities (*Almennyttige boligselskaber*) is strong, with over 1 million living in non-profit housing, most of which is in Copenhagen where it forms 45 per cent of the housing stock. Two-thirds of all cooperative housing being built is in the capital. Traditionally priority has been given firstly to families, then to childless couples and then to the retired. Since 1967 more of the authorities have built for owner-occupation, so most new construction is for this purpose. The non-profit-making sector has a quota of 25 per cent of all house-building although the 650 associations also participate in the construction of single-room apartments for students, the handicapped and the retired. There is also a slum-clearance company which is concentrating its attention on the 300 000 homes built before 1890, especially those in Copenhagen (Apelroth, 1974).

State and local authority housing is very limited (1.4 per cent of homes built) and confined almost entirely to the major centres, although schemes are frequently jointly managed with the non-profit associations. Low-income families receive grants from a fund which bases subsidies on income, actual rent and family size. Overcrowding, however, is avoided by withdrawing subsidies if there are densities of over two persons per room. Social housing is subsidized for up to 12 years but only 13 000 dwellings built each year benefit from the interest-free loans granted to developers.

(3) Norway

In contrast to Sweden, but like Denmark, the current emphasis in Norway is on providing private homes; 60 per cent of completions in 1974 were for owner-occupation, with only 19 per cent in cooperatives, 13 per cent provided by stock companies and 6 per cent from state and municipal housing. The role of the national government is to supervise the municipality which has a political and moral responsibility to provide housing leaving the building itself to other bodies. However, 70 per cent of all new dwellings are financed by the National Housing Bank which imposes limits on costs and floor space rather than on income or means. In this way rates of house-building are very high (up to eleven per 1000 population in some years) and 70 per cent of the production is small single-family homes (average size 89.4 square metres) while only 8 per cent are flats. Nevertheless the distribution of homes is still inappropriate with too many in the rural areas and the north and too few in Oslo, Bergen, Trondheim and, since the North Sea oil boom, Stavanger.

In 1976 a new urban renewal act enabled rehabilitation of homes to take place with municipal approval and assisted by Housing Bank loans. Further legislation concerning cooperatives has cut links between the organizations that build and those that manage housing developments, besides giving the representation to the municipality (Ministry of Local Government and Labour, 1976).

(4) France

Maldistribution of the housing stock is also characteristic of France, where housing policy has gradually developed along a set of predetermined lines without any fundamental policy reorientations (Duclaud-Williams, 1978). It was a policy created by the consensus of opinion that there was a grave housing shortage especially in Paris that has enabled policies to move forward since 1945. The owner-occupied sector was helped after 1950 when the Crédit Foncier was able to advance up to 60 per cent of the price of new homes. Later advances rose to 80 per cent of the total price enabling 1 million homes to be constructed through direct state intervention on behalf of a wide variety of social groups. After 1963 the Crédit Foncier scheme was restricted to those whose income fell below a ceiling, and further improvements in mortgage finance arrangements have enabled the share of owner-occupied homes to rise to 50 per cent in 1978 (Nationwide, 1979).

In the privately rented sector there are both controlled and uncontrolled sectors. The fixed rents of the prewar period had depressed rents to too small a proportion of the family budget, so rent levels were raised over a 6-year period at approximately 20 per cent per annum until they reached the new values. The government has tended to control the rents in the larger cities rather than impose blanket controls. In the same way within any city the control over rents in the centre is greater than on the periphery. As a result of this policy the number of controlled homes has fallen from 6.6 million in 1948 to 1.1 million in 1975. Building homes for rent has been encouraged by tax concessions to companies that construct the homes but, despite these concessions, this sector's share of housing in 1973 was only 20 per cent. These subsidies on building costs rather than land encouraged speculation which had the direct result in the townscape of the construction of luxury apartments in order that the high land costs could be recouped. The 16th *arrondissement* of Paris is littered with the results of this policy which has inevitably aided social concentration of the affluent in western Paris between Place Étoile, Charles de Gaulle and the Bois de Boulogne. Similarly in Belleville in the 19th *arrondissement*, a *quartier* was entirely destroyed as new apartment blocks rose because the municipal developers in this case were exempted from planning permission in zones pinpointed for rapid development.

Public-sector housing in France accounted for only about 15 per cent of homes, and 1.3 per cent of homes under construction in 1976, and is based on a policy of providing for the least fortunate and workers living principally by their salaries. The introduction of *Habitations à Loyer Modéré* (HLM) replacing the earlier subsidies on building for low-income tenants in 1947, administered not by the local authorities but by unpaid leading administrators, was given very low priority. In France municipal authorities do not build houses. However, the revelations on overcrowded households in the 1950s forced the government to consider the policy more seriously. The rents have nine categories which can be raised biannually and are based on a space formula. Qualifications for HLM homes were based on need and 70 to 80 per cent of the population were found to be eligible. In order to make sure that only the most needy gain access to this market in Paris an *arrête* has been used since 1968. In other words the *Préfet* prepares a list and 30 per cent of the new HLM places and 50 per cent of relets are allocated to people on this list. In other French cities the percentages vary. In addition there is a *sur-loyer*, or additional rent, as an incentive to leave if income is too high for the accommodation, which affects 8 per cent of HLM residents in the provinces and 20 per cent in Paris. Finance for HLM is aided by privileged interest rates. Cost ceilings imposed on the 1300 HLM agencies mean that there will be problems for lower-income groups affording rents and finding provision for families of five or more persons. There is much evidence to show that the poorest do not gain access to HLM housing and as a result the Barre Report has suggested the abolition of subsidies on building and the introduction of housing allowances to the poorest tenants (Duclaud-Williams, 1978). Since 1971 HLM can be constructed for both rent and owner-occupation; 20 per cent are built for owner-occupation. Because of the high cost of land to HLMs there has been a tendency to concentrate on schemes in the outlying areas thus increasing segregation. This is particularly the case in Paris where between 1959 and 1970 only one home in six built was social housing.

French housing policy has fluctuated less with the party in power than in Britain and has concentrated on reducing the shortage of homes. Overcrowding is still high by West European standards especially among young couples (17.4 per cent in officially overcrowded conditions). French homes have the lowest average number of rooms of all EEC countries. In Paris one home in ten is still overcrowded and 22 000 people were still living in *bidonvilles*. Efforts have also been made to redevelop the 38 per cent of the housing stock that was built before 1914 (the highest proportion in the European Economic Community) rather than engage in wholesale slum clearance. Despite devoting between 5 per cent and 6.6 per cent of her GNP to housing between 1962 and 1970, French housing policy has still to overcome the shortage of suitable homes.

(5) Federal Republic of Germany

In contrast to France, West Germany has achieved a national surplus of housing since 1972 and, as a result of the success of the postwar policies, more emphasis is being placed on owner-occupation of homes (Hallett, 1977). While one must always ask questions concerning the distribution of homes when statements of surplus are made, house-building has been a major achievement of postwar reconstruction. Approximately 39 per cent of homes are owner-occupied, but the growth of this sector has been limited by high costs resulting from building regulations and the importance given to meeting housing needs in other ways. By 1979 only 30 per cent of new housing was social housing compared with 40 per cent in 1964 and 54 per cent in 1954.

The rented sector has seen some of the most interesting developments with private and corporate landlords, cooperatives and non-profit-making corporations all providing both subsidized and unsubsidized accommodation while, at the same time, maximizing competition in the true sense of Erhard's social market economy. Rent controls did exist but these have been removed gradually since 1960 once the shortfall of home provision fell below 3 per cent of the housing demand, so that control continues only in West Berlin, Hamburg and Munich.

Subsidies for renting are related to personal need as a result of the 1956 Act and the more recent 1970 *Wohngeldgesetz*. The floor area needs per family are calculated as well as a 'tolerable' rent based on income and family circumstances which ranges from 5 to 22 per cent of the family income. The family can usually claim the difference between the actual rent and the 'tolerable' rent as a subsidy. Of the 8 per cent of households receiving allowances 68 per cent are pensioners (Lawson and Stevens, 1974). Of the 13.3 million dwellings built between 1950 and 1973, 8.8 million were built to let and of these 2.5 million, or 28 per cent, were built by the non-profit-making housing corporations. At least 50 per cent, in Hallett's estimation, was sponsored by private individuals.

The non-profit-making sector owned 3.1 million homes in 1973 and has maintained its traditions in German society. Its major strength lies in one enterprise.

This is *Neue Heimat*, the trade unions-sponsored institution that was reinstituted in 1950. Trade unions' involvement in housing commenced in Berlin and seventeen other cities in 1919 as a response to housing need. *Neue Heimat* concentrated initially on the repair and reconstruction of damaged buildings, new construction on bombed areas and the removal of housing need, with the result that some schemes were hastily conceived and aesthetically dull.

Neue Heimat has not confined its attention solely to housing having also turned its expertise to shopping centres, schools and department stores both in integrated schemes and single developments. It has its own research organization (*GEWOS*), and a separate urban planning section which enables the group to plan, build and manage whole developments in conjunction with city authorities. One such scheme at Munich-Perlach houses 80 000 people living in 23 000 homes. One-sixth of the 227 000 social housing units are provided by the *Neue Heimat* and 20 per cent of all private enterprise homes. *Neue Heimat* has taken advantage of tax provisions to build low-income family homes such as the 1600 built at Hamburg Hohnercamp. It is also able to keep its costs for tenants lower by purchasing land at 30 per cent below the land prices for the private sector. Despite this advantage, gained mainly by timing, land prices are a problem. Prefabricated building techniques have also resulted from high land prices and shortages. With over 90 completed schemes to its credit and a 4 per cent return on investment to the trade unions, *Neue Heimat* can claim that its policies have provided homes for all and a surplus that will result in the withdrawal of poor housing from the market.

Housing finance in West Germany has much more diffuse sources with only 16 per cent on average coming from the state (7.6 per cent in 1975), the rest coming from savings and mortgage banks and the building societies. Subsidies vary from *Land* to *Land* who pay up to 80 per cent of the subsidy. The cities tend to own between a quarter and a half of the land in their boundaries and much of the rest is owned by the non-profit-making housing groups, churches and charities so that finding the land is not difficult.

Since 1972 there has been yet another cooperative response to needs in inner city areas as a result of the *Städtebauförderungsgesetz* (urban development law) which has enabled areas to be renovated by non-profit-making organizations incorporating local authority membership and receiving federal subsidies for both renewal and redevelopment but ensuring that no landowner would profit. The 1975 urban development report stresses the need for conservation and modernization allied to the erection of some new dwellings in the inner areas (Monheim, 1979).

(6) Netherlands

Urban renewal has become an important aspect of Dutch policy in recent years. Owners can be compelled to make up for arrears in maintenance and repairs, and other proposals introduced in 1976 broadened renewal from merely slum clearance and the restoration of historic buildings. In cost terms, rehabilitation has been shown to be cheaper per unit than new buildings and means of assistance have been devised to prevent 'gentrification'. Nevertheless 6 to 10 per cent of the older houses need total renovation or replacement. Subsidies to help low-income tenants in these areas have been introduced and in Amsterdam purchase of lower-priced properties is restricted by the local authority to those who work in the community (Info Service, no date).

The housing stock is relatively modern with only 39 per cent built before 1945 compared with 42 per cent in West Germany. Similarly, owner-occupation is among the lowest in the European Economic Community although 65 per cent of 1976 housing starts were in the owner-occupied sector. It is planned for 65 per cent of all housing to be owner-occupied by 1990. The government involves itself totally in the finance of social housing, which is mainly provided by cooperatives with only a little municipal housing. An annual subsidy is also provided and is half the actual rent, reducing annually in relation to the compulsory rent increases. Subsidies will also be granted to others building for rent and sale. Private building can take place on public land so that speculation is more controlled. There are also individual subsidies (Theunissen, 1974).

(7) Belgium

Belgian housing policy has three major aims: (a) the encouragement of owner-occupation, as witnessed by its high proportion (60 per cent); (b) low rent for modest-income families; and (c) the promotion of slum clearance and improvement (Watson, 1971). There has been minimal planning control but since 1970 the government has acted to prevent speculation by placing a tax on undeveloped sites. There is a surplus of dwellings but these are mainly rural.

Low-income housing has been subsidized with restrictions to dwellings constructed and sold by the *Société Nationale de Logement* (13 per cent of house building) and the rural *Société Terrienne* (2 per cent of house building). The *Société Nationale* lets two-thirds of its dwellings and these gain rent subsidies based on family size and income which is reviewed every 3 years. In addition the Commune and the Public Association Commission can build homes. *Société Nationale de Logement* homes can be sold and about 1500 are built for agreed purchase. Government finance for social housing is also available in addition to funds from the *Caisse Générale d'Epargne et de Retraite*. Social housing loans are subsidised but only 5 per cent live in this accommodation. Owner-occupation is also subsidized through reduced interest loans.

The emphasis is on improving unfit dwellings in the coalfield cities of Wallonie where the average age of homes is 70 years, compared to 56 years in Flanders and 45 years in Brussels, reinforced by help through demolition grants, removal allowances, improvement grants, and loans and rent allowances to communes and households. However, the aid is about 2 per cent of government housing funds for 39 per cent of the housing stock (Power, 1976). Unlike other countries, demolition of old residential areas has continued, especially in Brussels where pressures for roads and office blocks that would help the city achieve the status of a European office centre, have had precedence over residences in the inner areas.

(8) *Italy*

Italy has continued to experience a housing shortage since the Second Wold War and current estimates suggest an approximate shortage of 5 million homes, a per capita shortage that in Europe is exceeded only by Turkey (Angotti, 1977). There are 2 million vacant units but these are either rural or luxury homes. Responsibility for housing has been dispersed between three government departments and a coordinating committee. Italy has relied on private construction and owner-occupation with 80 per cent of housing provided by private enterprise. Social housing can only be built by private cooperatives and comprises only 3 per cent of construction rising to 10 to 15 per cent of house construction in some of the larger cities. Three-fifths of the house building in the public sector is financed by a public institute (*Cassa per Depositi e Prestiti*). The funds are obtained by fixed percentage contributions from wages and salaries and a further government contribution. Bank loans are subsidized by the State Bank. Full financing is available for workers employed by the state and the large corporations. Social housing can be sold but few take advantage of the schemes. In Messina, social housing can be sold off thus increasing access for the poor (Ginatempo and Cammarota, 1977). Rent controls do exist and are set at eight levels according to the age of the property. However, they have been relaxed so that private rents have increased. The problems of rising land values especially in Milan, Naples, Rome and Turin where population growth has been four times the national average, have affected housing prices and rents. In Milan, for instance, land values have risen between five and seven times on the periphery and by ten times nearer the centre (Wendt, 1962). As a result a law passed in 1962 has been used to enable authorities to set aside zones to provide for up to 60 per cent of housing needs over the succeeding decade and to expropriate land at below the market value. The act enables up to half the land to be resold to private developers for building low-cost housing and commercial centres. The proceeds from these sales are supposed to pay for further land acquisition. A further law passed in 1971 enables the expropriated areas to include areas of existing building development.

(9) *Spain*

The involvement of the Spanish government in housing has gradually increased since 1957 when subsidies for dwellings built by public and private firms were introduced although this policy has met with little success (King, 1971). The homes that were constructed by the Housing Ministry (*Obra Sindical del Hogar*) were not of a suitable type and although the record looks impressive there is no data on the demolitions needed in the 1960s as a part of the programme. House-building has therefore tended to remain firmly in the private sector with 84 per cent for sale and 16 per cent for renting. More recently the proportion of social housing has reached 50 per cent, with some for sale as a result of a massive building programme of nine homes being built for every 1000 inhabitants, although house sizes are small by north-west European standards. This programme is especially concentrated around

Madrid and Barcelona (Borja, 1977; and Fuerst, 1974). The Third Development Plan's housing policy gives grants to developers rather than direct support to the occupiers, and the construction of the large housing estate is less complicated to execute than renovation and redevelopment which have fewer social costs. More so than in all other countries except Italy the authorities have not been able to deal with the shanty areas that are the natural response to housing shortage around the large cities. Pozo and Nueve Barrios (Madrid) and Montjuic (Barcelona) are three areas where the residents have won rights to remain and secure an infrastructure.

(10) United Kingdom

In his study of British and French housing, Duclaud-Williams (1978) contrasts French gradual incrementalism with British oscillations and fundamental modifications of policy while stressing the greater degree of local direction in the implementation of government policy. Compared with other countries Britain has a much more strongly developed social housing policy that had its origins in the 1919 Housing and Town Planning Act. Finance for social housing is obtained primarily from the private market aided by government grants and payment of loan charges together with an element from property taxes. In the field of social housing there was in the 1950s a general consensus on providing council housing; this has been replaced by a more sceptical attitude to social housing which was not reaching those in greatest need in, for example, the inner city, so that subsidies have moved to the individual, although this, in Duclaud-William's estimation, reflects a preoccupation with class. Despite large-scale provision, social housing is very standardized with only 2.3 per cent with three or more bedrooms. In the owner-occupied sector there is a much stronger support from both parties (for example, to building societies in 1973–74) although the tax subsidies are one of the best examples of a regressive tax concession in Europe which helps the wealthy and so supports the class system. Studies of the spatial patterning of mortgage finance have shown that building societies have been reluctant to lend for purchase in areas of older property and even General Improvement and Housing Action Areas (Boddy, 1976).

The privately rented sector in Britain is declining, in contrast to other European countries, due to a combination of frozen rents and security of tenure legislation which have forced properties off the market. Up to 90 per cent of property being sold in Islington in the early 1960s was formerly rented property. Only in the upper rental brackets has there been any increase in provision in cities in schemes such as the Barbican in the City of London.

As in other countries, attempts have been made to improve the worst housing conditions of inner cities through policies based on physical and area criteria used in Priority Area, Housing Action Area and General Improvement Area definitions. Similarly, attempts to promote solutions to the problems of inner urban housing through explanations that assume some of the problems have their origins in the characteristics of the population housed in the areas have always been popular. More recently, attention has been placed on the chances of gaining access to better housing although the studies of Sunderland, Oldham and Rotherham (Dept. of the Environment, 1974) still concentrated on physical, area and social explanations. The more recent works on Liverpool, Birmingham and Lambeth (see, for example, Wilson and Wommersley, 1977) do mention the working of the housing system but rarely discuss it in great depth. Part of the fault, though, must lie with those who formulated the original brief which assumed that physical factors dominated social ones in the inner urban areas.

Because methods of financing and constructing social and private housing are so different there has been a tendency for schemes in Britain to be both physically and spatially distinct. The postwar emphasis on cost yardsticks in the public sector and governmental anxiety to meet targets often forced policy decisions on local authorities which make the environments of social housing schemes so distinct. The 'no fines' techniques (concrete construction rather than bricks and mortar) that aided council policies to meet governmental targets in the early 1950s have left problem developments such as Bell Green, Coventry, where no one will buy homes even at extremely low prices. Likewise the high-rise revolution has produced a bristling of new developments that remain physically and socially distinct as for example Highfields, Coventry. Interurban mobility within this sector and security of tenure for the family of tenants are new steps actively under consideration following criticisms of the lack of opportunity to move (Bird, 1976). Gray (1976) has also shown how the selection procedures for council housing for people in slum-clearance areas, those on a waiting list and those wanting to move, involves eligibility filters that seriously discriminates against low-status tenants.

In West Europe as a whole, housing legislation, finance and allocation is a veritable jungle but it is possible to draw some conclusions. In some countries there is a surplus of homes although the distribution is not in the areas of greatest shortage. There is still a scarcity of particular types of accommodation for immigrants, large families and the elderly. On the whole, the creation of subsidized homes has not risen as fast as the rise in national incomes thus affecting the poor sections of society; to alleviate this problem subsidies are being shifted to the people rather than buildings. Owner-occupation is being encouraged but with a move to turn housing into a non-profit-making enterprise through attempts to control land speculation. Old properties are being removed or renovated and the latter is increasingly accepted as a desirable economic and social goal, although 'gentrification' is a problem whether in Islington (London), Gamla Stan (Stockholm), Île St Louis (Paris), or Joordans (Amsterdam). In all the literature there is comment on the dangers of increased social segregation resulting from policies. The segregation of foreign workers into 'ghettos' in Switzerland and West Germany and the *foyers* in France, the effect of regional economic policies on cities, and urban renewal that takes homes beyond the reach of former inhabitants, all affect the degree of segregation.

Policies in Action

Most of the literature on policies in action has concentrated on two types of scheme that reflect the success and failure of policies. First, there are solutions to the problems of housing shortage and the need to provide homes as cheaply as possible which has resulted in the proliferation of social housing schemes on the periphery of cities such as Sarcelles (Paris), Le Mirail (Toulouse), Osterholz-Tenever (Bremen), Neu Perlach (Munich), Råstätt (Jönköping), Wester Hailes (Edinburgh), Gran San Blas (Madrid) and Bijlmermeer (Amsterdam). Figure 6.2 illustrates the location of several such schemes with especial reference to German cities. The second policy is that of renovation and renewal in inner urban areas which has produced more euphoria in recent years particularly since renovation has replaced renewal in many city districts. However, there are still doubts about the benefits of these policies as applied within existing social constraints in most countries as Williams has shown in the case of Oporto (Williams, 1980).

Housing on the Urban Periphery

(1) Osterholz-Tenever, Bremen

Osterholz-Tenever was begun in 1970–71 as a development to house overspill population from the centre of Bremen. It succeeded an earlier scheme which was highly praised, Neue Vahr (Figure 6.2c). It was developed by the city and *Neue Heimat* with funds from the provisions of the *Städtebauförderungsgesetz*. By 1975, 2600 dwellings had been completed on 59 hectares. It is hoped that when the scheme is completed, 10 000–12 000 people will live here in 7000 dwellings at very high density. There is a third spatially more extensive scheme being developed in the south-west of the city.

One of the last of its kind to be built, Osterholz-Tenever is situated, rather unusually, in a city which did not have a history of high-density dwelling although its Social Democratic government has an impressive record of housing provision, building 110 000 dwellings between 1953 and 1974. Compared with other schemes Osterholz-Tenever has attempted to meet the criticisms of other high-density high-rise schemes. Owner-occupation has been encouraged in one-seventh of the dwellings but there are still problems in attracting people to live in the 'alternative town of tomorrow'. The 59 hectare site is 12 kilometres from central Bremen and the transport links are inadequate because it is beyond the present tram terminus. However, it is close to a new industrial zone which has attracted considerable investment. The physical form is varied with the units ranging from three to 23 storeys. Open space is found around the scheme but that within the scheme is rather formal in design and, despite discreetly placed vegetation, mainly concrete. Despite these attempts to alleviate problems, Osterholz-Tenever has one of the highest proportions of children under 15 of all the West German city schemes, 33 per cent, and less than 10 per cent of its population is over 60 years old.

(2) Gropiusstadt, West Berlin

This development designed by Gropius and built over the period 1962–75 on 264 hectares on the fringes of West Berlin-Neukölln houses 44 000 people in 19 000 units (Figure 6.2b). Its history of development again illustrates the problems with

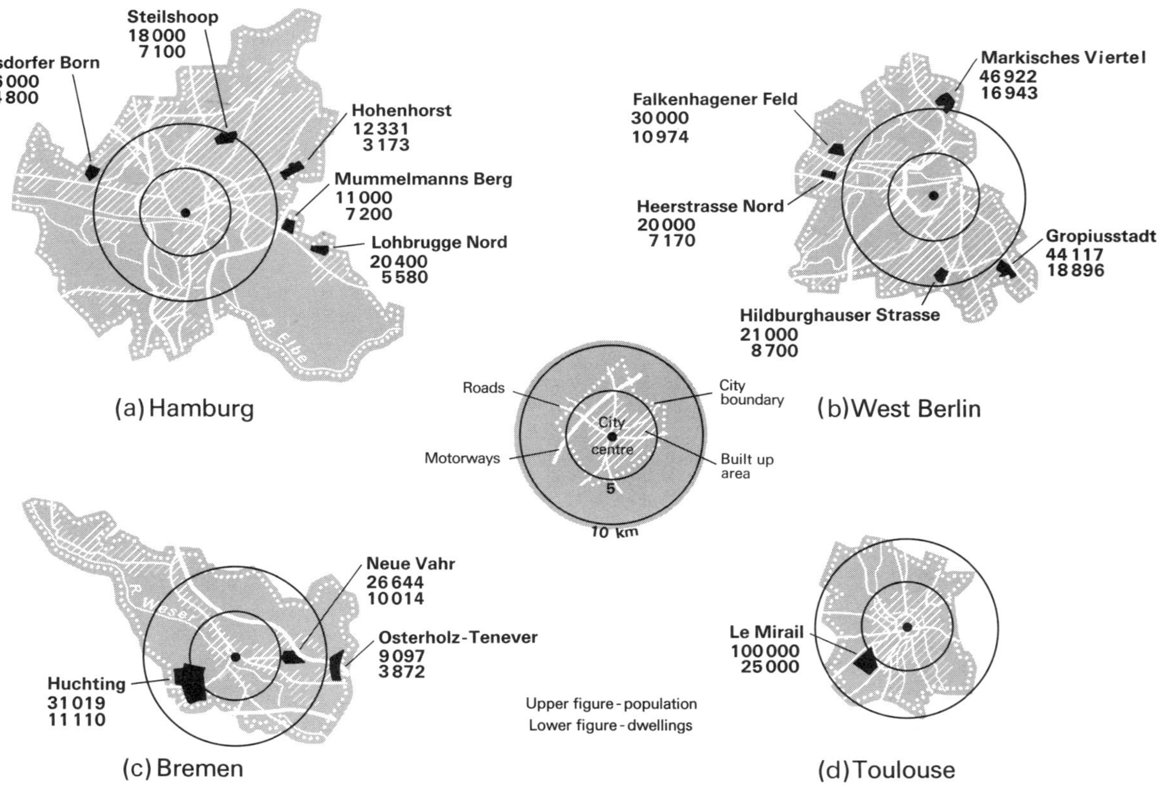

Figure 6.2 The location of peripheral estates in selected cities

which city housing authorities are faced. In the original plans of 1960 the 16 400 units were in low-rise blocks (74 per cent four storey or less) but by 1974 only 12 per cent were low-rise and 58 per cent were five to nineteen-storey blocks and 6 per cent nineteen to 31-storey blocks! In the final outcome 70 per cent of the 18 000 homes are in flat blocks (Becker and Kein, 1977). Play spaces for small children in this scheme are inadequate for a teenage population and private open space is generally absent except on balconies. Employment is sited elsewhere in the city and this makes it difficult for young mothers seeking employment, unless they can be employed in shops on the estate itself. More recently the lurid confessions of a teenage drug addict sensationalized in the press have drawn attention to the area's social problems. The social services in the *Bezirk* of Neukölln were more prepared than other cities for the problems of an estate where 75 per cent of the population was under 45 years old. Offices of the youth service, social psychiatry section and school health authority were placed in the development. With 95.7 per cent social housing being constructed and only 4.6 per cent for sale (including housing financed from the social housing programme) Gropiusstadt is very much a single social group housing development.

France—The Grand Ensemble

(1) Le Mirail, Toulouse

The development of Le Mirail, Toulouse (Figure 6.2d) was planned in 1961 with the realization that the city could grow into a centre for the electronics and aircraft industry; 700 hectares was set aside for a programme to build 25 000 homes for 100 000 people, 5 kilometres from the centre. A high-density housing area with pedestrian circulation, a university, a commercial centre and an industrial zone were planned but constrained by financial, legal, and administrative problems throughout its construction. The priority was to house people but the constraints resulted in cost-cutting exercises whose social consequences mirror those of other *Grands Ensembles*.

(2) Social Problems in a Grand Ensemble

Le Puits-la-Marlière at Villiers-le-Biel is a *Grand Ensemble* built between 1965 and 1967, 18 kilometres from central Paris. It included 1511 dwellings mainly in flats besides shops, two schools and an old people's home. Several problems of this type of development were highlighted in a subsequent report (Shankland Cox, 1971). The development is demographically unbalanced. The families are young with small children and there are few teenagers or old people; as the children grow up there is a lack of facilities for teenagers. For the young families, being placed in a new home had advantages but the general inexperience and absence of older families to assist in times of stress added to their problems.

The design of the flats did not encourage ease of social mixing with the result that many young mothers felt isolated during the day, a not uncommon phenomenon in any new social housing project, and labelled by the French 'Sarcellitis', after one of the largest *Grands Ensembles* (Lagarde, 1968). Despite subsidies the cost of housing was regarded as expensive particularly as husbands were now commuting back to Paris. Some flats had not been rented in the 2 years following completion and 20 per cent had changed hands, whereas the few houses had always been filled.

The housing environment was mainly liked for its quietness and countrylike atmosphere apart from the local amenities. However, the monotony of the blocks, poor maintenance, the lack of privacy caused by high density of blocks and poor noise insulation, the problems of public staircases and inadequate lifts and the lack of stimulating social life were the major criticisms advanced. It was particularly noticeable that actual play areas for children within the scheme were not always those designed for play. Actual unofficial play areas exceeded the planned ones by sixteen to five with three official areas being very much under-used. The need for parking had been underestimated and there were problems of on-street parking and noise for ground-floor residents. Private outside space, whether balconies or gardens, was valued and felt to be too scarce. The housing lacks the intimate small-scale spaces and multiple use so characteristic of older French towns.

These comments, while concerning one scheme, could be replicated in many other studies, but they serve to illustrate the social problems to be found in many such peripheral housing schemes, no doubt built with good intentions but with unforeseen social consequences which stem in part from the impact of the national policies outlined earlier in this chapter.

Recently most cities have decided to stop the construction of large peripheral housing schemes. In 1976 West Berlin curbed the size of a smaller scheme, Ruhwald, by 500 dwellings out of a planned 4000. The declining population, the problems of high-rise living and the costs of building which were not cheaper, have brought about a new look at social housing provision on the city fringes and a fresh approach to the older housing stock. It is a return to what Rappoport (1968) terms the vernacular tradition, from the grand technocratic design. The policy shifts have taken housing back to reinstating the vernacular tradition reflecting the life and activities of people.

Inner Urban Renovation in West Germany

(1) Ostertor-Remberti, Bremen

The renovation of this area of 6.8 hectares just to the east of the city-centre is being undertaken by the *Bremische Gesellschaft für Stadterneuerung, Stadtentwicklung und Wohnungsbau mbH* within the provisions of the federal *Städtebauförderungsgesetz*. The area was developed in the nineteenth century with distinctive housing called *Bremer Haus*. However, all the early attempts to provide an overall traffic plan for the city saw the area as lying astride an eastern inner ringroad around the central area. From 1967 onwards the east tangent became an accepted part of the planning strategy and planning blight occurred along the course of the planned road. However, in 1974 an urban renovation area (*Sanierungsgebiet*) was delimited on either side of the route. By 1976, however, the road plan was abandoned and as a result the renovation area was enlarged. The first attempts were made in one area in 1974, characterized by a mixture of residences and industry. Since then a whole series of studies have been undertaken (Bremische Gesellschaft, 1977) on the condition of the buildings, the environment and the social environment.

As one would expect in a blighted area, the proportion of immigrants (*Ausländer* is strictly a term applied to foreigners) rose rapidly from 6 per cent in 1970 to 18 per cent in 1976. At the same time the age structure was altering with fewer children and fewer in the 45 to 65 year age group, but more old people. The number of single-person households increased with an influx of students and the increase in the elderly to form two-thirds of all households, but there was also an increase in large households of the foreigners. Mobility in the area is twice that of the city as a whole.

As a result of the research programme by the interdisciplinary team, a six-part programme for the area phased from 1978–80 to 1981–83 was prepared, costing 39 million DM (£10 million at 1980 prices). Much of the plan for one of the phases for the 1360 inhabitants, 860 households and 135 industrial workshops, offices and retail outlets in *Sanierungsgebiet* was in the form of a social plan reinforced by federal government legislation in the form of seven acts. Much of the property (75 per cent) is rented by absentee landlords and the higher rents that renovation could bring are attractive to them. However, the financial assistance enables the existing population to remain and new groups to be encouraged to enter the area.

The changes are generally concentrated in small areas, often house by house, and conversion costs are paid. Loans are granted for modernization and repairs at 2 per cent below the existing savings rate and the highest rate is 4 per cent. In the first 10 years there is no interest payment. The personal contribution as a rule amounts to 15 per cent of the modernization costs and these are claimable against tax. For industries there is assistance to relocate. Throughout all stages the renters are made aware of their rights. Thus it has been possible to build new residential apartments and subdivide large single-family residences into three family apartments. The policy has been to encourage the letting of these to young families who work in the area. Rather than encourage ghettos of the old (*Altenghettos*), the *Generationshaus* (a house with an apartment for elderly relatives) has been encouraged together with the planning of an old people's day centre. The existing foreign-born population concentration is tolerated without encouraging a ghetto, yet acknowledging the desire to cluster. Schools will get special facilities for teaching foreign children. The size of the student population of the area is to be kept steady. The so-called social outcasts are also considered in the plan which hopes that no more will be attracted to the area, which is most unlikely once the rents begin to rise.

Ostertor-Remburti is one of nineteen special study areas for renovation (others in similar locations include zones in Karlsruhe-Alstadt, Hamburg-St Pauli, Berlin-Wedding and Osnabrück) funded jointly by the Federal and *Land* governments. In all, federal assistance is being given to 473 renewal schemes. The progress in the area to date is visible in the greatly improved external appearance of the houses. The cost of this scheme for the period 1962–75 was approximately 5 million DM. The social structure has been stabilized but only time will tell whether the danger of gentrification of the area's housing market has been avoided.

(2) Hamburg-Ottensen

Ottensen is one of four inner urban areas to which Hamburg has given priority treatment. It is under 6 kilometres from the centre of Hamburg but in terms of the city's history a nineteenth-century inner suburb of Altona which became part of Hamburg in 1937. It is an area where 60 per cent of the housing was built before 1918 and where the mixture of industry and housing was being altered by the flight of both employment and workers and the influx of foreigners. (In some areas there are 33 per cent *Gastarbeiter*). The area of Ottensen is much larger (207.7 hectares) than Ostertor-Remberti discussed above; also a nearby federal motorway had increased traffic flows through the area, which lacked open space. Ottensen has been the subject of intensive study since 1968 which led to the acceptance of a development plan for the district in 1977 (Ottensen, 1977).

The local aims of the plan were to renovate housing and to construct new apartments that partly compensated for dwelling losses to new industrial sites and transport improvements. In the sphere of the physical environment this demanded the creation of 'residentially oriented spaces', or open areas to serve the housing including the preservation and refurbishing of the urban landscape, especially the small squares. Commercial enterprises and traffic that detracts from an area's attraction for residence are to be moved from the area. Yet, at the same time, the diversity of work and small-scale factories had to be retained which could conflict with good environmental conditions. Similarly, conflict was foreseen between the preservation of dwellings and the provision of improved community facilities, and the dangers to other residential areas of traffic control measures in Ottensen. The population of 32 000 in 1975 was planned to fall to 26 000 by 1985.

Modernization began in 1975 with 21 apartments and then a second, larger area was tackled. In this area it was necessary to have some comprehensive redevelopment which was agręed with the participation of tenants and owners. Modernized homes in reorganized courtyards are a key point of the plan. Grants similar to those in Bremen are obtainable. Other areas will remain more mixed. The floor area for housing will rise due to the construction of dwellings but the share of dwellings in all floor space will fall due to increases in the intensity of use of the area for offices and businesses. Much of the housing that has been renovated has been assisted by SAGA, the city's public housing company, which encourages house-by-house renovation so that displacement is minimized. Over 500 homes have been repaired and 900 modernized, in addition to the construction of 400 new apartments especially on old factory sites. Factories have been converted, on parental initiative, into a kindergarten and an old people's day centre. These improvements in the social infrastructure together with the policy of 'renewal in steps' will, it is hoped, improve the housing conditions in this area where half the buildings are over 60 years old. The environment of deprivation is slowly changing to one of conservation and renovation.

Hamburg is able to contemplate the renovation of Ottensen because the city can now issue decrees requiring construction and modernization besides stipulating sides where buildings may not be demolished. Similarly, they can designate sites where only social housing or housing for those with special needs may be constructed. In addition, as we have seen in both the German cases, importance is attached to social plans which must be prepared and discussed. In the case of Hamburg, the discussions included interpreters to represent the foreign worker interests.

Not all inner urban schemes are exercises in renovation. In Mülheim (Ruhr) a housing scheme has been built since 1971 at the edge of the existing central area and incorporating a pedestrianized extension to the city's retailing space, a transport interchange, five multistorey car parks and four nineteen-storey residential blocks. Two of the residential blocks are for social housing and are now homes for 330 families in one to four room apartments. The scheme also includes other facets of social provision including two restaurants, a sauna, a swimming pool and children's play area. In other cities such mixed housing schemes have formed part of large-scale commercial developments to serve the inner suburbs such as Ihmezentrum, Hannover, and Hamburgerstrasse, Hamburg.

Old Housing in the Netherlands

In 1968 it was estimated that there were 375 000 slum dwellings, 250 000 poor dwellings in need of improvement and 50 000 oversize dwellings for which there is no demand in the Netherlands. On an age basis it has been calculated that 20 000 new buildings enter the above categories each year. The overall increase in slums in the 1960s was 10 000 dwellings per year. Over one in five slum dwellings and a quarter of those capable of improvement were located in the Rotterdam–Hague area of South Holland. Present policies represent a radical change in emphasis from expensive clearance and construction to a national and local policy of rehabilitation.

Of the homes that can be considered in need of improvement, 200 000 are already owned by housing corporations and municipalities and it is proposed to increase the number of those being improved from between 6000 and 8000 to 10 000 per annum. To achieve increased numbers of renovated houses it was suggested that the municipalities utilize their legal rights to make dwelling owners carry out the necessary improvements, for which government aid is forthcoming. Private individuals receive aid from the Premium Scheme for Improvement and Splitting of Housing and this aid can be boosted further in areas of high unemployment. Funds of up to 80 per cent of the cost are available for the worst slum clearance so that the municipality may redevelop the site. As a result of these policies renewal expenditure by the government has risen from 7.1 per cent of housing expenditure in 1971 to 11.9 per cent in 1976. In Rotterdam, eleven urban renewal districts have been designated within the provision of the 1965 Physical Planning Act and the 1976 Urban Renewal Act, containing a quarter of the city's dwellings, and in renewing the areas great emphasis is placed on local involvement and maintaining the existing population. It is intended to rehabilitate 1000 units a year and build a further 1500 units in the renewal areas giving priority to existing residents. In Amsterdam 13 000 dwellings are included within the city's major rehabilitation and conservation scheme.

French Urban Renovation

In 1973 it was estimated that 30 per cent of the population living in pre-1949 housing was living in unsatisfactory conditions; 16 million people in France would therefore appreciate improved housing, and over the years since the 1958 decree on renovation, several acts affecting housing renovation have been passed. The 1958 decree on urban renovation permitted the destruction of the housing stock of a *quartier*, alteration of landholdings and rebuilding, as in Belleville, Paris. The Malraux Act of 1962 permitted *Restauration immobilière*, exterior renovation with interior renewal, a form of conservation that is best seen in the Marais district of Paris. In 1967 the *Loi Amélioration de l'Habitat* permitted the improvement of hygiene, sanitary conditions, comfort and security of dwellings. The Vivien Law of 1970 was designed to tackle the worst insalubrious dwellings by relocation and destruction. Funds for renovation are obtained from *Fonds d'aménagement urbaine* which in 1977 funded renovations to the sum of 177 million francs. In addition, 170 million francs were set aside for implementing the removal of slums and a further 570 million francs for housing improvements (Urbanisme, 1978).

It is claimed that renovation of old areas has three major objectives, that of improving the value of the nation's real estate, maintaining social balance and reinforcing the old urban symbolism and distinctiveness of districts. Thus the schemes for public restoration began with areas in the more historical towns such as Avignon, Sarlat and Tours but some came to include areas in Lyons and Paris. However, no distinction is drawn between the true conservation of historic buildings and the renovation of dwellings. Many of the problems remain in Paris where 620 000 households still did not have exclusive use of toilet facilities in 1977 and these were inhabited by 237 000 pensioner households and 194 000 households from the lower socio-economic groups. The social characteristics for the 35 per cent of poor dwellings in large city areas resemble Ottensen or Ostertor but the pace of improvement does not match that of Hamburg or Bremen.

Housing in the Inner Areas of Liverpool and Greater Manchester

'The impression is of an area gone to seed, at the point where it needs a determined effort to lift the standard of the environment, and then keep it there for as long as the housing is to remain, or to abandon the attempt altogether and merely ensure that the resulting accelerated decay does not actually become dangerous' (Wilson and Wommersley, 1977). These lines describing Lodge Lane East in Inner Liverpool sum up the problems of old housing in the city (Figure 6.3). Here attempts have been made to alter the image of the 2000 privately owned Victorian houses. Initially policies were for clearance in stages, limited life improvements and for a small General Improvement Area. However, following the 1974 Housing Act, there was a change from slum clearance towards improving the remaining stock. To the General Improvement Area introduced in 1969, were added the concepts of Housing Action Areas where physical and social factors combined to cause stress and Priority Neighbourhoods—areas of unsatisfactory social conditions where Housing Action

Area status is inappropriate. The spatial changes which the policies brought about can be seen in Figure 6.3 although these are just part of a rolling programme that is restricted by financial stringency. Lodge Lane East is just one small scheme in a city where there are five categories of action area, as listed in Table 6.5.

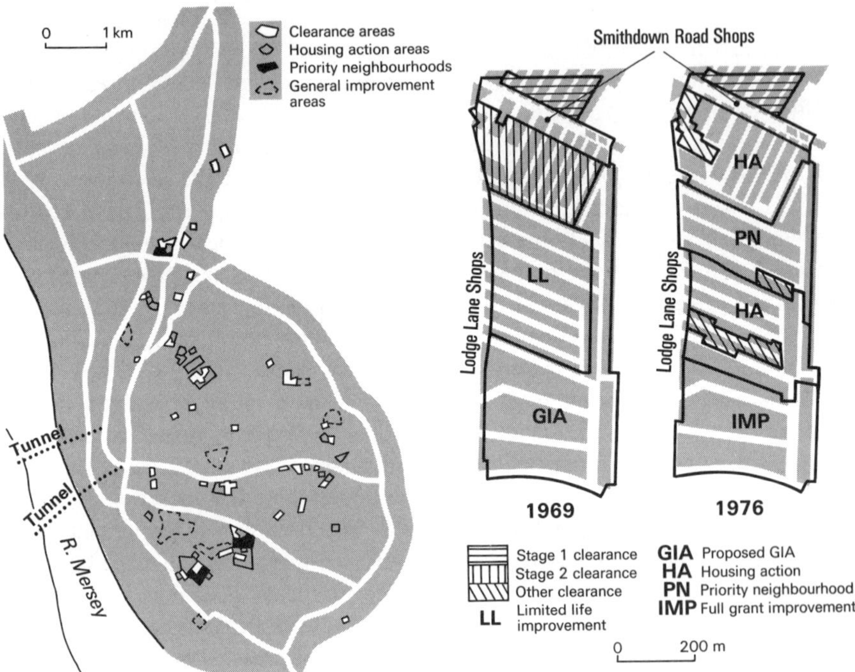

Figure 6.3 Housing programmes in an inner city area—Liverpool: (a) programme areas in Liverpool; (b) Lodge Lane East 1969–76 (both reproduced by permission of the Controller of Her Majesty's Stationery Office)

Table 6.5 Categories of Housing Action in Liverpool

55 New small clearance areas (includes remainder of Stage 1 clearances)	6150 dwellings
22 Housing Action Areas	4800 dwellings
3 Priority Neighbourhoods	1320 dwellings
13 New General Improvement Areas (plus the original GIAs)	5230 dwellings
Remainder where full improvement grants would be made available	64 500 dwellings

Source: after Wilson and Wommersley, 1977

Given this aid, continued deteriorations occur in inner areas for a variety of reasons. Incomes remain low in the inner area, building societies remain unwilling to lend on the pre-1919 property, while central government funds for local authority mortgages have been cut. The takeup rate for improvement grants has fallen since the 1974 recession. The population structure becomes older as the young adults leave. There has been no private house-building on any scale since the 1920s.

Liverpool also illustrates a further problem that inner areas are faced with in Britain, that of the neglected inner urban social housing projects built in the 1930s and 1950s. Schemes are now underway to sell, destroy or improve the worst cases in this city. The cosmetic policies at present operated in Liverpool for social and private properties did not prevent the project team from suggesting that the citywide housing policy requires changing to improve the chances of those at the bottom of the market. Stress was laid on the relationships of housing policies to more total approaches to the inner areas which, as we stated earlier in this chapter, involve new roles for central government in city planning. The discussion of a total approach to housing is still lacking in Liverpool and only a handful of British cities have attempted a complete plan for housing. Among these was the GLC's consultation document, *A Strategic Housing Plan for London* (Greater London Council, 1974) which looked simultaneously at all types of housing provision throughout Greater London.

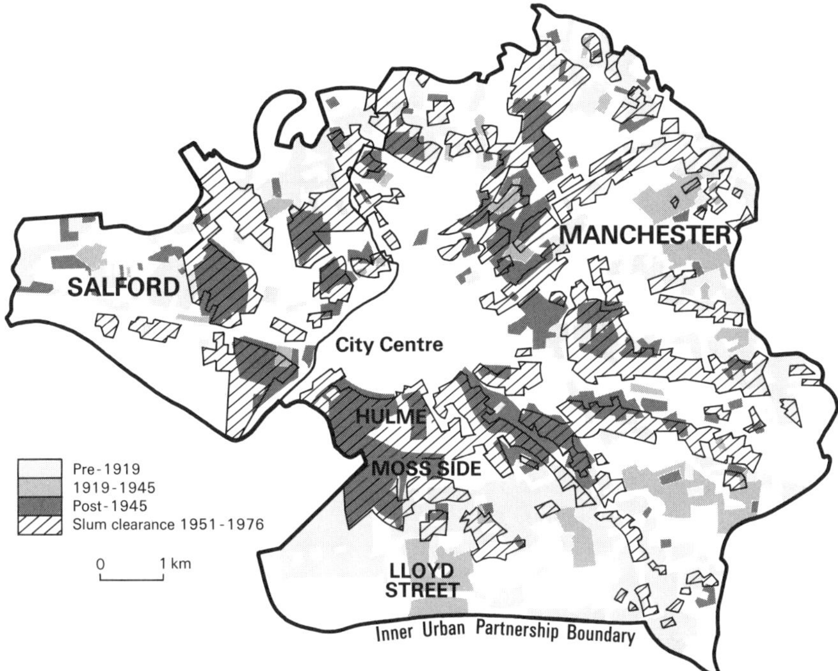

Figure 6.4 Slum clearance and age of buildings in the Manchester–Salford partnership area (reproduced by permission of Manchester and Salford Inner Area Study)

Similar patterns of change can be observed in Manchester–Salford, where the inner area has been subject to vast schemes of slum clearance and replacement by social housing schemes (Figure 6.4). Of the remaining undemolished housing stock about two-thirds is at risk because it is both pre-1919 and in private ownership in areas characterized by 50 per cent private renting where incomes of tenants and the many small landowners are low. Building societies are unwilling or reluctant to lend to council-nominated purchasers of pre-1919 housing, central government aid has been cut back, improvement grants are not being taken up; all these are contributing to continued deterioration. Sadly only 9400 houses are at present within the Housing Action Areas and General Improvement Areas in Manchester and Salford. Local authority housing has not been without its problems. Interwar council housing in, for instance, the Lloyd Street area of Manchester, is being improved. 'Walkup' flats of the immediate postwar period are difficult to let and in need of modernization while the pedestrian-deck access maisonettes such as the concentration of 2960 units in Hulme and Moss Side have achieved national infamy for vandalism, structural faults and problems for families with children. In all, 10 per cent of the social housing stock is difficult to let (Manchester and Salford Inner City Partnership Area Study, 1978), and it is no surprise that 48 per cent of Manchester's housing waiting list comprises inner area residents. Obviously the housing stress noted in inner Greater Manchester is part of a much broader all-pervading deprivation that characterizes the inner areas of British cities and some outer areas as well. Only when housing policies are related to investment policies, other social policies and to the needs of the city as a whole will the problem recede.

Bologna—Housing as a Public Good

In contrast to Liverpool and Manchester's sectoral approaches to housing, Bologna has provided housing within an overall plan for what the whole city needs (Angotti, 1977). Bologna's theoretical basis of housing provision is that the public good should be prevalent given the limitations imposed by the Italian economic and legal structure. The programme has attempted to stop speculation, to improve services and recreation space in the centre, to finance housing rehabilitation, and to maintain a stable socially mixed population. By 1972, a plan for the five areas of the historic city-centre had been proposed, which involved rehabilitation of residences in the centre where the costs of rehabilitation per square metre were 8 per cent lower than those of building on the periphery. The per capita costs of rehabilitation were one-third lower than those of developing at the periphery. While renovation goes on, the inhabitants are housed in special blocks of 33 apartments and seven houses (*casa parcheggio* or parking houses) until their dwelling is completed, thus permitting a rolling programme of renewal. Private house construction has slowed because the best land has been zoned for cooperative and public housing. An unsuccessful attempt was made to enable public funds for land expropriation for new building to be utilized to expropriate private owners in areas in need of restoration and renovation.

Renewal in privately rented dwellings now takes the form of a contract over 20 years in which rents are restricted to the level of those in social housing (that is, 12 per cent of average family income). Other conditions in the contract make it extremely probable that the property will be sold to the city or that the city will acquire more of the units. Corporate ownership is excluded. Not only is housing for low-income groups guaranteed in this way but also allied plans for social services and transport reinforce the renewal programme's comprehensiveness. Bologna's approach to the total urban environment, rather than to sections of it, is unique in West Europe although similar proposals are being utilized elsewhere in Italy, in Ancona, Bergamo and Ferrara.

Conclusion

Housing policies in West Europe are full of contrasts but certain distinct trends do emerge.

(1) The national and local municipal involvement in housing is very strong, although the exact nature of this involvement has been subject to changing political ideologies of those in power during particular phases of city development.

(2) There is a general movement towards the encouragement of owner-occupied housing in most cities although the socio-spatial dichotomy that this causes is of increasing concern.

(3) There is an acceptance that social housing schemes of the postwar period, which were based on the genuine desire to assist the lower socioeconomic groups, did not have the sympathy of design or an appreciation of the social bonds that tied people to the older housing stock.

(4) Housing policies are still governed by cost–benefit analysis rather than the shelter needs of society.

(5) The need to reinstate housing townscapes that are a part of a city's history and embody the physical elements of a nation's past ideologies has been appreciated more in the past decade initially for aesthetic and social reasons and, unfortunately, for purely economic reasons by the housing managers.

(6) Although we have tried to examine housing policy on its own, it is increasingly obvious that policies towards this sector of city planning cannot be isolated from other economic and social policies in the city or even the nation as a whole.

CHAPTER 7

Urban Conservation

Although there is a clear relationship between the physical form of a city, its buildings and patterns of streets and spaces, and the functions that a city performs, the physical fabric commonly outlives the functions for which it was created. Much of the distinctiveness of the West European city stems from the antiquity of its surviving historical forms. Houses often stand for two or three generations, public buildings frequently for much longer, while the patterning of roads and squares can survive for many centuries. The functions undertaken by the city, however, typically change their type, intensity and areas of operation much more frequently. The planning dilemma, therefore, is whether new urban forms should be built to accommodate the new functions, or whether the functions should be constrained to fit the existing forms. The first alternative assumes that the greater efficiency of a purpose-built urban fabric outweighs the financial, social and emotional costs of rapid and violent change in the city, while the second assumes that the aesthetic gains of preservation outweigh the costs of constraint.

The classical models which attempt to explain the internal structuring of cities largely ignore the existence of this dilemma. The North American cities from which these models were derived have had short histories dominated by rapid change, have consequently less of architectural merit worth preserving, and until recently are characterized by attitudes that equate the value of a building inversely with its age. In Europe, however, the character of the individual city, the civic pride of its citizens and the quality of life of its inhabitants has depended, to a large degree, on its relict buildings and 'there is a special consideration that the city is largely the custodian of Europe's cultural patrimony' (Hall, 1977). Conservation planning is therefore a central part of the whole process of planning the European city, not merely a constraint to be suffered in a few specified districts of the inner city. A conservation ethic will thus be found in many of the sectors described in this book—and only convenience causes the topic to be synthesized in this chapter.

The conserved urban form is the major tourist resource that the city offers and the experience of architectural and historical artefacts is the main motive for tourist visits to cities. The possible financial gains from tourism in turn provide an economic justification for conservation. In 1978 the European Economic Community's Regional Development Fund, whose grants can only be given to 'economic' enterprises that have a direct financial return, awarded a substantial grant to Lancashire County Council for building renovation in the city of Lancaster. After much deliberation on this test case, which will be followed by many other such grants throughout the EEC, it was accepted that tourism was an 'economic' justification for conservation, and suitable criteria for such applications have now been established by the Department of the Environment. This link, together with the inherent international character of both tourism and conservation provides the justification for considering in successive chapters the conservation of the urban fabric and the visitors who come to view it.

Pressures for Change

Change is of course endemic in any city that has not become a fossilized museum exhibit, and 1000 years of urban development in Europe has depended on the operation of a cycle of demolition and renewal. The last few generations, however, have witnessed a dramatic acceleration in the pace of change which has replaced a slow piecemeal renewal with a comprehensive redevelopment of large tracts of the city.

A fundamental change that affects the physical fabric of cities is fluctuations in the size, distribution and family structure of the urban population. Buildings exist to serve the needs of citizens and an increase in population leads to pressures for more or different structures, while a decrease in population leaves redundant buildings for which new uses must be found, or demolition ensues.

The well-documented flight of population from the central areas of cities to peripheral suburbs has left the inner districts of many West European cities, which normally contain a high proportion of the older building stock, with declining residential, retailing and employment functions. The islands in the lagoon that comprise the historic Venice (Figure 7.1) contained 47 per cent of the city's

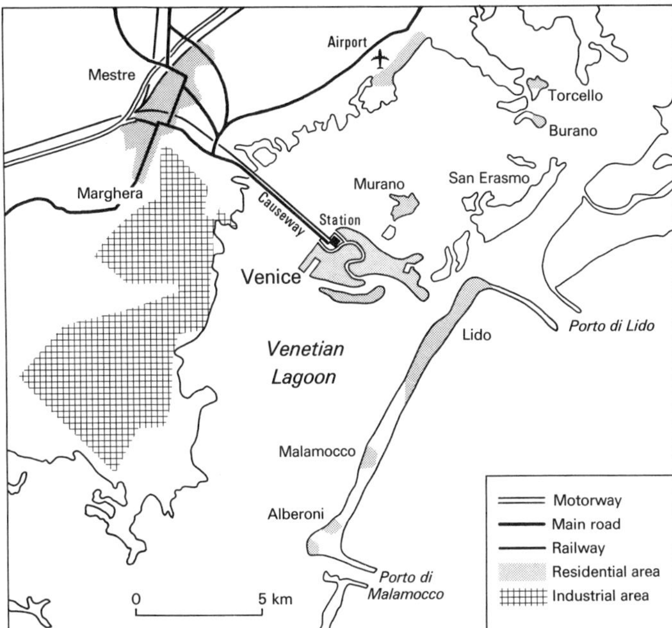

Figure 7.1 Venice urban area (reproduced from *The Geographical Magazine*, London)

population in 1951 but only 29 per cent by 1970, with 71 per cent of those under 45 moving out between 1951 and 1971. Less drastic, but equally marked has been the fall in the population of Paris *intra-muros*, Amsterdam within the *grachten*, Stockholm and many other major European cities. It can be argued that this trend removes some of the pressures on the inner city and releases buildings for preservation. It also, however, makes conservation more urgent, as much of the motive for private maintenance of property is removed, and successive dereliction and comprehensive clearance and development to serve new uses can occur. Large parts of even Europe's most acclaimed historic cities have been lost since the war because the time-lag between the flight of the resident population and the appreciation of the possibilities of restoration was long enough to make the latter prohibitively expensive. The Southgate area of Bath is a typical example of comprehensive clearance and redevelopment in the 1960s to fill a vacuum created by the outmigration of the resident population over the preceding 20 years (Figure 7.2).

Although the outmigration of people from the historic city-centres often leads directly to pressures for redevelopment, conservation may itself encourage such movement by raising the value of property and enticing existing residents to realize the value of their appreciating assets. The relationship between conservation and change in the social character of neighbourhoods is imperfectly understood but evident from many examples. In Venice, was it the expenditure on renovation of the residential districts of the lagoon city that encouraged the rich to acquire city-centre properties, and thus displace the lower income groups, or was it the movement of the working class to more comfortable and convenient flats in the mainland suburbs that left a vacuum, which in turn was filled by people more capable of bearing the costs of maintenance and renovation (O'Riordan, 1975)? Certainly the social status of neighbourhoods has a profound effect on the conservation of buildings to the extent that the amount of conservation activity in a locality often depends on the existence of a social class that appreciates its benefits and can bear its costs. It has been concluded from the French experience that 'although implementing conservation policies is likely to penalize the original occupants of city-centre areas, experience has shown that the French middle classes are eager to take up restored city-centre properties' (Kain, 1975).

While much of the motive for conservation is the desire to preserve the city as a monument to the past, a confident present will wish to leave a record of its existence in the fabric of the city. Paris provides one of the best examples in recent history of a government obliterating the past for political reasons when Napoleon III's attempt to create an imperial capital all but eliminated the record of the previous 1000 years of Parisian building. The wide boulevards and radial street patterns that Haussmann created are not a response to changes in the function of the city other than the need to reflect in stone and brick the grandiose and historian policies of the Empire, and to facilitate military control of the unruly Parisians. Even after the fall of the second Empire in 1870 the city authorities were content to complete the work that Haussman had begun, and the survival of some of the historic centre of Paris can be attributed to the practical difficulty of destroying it, rather than any desire to preserve it (Sutcliffe, 1970).

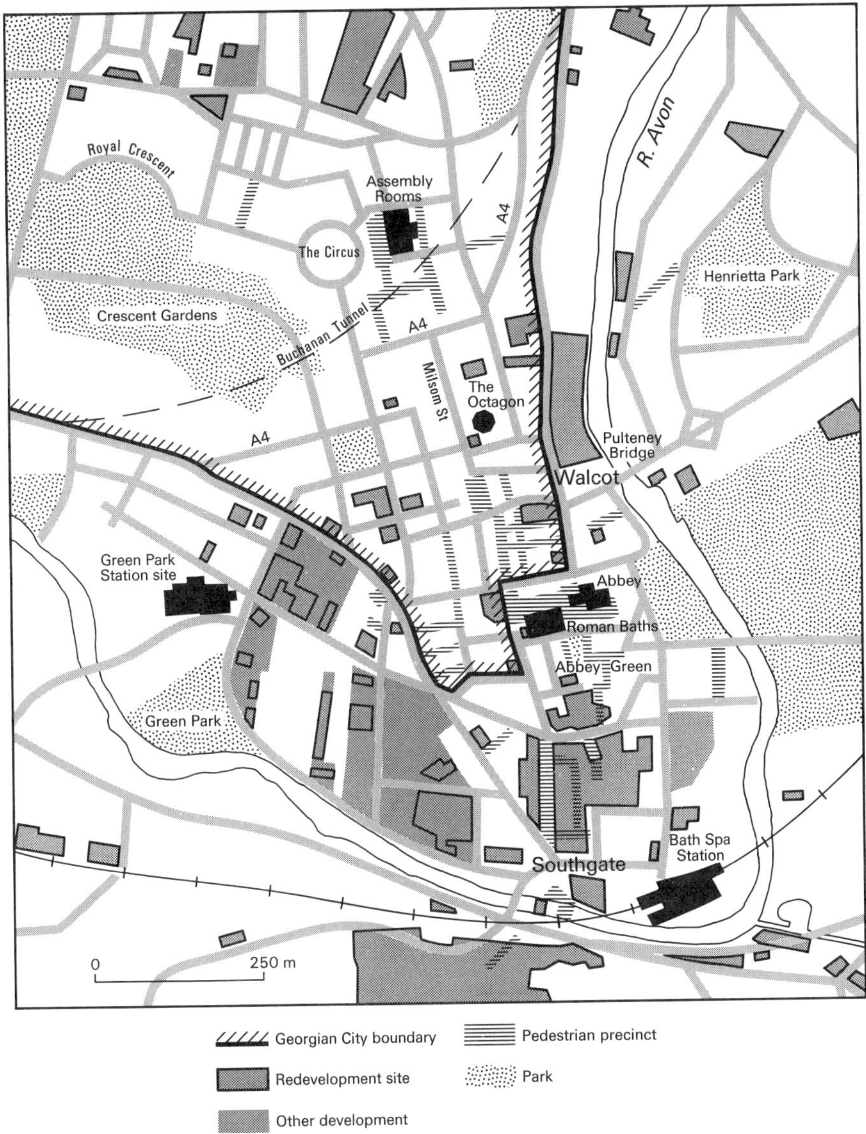

Figure 7.2 Georgian Bath and proposed developments in the city

Although few major European cities have been so completely reshaped in response to a change in government ideology, Paris had its contemporary imitators in other French cities, such as Lyons, and 'the spirit of Haussmann had also been abroad in London, Manchester, and Liverpool, and seems to feel itself just as much at home in Berlin and Vienna' (Engels, 1935). The same factor can be detected in the monumental building in Rome after 1870 which was considered appropriate for the new capital of the new Italian republic. It is not too far fetched to suggest that the large-scale office developments that transformed city-centres in the 1960s were prompted in part by the need for a visible symbol of a new political order, and the possession of a clutch of central high-rise offices was viewed as a sign of efficient urban government.

Changes in retailing, manufacturing industry and office employment in the last 20 years have all intensified pressures for change in the urban environment. The increasing dominance of the chainstore and the supermarket with their need for large selling areas and standardized recognizable façades, the demands of industry for access, and the requirement of the burgeoning office sector for large single-site complexes have been posed since the war in the form of two alternatives: the building of purpose-built modern structures on a scale previously unknown in the city, or the flight of many of these functions to the urban periphery. The first alternative promised demolition, the second dereliction.

In Brussels, where the office-building boom was triggered by the World Fair of 1958 and fuelled by the growing international role of the city, the demand was met by the first of Europe's 'Manhattan' business centres in the Noordwijk district completed in 1967. Other cities followed. Porte Maillot in Paris, the South Bank in London all involved demolition which in most cases could be justified by the condition of the existing property, but also brought a radical change in the skyline of the city and in the scale of building. Similarly, new trends in retailing produced the shopping centre and its associated carparks whose visual impact on the inner city was considerable. Hoog Catharijne which is a large part of the central area of Utrecht, is one of the largest and probably one of the last of its kind, but even relatively modest developments, such as Bath's Southgate Street cited above have changed the character of parts of the city.

The most insistent pressure for change, however, can be ascribed to the increasing consumer prosperity of Europeans over the last 20 years. Higher standards of amenity provision are demanded and are within financial reach. Above all, the private motor-car demands space both when it is moving and for the 95 per cent of its life when it is stationary. With levels of motor-car ownership in West Europe doubling in each decade since the war, the efforts of planners to keep traffic in towns moving caused the widening of roads, the loss of land for gyratory systems, parking lots and the destruction of a circulation system originally intended for pedestrians. New roads, the visual intrusion of the parked car which rapidly filled up the squares and piazzas, the vibration and atmospheric pollution which hastened physical decay all posed a threat whose implications only became clear in the mid-1960s. Policies of restraint offered as a solution denied citizens accessibility, which they had come to regard as a right and which was historically the main *raison d'être* for urban living, thereby hastening the flight of people, jobs and amenities from the inner city to the suburbs, where the motor car was both more acceptable and also more necessary.

The desires of a newly prosperous citizenry for more private consumption of urban space for transport and garaging has been paralleled by demands for more public provision, especially space for recreation. In the Gamla Stan district of Stockholm, for example, currently acceptable standards of public open space cannot be met within the crowded courtyards and narrow streets, and selective demolition is the only alternative to the loss of population to suburbs where such expectations can be met.

The Conservation Movement

Although the Protection of monuments and antiquities had been a preoccupation of the leisured classes in Europe for at least two centuries, as is witnessed by the establishment of societies of the Antiquarians in London, Paris and Berlin in the eighteenth century, the emergence of a coherent conservation argument as an alternative planning strategy is much more recent. Its growth can be attributed to consumer prosperity, intellectual fashion and a reappraisal of architectural standards, a growing concern for what became termed the quality of life and the availability of surplus disposable income to purchase this.

In West Europe, in sharp contrast to the cities of East Europe, much of the impetus of the conservation movement was local rather than national, and unofficial rather than governmental. Groups of citizens often, but by no means exclusively, drawn from the articulate middle classes drew together into pressure groups usually in response to an immediate threat to their local urban environment. One of the earliest was the Cockburn Society of Edinburgh founded in 1875 to protect the Georgian 'new town'.

The example of the Bath Preservation Trust is typical of many such groups (Aldous, 1972). The need to speed up traffic on the increasingly congested A4 main road that ran through the centre of the town led to an imaginative proposal in 1966 from the Buchanan consultants for a tunnel which would carry traffic underneath the Georgian Circus and Royal Crescent (see Figure 7.2). This proposal was the catalyst that united popular feeling in defence of the town's heritage, and focused a vaguely felt unease on a single issue. A classic confrontation of conservationists with developers was skilfully and successfully managed by the professional talents that rallied to the cry of 'Save Bath'.

Similar action occurred spontaneously in Brussels where the building of the ITT office block in 1972, which was little more intrusive than many other such blocks erected previously, provoked popular indignation as it overshadowed the *Abbaye de la Cambe*, one of the few surviving parts of eighteenth-century Brussels. Popular feeling coincided with the need of the *Front Democratique Francophone* for a new electoral issue, and opposition to the redevelopment of the 'Marolles' working-class residential district and the 'Sablons' square schemes led to the creation of both popular committees and a large measure of renovation in both cases (Culot, 1974).

Even as early as 1911, a 'Save Montmartre' movement—'the last hamlet in Paris'—had some success in preventing wholesale demolition and led in turn to the more broadly based Association of Friends of Paris and saw change in government attitudes embodied into the 1913 Law on historic buildings. More recently the creation in rapid succession of a number of uncompromisingly modern developments in the central city such as the Beaubourg Arts Centre, the Montparnasse tower, and the proposals for the Les Halles site and the left bank motorway, spurred Parisians to defend a Paris that had almost been lost. SOS-Paris was founded in 1973 to introduce an element of local participation into a planning system that has traditionally been among the least responsive to public pressure of any in West Europe (Fabre-Luce, 1976). Similarly, in the postwar rebuilding of Stavanger in Norway government action was met by local opposition which led to the establishment of a local preservation society for the 'Gamla Stavanger' district, which in turn set a pattern for delimiting the respective roles of government and amenity society in other cities.

In almost all cases, local reaction to a particular development preceded the establishment of formal associations, and locally based groups led to national organizations. The British Civic Trust established in 1957 had, by 1978, 1240 affiliated local societies and 33 local building preservation trusts, and was the archetype of other similar bodies elsewhere.

Curiously the two scales of conservation activity that are most evident are the local and the international. Architecture and history have an international appeal and foreign tourism has rendered the concept of a European Heritage familiar to large numbers. As early as 1963 the Council of Europe recognized that the protection of historic buildings was an important part of its work and established *Europa Nostra* initially to investigate a sample of 50 projects in as many cities (Council of Europe, 1974). As had occurred on the local scale, the international movement was fired by a reaction to specific threats. The 1966 floods in Florence and Venice revealed the vulnerability of some of the most famous European cities, the inadequacy of national governments to meet major catastrophes, and the depth of feeling in Europe and America. The sudden realization that cities such as Florence or Venice, or at least their historic centres, might not exist for the next generation inspired a crusade in which the international agencies were swept up. A series of international conferences beginning in 1971 in Split, and meeting in successive years in Zurich, Edinburgh, Bologna, Krems and Amsterdam, called for the establishment of conservation areas that would provide effective protection for districts rather than individual buildings, promoted the benefits of rehabilitation over demolition, and called in general for stronger national legislation. European Architectural Heritage Year in 1975 was an attempt to stimulate public opinion and give a European dimension to the problem as well as put pressure on national governments to initiate legislation. This initiative is to be followed in 1981 by the European Campaign for Urban Renaissance. In this campaign the main aim is to exchange practical experience, concentrating on the themes of the improvement of the quality of the environment; the rehabilitation of old areas; the provision of social and economic opportunities; achieving community participation and reviewing the role of local authorities. This is a wider brief than in 1975 but the choice of the historic centre of Durham and Greater Manchester's urban facelift serve to illustrate the conservation flavour of the British contributions.

The international movement has been effective in levelling up standards, which in practice has usually meant raising the standards of the legislation of Mediterranean countries to those existing in north-west Europe. In addition it has provided finance for key restoration projects and acted as a forum for the exchange of technical information. Equally, however, the limits of international action have become clear, especially as a result of experience in Venice, a city regarded not merely as the prime exhibit in a museum of European urbanism, but also seen as a model for the city of the future by planners as diverse as Buchanan, Mumford and Le Corbusier. Consequently UNESCO and a number of foreign private charities have been working in the city for 10 years (UNESCO, 1975). Money raised internationally can only be spent effectively within the framework of national and local plans and the ultimate success of the efforts of the international volunteers to save the city depends largely on action to remove the causes of change, which in turn depends upon the Italian authorities. The limits of international action have been demonstrated by the delay of the Venice commune and Venato region authorities to produce and implement the long-awaited plan for the city, which would both prevent a recurrence of the 1966 floods and solve the many long-term problems of the city, such as the rising level of the waters of the lagoon and industrial pollution. In addition controversy over the spending by the Italian state of loans raised internationally for the city has led to considerable frictions between the private and official, national and international authorities involved. The inviolable sovereignty of the nation-state within its frontiers removes much of the meaning from the concept of a 'European Heritage'. If Venice and Florence, or for that matter Nuremberg, Bath, Chartres and Salzburg, are an international responsibility, there must be some way that this responsibility can be exercised other than through national governments.

National Policies and Practice

There is a remarkable degree of conformity among the urban conservation policies of the West European countries, perhaps more so than in other aspects of planning. The pressures for change, the nature of the local response, the division of responsibility between government and pressure groups, and even the timing of the legislation is broadly similar with national differences being largely those of emphasis.

France, like Britain, initiated a system of listing buildings worthy of preservation before the First World War largely as a result of pressure from the learned societies, and improved this successively until the present day. As a result of the 1889 Act an inventory of buildings of national importance was drawn up and like Britain these are classified according to intrinsic merit with both the *monuments classes* and *monuments inscrits* approximating to grade 1 in the British system. Unlike Britain, however, far fewer buildings were listed—29 000 in 1970 compared with 170 000 in Britain. A large measure of protection and a high level of grant is thus awarded to the main 'set-pieces', and such protection is extended to a *zone protégé* up to 500 metres around the building. As early as 1913 the idea of a 'field of vision' (*champs de visibilité*) defined as being an area within 100 metres of a listed building, was introduced (Stungo, 1972). The centralized tradition of French government is reflected in the 'Malraux Law' of 1962 which moved from the protection of individual buildings to comprehensive conservation planning of urban areas. Some 50, of an envisaged eventual 400, of these *secteurs sauvegardés* have been designated

(Figure 7.3). Designation is undertaken by the central government and indeed can be imposed by it upon local authorities. Both major cities such as Paris which has eleven entire arrondissements designated, and the entire centres of small towns such as St Brieuc or Valence are protected. Zones range in size from 6 to 370 hectares but are on average considerably larger in extent than British conservation areas (Kain, 1975). Compared with Britain the French legislation has produced a more even pattern

Figure 7.3 Safeguarded towns and districts in France (reproduced by permission of Town and Country Planning Association)

of conservation with national criteria being centrally applied. Its critics, however, would also comment on its inflexibility, its continuing stress on the setpiece monuments rather than the more modest domestic buildings which *en masse* can play an important role in the urban landscape, and the unequal partnership between central and local governments. The creation of the restoration work itself is usually undertaken by a consortium, such as *SOREMA* in the Marais district of Paris, composed of the central government, local authorities and often private companies (Stungo, 1972). The comparable British legislation, the Civic Amenities Act of 1967, has led to over 2500 smaller conservation areas, (a much larger number), with much of the initiative being left to the city authorities resulting in a consequently greater variety in size and criteria (Dobby, 1978).

The Netherlands occupies an intermediate position between 'underlisted' France and 'overlisted' Britain. Around 45 000 buildings have been listed under the provisions of the 1961 Ancient Monuments Act. This Act also allowed the surroundings of buildings, including trees, canals and open spaces to be included, and was thus an appreciation of the importance of areas rather than individual buildings that predates both the British and French legislation. As in France, central government aid is generous, around 70 per cent of total costs, but like Britain much of the initiative comes from the towns themselves, with a resulting uneven distribution. Almost a fifth of all listings have occurred in Amsterdam, and more than a half in the Western Netherlands, which parallels the 44 per cent of British Conservation Areas found in South-East England. The 1976 Urban Renewal Bill gave the municipalities rights of land purchase, if necessary compulsorily, which has considerably strengthened the role of the local authorities.

Early demonstration of central government concern about the conservation of monuments can be seen with the Royal Commission of 1835 in Belgium. This resulted in the Law of 1836 that gave the provincial governments the power to act in this sphere. Very little, however, was actually executed despite a central government-inspired inventory of 1861, and the influence of Camillo Sitte (Chapter 2), whose writings on the concept of townscape found ready acceptance amongst the Belgian urban intelligentsia. The 1931 Law for the preservation of designated monuments offered protection rather than renovation, and the initiative has remained with the local conservation societies. Even the Grande Place in Brussels, which can be regarded as Belgium's best-known piece of townscape, and as the *îlot sacré*, a symbol of the capital city, was cleared of motorcars only by a vociferous local campaign to 'free the Grande Place'.

Again German practice contrasts with the centralized approach of the French, with responsibility for policy resting with the *Länder*, and for execution largely with the city authorities. Article 14 of the basic law of the federal republic states that 'property entails obligation. Its use should also serve the general well-being,' and the constitutions of seven of the eleven *Länder* refer specifically to their responsibilities towards conservation. Initiative stems, however, from the local authority, with the longest-established conservation office being in Cologne and the most recent in Frankfurt.

The 80 000 listed buildings therefore demonstrate considerable variety in their selection. In general, however, reconstruction is more usual than restoration with cities such as Nuremberg losing 90 per cent of its old buildings during the war. A reconstruction that captures the spirit of the original rather than a slavish detailed reproduction, was the model for Münster's *prinzipalmarkt*, and the central areas of Trier, Bamberg and Nuremberg. Where public enthusiasm, city initiative, and *Land* money have combined, the results have often been spectacular in their scale, quality of detailing and integration with urban planning as a whole. The restructuring of the Marienplatz district of Munich between 1965 and 1972 is an example where preservation, renovation and renewal have been successfully combined. Heidelberg, a largely untouched medieval town, by contrast demonstrates a systematic and meticulous conservation, with each building classified on a fourfold scale, and the city divided into zones of varying intensity of conservation effort.

The Scandinavian countries have lacked neither the national legislation nor the local will, only the basic resource for conservation—the buildings themselves. The use of wood as a building material, and the peripheral role of Scandinavia in the development of the European city has left these countries with less to conserve. The obvious exceptions to this general statement, Copenhagen and Stockholm, illustrate the dilemma posed by consumer prosperity and high standards of public amenity provision. These make the renovation of old buildings for housing difficult as contemporary standards of living space, parking provision, public open space and the like cannot be accommodated without considerable demolition.

The Italian situation is, in many ways, the reverse of this, with a surfeit of historical and architectural riches, which are entrusted to the care of a country relatively poor by European standards. There is an irony in the location of the cradle of European urban civilization in one of the European countries least able, either economically or in terms of the effectiveness of its governmental institutions, to conserve it. Conversely, however, relative poverty has protected Italian cities from some of the pressures for redevelopment. Legislation very similar to that already described in the countries of North-West Europe certainly exists. The fascist regime's interest in visible Italian history resulted in the 1939 Act for the classification of historic buildings and the creation of a national inventory. As in France and Britain, policy in the 1960s turned towards the delimitation and planning of areas, culminating in the 1967 Urban Planning Act and the 1971 Housing Act. The latter act was concerned with the residential use of the inner city which is more important in Italian cities where suburbanization is a relatively recent phenomenon.

It is the responsibility of the regional authorities to implement these acts of the central government. The national will and legal structure are therefore clear, but the reality is less impressive and depends for its success on the determination and skill of individual city governments. All too often those responsible for enforcing conservation norms have tended to accommodate rather than to oppose entrepreneurial initiative (Fried, 1973). Funds allocated by the central government are small and difficult to obtain and the administrative machinery often appears incapable or unwilling to implement existing legislation. Comprehensive plans with a major conservation component have existed for some years for such important historical towns as Venice, Genoa, Palermo, Siena, Urbino and Assisi, each embodied in a special law (Oaks, 1974). In each case, however, the necessary enabling legislation that must proceed the execution of the plan has been delayed.

In some cases it is clear that the three-tier local government structure of commune, province and region is particularly inappropriate to urban conservation planning. It is the city itself, most usually a single commune, that is most likely to have the motivation to preserve its heritage, enhance its civic pride and raise the quality of life of its citizens through a conservation policy. Many of the critical decisions, however, especially the financial ones, must be made by regional and' less often' provincial authorities. The region has less of a direct interest and in some cases may be hostile to the ambitions of the city, as a result of historic jealousies between cities in a country where until recently the city rather than the nation was the focus of patriotism, but also because the conservation of the historic cities often imposes restraints and financial choices that are detrimental to other parts of the regions. The results therefore depend on local initiatives and local political circumstances.

Small wonder, then, that Italy contains some of the most heartening and the most tragic case studies of urban conservation. Some of the small hill towns, such as Urbino and Arezzo in the Marches, and Bergamo in Lombardy have been skilfully preserved almost *in toto* and are in effect well-maintained open-air museums. A different sort of success has been achieved in the very much larger town of Bologna where the communist administration has endeavoured to both preserve the inner city, which is a single rigorously protected conservation area of 430 hectares restated most recently by the Law of 1977, without stifling the economic life of this growing industrial and regional service centre of half a million inhabitants (Figure 7.4). But against the successes, of which these are only a sample, must be set the tragedy of cities like Venice which still await effective legislation to arrest the all-too-obvious physical decay, and the major metropolises of Rome and Naples where plan has succeeded contradictory plan and little coherent intent has yet emerged.

The Issues

During the 1960s urban conservation planning was seen to be a relatively simple process. The justification was assumed more often than stated and the process was generally envisaged as being only the enactment and implementation of protective legislation. By the beginnings of the 1970s the legislation existed in some form or other in most West European countries and examples of its executions could be seen in a wide sample of European cities. This experience, however, revealed the difficulties and costs which previously had been either not known or naïvely assumed away, and conflicts between conservation and other aspects of planning became more evident.

To halt demolition and impose preservationist legislation may in itself cost little but the maintenance, repair and enhancement of old buildings, and their modernization to meet modern building standards is usually more expensive than demolition and replacement. The cost of restoration is only one part of the costs of conservation and, 'It does seem essential if proper attention is to be given to undertaking major areas of conservation work that the costs beyond a simple first

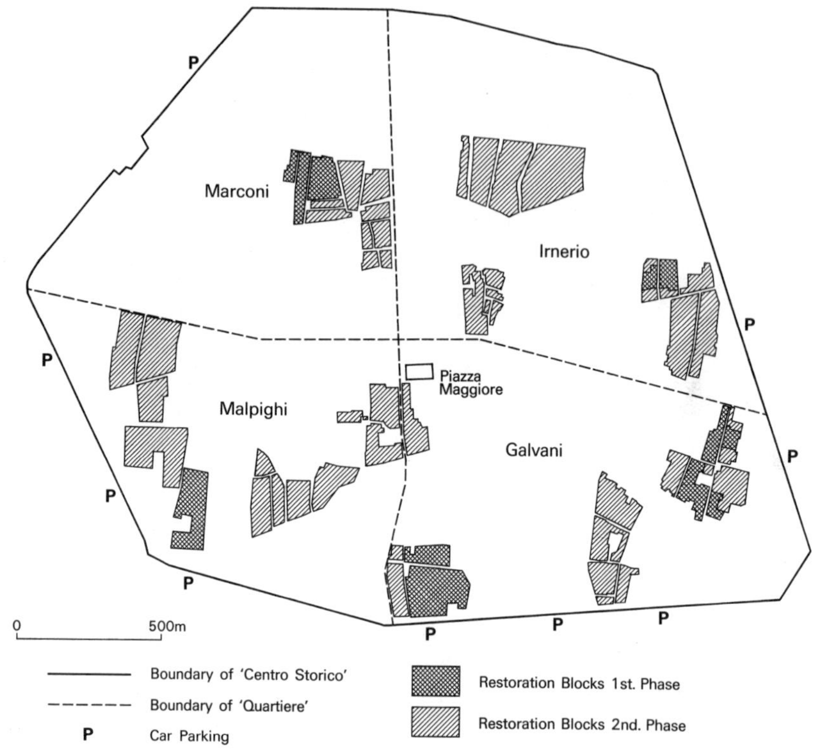

Figure 7.4 Bologna's *centro storico* restoration proposals

cost, which is only related to the dwellings, must be attempted' (Barnett and Winskell, 1977). The most intractable problem is generally finding new uses for historic buildings and new functions for historic quarters of the town. The demand that the buildings were constructed to meet in most cases no longer exists, and most modern functions could be more economically housed in purpose-built structures. The failure to find new uses condemns the historical city to an existence as an open-air museum without a residential or commercial population, a fate recognized in *Bruges le mort* 50 years ago. The extent to which this process of abandonment leaves the historical city as a series of perserved façades and empty buildings was revealed in the Ministry of Housing and Local Government conservation studies of York, Chester and Bath where up to 40 per cent of the floor areas of the historical city, especially the upper storeys, was empty. (Esher, 1969; HMSO, 1969; Insall, 1969)

Tourism and recreation are undoubtedly favoured choices for restored buildings. Military ramparts became parks, as in the Christiansborn district of Copenhagen; the defensive waterways, the *grachten* of many Dutch cities, became decorative amenity areas. The first series of *Europa Nostra* awards for outstanding conservation projects were announced in 1978, and eight of the nineteen diplomas were awarded for a new tourist use being established in a renovated building. These included two hotels (Croydon and Koutsounari, Crete), two castle museums (Portsmouth and Santander,

Spain), a palace museum (Stockholm), a tourist information centre (County Clare, Ireland), a cultural centre (Bremen) and a restaurant (Stavanger). This happy link between conservation and new tourist uses is not without problems. Although tourists are content to visit the historic city, many demand higher standards of overnight accommodation than old buildings can provide. The economics of the hotel industry, in any event, usually favours purpose-built hotels, accessible to airports and motorways, where a business as well as a holiday clientèle can be served. The Viking hotel at York or the Beaufort hotel at Bath, illustrate the dilemma of providing modern accommodation for visitors without unduly affecting the historic environment that they have come to see. The separation of the historic resources from the hotel quarter is a common solution, but this in turn exacerbates the problem of moving tourists into the historic centres, and leads to the sprawl of coaches and cars that surround many a European cathedral or palace.

The inner areas of most European cities have traditionally possessed important residential, commercial and industrial functions. The variety of buildings and the inverse relationship of age and cost, enabled the older parts of the city to offer relatively cheap and varied accommodation especially for low-income tenants who needed accessibility to jobs, and for small shops and workshops that valued cheap premises and a close contact with their markets. It has become clear that an unintended result of conservation has often been to alter the economic balance of the inner city and displace existing uses, many of which have difficulty in finding alternative accommodation. 'Conservation equals deportation' has been a slogan in recent Paris elections, largely as a result of experience in the Marais district where the sequence of restoration, higher rents and social change is well established and 20 000 people have moved out since restoration began. Whether higher land values are a result or a cause of the replacement of working-class housing and small workshops by high-rent apartments is, however, not clear. Similarly, in Venice the historic lagoon city has an increasingly eccentric social and age structure with twice as many managers and four times as many workers in the liberal professions as the national average, and a consequent smaller proportion of manual workers (Piasentin, Costa, and Foot, 1977). The residential appeal of the historic city is to the higher socioeconomic groups; only 4 per cent of the employees of the Marghera industrial complex choose to live in the lagoon city compared with almost 20 per cent of the managers.

A realization of this problem and a wish to preserve a social balance, or at least to avoid an accusation of expelling the population of the historic centre, has led to attempts to ameliorate this effect of conservation policies. As early as 1954 the master plan for the Christiansborn district of Copenhagen declared that the renovation of the eighteenth-century burgers' houses would not lead to a change in use, and that the district would remain residential. Despite the selective demolition of around 10 per cent of buildings to provide space for garaging and public parks, families have tended to move out to newer suburban housing, and have been replaced by students and other childfree groups. Experience in some West German cities, most notably Bremen and Hamburg, has indicated that the large houses of nineteenth-century merchants can be effectively converted into apartments and a residential function maintained, but that it is far more difficult to find tenants for the smaller, one or two-storey, nineteenth-century workers' houses. It is clear that a conservation policy must be conceived with the future use of the building. The Hearth Housing Association in Ulster is a good example of a number of similar institutions that combine private with public money to renovate historic buildings specifically for reletting, on a rolling programme that uses profits from the current function to finance further renovation (Shaffrey, 1975).

It is all too easy to see conservation planning in terms of social class. Much of the initiative stems from amenity and pressure groups whose membership is drawn overwhelmingly from the articulate middle-classes, who are then seen as moving in to 'gentrify' the historic quarters of the town. The policies of the communist-controlled cities of central Italy are thus especially interesting attempts to avoid these social effects. In Bologna, for example, the whole of the central city has been effectively conserved since 1969 with all demolition and change of use being subject to planning approval. The area has long been of importance for housing all classes including a high proportion of the poorer citizens. For ideological as well as practical reasons the decision was taken both to conserve the *centro storico* which had suffered from both demolition and neglect since the war, but also to maintain the function of the inner city as a residential area with a large amount of cheap accommodation. The weapons to implement these policies, which in most other West European cities had proved to be contradictory, were large financial grants, strict controls on changes of use and levels of rent, and the establishment of neighbourhood planning councils. The receipt of local authority finance is made dependent on the restored accommodation being made available to the original tenants at the unrestored rent, and the commune has considerable powers to press reluctant owners to maintain and restore. Practice still lags behind the powers available but strict preservation of the inner city has been combined with the maintenance of the pre-existing functions and social structure, and a transport and land-use plan has been prepared as an integral part of the conservation plan (see Figure 7.4) (Cervellati and Scannarini, 1973). The ideas developed in Bologna have been applied to some extent in other Italian cities such as Ferrara, Bergamo, and Ancona but of all the fifty Council of Europe European Architectural Heritage Year projects Bologna is the only one that guarantees continued tenancy to low-income residents (Angotti, 1977).

Both West Germany and the Netherlands have recently introduced rent subsidy schemes to partially offset increases due to renovation, while in Edinburgh a policy of making the level of restoration grant awarded vary inversely with the rateable value of the property, aims at impeding the 'gentrification' of the Georgian 'new town'.

A basic cost of conservation is the restriction such policies impose upon urban development strategies and the opportunity cost of strategies that are denied. In an extreme form the conflict between alternatives is illustrated in Venice where the situation of the historic inner city is dependent on restricting the development of the Marghera industrial area. The conservation of Venice is dependent upon controls on water extraction, pollution emission, navigation in the lagoon, and even in some schemes any access to the lagoon from the Adriatic (Fay and Knightley, 1976). All these would impose costs, probably prohibitively high costs, on the main sources of employment in the modern city. Even the development of new employment possibilities within the historic centre in an attempt to halt the flight of people and jobs presents problems. A large number of sites are available, most notably the *Arsenale* but any prospective entrepreneur must accept the inconvenience of the absence of road transport, for which *vaporetti* are a poor substitute, and a distance of at least half an hour from any public transport. Schemes for improving transport to and within the lagoon city, such as the Miozzi Plan of 1956, foundered on the opposition of the conservation groups (Rogatnick, 1971).

Small wonder, therefore, that conservation planning is an increasingly contentious issue in the urban political arena. The confrontation is most usually between middle-class groups concerned with residential amenity and working-class groups concerned with the amount and range of employment opportunities and the availability of low-cost housing. Although this alignment is still a common feature of town councils, two factors complicate, or even on occasion reverse it. As is clear from some of the policies described, successful implementation in many instances is dependent on controls over landownership and use which are typically associated with the left rather than the right of European politics, and communist (as in Bologna) or social democrat (as in Stockholm) councils have been among the most conspicuously successful. Similarly, the successful control of rent levels within conservation areas has weakened the link between renovation and rising property values. In summary, therefore, although it is the political right that still has the strongest motive for conservation, it is the left that has the more effective means of executing such policies. The result is often a confusing and seemingly inconsistent alignment of political groups. In Bologna for example, communists and socialists tend to support conservation while Christian democrats, which include many employers and small businessmen, usually oppose it. Similarly in Venice, republicans and communists, at opposite ends of the spectrum, have been the strongest supporters of attempts to curtail the damaging effects of mainland industry, while Christian democrats, socialists and liberals have generally opposed such attempts.

Continuity and Change

The city, as Lynch (1972) has said, needs both continuity and change, 'so that the comfort of the past may anchor the excitement of the future'. In the 25 years since the end of the Second World War more change was wrought upon the fabric of the European city than had occurred to most in all the preceding centuries of their existence. This change was both rapid, occurring within a single generation, and comprehensive in that whole districts were cleared and rebuilt. The replacement of war damage in Rotterdam and the German cities, and later the speculative land boom that produced the new skylines of Brussels, London and Paris was an abrupt break with the past that called forth the reaction of the latter 1960s and 1970s.

Conversely the absence of change can lead to the creation of the museum city where the preserved form becomes itself the city's main function. Bruges, Stratford-on-Avon and the whole city-state of San Marino are as unifunctional as any colliery town or fishing port. Preservation is a particularly likely fate for cities of homogeneous age. Georgian Bath, and on a smaller scale seventeenth-century Willemstad or the Zuider Zee towns such as Elburg and Enkhuisen, find evolutionary change difficult and easily become locked into their past.

If conservation planning is, as Ford (1978) has suggested, the 'management of change', then the need is to plan for cities which are capable of evolution, and can welcome the future and accommodate the present without severing the thread of continuity with the past. The best of the examples described above show that conservation planning is not planning for a sector of urban life, like planning for recreation or housing, nor is it planning for specific quarantined districts of the inner city. Rather it is a philosophy of change that can pervade all aspects of urban planning, and the balance that is struck between change and preservation is in the last instance, a political not a technical decision, taken in the council chamber not the planning office.

CHAPTER 8

The Tourist City

A traditional function of cities is the reception of visitors. Although it is convenient to think of the resort as a separate category of city, few resorts are unifunctional tourist towns and all towns have some tourist functions and are to an extent resorts. If a comparison is made between the population of towns and some indicator of their tourist significance, such as their capacity to accommodate visitors, a connection between the two can be established very similar to that found for any other central place function. Towns with more beds than their population would warrant are usually well known as resorts, but the resort function can be seen to be a relative rather than an absolute condition.

The rapid growth of tourism, especially foreign tourism, in Europe in the 1960s and early 1970s focused attention on the effects of tourism on other aspects of the city. Tourism was no longer regarded as a free bonus to the prosperity of the city but as an alternative strategy to be considered alongside other possible land-uses, types of employment and sources of municipal income. Although such a role may appear self-evident tourism is rarely viewed in this way except in resort towns. This can be attributed to the control and management of tourism by national government agencies. These are dominantly marketing bodies whose success is measured by their ability to attract ever-larger numbers of visitors, regardless of the impact of these visitors on the cities they frequent. Most cities do not consider it to be within their competence or authority to influence the size or direction of the tourist flow and confine their efforts to accommodating it. Even this attempt may be half-hearted:

> so far as inadequate planning for tourism is concerned, the structure of local government is largely to blame; the management of the cities is run on behalf of the residents by elected city councils or their equivalents. They undoubtedly equate the needs of the city with the needs of the city's residents and would suffer electoral embarrassment were they to do otherwise (Young, 1973).

It was not until well into the 1970s that planning authorities began to regard tourism as an urban function alongside others rather than a flow over which they had no control. The City of Westminster (1972) reflected that, 'policy guidelines have stemmed from consideration of specific problems which have arisen from time to time, rather than from a comprehensive appreciation of the needs of tourism'.

It is difficult to overstress the importance of cities, and the cities of Europe in particular, to world tourism. Of the 240 million foreign tourist visits made globally in 1978, about three-quarters were to West European destinations and the numerically most popular tourist 'honeypots' are not to be found among Mediterranean or Alpine resorts but in the large 'world cities'. London, Paris, Rome, Copenhagen and Amsterdam are, in that order, the world's top five tourist resorts, although none of these cities would regard itself as a resort as such, and in all tourism competes with other important economic activities. Planners in these and other lesser tourist cities have responded sluggishly to this vast annual temporary migration, which often exceeds the size of the resident population. This can be attributed in part to the rapid growth of tourism in general which has increased at between 6 and 12 per cent per annum for most of the last 15 years. In part also, however, the sharp shifts in popular fashion that are features of tourism outpace the capacity of the more slowly moving planning system to respond. The staid, protestant, and rather dull cities of London, Copenhagen and Amsterdam were transformed in a few years in the mid-1960s into the 'swinging', pornographic and youth capitals of Europe, a process seen earlier in the creation of Rome's *dolce vita* in the late 1950s or even 'Gay Paree' in the 1890s.

Two inventories of the tourist resources of Europe, one from a French and the other from a German source (Figure 8.1), show the importance of cities on the tourist itinerary. The two maps are almost plots of the distribution of towns in Europe with the significance of the cities of the Low Countries and Rhine valley being enhanced, and that of the older industrial areas being diminished. Again the size of the city correlates strongly with its tourist importance, the major European cities being also major centres of tourism with the exception that some smaller historic towns have an inflated significance to the tourist. It can also be concluded that cities with important tourist functions tend to agglomerate, with isolated centres such as London or Paris being less typical than clusters of towns in a recognized tourist region, such as the art cities of Flanders, Holland, Northern Italy or the middle Rhine valley.

The nature of the tourist attractions offered by cities varies widely, and different cities are seen as offering distinctly different holiday experiences to visitors. A study of the images projected by the main West European cities (Figure 8.2), for example, revealed that some were seen by potential tourists as 'historical', being open-air museums full of viewable relics of a past relevant to the visitor—such was the dominant image of Rome or Leiden. Other cities projected a 'beautiful' image, of peaceful, quaint tranquillity, typified by Delft or Florence. There were cities whose reputation was for chic, dignified sophistication such as Vienna or The Hague. A final category was the lively, modern, exciting cities such as London, West Berlin or Amsterdam which had built up reputations as permissive trendsetters. Clearly the tourist image of most European cities is composed of a number of strands which combine in a composite reputation, that in turn affects the numbers, characteristics, and expectations of visitors, and the nature of the tourist industry developed to accommodate them. It is worth noting that urban governments have some control over the creation of the tourist image as well as over the provision of facilities. But, in practice, few exercise this power in a positive manner, and marketing is commonly divorced from planning within the city administration.

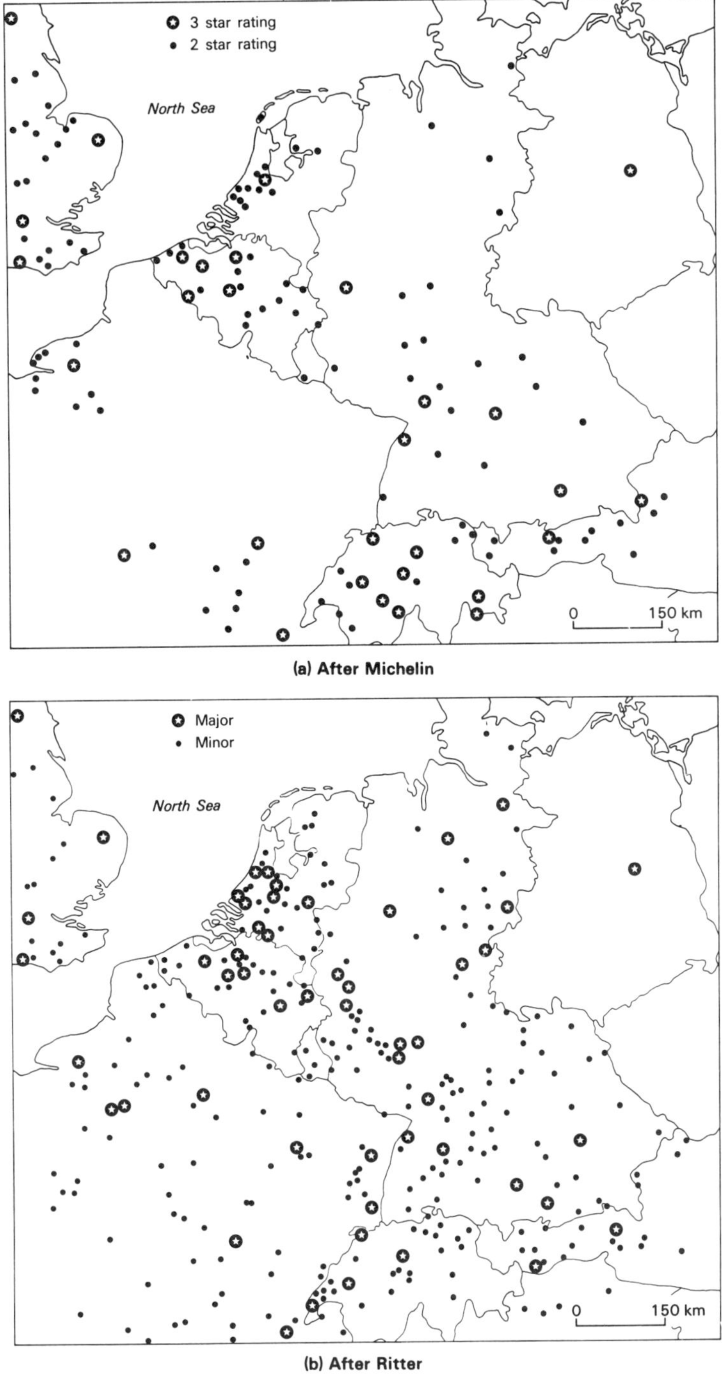

(a) After Michelin

(b) After Ritter

Figure 8.1 West European tourist resources based on alternative sources

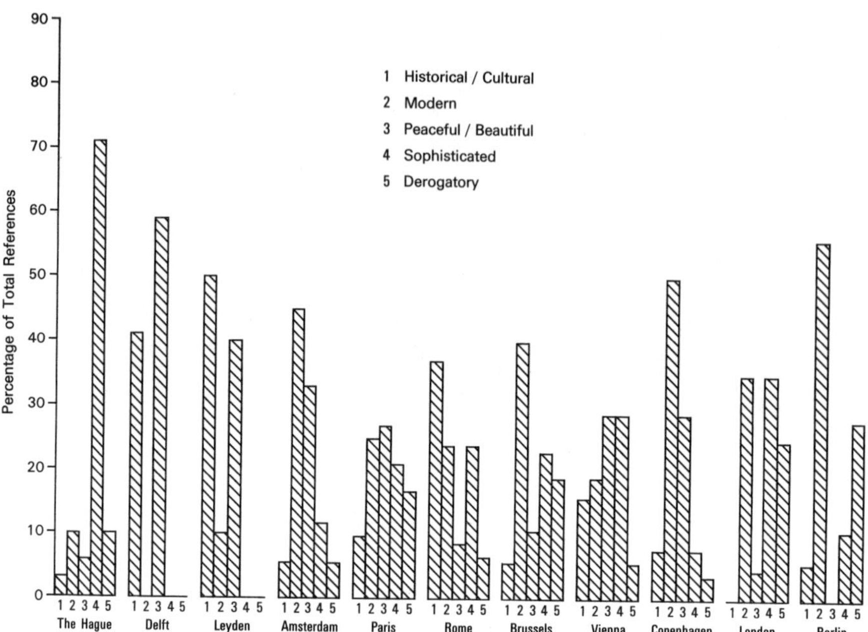

Figure 8.2 Images of West European cities

The Urban Tourist

The city attracts a wide variety of visitors and an understanding of their general characteristics and behaviour is a necessary preliminary to the planning and management of their visit. Visitors attracted by the tourist resources of the city travel further than visitors to other holiday destinations. A higher proportion of the total visitors to the European city are foreign compared to visitors to inland rural and beach resorts; 86 per cent of visitors to Brussels, for example, are foreign, compared with only 9 per cent of visitors to the Belgian coast resorts. Similarly in Britain, although domestic holidaymakers outnumber foreign visitors by more than three to one, just under two-thirds of tourists in London are from overseas. The importance of the foreign element in the tourist industry increases sharply with the size of the city, with capital cities forming an exclusive league of world tourist centres. Capitals are endowed with a disproportionate share of accommodation, museums, theatres, and national art collections and serve as national symbols so that to visit Britain but not London, or Denmark but not Copenhagen, becomes unlikely. Small wonder then that more than a half of all foreign visitors to the Netherlands stay in Amsterdam, and two-thirds of all foreign visitors to Britain visit London with 40 per cent visiting nowhere else (English Tourist Board, 1975; and Central Bureau Statistics annual). Only West Germany and Switzerland with their lack of a 'cultural' capital, and Austria with its capital so distant, physically and metaphorically, from its Alpine tourist resources, and Spain with its dominant littoral tourist developments are exceptions to this pattern.

Not only does the city appeal to foreign as well as domestic tourists, it also attracts intercontinental visitors as well as near neighbours. In Paris, for example, 32 per cent of all tourists are American, while less than 5 per cent of foreign visitors to the coast are American, compared with neighbours such as Germans, Dutch and Belgians who comprise 30 per cent of foreigners in Paris but 63 per cent of visitors to the coast. The same pattern is evident in London, Brussels, Rome and Vienna, where the tourist industry is dominated by the long-haul North American, Australasian and Japanese tourist, in contrast to the smaller cities where European visitors dominate.

Unlike other tourist areas, however, a high proportion of visitors to the cities are there for business rather than pleasure. The amount of business travel generated relates strongly to the size and economic importance of the city with a particularly large volume of traffic being generated by the major financial centres such as Frankfurt and Zurich, and by the cities with international administrative functions such as Brussels, Strasbourg, Geneva and Luxembourg City. In addition, the periodic trade fairs at such cities as Utrecht, Frankfurt and Hannover attract large numbers of visitors. Conferences combine tourist and commercial motives for relatively high-spending visitors, and are an increasing and profitable business on both national and international scales. London, for example, earned around £150 million from conferences in 1978. Business visitors make use of many of the same facilities as tourists, and especially provide a 'baseload' for hotels, which is less subject to the seasonal peaking of the holiday industry. The larger hotels, especially those belonging to the main chains such as Hilton, Sheraton and Intercontinental, are particularly dependent on a commercial clientèle which is a major influence on their location.

The appeal of the cities to particular tourist markets is, in turn, the main determinant of the length of stay, timing of visit, choice of accommodation and pattern of expenditure—factors which themselves are the main determinants of the character and extent of the impact of the industry upon the city, and also provide many of the opportunities for the operation of planning policies. Visitors to the city do not generally stay long. In Amsterdam the average length of stay of foreign visitors is only 2.2 days, compared with over ten days in the nearby North Sea coast resorts. A similar brevity is found in Paris (3.5 days) and London (3.3 days). The typical business trip is short and holidaymakers can grasp the attractions of the city in a few days, or even a few hours in the smaller historic cities such as Delft, Bergamo, Chartres or Canterbury. The city tends to be a staging post in a circuit of similar attractions rather than the location of the whole holiday, with even world-renowned centres such as Leiden, Versailles, Bruges or Stratford-on-Avon entertaining the holiday excursionist lodging elsewhere, rather than the staying visitor.

In terms of seasonality, which largely determines the profitability of the industry, urban tourism is less dependent on the vagaries of the weather and less tied to the traditional short summer season of the beach resorts. Consequently the season has less pronounced peaks and continues from spring well into the autumn (Figure 8.3). The nature of the clientèle, however, changes significantly with intercontinental visitors dominating the cities in high summer, while near neighbours and domestic

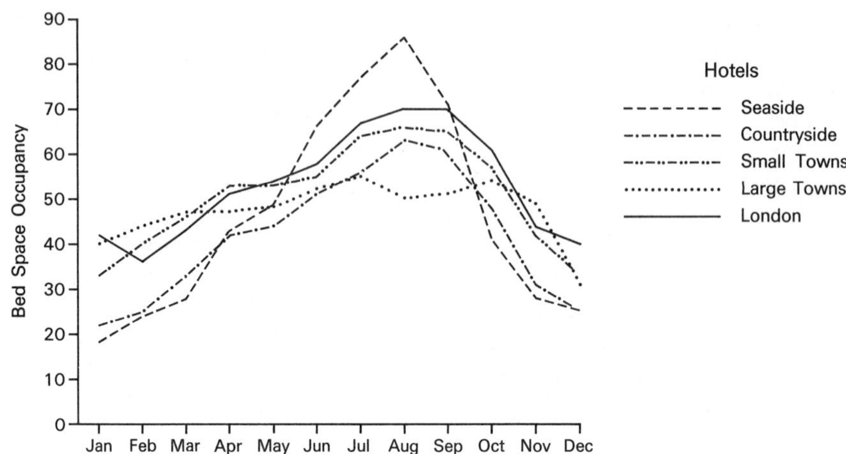

Figure 8.3 Seasonal variations in hotel occupancy, Great Britain

tourists predominate in early and late seasons (Ashworth, 1976). Foreigners make up two-thirds of visitors to Paris in August, but only a half in May. Despite the relatively elongated season, however, still 40 to 50 per cent of the annual intake of visitors to London, Paris and Amsterdam are received in the three months of July, August and September, which concentrates the impact of the industry upon the city and its inhabitants.

Visitors to cities spend more freely than tourists in other destinations, spending around twice as much each day as visitors to beach resorts. In part this is a reflection of the relatively high age and socio-economic status of the tourists who are attracted by urban history and architecture, and in part a result of the high spending of conference and business visitors. Similarly, visitors to the city choose hotel rather than cheaper self-catering accommodation. Camp and caravan sites and self-catering villas do exist in and around the European city, but hotels account for more than half of visitor-nights in Paris, London and Amsterdam, in each case a percentage more than twice as high as the national average.

A picture, then, emerges of short-staying, high-spending, hotel-based, often intercontinental visitors that differs little in its characteristics, or in the behaviour of the visitors throughout the major tourist cities of the continent.

The Location of Tourist Facilities

The impact of tourism upon the city is magnified by its concentration in space as well as in time, and it is this concentration rather than the absolute numbers of tourists that presents most of the planning problems. The concentration of tourist activities can be related to three distributions in the city: the location of the tourist attractions that have drawn the visitors to the city, the location of the hotel and catering facilities that accommodate and feed them while they are there, and the pattern of behaviour of the visitors in the city.

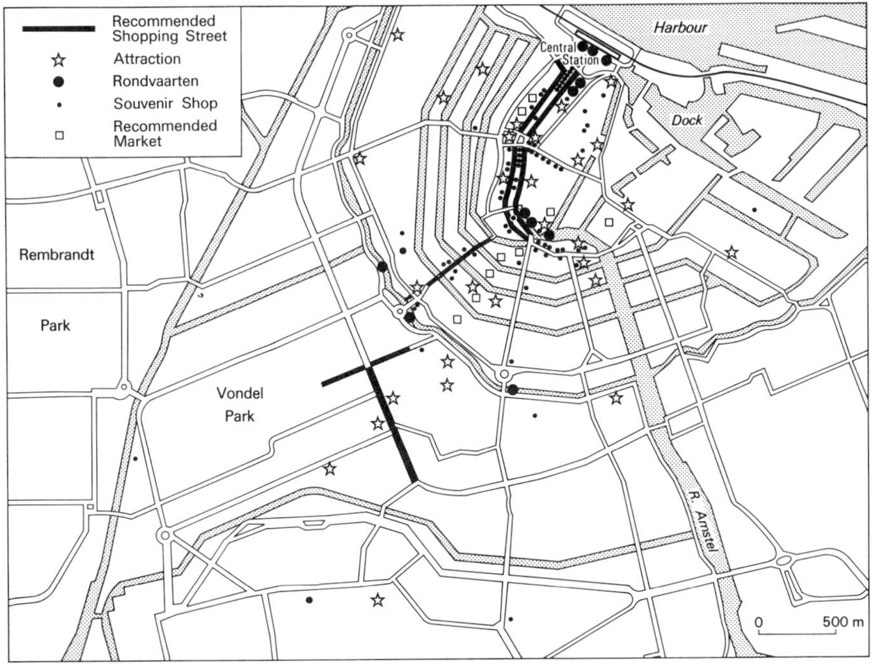

Figure 8.4 Major tourist attractions in Amsterdam

Figure 8.4 shows the location of the main tourist attractions of Amsterdam, and Figure 8.5 those of Paris, the former as defined by the city's tourist authorities and the latter as selected by the visitors themselves. Neither of these inventories is exhaustive but they include the museums, art galleries and historic monuments that dominate the typical tourist visit to the European city. In addition to these points of interest which are generally located in distinct clusters, tourists make use of linear facilities such as specialized shopping streets like Kalverstraat (Amsterdam), the Champs Elysées (Paris), and Konigsallee (Düsseldorf), canal excursions and river embankments. The extensive concentric growth of the city in the nineteenth and twentieth centuries has left most of the historical attractions concentrated in a small area of the inner city, often clearly delimited by old defensive walls or waterways. Even museums which could conceivably be located anywhere in the city, tend in practice to occupy historic premises and locate near the historical city-centre that they illustrate and document. In the smaller cities the pattern is often simple with the current commercial centre and the historic centre coinciding, as in Delft or Florence. In the larger cities, however, a distinct museum quarter may have developed, such as South Kensington in London or EUR in Rome. In Amsterdam, the Rijksmuseum complex of three major galleries, two associated parks, and a linking shopping street (Pieter de Hoochstraat) specializing in artware and antiques was consciously encouraged by the city planners on a site two kilometres from the traditional city-centre. Similarly, the migration of the central business district can leave the

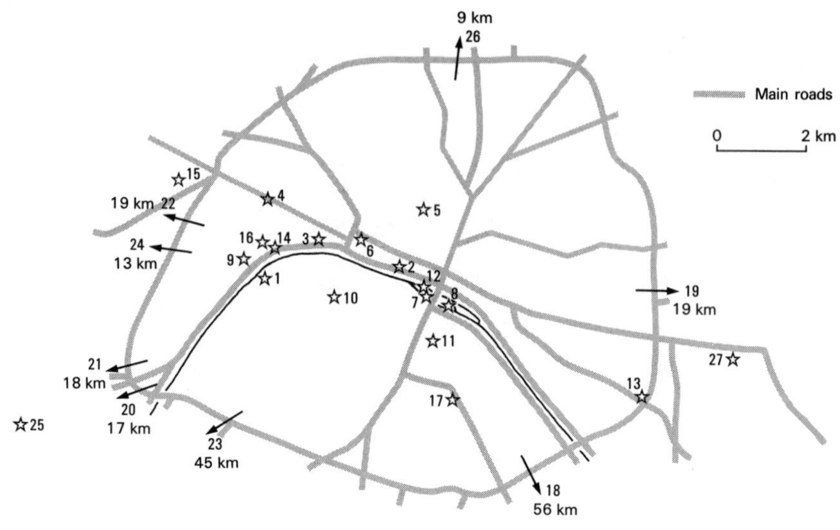

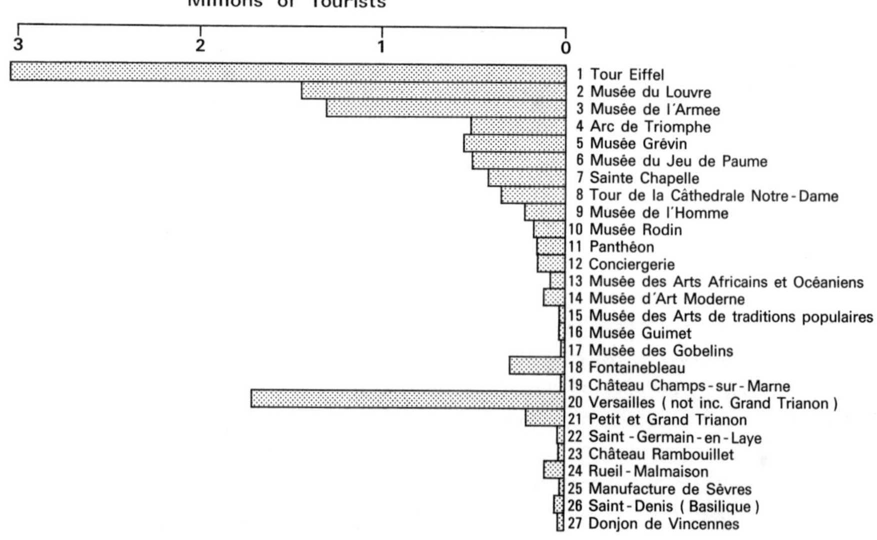

Figure 8.5 Major tourist attractions in Paris

redundant historic centre to tourist functions alone. This is most obvious in hilltop towns such as Bergamo, Bar-le-Duc or Arezzo where modern communal functions have migrated to more convenient low-level sites, leaving the old 'upper town' to tourism alone.

The traditional location for hotel accommodation in the city is as an integral part of the central business district in close proximity to the historical attractions, and this pattern remains typical of both the small and medium-sized town. Even in a city the size of London 45 per cent of all hotels are located in the single borough of Westminster and a further 20 per cent in the borough of Kensington and Chelsea. The tendency for hotels to become larger in response to changes in the economics of the industry, and the high costs of expansion on city-centre sites, together with changes in the mode of travel of visitors, has encouraged migration to new sites where land is cheaper and accessibility better. This is by no means a recent process. The railway station, generally located just outside the historic city-centre, often attracted substantial hotel development in the late nineteenth century. The distribution of hotels in prewar Berlin, for example (Figure 8.6), shows a distinct clustering around the three main railway stations which themselves are located just outside the historic *altstadt*. Some diffusion of the hotel quarter westwards along the Tauentzienstrasse and Kurfurstendamm can be seen before 1945, but by 1976 this trend, strongly reinforced by the political division of the city, has resulted in the virtual abandonment of the railway station sites, especially in Kreuzberg, in favour of Tiergarten in particular, a pattern that is clearly repeated in Munich.

More recently the importance of access to motorways and airports has encouraged the establishment of out-of-town hotels. These trends have been reinforced in some instances by the planning policies of urban authorities. In Amsterdam, for example (Figure 8.7), a large number of hotels remain in the central city within the Singelgracht, but severe restraints on hotel development and new access requirements have determined that all new hotels built since the mid-1960s have been located outside the city, notably the 'Amsterdam motel' at Osdorp and the 'Schipol motel' at Haarlemmermeer. The two London boroughs of Westminster and Kensington and Chelsea have more recently imposed similar restrictions (Greater London Council, 1978). Similarly in Paris (Figure 8.8), the hotels of the central *arrondissement*, such as those off the Boulevard St Michel on the left bank, tend to be small, located in converted rather than purpose-built buildings and family-owned and managed. By contrast the larger purpose-built hotels constructed since the war have been located at such sites as Porte Maillot with access to the national motorway system and the *Boulevard Périphérique* and in new redevelopments such as Fronts du Seine. The pattern of hotel accommodation at the city-region scale is illustrated by South-east England. Successive rings can be identified including a hotel-rich central city, a hotel-poor suburban ring, and a hotel-rich outer zone including distinct hotel clusters around Heathrow and Gatwick airports.

Visitor accommodation is clearly not homogeneous in quality or function, and these differences lead to distinct differences in location within the city. In particular the small hotel and pension sector usually form a distinct quarter near but outside the historic centre, and often associated with areas of large, older housing suitable for conversion. Planning policies that restrict changes of use to guest-houses will further concentrate accommodation into clearly delimited quarters. This feature can be seen in Nuremberg (Stadt Nürnberg, 1976), while in Amsterdam (see Figure 8.7) it is located especially around the Vondelpark two kilometres from the city-centre.

In many cases, therefore, the accommodation resources of the city are located some distance from the attractions, and the distance between the two is likely to widen as increasing constraints on hotel development are imposed on the centre, and

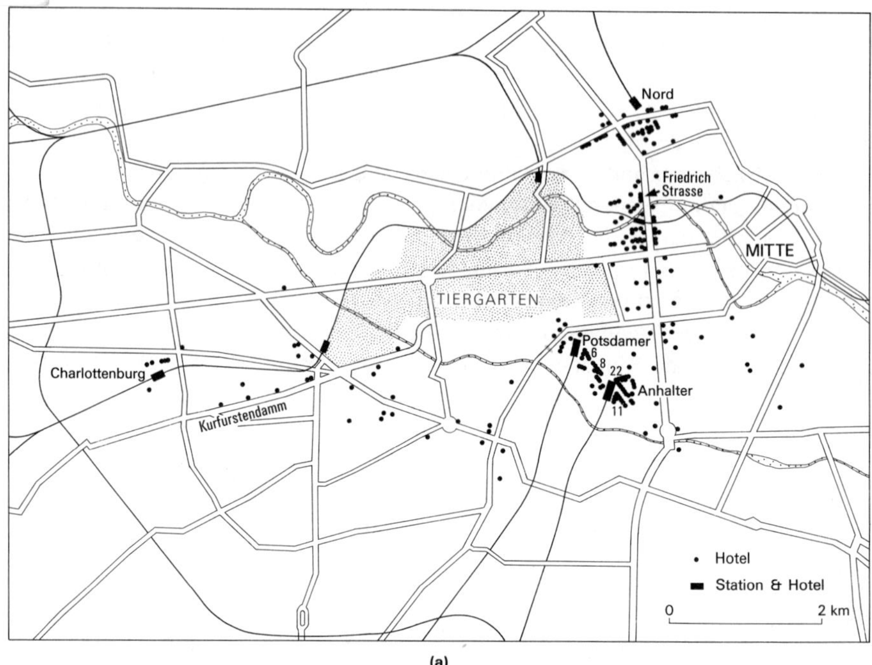
Nord
Friedrich Strasse
MITTE
TIERGARTEN
Potsdamer
6
8
22
Anhalter
11
Charlottenburg
Kurfurstendamm
Hotel
Station & Hotel
0
2 km

(a)

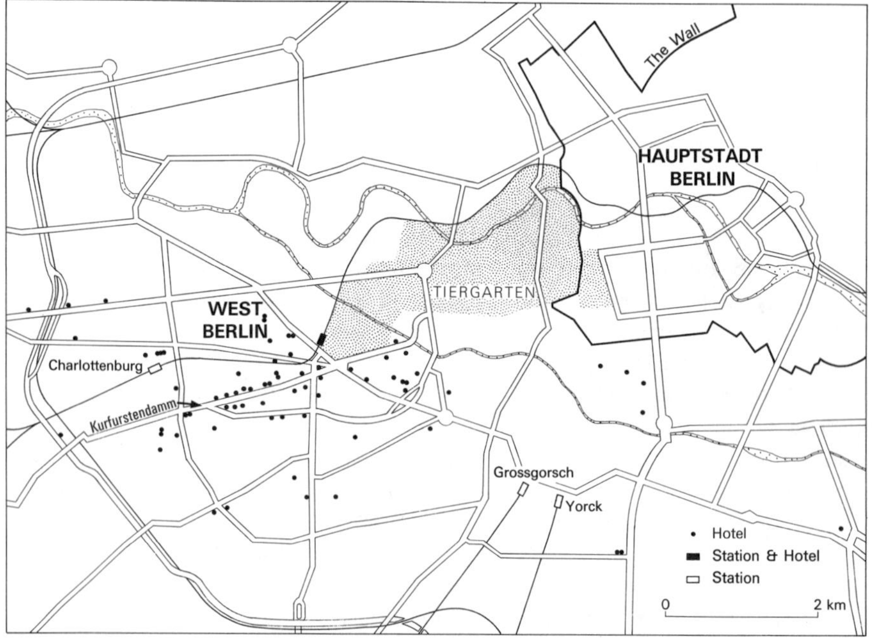
The Wall
HAUPTSTADT BERLIN
TIERGARTEN
WEST BERLIN
Charlottenburg
Kurfurstendamm
Grossgorsch
Yorck
Hotel
Station & Hotel
Station
0
2 km

(b)

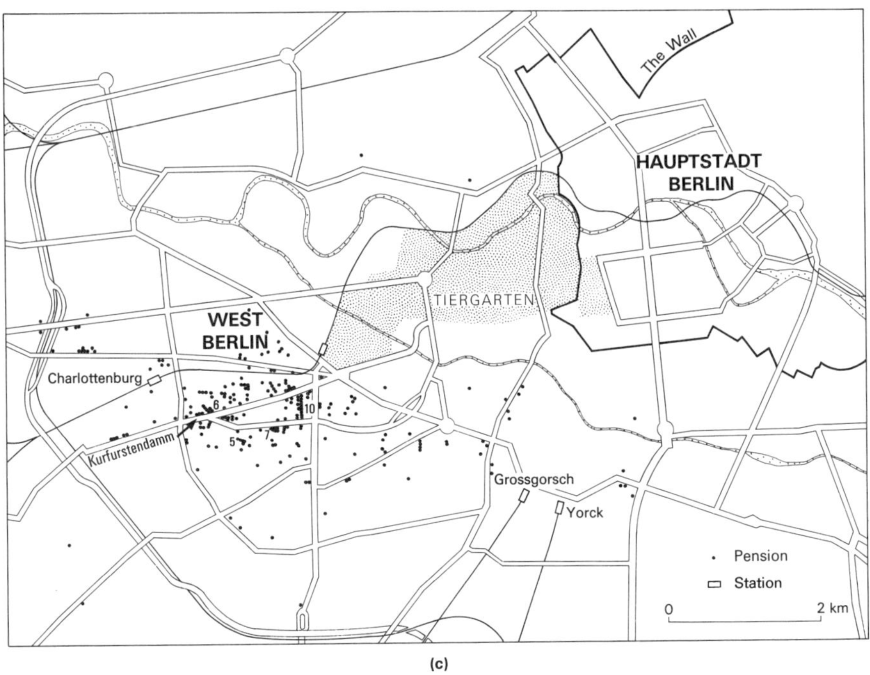

Figure 8.6 Changing hotel locations in Berlin 1943–76: (a) hotels (1943) in Greater Berlin; (b) hotels (1976) in West Berlin; (c) pensions (1976) in West Berlin

hotels relocate closer to the road and air transport nodes on the urban periphery. The movement of visitors from their hotels to the city-centre, usually by coach, poses particular and, in many cases, intense problems of traffic management, such as can be seen around the Amsterdam Rijksmuseum or London's Parliament Square. In London, where coach-parking spaces in the central city are estimated to cost around £30 000 each to provide, a standing liaison committee of the GLC and tourist interests has been established to monitor the problem, and for a time, in 1978, licences to visit key tourist sites such as Buckingham Palace were issued (Greater London Council, 1978).

The third variable affecting the agglomeration of tourism within the city is the behaviour of the visitors themselves. Visitors, especially foreign visitors, have a very restricted image of the city composed of a few world-famous tourist sights that are fixed in the popular imagination by guidebooks and tourist publicity. Most cities are reduced in the mind of the visitor to a handful of essential experiences. The Louvre, the Houses of Parliament, Dam Square and similar sights will therefore attract a very high proportion of the total visitors to their respective cities, and few visitors will extend their search much further. The longer the distance visitors have travelled, the more restricted is their information field likely to be. As many American visitors to Amsterdam take the traditional canal *rondvaart* as are registered in the city's hotels. Similarly, in Paris intercontinental visitors make up less than one-third of the city's

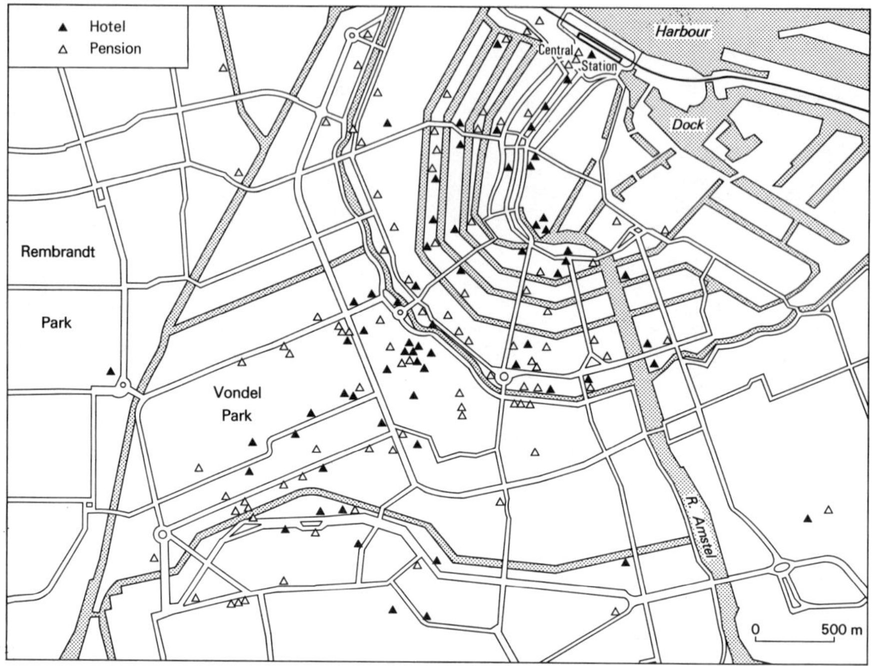

Figure 8.7 Hotel accommodation in Amsterdam

foreign tourists but over two-thirds of foreign visitors to the Louvre. As well as a fragmentary mental map, the visitor has only short stays and lacks personal transport. The absence of the private car and a lack of familiarity with public transport further confines visitors to the areas they are prepared to explore on foot, or those that coach tours choose to show them, which again are usually the sights visitors expect to see.

Consequently the tourist city covers only a small fraction of the area of the residents' city. In smaller towns such as Delft, where the length of stay is measured in hours, visitors when questioned (VVV Delft, 1972) had a very hazy perception of the town beyond the market square and the Royal Porcelain Factory. Even in larger cities such as Paris the tourist city is confined to a limited area of the inner city, in this case not a single district but a collection of areas, such as Montmartre, the Latin Quarter, Eiffel Tower and Étoile, joined in some cases by tourist 'corridors' such as the Champs Elysées.

It is possible, therefore, to conceive of a 'central tourist district' which occupies only a small proportion of the city's area but contains most of the tourist facilities. In the smaller historic towns such a district usually shares the city-centre with other central business district functions, while in the larger cities tourism can develop as an exclusive use over extensive areas. In Utrecht (Figure 8.9), which accommodates 20 000 staying foreign visitors annually, the dense concentration of facilities in the old city within the ring canal (*grachten*) is clear, with only a few hotel and pension

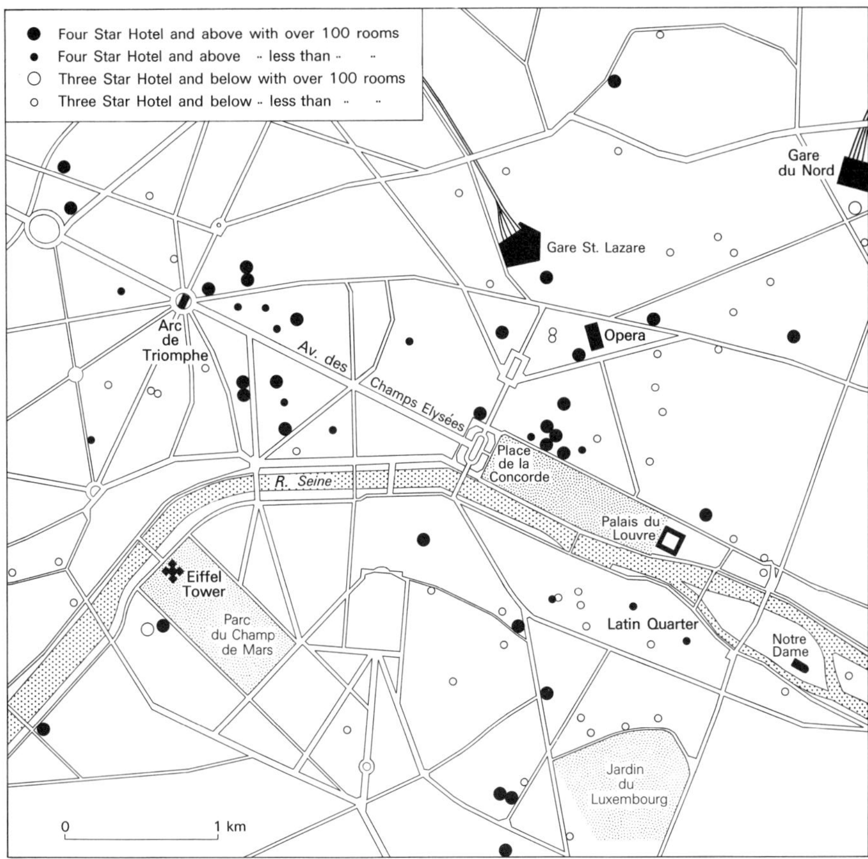

Figure 8.8 Hotel accommodation in central Paris

outliers near the railway station and in the eastern residential suburban district. There is also no clear distinction between attraction and accommodation districts. By contrast in the larger and more popular city of The Hague (Figure 8.10), which attracts 150 000 staying foreign visitors each year, the tourist district is more dispersed, forming a number of clusters on an east–west axis, running from the 'SS' railway station, through the city-centre to the sea at Scheveningen, with the historical and shopping attractions being clustered in the historic centre around the west of the *Binnenhof*, and accommodation being concentrated around the station, the coastal resort, and more widely dispersed through the woods west of the city.

Planning for Tourism

The planning problems posed by tourists are viewed by many city authorities as a matter of accommodating, with as little possible expense or political disturbance, a flow of unknown size over which it has no control. Even in ostensibly resort towns

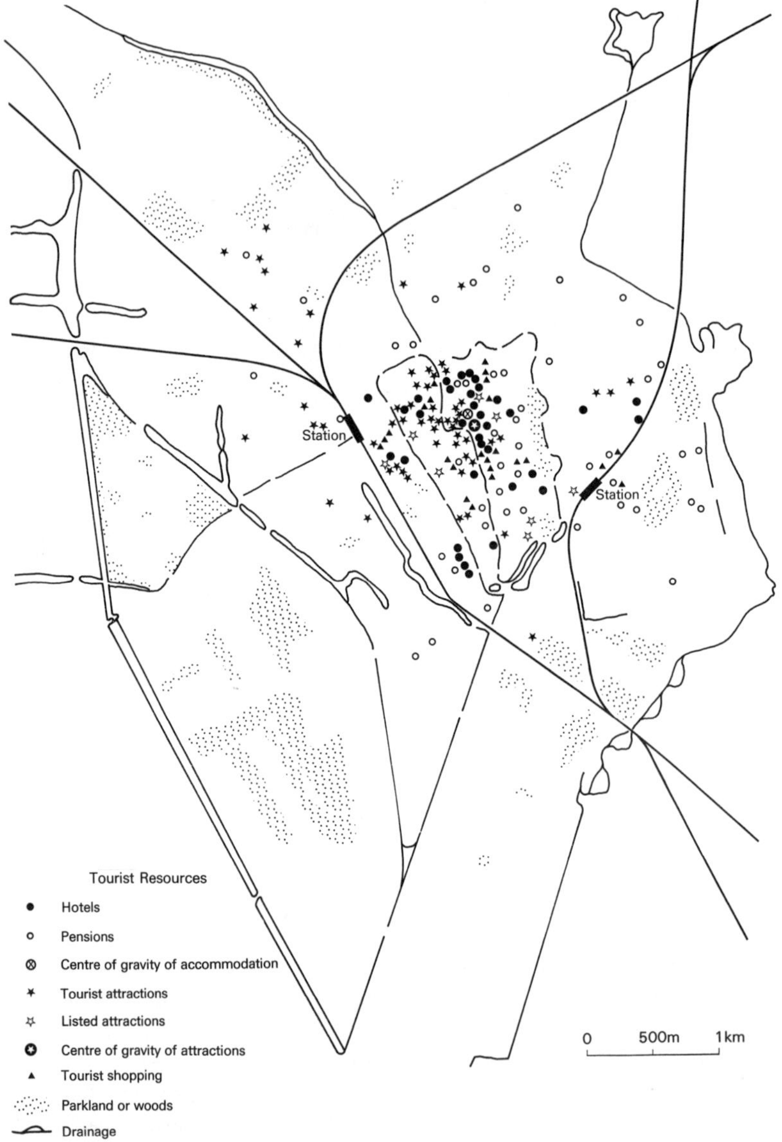

Figure 8.9 Utrecht old city tourist district

this defensive cost-reducing approach is adopted by the planning authority, while the benefits are assumed to accrue to the private sector. A rather more sophisticated approach is to attempt to maximize benefits while minimizing costs, but few authorities have reached the point where they attempt to influence the size, timing and composition of the tourist flow in order to achieve a desired cost–benefit ratio.

Many costs are imposed by tourists on the local area, but those that city planners

Figure 8.10 The Hague's tourist district

can be expected to mitigate concern the allocation of urban resources, especially land, and the pressures imposed by visitors on an urban infrastructure that was built for residents alone.

A common problem in the first category is the 'homes or hotels' controversy that has featured in the local politics of many cities, most recently in London and Amsterdam. The rapid increase in the demand for hotel beds in the major European cities in the late 1960s and early 1970s, coupled with the existence of rent controls on residential rented property in some form or other in most of West Europe (Chapter 6), made the conversion of property to serve visitors rather than residents economically attractive. In some countries the existence of government subsidies for the creation of new hotel beds increased the incentive. Districts composed of large, old, multiple-occupancy housing close to the city-centre proved especially vulnerable to what has been termed 'creeping conversion' (Greater London Council, 1978).

The city of Westminster, for example, allowed the conversion of 1240 dwelling units between 1965 and 1971, while the London Borough of Camden, which has a particularly long housing waiting list, lost many privately rented flats in the Bloomsbury area to small hotels in the same period. By the late 1970s it was estimated that around 1000 residential 'bed spaces' were lost to hotels each year. At the same time, of course, many hotels and guesthouses, especially those with less than ten bedrooms, were similarly lost to other uses. Between 1961 and 1971, 2800 beds in these establishments were no longer available to visitors in London (Lavery, 1975). In the overall context of this growth of demand, however, the various predictions of hotel shortage announced by the Greater London Development Plan (15 000 beds short) in 1967, the GLC (200 000 beds) in 1972, and Lavery (1975) (280 000 beds) were understandably alarming, especially as the last prediction would require around one square mile of land to satisfy (Young, 1972). More recent predictions are less dramatic but even a modest 10 000 new beds (Sandles, 1978) would require 20 new large hotels. Similarly in Amsterdam, the number of hotel-beds available doubled between 1965 and 1975, and in 1971 a further doubling was predicted by 1985. The large mainly interwar housing to the south-west of the city-centre proved particularly suitable for conversion into small hotels and pensions (see Figure 8.7). This situation has most of the ingredients of a popular political issue. Relatively rich tourists could be seen as usurping an increasing share of a scarce resource from relatively poor residents.

Reality, however, was rarely as simple as the slogan 'homes before hotels' suggests. Planning authorities had the ability, through their development control powers, to prevent many of these changes of use, but rarely did so, and their reluctance to intervene cannot be explained solely by the pressures placed on them by national governments, to earn foreign exchange. The districts of the city which were ripe for conversion in this way were generally those located in a transition zone that was already losing population and tourist uses were here, as in the city-centre, often filling a vacuum created by the flight of jobs and residents to the suburbs, and only rarely can residents be seen to be supplanted by visitors. In Edinburgh, for example (Figure 8.11), the streets on the edge of the Georgian 'new town', which are composed of substantial terraced housing built in the first half of the nineteenth century, have been widely converted to small hotels. But it is these streets that have proved the least attractive to residential uses and make up what has been termed the 'tattered fringe' of the conserved area (Youngson, 1966).

Tourism is a new source of employment as well as a new land-use, and some have seen tourism's need for large numbers of seasonal and relatively lowly paid workers, around 150 000 in London, as a 'threat to the local employment structure' (Young, 1973). 'The danger is that tourism will call for precisely the sort of job opportunities we do not want: unskilled work, seasonal work, badly paid work, work without prospects' (Greater London Council, 1971). In addition the prosperous cities of West Europe need to import much of this labour from low-wage countries, and tourism

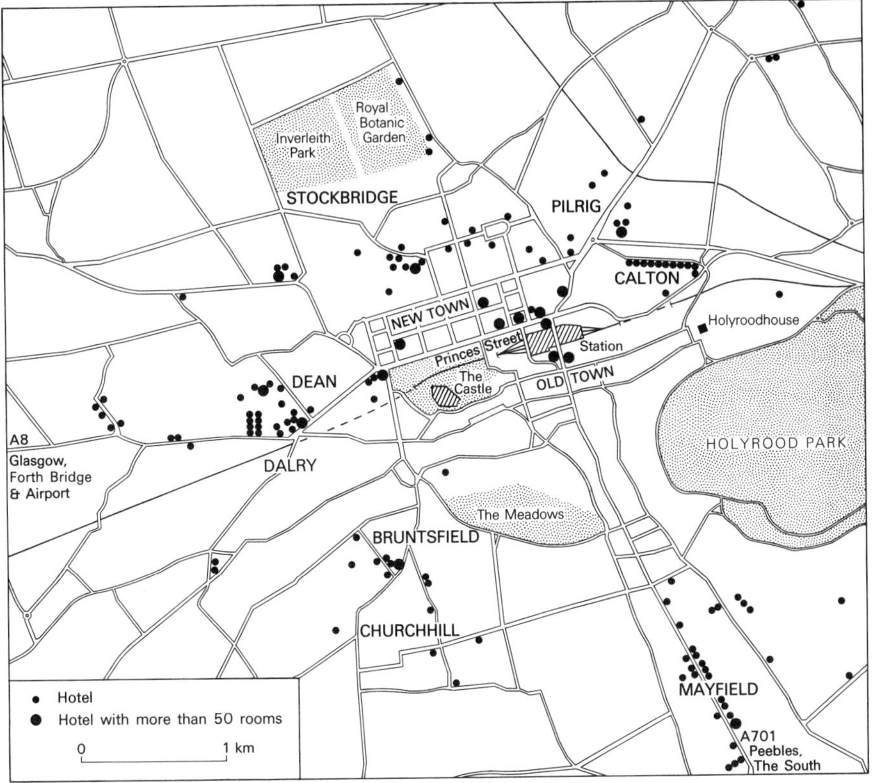

Figure 8.11 Hotel accommodation in Edinburgh

has been credited with contributing to the 'immigrant problem' and encouraging the creation of a pool of cheap labour in the inner city. Again, in reality, cause and effect are often reversed with tourist functions, especially in the hotel and catering industry, mopping up existing surplus labour that has been marooned in the inner city by the flight of jobs to the suburbs, rather than bidding away labour from more profitable occupations. The action of planning authorities who often react in defence of residential interests by containing hotel and catering functions within designated areas, aids the creation of specific ethnic districts which form the 'Chinatowns' or 'Little Italies' that feature in the central area of many European cities. It should also be noted that without the Chinese, Indian, Indonesian, Greek, Turkish, Italian and other similar communities that staff the catering facilities of Europe's cities, the traditional function of the city as a place of evening entertainment would effectively lapse.

Another source of conflict is the demands that visitors make, in competition with residents, on public services in the city, of which the most obvious is usually its transport facilities. Visitors demand road space at points in the city where it is scarce and their lack of familiarity with public transport ties them securely to car, taxi and hired coach. The 'Venice solution', where visitors' cars are compulsorily parked at the head of the causeway or at the *vaporetti* terminals, is sometimes quoted as an ideal, for the visitors must explore the city by foot or gondola. This situation arose as a result of the unique circumstances of the lagoon city, and imposes a substantial cost upon residents as well as visitors. Peripheral tourist car-parks as in Bologna, high-capacity city-centre car-parks as in Paris, car-routing systems for tourists, and even special multilingual tourist guides for public transport as on Amsterdam's trams, are all management strategies.

The pressures caused by the physical presence of visitors in large numbers, in specific limited areas of the city, are less amenable to planning measures. The physical congestion of pavements and squares may be compounded by cultural and linguistic differences between visitors and citizens, and by contrast in the leisure behaviour and spending patterns of visitors and residents. The result can be the alienation and resentment of citizens who feel themselves foreigners in their own city as they compete for space and the use of facilities, a not unfamiliar reaction in London's West End. There is usually little that city authorities can do to mitigate this reaction in detail, apart from mounting 'courtesy campaigns', as was attempted with little success in Paris in the early 1970s. Irritation which can develop into hostility often stems, however, from errors and omissions of a more tangible nature which are within the competence of planners to correct. In general terms, planners need some way of relating the number of visitors to the available resources, so that a saturation level, beyond which conflicts of this kind occur, is not exceeded.

Planning for tourism in most cities has not yet passed beyond the stage of responding to particular incidents of imbalance between the demands of visitors and the supply of facilities. Symptoms are eased rather than problems solved. A few cities with a major economic interest in tourism have constructed schedules of costs and benefits with the intention of minimizing the former while maximizing the latter (Eastbourne Tourist Board, 1977; Union of Dutch North Sea Authorities, 1971). It frequently appears, however, that the benefits accrue principally to the nation as a whole, while the costs are incurred mainly by the individual city. Such a distinction goes a long way towards explaining the differences in approach of national tourist agencies, such as the British BTA, Dutch NTB or Italian ENIT, and individual city governments. Again it is evident in many of the individual studies that while the benefits are relatively easy to quantify in terms of visitor expenditure and increased local incomes and employment, the costs, on the other hand, are far more diffuse and expressed in terms such as 'social alienation', 'cultural degradation' and lost alternative opportunities that are difficult to quantify. The equating of demand with supply depends in turn on accurate assessment of the capacity of the city of absorb visitors, as the ratio of costs to benefits will alter with the size of the visitor flow. The marginal cost of visitors to under-used facilities is low, but once a saturation level has been attained the extra costs incurred by the marginal visitor will exceed the extra revenue earned. Unfortunately, it has proved very difficult in practice to estimate capacity. Different facilities have different saturation levels and the sharp temporal fluctuations in the tourist flow make for a rapidly changing pattern. Thus, even when the number of visitors to Westminster Abbey have far exceeded comfortable levels, the Royal Parks will be capable of absorbing more without conflict. A shortage of hotel beds in the city-centre may coexist with a surplus in the suburbs, and museums crowded in August or on a Sunday may be empty in February or on a Monday.

The first requirement of the tourist planner, therefore, is information on the size and characteristics of the tourist flow and the capacity of the city to accommodate it. In practice, statistics on both are scarce and rarely can either be quantified with any accuracy. An additional problem that complicates the planners' attempts to equate supply with demand is the volatility of the latter and relative sluggishness of the former. Although holidaymaking itself may be an habitual activity, the type of holiday taken and its timing and location are very volatile. Most of the tourist facilities of the city, however, are relatively immobile in their siting and inflexible in their size. Whereas visitor numbers can fluctuate from one season to the next, new investment in hotels and transport installations take a number of years from inception to operation. The British Hotel Incentive Scheme that ran from 1969 to 1973 was devised in part to relieve the pressure of demand for hotel beds in London, mainly from transatlantic visitors whose numbers had increased dramatically in the late 1960s; 40 000 largely high-quality, new hotel beds in London received subsidies under the scheme, more than half the total for the United Kingdom as a whole. The benefit of most of this new investment was not felt until well into the 1970s, by which time much of the intercontinental demand for which it was created had slackened off, to be replaced by demand from West European visitors, many of whom favoured cheaper or self-catering accommodation forms outside as well as inside London. Short-term prediction has proved a hazardous, albeit necessary, procedure.

In practice, the main task of the tourist planner is to spread tourist demands on the city in time and space in order to raise the overall level of occupance of tourist facilities. The timing of holidays is influenced more by factors in the place of origin than the destination but cities have been more successful than most holiday areas in identifying and capturing off-season markets. Major cities such as London, Paris, West Berlin and Amsterdam have managed to attract both their own nationals and a substantial international clientèle in the off-season. Encouraging the spatial spread of visitors through the city usually proves to be much more difficult. Visitors have a clear idea of what they have come to see, and the heights of Belleville are no substitute for the Eiffel Tower, nor Southwark Cathedral for Westmister Abbey, regardless of the intrinsic merits of the attractions. Some success has come in the Tower of London area where tourists have been diverted into the adjoining St Katherine's dock area. Similarly, the competition for foreign visitors is between the major international centres rather than between all cities in one country, so that tourists dissuaded from visiting Paris, will switch their interest to Amsterdam or Rome, rather than Lyons or Marseilles. Nevertheless, the restricted fields of information of visitors, and their relative immobility within the city presents planners with a potent instrument of management. By influencing the flow of information through official guidebooks, information centres and signposting, tourists can be encouraged to visit some sites, discouraged from visiting others, and enticed along particular tourist corridors.

Tourism and Conservation

The tourist is thus drawn to the city by its relict forms and spends his stay among the conserved buildings and monuments. The 'central tourist district' is, in most cases, co-terminous with the conserved city. It has often been argued, however, that the demands of visitors in large numbers are incompatible with urban preservation, and that ultimately tourists will damage, by their presence alone, the sites that they have come to experience. In many instances this is indisputable. The thousands of visitors shuffling around Westminster Abbey's one-way system on a summer afternoon have little chance of enjoying the spiritual experience that its builders intended and the Tower of London, when filled with visitors, is more reminiscent of a carnival than a forbidding fortress. Yet conservation needs a consumer or the question 'conservation for whom?' will remain unanswered. The concept of a European Heritage, celebrated throughout the continent in 1975, has little meaning unless that heritage is accessible to all Europeans. The alternative policy of preservation without access is the architectural equivalent of locking paintings in a bank vault, and it fails to satisfy either the intentions of the builder or the motives of the conservationist.

The 1978 conference of *Europa Nostra* noted 'with satisfaction the growing recognition that tourism and conservation are greatly dependent upon one another and therefore stand to gain from close and effective collaboration'. But if tourism is the moral justification for conservation, it is also its greatest threat. Tourism provides much of the initiative, the money and the human occupation without which the conserved city could become a lifeless exhibit. It also provides physical and psychological damage by its intrusion. This is the dilemma that makes planning in this field so difficult, yet so necessary.

CHAPTER 9

Urban Recreation Planning

A traditional function of cities has been the provision of opportunities for the recreation of citizens and visitors from the city-region. One of the earliest pieces of urban planning legislation in Britain was the fourteenth-century government injunction that towns must make land available for archery butts. The town market, credited by Weber (1958) as being one of the main reasons for the existence of the medieval town in Europe, was, to most of its participants, an occasion for entertainment and recreation as much as for trading. The utopian planners from More to Abercrombie regarded the recreation facilities of the town as a major determinant of the well-being of citizens, and critical for the success of their schemes. Both the planned garden city, and the more spontaneous flight to suburbia were essentially motivated by a desire for better access to the recreational amenities of the countryside, which are themselves a major component of the almost universal private dream of the 'good life'.

The interest of public bodies in the planning and management of recreation was largely a response to the growth in demand for it. The limited attentions of central governments, reflected in Britain by a handful of acts of parliament since the war, were essentially attempts to channel and organize activities that had developed largely spontaneously. Meanwhile local authorities had acquired their large collection of diverse recreational interests by a slow accretion of functions undirected by any overall concept of the role of the city government in this field.

The period from the middle of the 1960s to the early 1970s posed a special challenge to city authorities throughout Europe. A very rapid growth in almost all demands for recreation and predictions of further large increases, typified by Dower's (1965) 'fourth wave', was accompanied by a popular feeling that it was the responsibility of public authorities to satisfy this demand. The provision of libraries, swimming pools, playing fields and public gardens had long been regarded as a responsibility of the city government in most European countries, but to these functions were now added a whole range of new facilities including sports centres, boat marinas, caravan parks, day recreation centres, picnic sites, and even theatres and concert halls. Although the pressure of citizens' expectations was the main spur to the growth of local authority leisure facilities in this period, there was in addition in most countries national legislation that imposed new obligations on cities. In Britain, the 1968 Access to the Countryside Act, and the 1969 Development of Tourism Act both depended to a large extent on implementation at the local level.

The urban planner found himself faced with a new set of tasks. The traditional fields of the urban planner can be summarized as 'work', 'housing' and 'transport': to this trilogy must now be added 'recreation'. In most cities this set of tasks was composed of three elements: First, to tidy up the results of the incremental growth in city responsibilities by devising new administrative structures such as, for example, the 'leisure directorates' that many British cities established after 1974, as amalgamations of the recreation interests of many different departments. Second, it was necessary to define the limits of public provision and to delimit the proper spheres of commercial and municipal enterprise. In practice, this has been commonly done on an *ad hoc* basis rather than as a result of a coherent philosophy, and the differences between cities, even within one country, are consequently great. For example, West German and French cities are more likely to regard this area as suitable for direct municipal enterprise than is commonly the case in Britain or Belgium. Third, the question of how much to provide was constantly posed by the rapidly rising levels of demand. The public commitment to provide facilities was rather 'open-ended', the demand itself was often stimulated by the supply of facilities, and the question of what is 'enough' could, in practice, only be answered comparatively.

Urban Parks

The park is probably the oldest feature of the city created specifically to serve the recreational needs of citizens. It can trace its ancestry back to both the common, whose function was essentially utilitarian, and to the private garden. The one provided the idea of free public access, the other that of relaxation among the works of nature. Examples of private gardens used for leisure rather than agriculture can be found in many cities of medieval Europe. The plucking of the roses in London's Temple Garden at the beginning of the Wars of the Roses shows public assembly in an area cultivated for pleasure rather than food in the heart of the city (Shakespeare, 1978). It was not, however, until the sixteenth and seventeenth centuries that substantial tracts of the city were laid out as parks for the enjoyment of rulers. The royal parks of London (Hyde Park, St James's Park and Kensington Gardens), Paris (Tuileries, Luxembourg Gardens), Berlin (Charlottenburg, Tiergarten), and those of the lesser dignitaries, monastic orders and universities, have remained a major element in the land-use of the central areas of cities, and much contemporary public benefit derives from the survival of these relics of past privilege.

The opening up of the private parks to the citizenry as a whole was usually a slow process that spanned the seventeenth to the nineteenth centuries. The idea of building new parks in imitation of the private estates, to be provided on a commercial basis to satisfy the demands of the middle classes, led to pleasure gardens such as London's Vauxhall and Ranelagh Gardens and Copenhagen's Tivoli. These, in turn, can be considered as the direct ancestors of such pleasure parks as the Battersea Pleasure Gardens opened in 1951. The vast majority of the citizens of the 'Coketowns' of the nineteenth century had access neither to private gardens around their houses, nor to the public commercial pleasure gardens of their social superiors. A report of the health commissioners in Lancashire reported in 1842 that 'there is only one public park in the county and that at Preston' (quoted in Ward, 1976). The Victorian municipal park was created to serve these people. They were founded for a mixed set of motives which included a utilitarian belief in the value of recreation as a spur to the higher productivity of labour, a romantic notion of the need to bring nature back into cities, which for the first time in European history were divorced from the countryside, and an urban pride which made the endowment of a city park a prestigious as well as an humanitarian gesture. By the end of the nineteenth century most cities in Britain had acquired, through private philanthropy or public enterprise, municipal parks freely open to all citizens. In London, Victoria Park, situated between Hackney and Bethnal Green, was established in 1845 as a deliberate attempt to provide in the East End some parks to balance the royal parks in the West. This was a forerunner of many other 'Victoria Parks' established in the provincial cities of Britain over the next 50 years. The City of Leicester, for example (Figure 9.1), created a network of six parks between 1882 and the end of the century, and between 1859 and 1906 there were four Acts of Parliament which encouraged local authorities to establish parks. These were generally laid out as small-scale imitations of the private estates of the gentry with winding paths between herbaceous borders. The behaviour expected of the public was generally the promenade and quiet appreciation of nature developed in the private garden, rather than more active recreational pursuits, and a battery of byelaws, and regulating notices were enforced by railings and uniformed officials.

Thus the West European city has inherited a variety of public open spaces created to satisfy the recreational needs of various groups of citizens at various times in the

Figure 9.1 The age of parks in Leicester

last 500 years. This legacy often included the fortuitous addition of disused fortifications, as in York, canal and river banks and waterfront areas, such as in Geneva or Hamburg, which became parks by public usage rather than design. It is hardly surprising, therefore, that the quantity, type and distribution of urban parks did not correspond with the patterns of leisure demand in the modern city. In particular, the increased volume of use, due largely to increased leisure-time during the day and at weekends, the demand for space for more active recreational pursuits than can be accommodated in the traditional park, and the redistribution of population within the city, have all posed problems. In the interwar period a number of enlightened cities, such as Leicester (Figure 9.1), reviewed their stock of parks and created new peripheral parks to cater for the expansion of the town. In other cities, however, there was a body of informed opinion that regarded this inheritance as largely irrelevant to the needs of the twentieth-century city. Two ideas can be credited with saving the urban park and revitalizing the concept. First, the desire to beautify the city by providing open space as a setting for buildings survived, and was justified by such phrases as 'lungs for the cities', sometimes with the addition of often spurious counter-pollution motives. Secondly, the importance of space, preferably green space, to children's play was stressed by developmental psychologists (Mercer, 1976), with increasing insistence in the postwar period.

Two main questions confronted urban authorities when they attempted to review the adequacy of their park endowment and remedy its deficiencies. How much public open space should be provided and where should it be located within the city? The two questions are clearly related as any estimate of the adequacy of provision will depend upon the distance visitors to parks will travel. As a high proportion of these visitors will be either old or very young this distance is often short. The question of how much public open space to provide is answered in most countries by the acceptance of conventional standards of provision. In Britain, these are generally quoted in the form of 2.8 hectares of public open space, of which 0.4 hectares are ornamental gardens, for each 1000 of the population. First devised by the National Playing Fields Association in 1925, this standard has been repeated in successive urban plans through to the most recent (Hampshire County Council, 1978). In London, successive plans have reconstituted the figures. The London County Council standard of 1.7 hectares per 1000 population with an additional 1.3 hectares provided outside the LCC boundary, was superseded by the 1951 development plan which proposed 2.9 hectares per 1000 within the county boundary. The Greater London Development Plan of 1967 increased this figure but recognized that 1.6 hectares was a more realistic target in the more densely populated boroughs. None of these targets was realized (Greater London Council, 1967a).

Most West European countries have similar standards, although they are rarely so explicitly stated. In Paris, for example, the target of 100 square metres for each citizen has been used to highlight an overall deficiency. Such standards are more often plucked from the air than based on any detailed understanding of the nature of the demand. They have, however, been effectively used to point out gross inequalities of provision between cities. A study in Paris, for example (Conseil de

Paris, 1971), demonstrated that this city devoted only 7 per cent of its area to 'green space', half as much as London or New York.

Similarly, a study of the nine largest cities in West Germany showed wide variation in provision from the relatively lavish 22 square metres in Munich for each citizen, 24 square metres in Cologne, and 32 square metres in Bremen, to the more parsimonious provision in Düsseldorf of 15 square metres, and in Essen and Stuttgart of 14 square metres each; there is no obvious explanation for these differences in terms of the age of city development, or employment structure (Stadt Köln, 1978). In the same way a British study compared all towns with more than 100 000 inhabitants and showed that not only did few cities in the country approach the 50-year-old NPFA standard, but also that large discrepancies existed at the extremes (Lever, 1973).

Such standards are, however, of limited use in planning the location of parks within the city. They assume a homogeneous demand without variations in need due to the age and family structure of the population and the amount of private open space provision. They also assume a homogeneity of provision within the park whereas, in practice, parks provide many different facilities which often have different hinterlands. Consideration of these problems led planners in a number of countries to move away from a search for overall standards of provision in terms of area per head, towards the creation of an ideal park system in which the individual parks are arranged in a hierarchy. Dutch planners had produced a theoretical park hierarchy by the middle of the 1950s which combined the size and nature of facilities provided in the park with the range and character of the demand for these facilities. The result (Table 9.1) is a theoretically neat and comprehensive framework which was seriously applied within the Randstad during the 1960s. The most successful attempt to carry through such a schema was in the province of South-Holland which includes the Rotterdam conurbation (Provinciale Bestuur van Zuid-Holland, 1967), where plans for the complete range of the hierarchy were drawn up and, in large part, implemented. This approach to park planning proved attractive to planners in many other parts of Europe, who applied it, or at least its central idea if not all its implications, with varying degrees of comprehensiveness. Clearly, the size of parks at various levels in the system and the nature of the facilities provided, as well as the distance travelled by visitors, varies nationally, and is usually separately calibrated in each example, so that the plan for Bologna (Figure 9.2) must, of necessity, vary greatly in these details from that for Rotterdam.

The largest European city to make a conscious attempt to plan for a complete hierarchy is London. The Greater London Development Plan (Greater London Council, 1967a) based its proposals for public open space squarely on the concept of a hierarchy that ranged from the neighbourhood park drawing visitors from less than a mile away, to major recreational centres, such as the Lee Valley Regional Park which would have a city-wide hinterland. In this respect recreation planning mirrored the similar use of hierarchies in other aspects of the city's planning such as that for shopping centres.

The problem of the scale of administrative control often makes the application of such a theoretical schema very difficult in practice. While parks at the

Table 9.1 Hierarchy of public open space in the Netherlands

Type	Responsibility	Requirement	Size	Range	Transport Facilities	Other features
Neighbourhood	Gemeente	4 square metres per inhabitant	1–4 hectares	up to 0.5 kilometres	Paths	—
Local	Gemeente	8 square metres per inhabitant	6–10 hectares	0.5–1 kilometres	+ Cycle tracks	Toilets/kiosk
District	Gemeente	16 square metres per inhabitant	30–60 hectares	1–3 kilometres		Cafe
City	Gemeente	32 square metres per inhabitant	200–400 hectares	3–5 kilometres	+ Car parking	Restaurant
City-region	Gemeente/ Regional authority	65 square metres per inhabitant	1000–3000 hectares	5–20 kilometres	+ Public transport access	
'Country'	Province/ state	125 square metres per inhabitant	10 000–30 000 hectares	50–100 kilometres		Hotel/campsite
National	State	250 square metres per inhabitant	60 000–10 000 hectares	100 + kilometres		

Source: Rijksplanologische Dienst. Netherlands, 1965

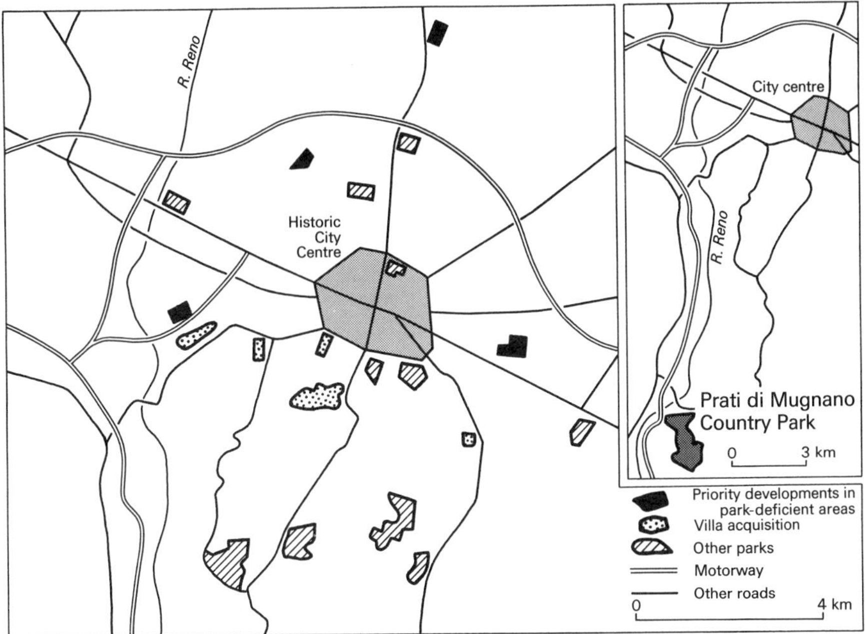

Figure 9.2 Public open space plan for Bologna

neighbourhood level are usually provided by the city authorities, those at the level of the city-region are usually the responsibility of the county or province. In the London example the metropolitan boroughs, the Greater London Council, and the neighbouring county councils were involved. In addition, there is often, as in Britain, a division of responsibility between the local authority housing departments which plan and sometimes manage the small recreation sites and play spaces in association with its housing developments, and the parks or leisure departments which are responsible for the larger tracts of public open space.

It was not these administrative difficulties alone, however, that caused doubt to be cast on the proposals for London. The public enquiry into the Greater London Development Plan concluded that, 'Our view is that both old (ie global standards) and new (ie hierarchies) systems have defects in that they largely ignore the density of population and accessibility to public transport' (Greater London Council, 1967b). The last point in particular posed a cogent argument against the meticulous application of a detailed structure. In many cities, including London, however, the most commonly heard argument against imposing any overall planning model is that the deficiency in public open space is so great that almost any additional provision, in almost any location, will meet a need, and that most cities must proceed in an opportunist manner utilizing relict space wherever it occurs.

In practice, therefore, park planning has been more successful in identifying areas of gross deficiency within the city and ameliorating these than in creating idealized patterns. This lack of subtlety matters less when the anomalies between districts within the city are so great. In Paris, for example, it is not so much the overall deficiency of public open space compared with other cities that has prompted action as the demonstrable discrepancies in provision between parts of the city. The inner city (especially the 9th to 12th *arrondissements*) have less than 0.3 square metres of public open space for each inhabitant, compared with the better-served western districts (1st, 5th and 6th *arrondissements*) with more than 3.5 square metres (Figure 9.3). The task of the planners here is to insert green space into a densely developed environment when the opportunity occurs. This policy in Paris can be traced back to the Second Empire, when the prefect Haussmann, better remembered for his destruction of large parts of the city (Chapter 2), created a number of parks, such as the Buttes Chaumont and Parc Monceau, in working-class districts. In addition he attempted to recreate in Paris the small parks of London's West End squares, many of which had begun as 'subscription gardens'. According to Chadwick (1966) his efforts earn him the title of the 'creator of the first real urban park system'. More recently, similar initiatives have used a large part of the old Citroën works, the military training grounds at Île St Germain, and the Sèvres quarries for park development, although the attempt to locate a 5-hectare park on the Les Halles site in the heart of the city has met with political problems.

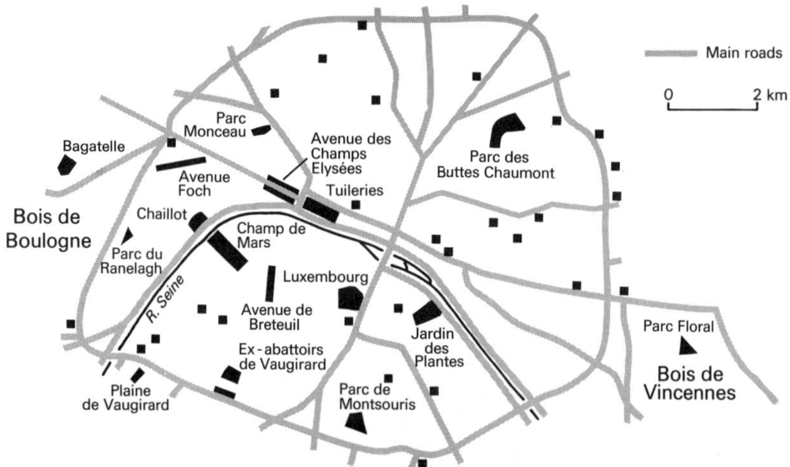

Figure 9.3 The Distribution of green space in Paris

Similarly, in Cologne (Stadt Köln, 1978), a detailed inventory revealed discrepancies which ranged from 14 square metres of public open space, for each inhabitant of the *altstadt* district to 177 square metres in the spacious suburban Pesch district. In Hannover (Ulfert-Herlyn, 1977), a similar disparity in provision was compared with other variables, and a paucity of public parks was strongly correlated with an absence of private gardens, and with the lack of a whole range of other neighbourhood amenities. Park planning was thus seen as only one facet of planning for 'positive discrimination' in favour of the traditional working-class inner suburbs such as Linden-Mitte and Kleefeld.

It has often proved necessary to demolish existing buildings and lower the existing density of housing in order to insert new public open space. Thus, part of a district is cleared so that the remainder can be raised to modern standards. Frequently this has involved retaining the buildings flanking the residential blocks while clearing the back streets for parks, as in Vienna's Lichtental district (Figure 9.4). Similarly, in the 'bridge quarter' of Copenhagen the policy of retaining the historical atmosphere of the district and also its function as a residential quarter necessitated the clearance from the courtyards of the eighteenth and early nineteenth-century housing blocks of later accretions, and using these yards as well as a number of pedestrianized streets as a system of 'miniparks' (Christiansen, 1978). Such work is normally carried out as an integral part of a more comprehensive inner-city renewal programme such as discussed for Hamburg in Chapter 6.

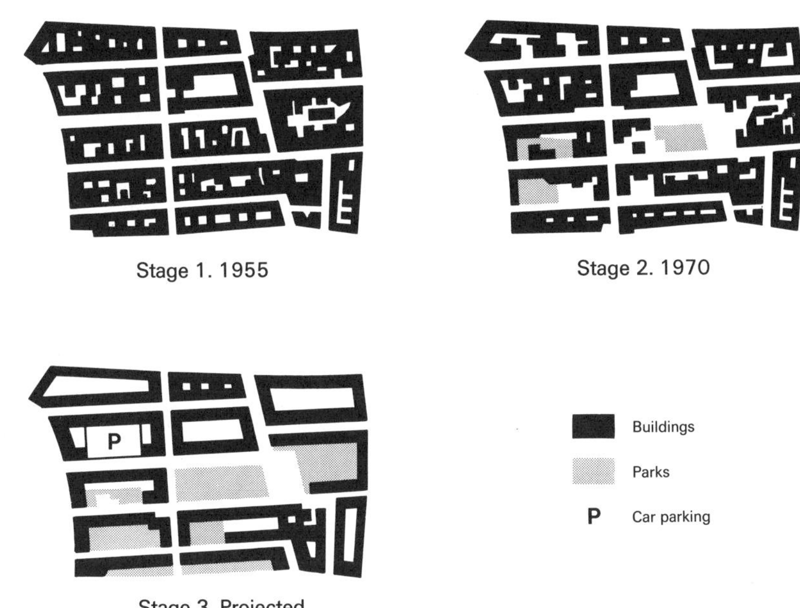

Figure 9.4 Park insertions in Lichental district, Vienna

Consideration of the quantity of public open space was rarely matched by an examination of its use. 'In orthodox city planning neighbourhood open spaces are venerated in an amazingly uncritical fashion, much as savages venerate magical fetishes' (Jacobs, 1962). Studies in many different European cities during the late 1960s and early 1970s were broadly agreed that distinctly different markets existed. Parks were open-air dining rooms for the central business district office worker, open-air playrooms for small children, and open-air sitting rooms for the old in search of company during the day and for the teenager in search of privacy in the evening. Frequency of habitual use varied widely between cities, suggesting an element of national custom. In Paris (Leusse, 1976), for example, only a minority of citizens made a regular visit to a park, while in London (Greater London Council,

1976b) there were 1004 visits per annum for each 1000 of the population. There was, however, a large measure of agreement on the average distance travelled to neighbourhood parks.

Leisure in the City Region

There is a long-established tradition for citizens using the rural environs of the city for recreation. Even before the dawning of the age of mass leisure the European city was typically surrounded by the hunting lodges and rural retreats of the richer citizens. Henry VIII's Nonsuch House, Louis XIV's Palace of Versailles, Fredrick the Great's Potsdam Palace and, further down the social scale, the country seats of the seventeenth-century Amsterdam merchants on the Gooi ridge, were all attempts to combine access to the centres of political and economic power in the city with the recreational opportunities of the countryside. The modern daytrip to the country, and the ownership of a holiday home outside the city are the reactions of a newly prosperous middle class motivated by the same desire for space, landscape beauty, and a possible return to a long-lost rural past as their social superiors in a previous age.

Understandably, therefore, the relationship between urban and rural areas and the nature of the interface between the two has been a preoccupation of urban planning since its inception. The experience of utopians from Plato to Sir Thomas More was of cities small in physical extent, and they understandably assumed that the built-up area contained within its defensive walls would be surrounded by a countryside that was easily accessible on foot to all citizens. Many later visionaries, including those as diverse in other ways as Howard and Le Corbusier, implied that placing the city in a rural setting was in itself sufficient to provide for the demands of citizens upon the rural hinterland.

The designation of a green belt around London, proposed in 1935, legalized by the 1938 Green Belt Act and demarcated as part of Abercrombie's 1944 plan, gave a name to the city's rural hinterland and initiated a continuing discussion on its purposes. As early as 1580 a ban on building on new sites within three miles (4.8 kilometres) of the gates of London had been instituted, although ineffectively enforced, principally in order to create a *cordon sanitaire* that would check the passage of disease. The 1938 legislation was similar, defining a green belt as 'an area of land near to and sometimes surrounding a town, which is kept open by permanent and severe restriction on building' (Ministry of Housing and Local Government, 1962), but had different purposes. Its two functions were: first, to prevent the outward spread of the city by containing it, and second, to provide a peripheral zone with space for the recreational needs of citizens. Although both purposes were mentioned with almost equal emphasis in the 1935 proposals, the later Act and the Abercrombie Plan in practice stressed the former. After the 1947 Town and Country Planning Act other British cities were empowered to establish green belts and by the early 1960s they were included in the plans of seven city-regions. In all, however, there was a tendency to regard them negatively, as means of containing growth and conserving rural areas, rather than as opportunities for a conscious development of the urban periphery for recreation. Although, in practice, sites in the green belt such as Box Hill or Epping Forest had long been favoured by London trippers and many London colleges and clubs located their sports fields in the green belt, there were, in fact, no automatic rights of access, and the implementation of the conservation motive could, on occasion, frustrate the construction of recreation facilities, such as camp and caravan sites and commercial entertainment centres.

The London green belt had many imitators outside the United Kingdom, although the scale and the emphasis upon the twin purposes of containment and recreation were frequently quite different. The Copenhagen Land-Use Zoning Plan of 1962, for example, designated a belt around the conurbation from Helsingør to Køge up to 50 kilometres wide, stretching completely across Sjaelland and including about half the island. Areas within this belt were specifically designated for public open space, day recreation centres and second homes.

In Paris, a modified form of green belt planning was included in the 1965 *Schéma Directeur* for the city. Green spaces, known as *zones des discontinuités* were established between the main axes of centrifugal urban expansion. After a decade's experience of the operation of this plan a reassessment published in 1975 (Préfecture de la Région Parisienne, 1975), concluded that as barriers to urban expansion these zones had proved to be too vulnerable to pressures for development. In addition it was clear that it was not sufficient merely to preserve green space without considering what use should be made of it. Space alone did not create a recreation zone. A further problem, not unique to Parisian planning but recognized more explicitly in this city than elsewhere, was that the 1965 proposals regarded rural areas as empty space to be manipulated in accordance with the planning needs of Paris, whereas the *zones* had substantial populations and planning problems of their own.

The 1975 proposals reasserted the role of the rural–urban fringe as a barrier to the undesirable outward expansion of the city's built-up area. A series of *fronts rurals* marking a sharp but narrow green buffer were established at points around the edge of the city where outward expansion would be resisted. The previous *zones des discontinuité* were renamed, and redrawn in detail, as *zones naturelles d'équilibre*, and given a more clearly conceived set of functions and a positive strategy for development. The six *zones* (Figure 9.5) together account for 250 000 hectares, or 30 per cent of the area of the Île de France planning region. The new *zones* will include positive provision for outdoor recreation, as well as attempts to accommodate the needs of the existing settlements and occupations, especially agriculture. The new recreational functions are to be grafted onto the traditional land-uses by a process described as 'controlled evolution', the success of which can only be judged in the next decade.

With large conurbations, however, it is clear that a peripheral green belt bestows benefits of recreational and residential amenity unequally upon citizens. Accessibility to it is easiest in the outer residential areas, which often also have relatively high standards of public and private open space provision, and most difficult in the central districts of the conurbation where the need for recreation space and usually also

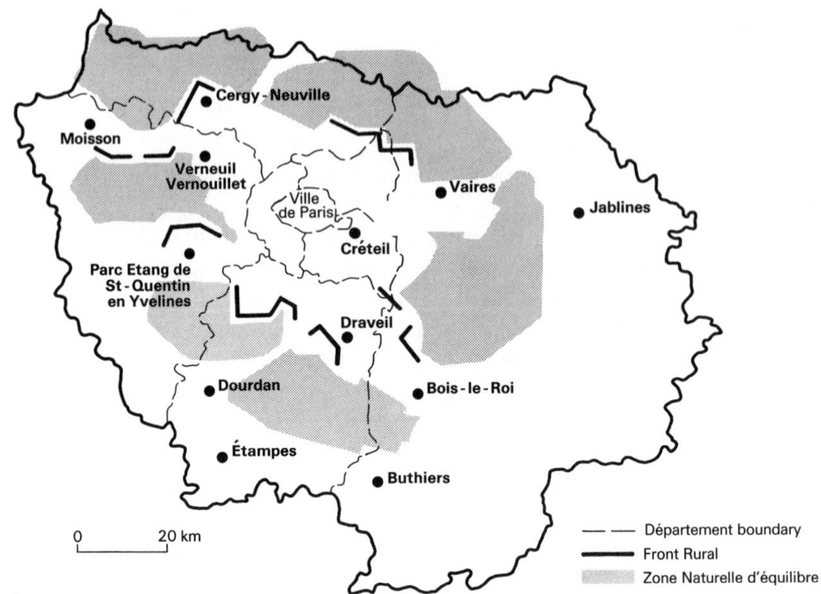

Figure 9.5 Green space planning in the Paris region

levels of car-ownership are typically low. The problem was how to bring the green belt closer to all parts of the city. One solution was the 'green wedge' driven deeinto the built-up area (Figure 9.6). Cities which had developed radially outward along transport routes found it relatively easy to designate the less built-up interfluves between the developed fingers as green wedges. In Bologna, for example, the site with its steep range of hills to the south and west threaded by the settled valley of the Reno river allowed the conservation of the upland spurs as recreation space quite close to the city-centre and well served by public transport.

If the wedges can be continued right across the city to join the green belt on the other side then clearly even better access to green space can be achieved especially for the central districts of the city. Such an arrangement, known variously as 'green corridors', 'green binding zones' or 'green axes' is particularly attractive when an objective is to prevent the coalescence of a number of distinct urban centres within a conurbation. It is not surprising, therefore, that such ideas have been most extensively pursued in the two largest multicentric conurbations of Europe, the West German Ruhr and the Dutch Randstad.

In the Ruhr the problem of poor access to open space caused by the rapid population growth in the years before the First World War was particularly acute, and the threat of the coalescence of the individual towns along the Hellweg from Duisburg to Dortmund into a continuous built-up conurbation was very real. Fortunately a regional planning authority, the *Siedlungsverband Ruhrkohlenbezirk* (SVR) had existed since 1920, and the idea of forcing green corridors between the urban nucleii was implemented in the 1960s (Siedlungsverband Ruhrkohlenbezirk, 1966). The overall plan designated general conservation measures in a wide zone

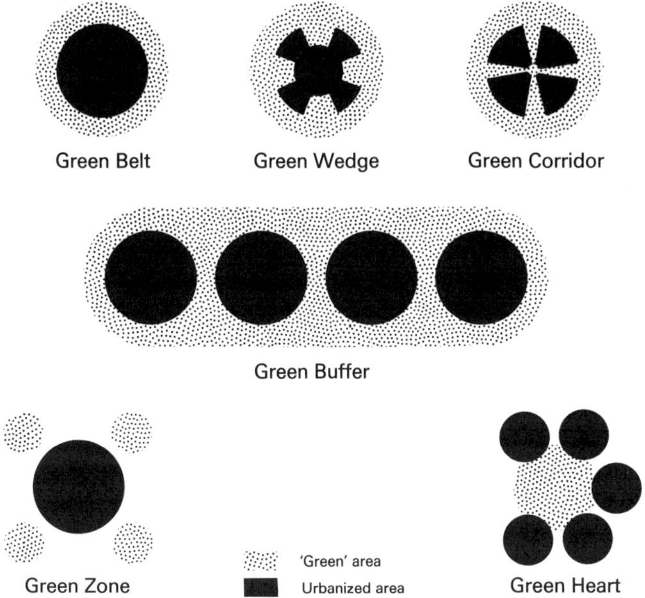

Figure 9.6 A typology of 'green' planning

surrounding the conurbation which, in practice, has been more complete in the north and south than in the east and west. The alignment of the Ruhr towns broadly along an east–west axis has determined that the corridors separating them shall run from north to south. Six of these are proposed, most of which exist as through routes although the corridors narrow dramatically to a width of only a few hundred metres in their central sections (see Figure 11.6, page 246).

In the West Netherlands there was a similar desire to both provide easy access to open country for the leisure pursuits of city dwellers and also to preserve the spatial integrity of the individual towns from coalescence into a single urbanized area. Again, both objectives were seriously threatened in the decade after the Second World War by rapid population growth and the increasing demands for land of industry, housing and transport. The arrangement of the major urban centres of the West Netherlands in the approximate shape of a horseshoe suggested the concept of Randstad, which was propounded in detail in the first National Structure Plan of 1962. This plan had three main objectives. The character of the relatively less developed areas beyond the urban rim (or *rand*) would be maintained as a sort of green belt and would include the Rhine Delta islands of South-Holland and Zeeland and the eastern and southern sandy heathlands of Utrecht, Gelderland and Noord Brabant. Thus, the West Metropolitan Netherlands would be kept spatially apart from the expanding conurbations of the Rhine–Ruhr and Brussels–Antwerp. Secondly, the cities of the rim would be separated from each other by 'green buffer zones'. In some cases this function was performed by the rivers, as south of Utrecht, while in others planners hoped to prevent development in narrow zones of a few kilometres width such as between Delft and Rotterdam, or Rotterdam and The Hague. Thirdly, the area within the rim, optimistically designated as 'the open-heart', was to be maintained for agriculture and for recreation. Thus, what has been called the 'greenheart metropolis' (Burke, 1966), promised a novel and imaginative juxtaposition of town and country.

This promise, unfortunately, could not be fulfilled. Growth in the demand for land in the 1960s, not least in the demand for building land within the 'open-heart', led to a radical rethinking of the Randstad concept and its replacement by an arrangement of built-up 'wings' (or *vleughels*) and 'open corridors' (Figure 9.7). The northern 'wing' recognized the emergence of a 'Greater Amsterdam', stretching from the sea at IJmuiden through the Gooi ridge to Utrecht. Similarly, the southern 'wing' extended from the sea at The Hague, through Delft, and Rotterdam to the *Drechtsteden* on the rivers. The third structure plan (1978) regarded the extension of these wings eastward to Arnhem and Nijmegen, and south-eastwards through the Brabant towns to Den Bosch and Eindhoven, as largely inevitable, although attempts are still being made to insert narrow buffer zones between the component nuclei in each 'wing'. The 'open-heart' has thus become a series of corridors running through the middle of the metropolitan region and linking it to the peripheral green belt. These corridors are devoted mainly to agriculture but increasingly also include

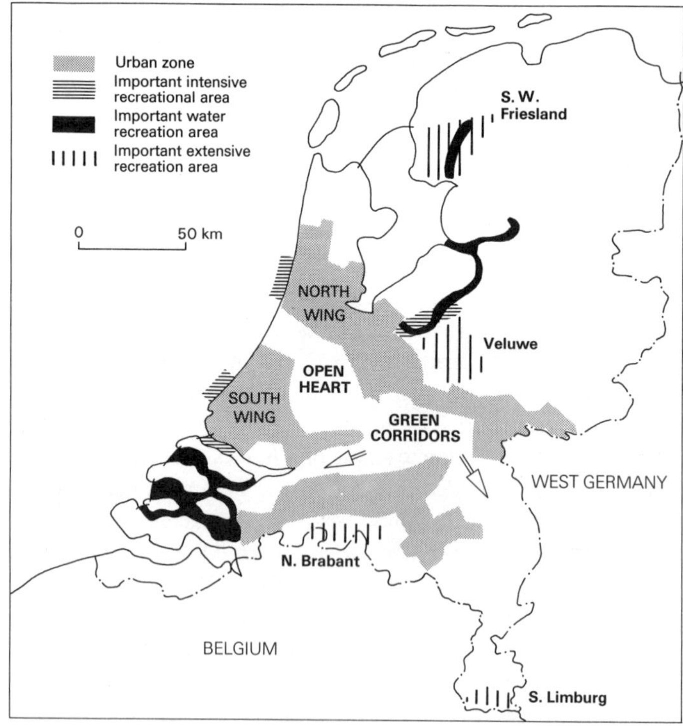

Figure 9.7 The West Netherlands open space plan

natural landscape parks and other recreational areas. They extend from the Holland coast eastwards along the rivers to the heaths and forests of the Veluwe, south-eastwards to the Kempen and Peel of Noord Brabant, and southwards into the islands of the Rhine Delta.

The comprehensiveness of the scheme for open space provision in the West Netherlands, as outlined in the three successive national structure plans, is unequalled in West Europe. Despite some difficulties in the application of the proposals at provincial and district levels (Steigenga, 1968), it is a successful fusion of both peripheral green belts and green corridors. Many other urban areas, however, including cities much smaller than the metropolitan Netherlands, have attempted to plan for what they term 'green systems'. Land both on the periphery and within the city, whether designated formally for recreation or for other uses which include an informal recreation use, is linked both functionally and spatially. A large number of the medium-sized West German cities are active proponents of the idea, including Bremen, Munich, Nuremberg and Mannheim. The last-named city has applied the idea most rigorously in the city-region plan (Stadt Mannheim, 1977); it included not only a carefully graduated hierarchy of open space provision from the regional to the neighbourhood scale, but also introduced 'green binding zones' that link the parks not only with each other but also with the pedestrianized areas of the central city thus providing continuous walkways through both the natural and built-up environments. This idea has been implemented in towns as diverse in their size and history as Vienna and new towns such as Harlow and Evry.

Until quite recently planners in many cities considered that they had discharged their obligations to the recreational needs of citizens in the rural periphery once they had conserved areas designated for this purpose, and that the recreational facilities themselves would be provided either by private enterprise, or that recreation could be accommodated on an informal basis on land officially designated for some other purpose such as agriculture or forestry. In the Ruhr, for example, until the mid-1960s the *Siedlungsverband Ruhrkohlenbezirk* considered its function to be to secure land in the periphery upon which casual and unorganized recreation might take place, and only in the last fifteen years has it attempted to actively encourage and organize recreational activities, in a ring of recreation centres from Villa Hugel in the south to the Haltern nature park in the north. Similarly, in the London green belt, the conservation of land in itself created neither community ownership nor public access and facilities for recreation were provided by private clubs and institutions. Golf courses, both private and municipally owned, are a particularly favoured use, the extreme case being Edinburgh with its 22 courses in the green belt within the city boundary.

By the middle of the 1960s it was becoming clear to many that this largely unplanned provision of facilities in green belts was inadequate on two counts. First, it was feared that a rapid increase in demand by urban populations for rural recreation would overwhelm a more slowly growing supply. In particular, the growing demand for the daytrip to the country was strongly associated with the increase in motorcar ownership in the two decades since the war. Wippler (1966) produced the classic study of the day-visitor demands of urban populations, using the case study of Groningen in the Netherlands, and formulated a series of predictions, later replicated for Rotterdam (Provinciale Planologische Dienst. Zuid-Holland, 1969) that caused considerable alarm. In summary, it was predicted that between 20 and 30 per cent of households in Dutch cities of over 100 000 inhabitants would seek recreation in a zone from 15 to 30 kilometres from the city during a typical summer weekend. Although pioneered in the Netherlands this type of study was rapidly imitated in many cities. It was not surprising, therefore, that planners responded to this increasingly clamorous chorus of predictions warning that urban recreation demands were about to overwhelm the countryside surrounding the cities.

Secondly, the tradition of accommodating recreation on land designated for other uses was breaking down as a result both of the increasing numbers of recreationists, and also because of changes, especially in agriculture, that were rendering these informal multi-use schemes less acceptable to both visitors and landowners. By the early 1970s, the National Farmers Union in Britain was complaining that informal recreation was effectively sterilizing agricultural land on the immediate periphery of urban areas. Increasingly, recreation was to be included as a land-use in its own right needing specific planning policies.

Around many European cities this planning took the form of establishing recreation 'honeypots' at defined distances from the city to 'soak up' the visitor exodus. In the Ruhr, for example, six major recreation centres, each larger than 300 hectares, and each containing a range of facilities for car-borne daytrippers have been located in a ring from 20 to 30 kilometres from the urban centres they are intended to serve. All but one are on lake or reservoir sites. Similarly, in the West Netherlands, high-capacity day-recreation centres have been specifically designed in the countryside at the critical distances from the city revealed in the research on visitor demand. In the Netherlands, these distances tend to be both shorter and better served by public transport than in the other major European conurbations. Sites such as Brielsemeer for Rotterdam, Kennermerduiner for Amsterdam and the Loosdrecht Lakes for Utrecht were sited in the 1960s in the peripheral green belt and interior 'greenheart'. Later plans in the 1970s continued the policy of providing intensive 'honeypots' but the outward growth of the urbanized area and increasing car-ownership led to the second generation being developed further from the western cities along, for example, the IJsselmeer *randmeren*, the Gelderland rivers district and in the Veluwe.

Both London and Paris were some years behind the Ruhr and the West Netherlands in day-recreation planning. In Britain, it was not until the 1968 Access to the Countryside Act that local authorities could be reimbursed for the creation of what were termed 'country parks' and the smaller 'picnic sites'. These were publicly owned and managed recreation centres offering a range of facilities to car-borne day visitors from cities within an hour's drive time. Although individual local authorities were already active in developing such demand-orientated facilities, most notably the Greater London Council with projects such as the Lee Valley Regional Park, and the English aristocracy had turned their country seats at Beaulieu, Longleat, Woburn and elsewhere into broad-based day-recreation centres, the 1968 Act was a spur to the development of a rational system of such centres around British cities.

More recently, the 1974 White Paper on Sport and Recreation did not encourage the creation of major honeypots some distance from the city. Concern about the carless inner city population and the increasing costs of petrol led to a reassessment of the recreational possibilities of the immediate urban–rural fringe.

In the Paris region, the 1975 plan (Préfecture de la Région Parisienne, 1975) made specific suggestions for the development of day-recreation centres, usually within the six *zones naturelles d'équilibre* and these proposals are now being implemented. Twelve *bases de loisirs* will be established at distances from 20 to 40 kilometres from central Paris (Figure 9.5). Each will be large, between 200 and 600 hectares, and contain facilities not only for parking and exploring the countryside, but also provision for active sports. The first four, at St Quentin-en-Yvelines, Cergy-Neuville, Jablines and Bois Le Roi near Melun, have already been opened; three of these are in new towns, thus reinforcing the regional role of the new towns in the overall regional plan. The remaining eight, mostly in the south and west of the city, will follow in the next few years.

Thus, the major West European conurbations have successively conserved their respective rural peripheries and made positive provision for day-recreation in them. But such planning has been by no means confined to the large metropolitan areas and similar ideas, on more modest scales, are now found in the plans of most medium-sized cities. Many have *de facto* green belt policies and have created facilities in them for the recreation of their citizens. Hannover has its Steinhüder Meer, Edinburgh its Pentlands Park and Turin its Villa Real.

Sports Provision

The systematic provision of sports facilities is a responsibility that has only recently been assumed by city authorities, and then more usually as a result of pressure from the local electorate than in response to specific government legislation (Windle, 1981). As with the planning of parks, the first problem is to determine need and the second to devise policies to satisfy these needs that can be accommodated among the existing land-uses. Studies to determine the propensity of populations to engage in active sport, and to establish the distances participants were prepared to travel proliferated after the middle of the 1960s, and in turn led to the creation of theoretical hierarchies of provision based on various optimum catchment areas. A study in Edinburgh, for example (Cargill and Hodgart, 1978), produced a series of locations for a variety of sports facilities that minimized travel distances for potential participants, while in Glasgow (Robertson, 1978) a study produced the ideal locations for both large multipurpose sports complexes, each serving a hinterland up to 6 kilometres wide and containing more than 50 000 people, and also for smaller local centres serving communities of less than 25 000 people. Similarly, in many medium-sized German cities, a comprehensive range of standards of provision has been devised in terms of space for various sports for each inhabitant to be provided within a defined distance of home, (Stadt Köln, 1978). A simple but completed example of the execution of such policies can be seen in Zurich (Figure 9.8) where a comprehensive cover of the city using hinterlands of 15 to 20 minutes' travel time has been attained.

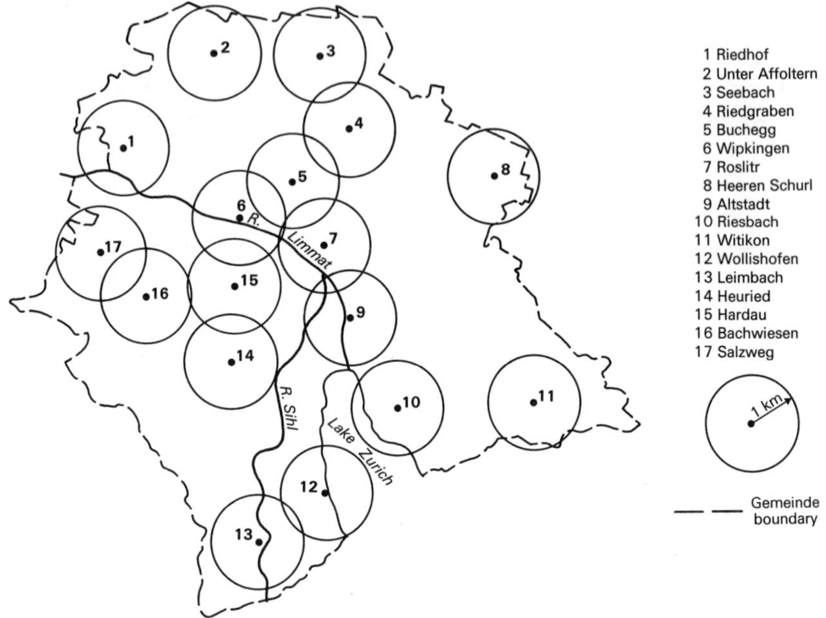

Figure 9.8 Catchment areas for sports centres in Zurich

Such analyses of demand are, however, prone to all the difficulties of application that have already been mentioned in the discussion of public open space planning. In addition, spending on sport has generally been low in the priorities of local authorities; many facilities are too demanding of land to utilize small infill sites, and large multipurpose sports complexes have proved very expensive to build and operate. Consequently, there is a great variety in provision between and within cities, with the presence of facilities being often a result of political will or the adroit opportunism of planners in responding to the fortuitous availability of sites (Windle, 1980). In Britain, the Albemarle (HMSO, 1961) and Wolfenden (1960) reports gave central government encouragement to the building of large sports centres but the initiative still remained with the local authority. The first was opened in Harlow in 1963 and there were 41 in use by 1968 (Molyneux, 1972). An assessment of provision in the county of Hampshire in the late 1970s, for example, revealed wide discrepancies between the cities of the region (Table 9.2). A growing feeling that the concentration on building large multipurpose centres with a city-wide hinterland was bound to produce an uneven pattern of supply, together with the greater financial stringency of the 1970s, prompted a major shift in policy in Britain away from the expensive sports centre with its specialized equipment and private car-serviced hinterland, towards the lower end of the hierarchy. The Sports Council's 'Sport for All' campaign coincided with government encouragement for relatively simple

Table 9.2 Sports centre provision—county of Hampshire

Districts	Existing	Needed	Deficiency
North-East Hampshire	2	3	1
Mid-Hampshire	2	3	1
South Hampshire (including Portsmouth and Southampton)	1	8	7
South-West Hampshire	1	1	0

Source: Hampshire County Council Policy Analysis and Review Recreation Programme Areas, 1976

neighbourhood facilities, usually in converted premises, located close to the demand, and serving neighbourhoods of not more than 25 000 people. The fact that this figure also happens to be the size of a secondary school catchment points the way to a more effective dual use of facilities at the community level. Although Britain, and especially the urban authorities of central Scotland Edinburgh and Glasgow were early to appreciate these possibilities, the cities of Scandinavia, the Netherlands and West Germany provide similar examples.

British cities have reacted more strongly against the idea of the large sports complex than most continental cities, many of which are still pursuing such policies, but the increasing use of the urban–rural fringe for formal sport provision is a more universal trend, reinforced in Britain by the structures to this effect in the 1975 White Paper on Sport and Recreation. So pressing has been the demand for the use of the immediate urban periphery for sport that, in the case of one category of facilities, the Countryside Commission has recently expressed its unwillingness to see any further golf courses developed in this zone despite the obvious conservational advantages of such courses (Davidson, 1978).

Beyond the urban fringe the city's inhabitants make demands on the surrounding region for a wide variety of sports, and for the more specialized activities often at a considerable distance from the city. Numerous examples of the link between particular cities and resource-orientated sports facilities can be found. The sporting potential of mountains links the cities of South Lancashire and the climbing possibilities of Snowdonia, the Lancashire and Yorkshire conurbations with the caves of the Pennines, and the cities of Turin and Milan with the ski slopes of the Val D'Aosta and Lombardy Alps respectively. The marinas and associated boat facilities of the Solent coast are strongly patronized by boat-owners from Greater London, as are those of the Zeeland Lake from Rotterdam, and the IJsselmeer *randmeren* from Amsterdam. If the car-borne day-visitor in search of general countryside recreation travels 30 to 60 kilometres from the city for more specialized activities, the range of the recreating citizen is much greater and extends to yachtsmens' cottages, campsites and second homes in a recognizable 'weekending zone'. The use of the Veluwe by the Dutch, the New Forest by Londoners, and the Bavarian Alps by citizens of Munich becomes an integral part of the recreation industry.

Planning for sport in a city whose influence is so extensive poses major administrative problems and often distinct differences of approach by the government of the city and of its region; while the city may regard the region as its legitimate hinterland for these sporting activities, the region may view the influx of recreating citizens as an unwelcome and unprofitable invasion.

Entertainment

Planning for the provision of entertainment and cultural facilities is again an aspect of urban life that was not regarded as a responsibility of local authorities until quite recently. Although the entertainment of residents and visitors has always been an important function of cities, most facilities are provided by commercial enterprises and even when public money is involved little attention has often been given to planning considerations.

In the course of the 1970s the Council of Europe took an interest in national variations in cultural provision and instituted a long-term study of a sample of fourteen European towns (Mennell, 1976). The gist of their argument was that they 'expect local authorities increasingly to shoulder the burden of public patronage of culture and leisure—highbrow, lowbrow and middlebrow. ... So how is a town to distribute its limited resources to best advantage?' Attempts over the study period to estimate desirable levels of provision and isolate sections and areas of underprovision, have generally foundered on the large variation in the popularity of entertainment media, and the differences in responsibility assumed by urban authorities. For example, theatre-goers formed 1 per cent of the inhabitants of Stavanger but 10 per cent in Stockholm and only one-half of 1 per cent in Bologna. But local government per capita expenditure on public entertainment was four times higher in Bologna than, for example, in Exeter. After almost 10 years' study it was concluded that it was not possible 'to develop one ideal cultural policy as a model to be copied by other towns. Obviously that is impossible—towns and people vary too much for that.' But policy in this relatively unfamiliar area of urban planning may still be assisted by the development of 'a set of methods by which the effectiveness of cultural policies can be judged and evaluated' (Mennell, 1978).

Attempts to allocate entertainment facilities, especially those with a national or regional catchment area, vary from country to country. In France, the central government inspired and substantially financed a network of *maisons de culture* from the mid-1960s to serve as regional cultural centres. That at Grenoble, for example, served a region of more than a quarter of a million, while more recent foundations at Caen, Bourges and St Étienne have been rather less successful, perhaps largely due to the lower level of local enthusiasm for the project. If French policy suggests a missionary endeavour by the central government in stimulating *animation* in the provinces, the British government, in contrast, relies heavily on supporting local initiatives, usually from local authorities. Although the Arts Council have developed some guidelines, especially in their sponsorship of 'regional' theatres, and through the International Festivals Society, of regional Festivals, there is nothing to compare with the French or Scandinavian policies of seeking spatial equity in arts provision.

If public authorities in most countries have been only sporadically interested in the allocation of cultural and entertainment facilities between cities, they have become much more deeply concerned with their allocation within the city. Public entertainment facilities show a strong tendency to agglomerate in particular quarters of the city. Many of these facilities, especially cinemas, theatres and concert-halls are serving a city-wide, or even an international, hinterland. Similar facilities will tend to cluster together in response to the behaviour of customers who will seek out a district where comparisons can be made, rather than an individual establishment. Each type of entertainment facility provides only a part of the total 'night-out' package assembled by the customer. Therefore, different sorts of entertainment, such as theatres, restaurants, nightclubs and bars, will tend to cluster near each other, so that together they form the entertainment quarter, or nightlife district, that the customer seeks. Once established this concentration in a particular district will be reinforced both by popular sentiment that advertises the area to those in search of entertainment in the city, and also by planning decisions. Many such facilities are 'bad neighbours' and will tend to repel other functions. Planners will frequently endeavour to contain the nuisance by opposing its expansion into other areas and encouraging all such facilities to locate within the existing entertainment quarter.

The existence of the nightlife district has long been an important function of the European city, and for many visitors is the main reason for their visit. While the city's residential and employment functions have increasingly fled to the suburbs, the entertainment function has remained firmly rooted 'downtown'. A closer investigation of its component elements in a variety of cities is needed.

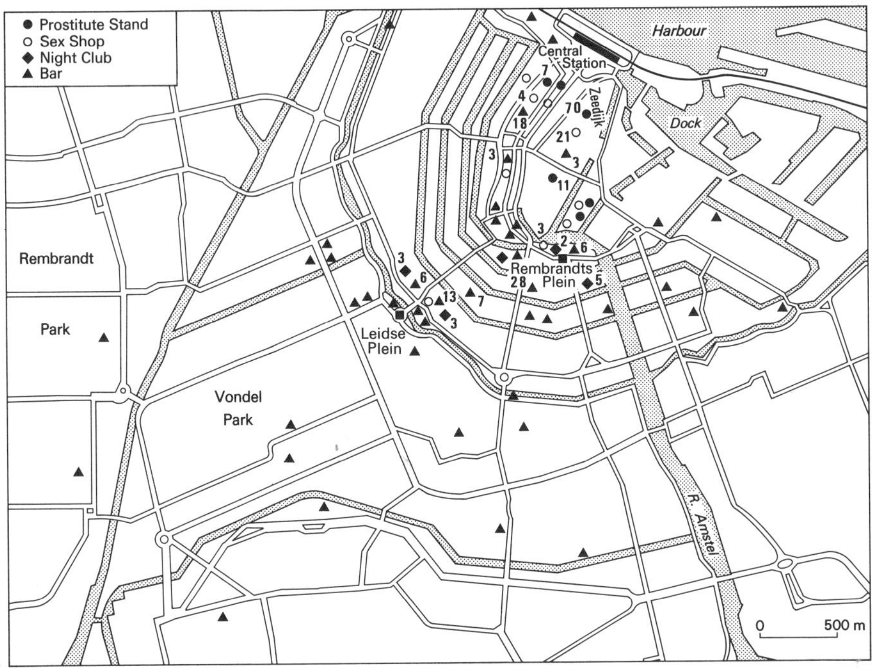

Figure 9.9 Nightlife in Amsterdam. Numbers refer to the total of each function at that location

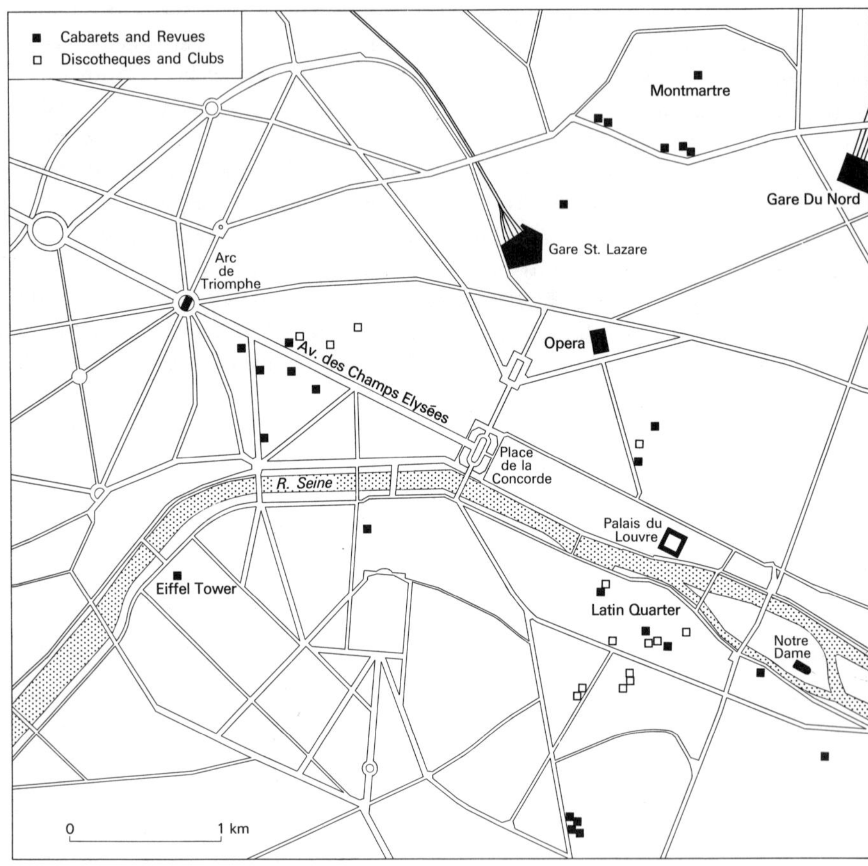

Figure 9.10 Nightlife in central Paris

A map of the distribution of licensed bars in Amsterdam (Figure 9.9) reveals an 'export' surplus in the inner quarters of the city, especially in the Zeedijk and Rembrandtsplein areas. If nightclubs are examined, a more restricted pattern emerges with a concentration around Rembrandtsplein and Leidseplein. In the much larger city of Paris nightclubs are concentrated in three distinct areas (Figure 9.10), north of the Champs Elysée, Montmartre, and on the left bank around the Boulevard St Michel. Work on the gastronomic geography of Paris (Bonnain-Mœrdyk, 1975) reveals a similar clustering of high-class restaurants in the same areas but with a quality gradient descending from west to east of the city. Similarly, in Copenhagen the streets west of the Tivoli contain most of the city's nightclubs. All these examples delimit what can be termed 'west-end' entertainment which occupies relatively expensive sites (Figure 9.9) in high-prestige districts.

A different sort of nightlife district, however, may also exist near to, or spatially quite distinct from, the 'west-end'. This may offer cheaper and more explicitly sexual entertainment often including commercial prostitution. Such redlight districts have long been a feature, if largely unacknowledged, of the European city, and although some citizens may prefer to ignore their existence, planners must increasingly include them in their plans. In Amsterdam, for example, the Zeedijk district near to, but one street separated from the main commercial thoroughfare, has entertained visiting sailors since the seventeenth century, and today continues the tradition for an international clientèle. Figure 9.9 shows that sites used for prostitution, and also shops selling sexual equipment, are strongly concentrated into this one small area. Relatively low rents on the eastern side of the central business district compared with the equivalent area to the west, the availability of suitable premises in what is still a working-class residential area of largely privately rented accommodation, and the international reputation of the area which removes the need to advertise, have all tended to maintain the existence of this function in this clearly defined district.

The response of the city planners has been ambiguous combining both the absence of any specific mention of the activities of the redlight district as a central business district function, with an implicit toleration of these activities as long as they remain confined to Zeedijk. The city's tourist authority regards the area as a major tourist resource, a major contributor to the image of exciting Amsterdam and organizes tours for interested visitors. Many other major European cities contain similarly clearly defined districts that are regarded by planners partly as legitimate extensions of the entertainment function of the city and a major tourist asset, and partly as an indicator, alongside others such as crime and vagrancy, of the social malaise of the urban 'transition zone' first recognized by Burgess (Burgess and Park, 1925) when he wrote 'vice district' on his famous map of urban functional areas in Chicago.

The existence of redlight districts in large cities such as London (Soho), and Hamburg (Reeperbahn) is well known but their presence in smaller towns is less well documented despite the major problems they pose to urban planners. In Arnhem, for example, a city of only 150 000 inhabitants, the Spijkerkwartier, a district of the inner city just to the north-east of the central business district, shows the same features as Amsterdam's Zeedijk on a smaller scale. A district of working-class rented housing contains a dense concentration of prostitution sites within a clearly defined area, situated close to but distinct from, the legitimate 'west-end' entertainment zone (Figure 9.11). The Spijkerkwartier has the problems of declining population, ageing housing and a lack of a stable community typical of many such inner city wards, but its rehabilitation is made more difficult by its redlight function which tends to repel other commercial and residential uses (Sociografischdienst gewest Arnhem, 1975) and locks the area more firmly into its role of accommodating the poor, immigrants and the socially deprived.

There is little reason to assume that Arnhem is unique in this respect. The Guillemins district of Liège, the Waalkade district of Nijmegen, the Grassmarket area of Edinburgh, the streets south of Kurfurstendamm in West Berlin, and the Derby Road area in Southampton all house similar functions and pose similar problems.

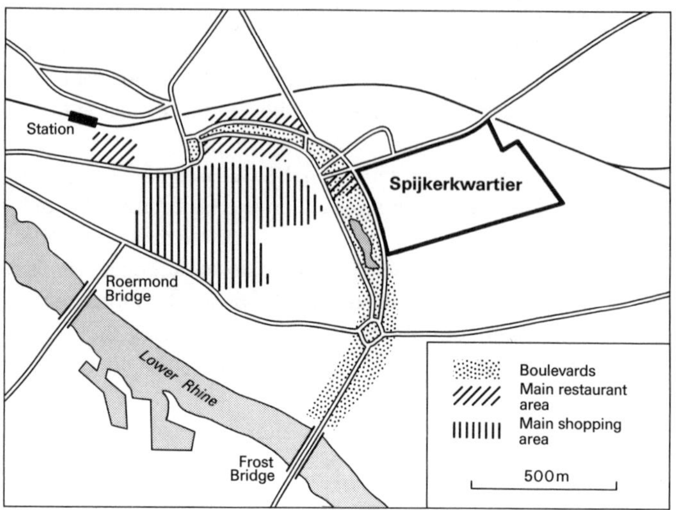

Figure 9.11 The Spijkerkwartier district, Arnhem

Conclusions

Throughout the wide field of leisure provision, planners in cities all over Europe found the problem of defining their role complicated by the size and recentness of the increase in leisure demands, and the essentially spontaneous rather than regulated nature of the activity. Planning for housing, transport or employment has a longer history and a tested body of practical experience. Consequently local authorities have acquired responsibilities for the bundle of very diverse activities outlined in this chapter without any clear idea about their function. As to the justification of the choice of activities, 'historical accident plus the concept of "worthy" leisure provides the only explanation' (Roberts, 1974). The limits of public responsibility are equally difficult to trace. 'Thus private enterprise has offered us the frisbee, grouse shooting and Summerland, while Epping Forest, the Royal Festival Hall and our local tennis courts are by courtesy of the public purse' (Roberts, 1974).

The earlier involvement of American government authorities in leisure planning and the quality of the work produced in the United States, most especially the ORRRC (Outdoor Recreation Research Review Commission) reports of 1956–69 were of little practical help to the European planners. The different balance between private and public responsibilities traditional in Europe, the shorter distances travelled to leisure, and above all the much greater constraints on the availability of land in the European city, made the American experience difficult to transfer. The European city had to devise its own methods of analysing the problems and create its own policies for their solution.

However, in all the diverse activities discussed above, urban planners have responded in a similar way throughout Europe. Administrative fragmentation of recreation responsibilities, both within cities and between the urban and other levels of government, has occurred as a result of the ad hoc expansion of planning interests.

In Britain and Italy, the solution has been sought largely through integration at the city level, whereas in Germany the region, represented by the *Land* government, has tended to assume this role. In both France and the Netherlands strategic planning has been largely assumed by the regional authorities, leaving the city with the task of implementation.

The need to establish the appropriate quantity of provision has led to a search for standards. Although based often on little more than intuition, such standards have been used to highlight comparative deficiencies, or surpluses, in facilities as diverse as parks, sports centres and theatres. Attempts to create international standards allowing comparisons between cities across national boundaries, has really only been tried in the arts and here with little success.

Attempts to monitor the adequacy of provision of many different recreational activities has led to the study of the effective range of demand, the drawing of catchment areas, and ultimately the creation of a hierarchy of provision which varies in scale from the local to the international. Finally, studies of adequacy have led to the application of policies of territorial justice and, in some instances, even policies of positive discrimination in favour of certain areas. These ideas of spatial equity are still weakly developed and found most commonly at the intra-city rather than inter-city level, especially in public open-space provision where deficiencies are usually visually obvious and demonstrably socially damaging. It can be expected with some confidence, however, that as recreation planning 'comes of age' in the European city, that such ideas will be extended to other activities and to other planning scales.

Part III

CHAPTER 10

Urban Planning: National and International Influences

City planning in West Europe has been part of a growing trend towards intervention apparent in almost all West European countries in the period since 1945. Government intervention in most areas of the economic and social life of the nation on behalf of citizens has had both direct and indirect effects on city planning. While direct involvement by central government in city planning is rare, for almost all the West European nations it is true to say that various forms of economic policy, such as those towards regional development or national transport, have been incorporated in city policies. Similarly, social policies towards housing, higher education and welfare are generally implemented by local authorities with the consequence that the city structure plans cannot avoid these impositions of national ground rules and planning law.

A clear and often dramatic example of this is provided by the university towns of Europe, where national educational institutions, centrally financed, have a massive impact on the economy, society and physical appearance of their host cities, and become a major item in the attention of local planners. When a large national institution is located in a relatively small city the result is often spectacular. In Groningen, for example, the state university has 15 000 students in a town of 160 000 inhabitants. The employment of about 4000 staff makes it the largest employer not only in the city but in the entire north of the country, while the spending of £400 million by the university and another £100 million by students makes it the most important channel of government money in the region (de Jong, 1969). The impact on the demographic structure, with three times as many people in the 20–24 years age group as in the 40–44 or 0–4 years age groups, is obvious on the streets, but equally pervasive is the effect on the housing and land markets, retailing and social attitudes. The traditionally conservative calvinist city now has a strongly entrenched socialist city council, and the highest proportion of declared 'non-religious' of any Dutch city (51 per cent). Although this is perhaps an extreme case, it is not unique. National educational institutions play a similar role in cities as varied as Münster, Edinburgh, Florence or Louvain. Similarly other sorts of national institution, such as defence installations and major hospitals, as well as government departments and agencies, will exercize local influence but be largely outside the competence of the local planners.

Thus the ideology and actions of the country's governing party can influence urban developments even in cities governed by parties subscribing to alternative ideologies and committed to alternative actions. Nevertheless there are certain national planning policies and goals which have evolved in a particular fashion to provide a relatively distinctive and continuous impact on urban development within each country. It is also true that there is an even broader scale of physical planning that has emerged at an international level with the developing role of the enlarged European Economic Community.

International Influences

The movement towards European integration has focused attention on the urban system of the European Economic Community especially in the highly urbanized core of the original community of six. Until after the Second World War attempts to view the national urban systems were beset by problems of the intervening national boundaries and very little attempt was made to recognize the impact of extra-territorial urban developments on the cities and towns of the country. Therefore the few city planning statements that existed were usually focused on the city itself rather than its relationship either to the broader region or to other cities. For instance, the interdependence of cities in the Maastricht–Liège–Aachen triangle, which is readily recognized today, was affected by the nationalistic views of territory in the early twentieth century. In addition, the problems of cities located on the national periphery, a long way in both physical and time distance from the core of the state, has slowed the development of many cities in the past. This has been the claim of Nancy, Metz and Saarbrücken (Burtenshaw, 1976a and 1976b).

With integration in the European Economic Community, many authorities have begun to consider the cities of West Europe as the parts of a potentially integrated system. Given the acceptance of this concept, it is possible to see each individual urban plan within the context of a much broader vision of urban development. Kormoss (1976) recognized this in the area covered by the North-West European Physical Planning Conference (Belgium, Netherlands, Luxembourg and parts of West Germany and France). He noted that there were 43 conurbations of increasing dominance in the region from the Ruhr at one end of the scale to Leiden at the other which housed 40 per cent of the region's population.

The cluster of clearly interdependent towns and interrelated planning problems that exist on either side of the arbitrary border between Belgium and the Netherlands, was an obvious testbed for early experiments in international cooperation. Indeed the Benelux treaties of 1949 made particular reference to joint planning policies and established a governmental committee at a senior level to encourage their creation and implementation. The need was emphasized by a frontier in Limburg that separated the city of Maastricht from its hinterland to the west and south, and separated home from workplace for many in the settlements along the Maas. To emphasize that, the two regions of Dutch Limburg and Belgian Limburg although peripheral to their nation-states, could be viewed as central when taken together. The joint region was called the Benelux–Middengebied.

The experience of cooperation has, however, not fulfilled the expectations. Study groups have reported (Verbeck, 1973) and plans proposed, but in the last analysis the future of the two regions has until now always been determined by the policies of their respective central governments. The quite different strategies for the development of the divided Limburg coalfield settlements on each side of the frontier is a major example. Such cooperation that is apparent on the ground, such as the Belgian–West German motorway link across Dutch Limburg or the joint recreation proposals for the Maas valley, could, one is tempted to believe, have occurred without the panoply of joint committees. If planning cooperation between two friendly countries linked by treaty has proved so difficult in practice, there are grounds for pessimism about the results of similar joint projects elsewhere in Europe.

The concept of interdependent national urban systems was taken a stage further by Michels (1976) who drew together the various national and regional urban systems to produce an international system of development axes and growth points for north-west Europe. He examined the Dutch planning structure with its proposals for grouped deconcentration (*geburdelde deconcentratie*) and hierarchies of centres (Buursink, 1971). Similar policies for an urban hierarchy and sectoral growth poles for particular developments in Belgium together with a linking transport net, were considered alongside German and French studies. While differences between individual national policies, which we will examine later, were apparent in terms of the number of levels in a hierarchy, and the French use of the concept of discontinuously urbanized axes, it was possible for Michels to propose a basic axis development point system (*Achsen–Schwerpunkt System*) that harmonized with the identical German system developed a decade earlier (Figure 10.1). Three major ranks of centre are distinguished and related to the two levels of axial links between the centres. He proposes a series of city-regions which, despite the efforts at integration, somewhat paradoxically recognize national boundaries. Thus the 178 cities classed as development centres, which include 47 metropolitan centres, 35 primary centres and 96 secondary centres, are able to formulate plans in relation to this wider supra-national view of urban development.

Another practical example of the supra-national character of urban planning is the case of Geneva which is surrounded by a 103 kilometre boundary with France and only a 4.5 kilometre-wide strip linking it to the rest of Switzerland. It is a city that attracts 25 000 frontier workers into the city from the French *départments* of Ain and Haute Savoie. Here in 1973 a Franco-Swiss Consultative Committee was formed to study topics such as frontier workers, transfrontier planning, transport and noise pollution from the international airport (Republique et Canton de Genève, 1977). As a result of these initiatives the 1975 *Plan Directeur Cantonal* does include reference to developments on French territory that are an integral part of the overall structure of the Geneva city region (Republique et Canton de Genève, 1975). This plan will be examined in greater detail in Chapter 12.

A third example of cooperation can be seen at the heart of the European Economic Community where the plans of four countries acknowledge the common problems, needs and aspirations of the people's living within the area of the Saar–Lor–Lux Triangle (Burtenshaw, 1976a). Here the development programmes for the Saarland, Rhineland Palatinate, the Grand Duchy of Luxembourg and Lorraine all acknowledge the existence of two major axes of development. The first

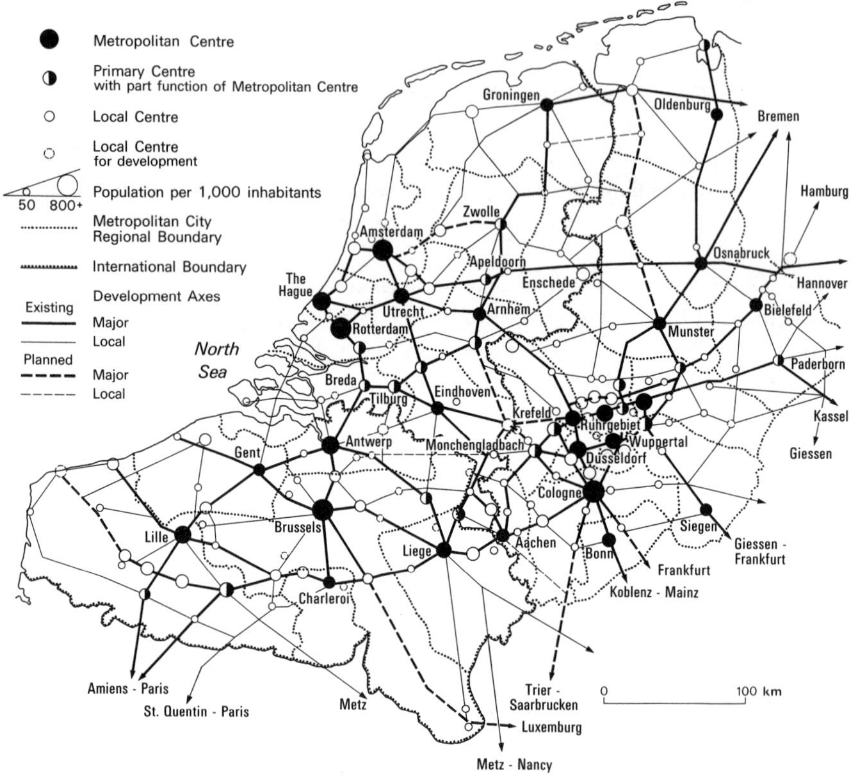

Figure 10.1 The axis–central place system in north-west Europe (after Michels, 1976) (reproduced by permission of Bundesforschungsanstalt für Landeskunde und Raumordnung, Bonn)

runs south from Luxembourg City, through Esch-sur-Alzette, Thionville and Metz to Nancy, while the second extends from Kaiserslautern through Saarbrücken, Forbach and Saarlouis towards Luxembourg. Between these two axes and beyond them to the west and north lie the recreational zones of the triangle. Given this agreed international view of the directions of growth, the individual cities of the region have a set of unique guidelines for the future so that the plans for the expansion of Saarbrücken, for example, accept the constraints of the broader strategy.

The measures of regional aid dispersed by other international bodies have also had an effect on urban growth and change. The European Coal and Steel Community (ECSC) and the European Investment Bank (EIB) have both been involved in regional development. The ECSC has confined its attention to regions affected by structural problems and particularly the coalfield industrial towns of France, Belgium, the Netherlands and West Germany. The EIB has also been involved in loans for the specific purposes of regional development. Pinder (1978) has shown how the development loans show a spatial concentration in southern Italy and particularly around Naples and Rome. Strasbourg in particular and Alsace-Lorraine

Figure 10.2 European commission zones qualifying for regional development fund aid (reproduced by permission of Oxford University Press)

in general have benefited from investment in France. The European Regional Development Fund which was set up in 1973 has also affected the development of cities in those areas of West Europe that qualify for such assistance (Figure 10.2). The funds available are small but towns and cities are benefiting from the policy which has favoured the rural periphery and those regions suffering from severe structural problems. Thus schemes in Liverpool, Brest, Naples and Groningen can receive aid, but cities within development regions according to their own country's criteria for assistance such as Saarbrücken, Metz and Mons are excluded (Burtenshaw, 1976a).

National Influences on Urban Planning

Within each country there are overall policy guidelines, some of which are often not intended to have a direct impact on towns and cities, that govern the expansion and development programmes of cities. While it is true to say that central government involvement in city planning has grown throughout West Europe, the actual course of this involvement has varied considerably. In some countries there has been a consistent pursuit of a set of social goals which have resulted in an equally consistent set of policies. Such consistency has been realized in Sweden, for example, through a continuous period of government by one party until recently, whereas as we saw in France in the area of housing policies it has been maintained despite changes in government. On the other hand, policies have oscillated in the United Kingdom with changes in power while policies in Italy have been slow to be created and, more important, slow to be implemented due to the inability of the administration to make effective decisions.

(1) Great Britain

Bourne (1975) has drawn attention to the impact of national policies on urban development in both the United Kingdom and Sweden. Early attempts at regional planning in Britain included restriction of growth in the overcrowded south-east bringing with it a policy of limiting first industrial development and, much later, office development. In line with the recommendations of the Barlow Commission of 1940 the policy of decentralization implied the restriction of growth of London and the transfer of development to the development regions and, ironically as it transpired since it was so successful, the rest of southern Britain (Barlow Report, 1940). The new towns, partly a reaction to another Barlow recommendation and the result of half a century of campaigning, were another policy decision that has influenced subsequent British urban development. The impact of post-Barlow policies on London have been well documented. For example, industrial employment declined, office rentals rose following restrictions and there was a reduction of over 200 000 commuters a day into the capital. Beyond London the legion of industrial estates in the south-east with factories built to avoid the restrictions on floor space, and later the sudden interest of property developers in the outer suburban centres such as Croydon, were tangible effects on urban areas of national policies. The changed central area townscapes of Reading, Ipswich and Swindon also reflect the effects of office policies on medium-sized cities. Further afield the movement of the growing number of civil service posts, for example from London to Newcastle and Durham, was altering the social geography of cities in the development regions (Hammond, 1968).

Since 1974 national policies have been implemented which direct attention to the inner city and particularly the revitalization of inner zones of cities. The Inner Urban Areas Act 1978 has given aid to named local authorities to attract industry. These named Partnership Areas are London's docklands, Lambeth, Hackney and Islington, all in the metropolis, and the inner areas of Birmingham, Manchester, Liverpool, Newcastle and Gateshead, and parts of inner Glasgow. In addition parts of Bolton, Bradford, Hull, Leeds, Leicester, Middlesbrough, Nottingham, Oldham, Sheffield, Sunderland, Tyneside, Wolverhampton and Hammersmith (London) have been designated Programme Districts with fewer powers to attract industry (Figure 10.3).

Since the change of government in 1979 the assistance to the development regions is to be reduced and the areal extent of these regions is to be contracted by 1982 (Figure 10.3). The Location of Offices Bureau (LOB) has been disbanded, and

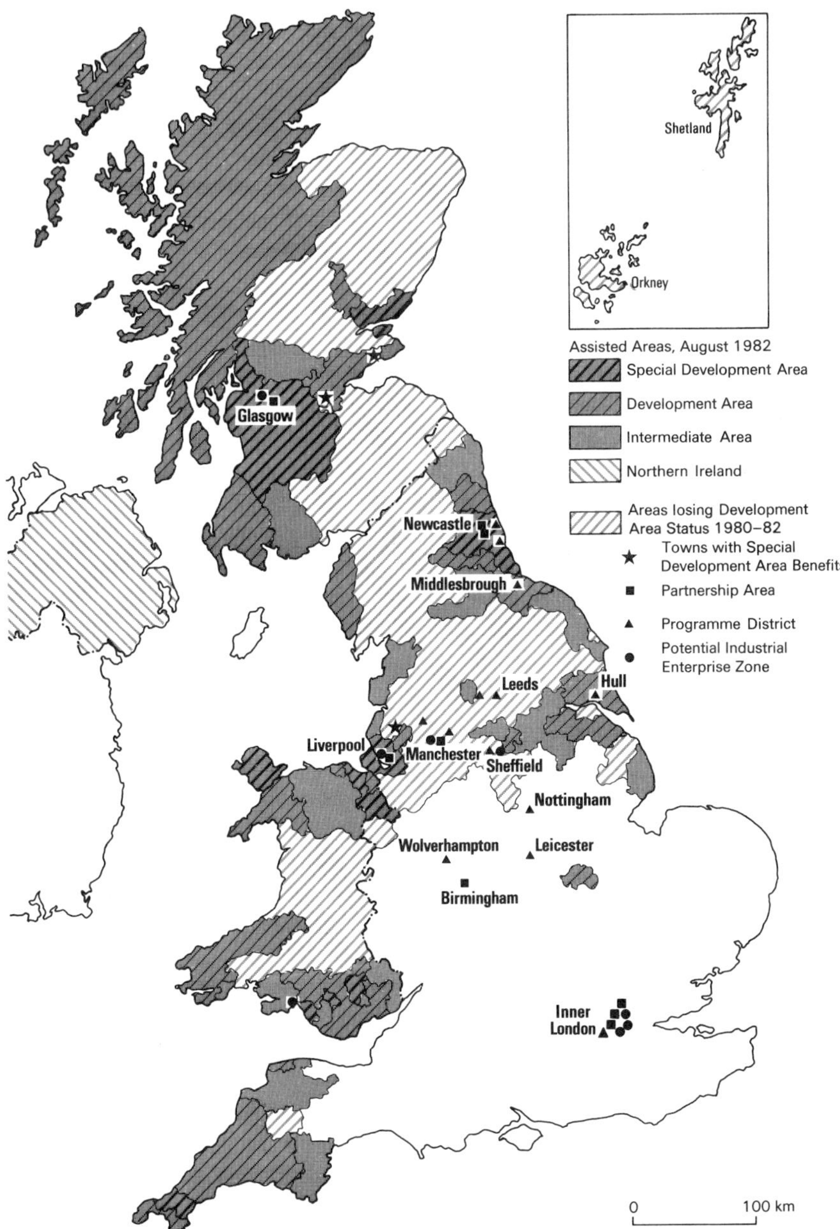

Figure 10.3 Regional development in Great Britain

tions of the civil servants planned to such cities as Glasgow and Swansea will be less necessary in a severely pruned service. However, there is a realization that the inner cities house the most severe economic and social problems. The introduction of Industrial Enterprise Zones to encourage industrial growth with the minimum of red-tape and the proposed Urban Development Corporations for London's docklands, inner Merseyside and the inner eastern area of Glasgow are the latest parts of the inner city strategy (Figure 10.3). The effects on city development throughout Great Britain, and especially the areas of changed status, will take time to emerge, but no doubt, the changed direction of policies will have repercussions on urban development far beyond the immediate policy objectives.

(2) *Sweden*

In Scandinavia, increasing concern has been shown at the growing imbalance between the metropolitan centres with their increasing share of resources and the rest of the country, especially the north of Norway, Sweden and Finland. In Sweden, this led to a policy to limit the growth of the three major centres, Stockholm, Gothenburg and Malmö (Bourne, 1975). Even though it could scarcely be argued that major congestion problems exist to parallel those in the north-west European agglomerations, the national disequilibria were such as to bring about this action. It is the continuing aim of Swedish regional policy to bring about increased economic, social and cultural equality between people in different regions. An additional aim is to provide security for the individual faced with the consequences of structural changes in the economy and economic expansion. The Swedish regional planning response has been to encourage the development of labour market areas of a sufficient size to provide diversity of employment and other opportunities. In 1972 the Riksdag designated 23 *primary centres* outside the three *metropolitan centres* to provide the nuclei for services and economic activities such as Umeå and Gävle. There has been a redistribution of government office jobs with encouragement to locate in disadvantaged locations particularly in the north, which had been an assisted area since 1965 (Ministry of Housing and Physical Planning, 1976). Below this level there are 70 *regional centres* with a population threshold of 30 000 to function as small-scale growth centres which could offer some employment stability and reduce outmigration. The final tier of 120 *municipal centres* was designated to act as small-scale activity nodes (Figure 10.4). This policy, by being selective in its designation of centres at each level, has ensured that some centres would grow possibly at the expense of more peripheral locations. The selection of the centres themselves obviously involved many intricate political considerations.

(3) *Norway*

In contrast to the Swedish policy, encouraging urban concentration at particular levels in the urban hierarchy, is the policy of the Norwegian government. Although regional growth points have been designated, the emphasis is rather more on maintaining the viability of the peripheral and rural communities (Hansen, 1972;

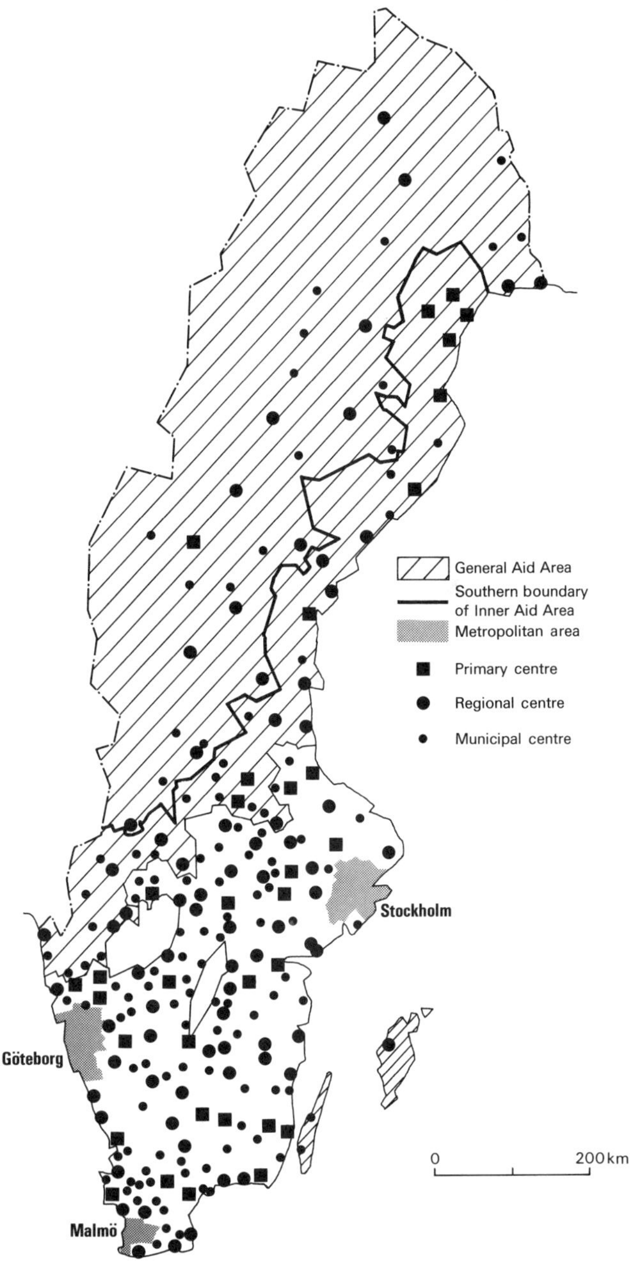

Figure 10.4 Swedish development regions

and Knox, 1973). The basis of Norwegian planning is that the whole population must have, as far as possible, equal access to social and cultural possibilities for rewarding well-paid employment and a wide choice of jobs. To do this the preservation of the existing settlement pattern and a continuation of the existing balance of population are just slight restatements of the planning aims of their neighbours. Perhaps more than their neighbours the Norwegians stress the social basis of regional planning and that economic growth is not an end in itself (Ministry of Environment, 1975). Resource utilization and conservation, full potential for public participation, and informed politicians are all aspects in the latest planning act that suggest a broadening of the existing social emphasis (Norway, 1977). There had been the obvious problem of overconcentration of population (19 per cent in 1974) and service sector employment in Oslo, and a part of the regional development policy pursued since 1961 has been to control further growth in this city. The growth of government office activity itself, which accounts for 45 per cent of the increase in service sector employment between 1960 and 1970, underlined the need to redistribute this growth away from the capital. The headquarters of the government agency administering Norway's North Sea oil interests has been located in Stavanger, a city already housing a large number of expatriate oil workers, but this is one of the few decentralization schemes which has taken place. The fastest population growth is now in the four provincial centres of Bergen, Kristiansund, Stavanger and Trondheim. Nevertheless, the levels of regional support do suggest that the Norwegian strategy is more anti-urban than that of Sweden and designed more to favour the stabilization of the rural community.

(4) Finland

Policies in Finland are concerned with the same problem as its Nordic neighbours, that of a southward drift of people. Aid for industrial development from *Kehitysalverahasto*, the regional development fund, is most favourable in the north and north-east besides the Aaland Islands. The area bounded by Oulu, Pori and Savonlinna has smaller grants but has taken the lion's share of successful developments, cash and jobs created, including the regional development fund's office at Kuopio. However, the social democrat element in the Finnish coalition are more concerned with the impact which the 5500 schemes might have had if they had been located in Helsinki or Turku, where some of the industrial areas are showing signs of decay not unfamiliar in other cities where decentralization has been encouraged by regional policies.

(5) Denmark

Denmark provides a further example of the dominance of one particular regional problem in urban development, namely, the overwhelming importance of Copenhagen which houses approximately one-third of all the Danish population.

The original Regional Development Act dates from 1958 but the latest Act on National and Regional Planning in 1973 excluded Greater Copenhagen which was the subject of entirely separate provision in 1974. The reforms of planning have tended to reinforce the need to cater for the concentration of population in the capital region, the three major centres Aarhus, Aalborg and Odense and the other 20 medium-sized towns of 20–80 000 people. More responsibility has been devolved to the new administrative units (Ministry of Housing, 1976).

(6) Belgium

The liberal philosophy that had created the Belgian state out of the Greater Netherlands did not encourage central planning and Belgium has been slower than its Dutch neighbour to enact regional planning legislation. The Regional Development Act of 1959 and 1966 and the national plan of 1962 were, however, a beginning upon which subsequent legislation, such as the 1974 law for open space preservation, has been built.

In Belgium, however, the problem of planning the national capital has dominated the attention of the country's city planners, in this case not been only because of its size relative to the other Belgian cities, but also because of the drastic constraints imposed by the country's nationality dispute. Although Brussels lies to the north of the line demarcating Flemings from Walloons, it has been officially designated as a bilingual area since 1932. Legal bilingualism has not, however, prevented immigration, or the aspirations of parents, and the influence of international firms and institutions have all encouraged a trend towards the consolidation of the French language at the expense of the Flemish. The intractable planning problem arises with the physical expansion of the city into the surrounding province of Brabant. Such urban spread, which has occurred in the other major European cities, is unacceptable to the Flemish politicians who fear the consequences of an extension of French-speaking suburbs into previously Flemish-speaking rural areas. The threat of the spreading Brussels 'oil slick' provokes a determined and sometimes violent response. On the other side, attempts to contain the legally defined city of Brussels within the 'iron collar' of its 50-year old boundaries is seen as unrealistic, and unfair to those French-speaking citizens whose suburbs are still legally defined as being within the Flemish language area, with obvious consequences especially for education. Numerous attempts to seek compromises that would allow the existence of some form of 'Greater Brussels' have ended in failure, frustration on both sides, and the fall of more than one Belgian government (Ashworth, 1979).

The nationality dispute has not only hindered the effective planning of the capital but is also always a consideration that haunts the planning of the other Belgian cities. The necessity for governments to be seen to be fair in the allocation of resources between the two national groups adds to regional planning a criterion other than need (Riley and Ashworth, 1975). It also enhances the importance of Antwerp and Liège as 'national' capitals, and in one dramatic instance led to the creation of a new town—Louvain-La-Neuve—when the French-speaking faculties of Louvain University were compelled to migrate across the language frontier.

(7) *Netherlands*

In sharp contrast to its Benelux partner, the Netherlands has evolved an urban system in which there is no single primate city but rather a primate urban region composed of three large and many more small and medium-sized towns located close to but separate from each other. On the national scale, Dutch thinking has focused on two obsessions, the preservation of the unique character of the urbanized western provinces of North and South Holland and Utrecht, and the stimulation of the economically and spatially peripheral regions of the south, east and north.

Detailed discussion of the planning policies for the Metropolitan West Netherlands is found in Chapter 11, but the accommodation within this urban region of around one-third of the Dutch population, and the country's most important industrial concentrations, has given planning policies a national rather than purely local significance. Planning objectives for the west have altered little since 1945, but the chosen instruments for their achievement have varied considerably; they have swung decisively in recent years away from policies of persuasion by providing incentives and financial support for the periphery, towards policies of prevention of growth in the west.

Policies for the stimulation of the peripheral regions have been reformulated many times since the war (Tamsma, 1972), but have consistently focused on the development of urban centres, variously termed, according to the fashion of the time, *growth poles* (*groeckernen*), *growth cities* (*groeikernen*) and *counter-magnets* (*tegenpolen*). There has been considerable uncertainty, however, about the sort of urban hierarchy that will most promote economic growth. Opinion during most of the 1960s favoured the development of a large number of relatively small centres, in accord with the principles of *grouped deconcentration* favoured by the Second Structure Plan (1966). More recently, opinion has swung in favour of the encouragement of fewer but larger urban centres and the concentration of investment in such urban regions as Groningen and Delfzijl–Eemshaven in the north, Arnhem–Duiven–Westervoort in the east and Breda and Eindhoven–Helmond in the south (Rijksplanologische Dienst., 1976).

The link between regional and urban planning is perhaps more evident in the Netherlands than in the larger West European countries. The size of the country makes it particularly difficult to distinguish between policies designed for the city-region and those concerned with regional imbalance on the national scale. Similarly the success of Dutch regional planning—and it can be shown to have had a large measure of success in reversing the internal migration flow and equalizing standards of living and welfare between regions—can be attributed to change at the city-region level. The expansion of the West Metropolitan area southwards into the northern part of the Rhine Delta, north-eastwards into Flevoland, eastwards towards Arnhem–Nijmegen and south-eastwards into Brabant, has improved the economic situation of the more accessible parts of the peripheral regions. Only the Westerschelde area in Zeeland, the provinces of Friesland and Gronigen in the north, the old textile area in Twente in the east, and the old coalmining area of South Limburg in the south remain outside the metropolitan orbit. It was made clear by the van Agt government in 1979 that the economic future of these regions must now largely depend on the economic success of the country as a whole, rather than on large-scale decentralization of functions from the west.

(8) France

In France the national policy was designed to limit the growth of Paris which like the

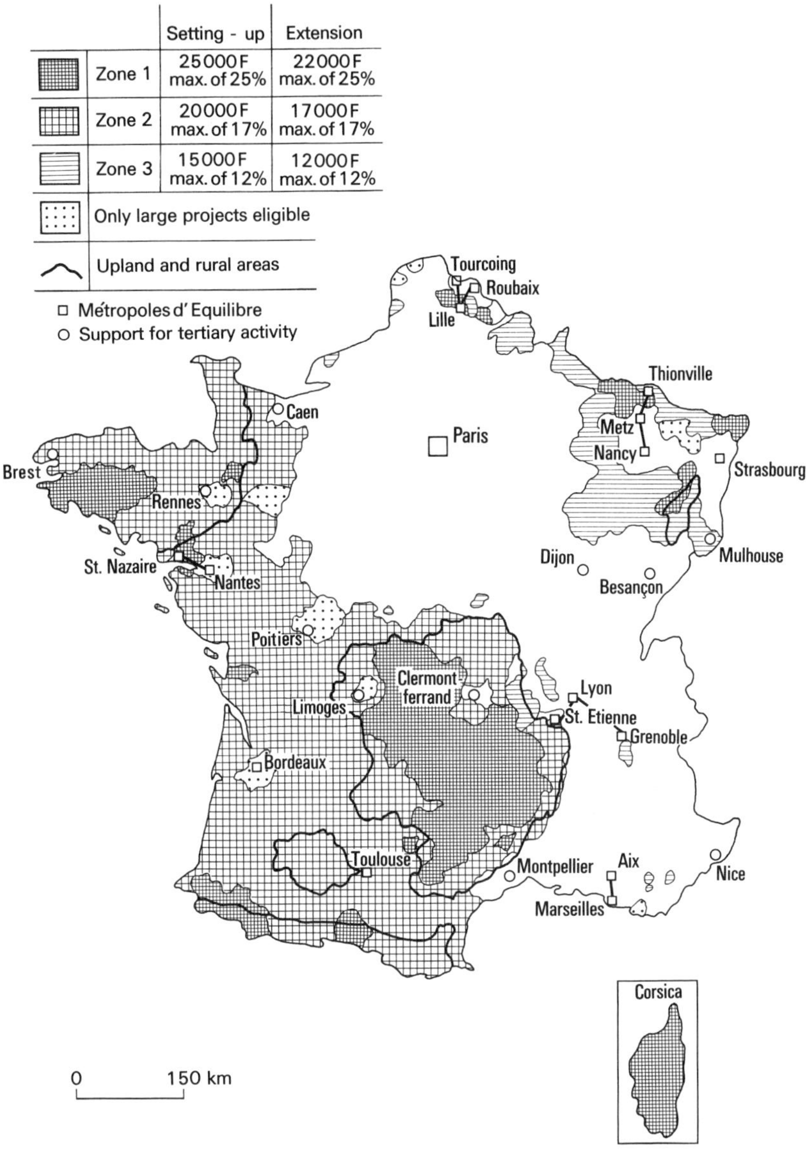

Figure 10.5 Urban and regional development policies in France

capitals of the Scandinavian countries was dominating the country. The concern was most aptly expressed in the title of Gravier's book in 1947, *Paris et le désert Français.* The regional policy outcome in 1964 was the creation of the eight *métropole d'équilibre* as counter-growth magnets that would take a share of employment growth, particularly in the tertiary and quaternary sectors, which might otherwise have gone to Paris. The centres themselves were an assorted collection of urban areas ranging from single nodes such as Marseilles to 'composite nodes' such as Lyons–St Étienne–Grenoble (Chapter 12) or Nancy–Metz–Thionville. These provisions within the fifth-plan period were an attempt to distribute services more rationally throughout France. An attempt to give greater status to the regions was the creation in 1964 of 22 regions empowered to coordinate regional development, financed since 1972 by a modest budget.

However, the policy of *métropoles d'équilibre* did not meet with great success, and by 1970 it was being questioned especially by those who favoured the development of what was termed the *ville moyenne* or town of from 50 000 to 200 000 people. An influential report to the *Conseil économique et social* (1973) suggested that the aims of regional planning, especially the maintenance of the population and infrastructure of the peripheral regions, would be better served by encouraging the development of the smaller towns rather than the less numerous and more widely spaced *métropoles.* It has been strongly argued by commentators such as Lajugie (1974) that the smaller urban centres are better equipped both to fulfil the goals of French regional planning and provide for a richer quality of life for citizens: *'L'emploi, l'habitat et les equipments collectifs, l'appareil d'education et de formation, les moyens de communication, les relations avec l'espace rural, tel sont les principaux domaines sur lesquels l'effort devra porter si l'on veut mettre les villes moyennes, en mesure d'assumer leur role dans l'aménagement du territoire'* (Lajugie, 1974). These arguments, he would add, have been convincingly endorsed by the French people. For whereas the population of the Paris agglomeration grew by 1.3 per cent per annum in the 1960s, and the population of towns under 80 000 by only 1.1 per cent, the *villes moyennes* grew by an average of 2.1 per cent per annum.

On the other hand, there was a feeling that the role of Paris as an international centre had to be strengthened (DATAR, 1973). Therefore the old strategy was no longer given priority in the Sixth Plan and the emphasis shifted to the medium-sized towns with contracts to develop signed with the state. In all, just over 50 contracts have been signed (Chaline, 1978). Even this policy, designed to spread growth, was felt to be confined to too few urban areas and in 1975 a third strategy for assistance to small towns was initiated. By 1978 agreements had been signed with 140 towns. This latest strategy reflects an increasing polarization of French regional planning, first to supporting Paris the international centre (the subsidy for Paris transport is still greater than the regional premiums), and second an increasing emphasis on the rural areas where much governmental political support could still be found. So the medium and small towns' strategies cannot be understood without also noting the policy for preserving coastal areas introduced in 1976, the mountain area policy of 1977, and the declining rural areas policy.

French policy has succeeded in slowing the growth of Paris, and it has enhanced its reputation as an international centre for the multinational companies due in part to a policy of making the French computerized telephone system among the most modern in the world and so proving more effective than London in this one apparently small, but very important factor in office location decisions. On the other hand, the rapid growth of Alsace, Provence and the Côte d'Azur plus the positive migration balances of the Massif Central and the south-west in the period from 1968 to 1975 do suggest some success. Some would point to the policy to date as a purely economic phenonemon, while socially and culturally there are still great differences between Paris and the *désert* (Chaline, 1978). These policies, which reflect the evolving thinking of French governments that have been consistently centre-right in political stance, are the context for Parisian planning (Chapters 11 and 13) and those of Lyons, Grenoble, Lille, Rouen and La Grand Motte (Chapter 12).

(9) Italy

Italian urban and regional planning has been traditionally weak in comparison with that of France or the Scandinavian countries primarily due to deep-seated weaknesses in the administrative structures despite many attempts by both the ruling and opposition parties in parliament. The result was that planning too often became an emergency response to pressing problems and responsibility is divided among governmental agencies, a process aptly termed 'Balkanization' by Nanetti (1972). In 1972, town planning became the responsibility of the regions. The problem of the south has dominated the regional programme but much of the help has concentrated on the rural areas, despite the emphasis given to urban development in the Bari–Brindisi–Taranto region.

It was not until 1965 that Italy passed its first National Economic Plan, 1970 before regional administrations had been formed to provide autonomous administration of economic development, and much later before this reorganization was actually implemented. This reform gave Italy a three-tier local government structure, composed of commune, province and region. Although this provided a range of scales for government services, including planning, it has proved to have a number of weaknesses. The communes, at the lowest level, range in size from groupings of rural settlements to large cities such as Milan or Turin with a proud tradition of independent nationhood. The province is both too large to attract the loyalty that is given to the commune and also generally too small to be the unit of effective regional planning. The region is the newest authority and has yet to be accepted in the popular imagination. The possibilities for confusion, bureaucratic procrastination, and conflict between the three levels are obvious, and compounded in a country where centralized government was imposed on traditions of local independence only a hundred years ago.

The second national plan of 1970 did include urban areas and noted the need to control the growth of the largest cities. This was an admission that policies had been ineffective in slowing the growth of Rome (2.8 million), Milan (1.7 million), Naples (1.2 million) and Turin (1.2 million) and that the various local controls were powerless to structure effectively urban growth, primarily due to a lack of local finance. Local planning was relatively uncoordinated except for some intercommunal schemes to create outlying business centres (*centri direzionali*) as in Rome or to build selfcontained peripheral large-scale developments (*quartieri organici*), as around Rome, Bologna and Milan.

The overriding dominance of the north-south distinction makes it difficult to generalize about the character of Italian cities or the nature of their planning. The problems and responses of Milan have more in common in many ways with the cities of central Europe such as Munich or Zurich than with Mediterranean Naples or Syracuse. Nevertheless, despite the inability of Italian regional planning either to slow the growth of the large cities or to effectively reduce the Mezzogiorno problem, there is still a strong tradition in favour of state control. The tradition of the sovereign state has its origins in the Roman Empire and is part of the traditions of the Catholic church. It embodies the view that the state is above the individual view or that of sectors of society and that the state operates more competently and satisfies a more genuine public interest. Thus the reforming zeal of the socialist governments of the cities of the Romagna such as Bologna can be seen as sectoral, and state policies which severely limit the power of the local authority as policies in the public interest. On the other hand, the growth pole policy in the Mezzogiorno has had a definite impact on urban development of a few cities, such as Taranto and Bari.

Federal Influences on Urban Planning

(1) Switzerland

The relationship between national economic, social and regional policies and urban development is different again within the federal states. For in countries such as Switzerland, Austria and West Germany the relationship between the various tiers of government are enshrined in the constitution, with the result that increased central government activity is vigorously opposed at the more local level. Switzerland has often been called a 'Referendum democracy' and the 1976 federal *Raumplanungsgesetz* (Area Planning Law) was a casualty of such a referendum (Elasser, 1979a and b). The strength in regional planning terms still rests with the 26 cantons and the 3000 *gemeinden* and the federal government confines its regional policies to the mountain region and the Jura watchmaking area (*Uhrenregion*). At the cantonal level there are disparities in taxation and wealth which lead to disparities in urban growth.

Regional development has concentrated on three issues. First, the problems of the mountain areas, including the Jura, which cover 66 per cent of Switzerland and are the home for 10 per cent of the population, are the prime target for government coordination. Secondly, the government is aware of the strong city–town division and the problems of the rural areas in an affluent society that must be able to survive in isolation in wartime (Burtenshaw, 1970). The third problem is that of the cities and agglomerations, five of which—Zurich, Basle, Bern, Geneva and Lausanne—house 30 per cent of the country's 6.3 million people. Here the emphasis is on the rapid growth of the city-regions (710 000 living in the Zurich city-region in 1978), the consequent problems of the pressure on the central area, transport and pollution, and increasing segregation of the immigrant workforce that comprises 15 per cent of the population (Elasser, 1979). The settlement structure of Switzerland is shown in Figure 10.6. It distinguishes the five major centres, the development bands linking these, the fourteen medium agglomerations and 34 minor agglomerations and urban areas. Also plotted are those areas regarded as underprovided with urban facilities. Swiss planners would like to see a reduction in the concentration of populations and employment in the five major agglomerations, but they realize that as long as cantonal powers exceed those of the confederation then a truly national rather than 'Vaudoise', 'Genevan' or 'Basler' policy will be difficult to achieve.

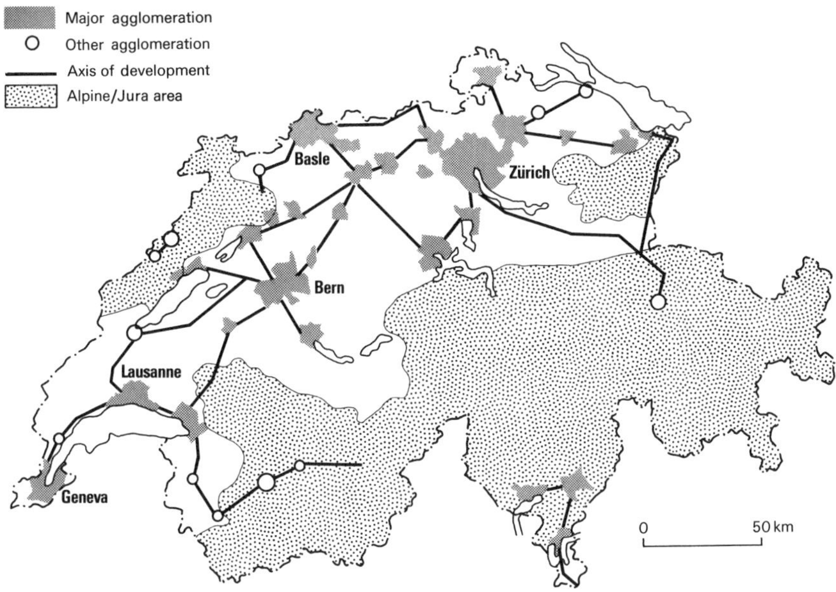

Figure 10.6 The settlement structure of Switzerland

(2) *Federal Republic of Germany*

The history of Germany, as firstly an agglomeration of a large number of important and lesser kingdoms and principalities and, more recently, a federal state, has meant that West Germany like Switzerland has developed an urban and regional policy that reflects the imprint of history and present national ideology. In the immediate postwar years there was a dominant mood that saw planning as an evil associated with the Nazi period and as a result any physical planning was purely local and rarely related to national needs other than that of re-establishing urban life as rapidly as possible. Once the *Wirtschaftswunder* had passed and some of the realities of late twentieth-century economic and social change began to emerge in the late 1960s coinciding with the rise to power of the SPD (social democratic party), the need for an overall urban and regional programme became more apparent. Besides the definition of regional action programmes that encompassed problem rural areas, the politically sensitive eastern border region and declining industrial centres, the federal programmes also defined the major population concentrations and growth areas (*Verdichtungsräume*) which could include development regions, and the major axes (*Achsen*) that linked these to other cities and towns in the hierarchy (Figure 10.7).

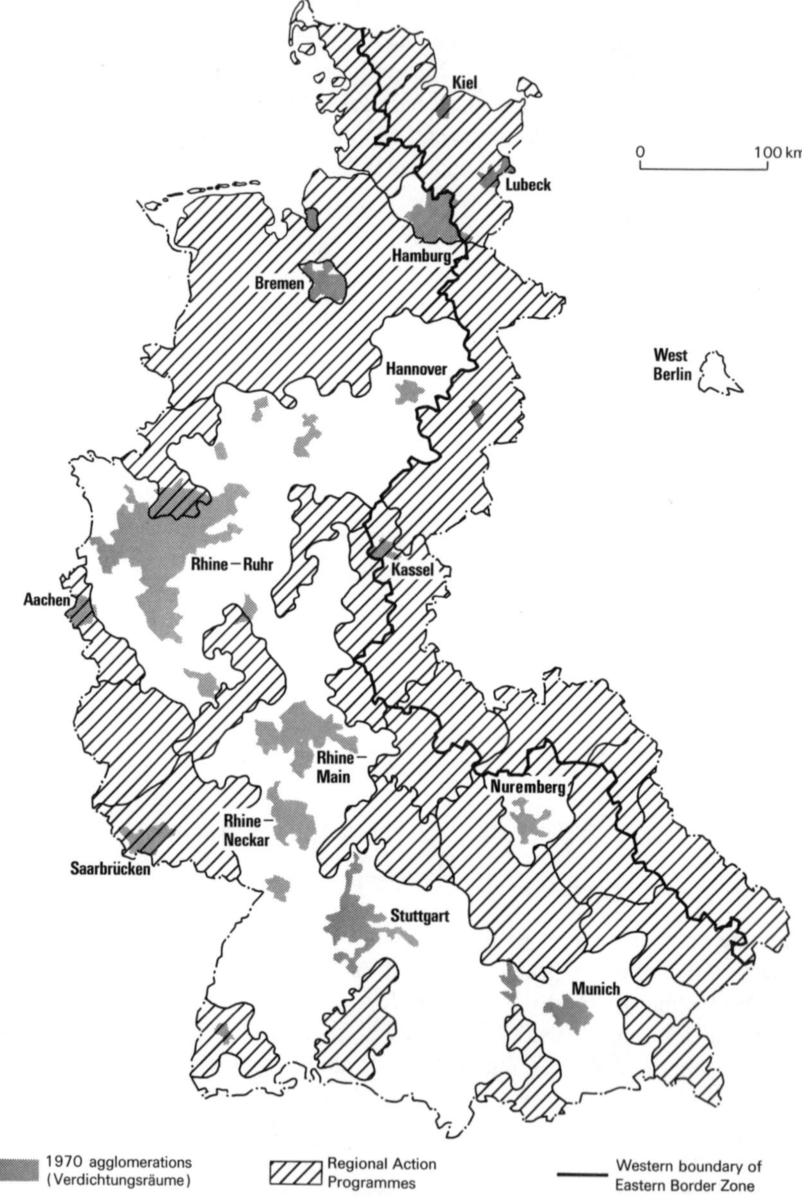

Figure 10.7 West German regional development and growth zones (from Burtenshaw, D. (1974) *An Economic Geography of West Germany*, by permission of Macmillan, London and Basingstoke)

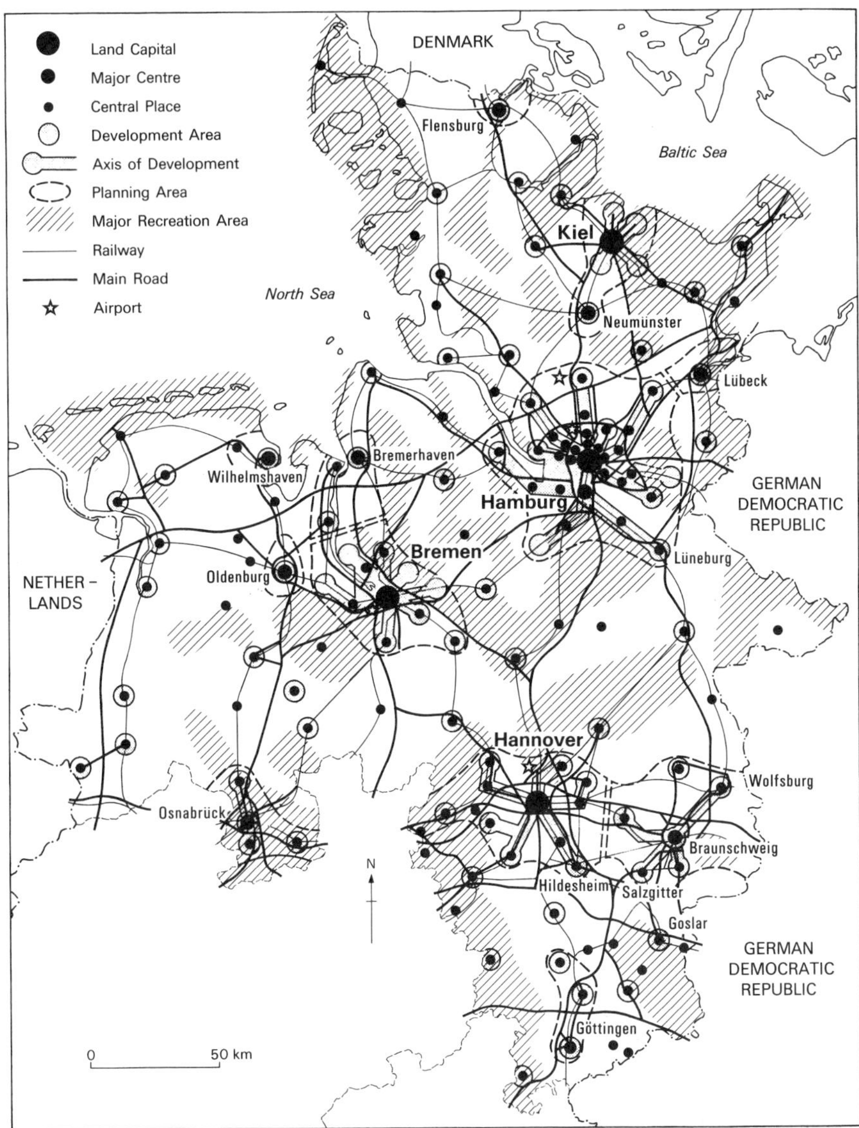

Figure 10.8 *Raumordnungspläne* for four north German *Länder*

Verdichtungsräume were first designated in 1968 and were the latest attempt to define the regions of most rapid urban change and development that go back to Isenberg's 1957 *Ballungsraum* and before that Schott's *Agglomerationen* of 1912. It is these twin concepts that then govern each *Land's* attempts to prepare a *Raumordnungsplan* which outlines the basic structure of spatial organization including urban development. Figure 10.8 illustrates the main aspects of the *Raumordnungspläne* for the four north German *Länder* which have a bearing on the city structure plans of Bremen, Hamburg and Hannover considered in Chapter 12. While the proposed structure on the map might look organized, the political rivalry between the *Länder* has brought agreement on proposals more quickly between Hamburg and Schleswig-Holstein than Hamburg and Lower Saxony (Bahr, 1976; and Hollmann, 1977). In the 1970s the growing emphasis on the quality of life ('Quality of life is more than standard of living'—Abress, 1974) resulted in the introduction of further policies for urban renewal and improvement which, like the earlier policies, continued to be administered by the federal *Länder* each with their own political complexion.

The emphasis on a federal structure has maintained West Germany as a multicentred urban system undominated by any one city as are Britain, France, Denmark or Austria. The largest urban agglomerations, Rhine–Ruhr and Rhine–Main, contain respectively the capital Bonn, only officially recognized in 1971, and the commercial centre Frankfurt. However, the rank-size order is dominated by West Berlin, a city whose unique political and geographical position separates it from the national system. The *Land* capitals have added status and as a result a greater diversity of employment, but not all are as high in the rank-size order as Hamburg (2nd) and Munich (3rd). Kiel, for instance, is 20th and Wiesbaden is 23rd. Other centres such as Cologne (4th), Nuremberg (11th) and Mannheim(17th) have remained prominent, with activities of national significance located in them such as the insurance offices in Cologne and the federal labour office at Nuremberg. Thus, in contrast to many of her neighbours, West Germany has developed a much more polycentric city system (Michael, 1979).

(3) Austria

The third federal state, Austria, has also devolved planning matters to the nine *Länder* although there is an overall coordination role for federal regional planning. Urban planning had its origins in Vienna in the nineteenth century, as we saw in Chapter 2, although its modern origins lie in the period after the First World War when Vienna became the capital of a country one-eighth the size of the old Austro-Hungarian empire. Vienna has continued to dominate the urban system, housing 20 per cent of the population, although its dominance has lessened slightly with decentralization. Only since the signing of the Austrian State Treaty in 1955 has urban and regional planning developed, at first to provide housing for refugees and to equalize growth between the regions and especially the problem *Ö Grenz*, the eastern frontier zone (Figure 10.9). Thus the growth of *Land* capitals such as Salzburg, Klagenfurt, and Bregenz, which are part of the seven recognized *Ballungsräume* growth areas, has been encouraged in preference to maintaining people in the rural areas. Decentralization from the administrative area of Vienna to the surrounding districts is fostered alongside a policy to give the city a new international role commensurate with the country's neutrality (Burtenshaw, 1981). As in West Germany, history and the search for a new national ideology in the wake of the tragedies of two wars has produced a distinctive national urban and regional strategy.

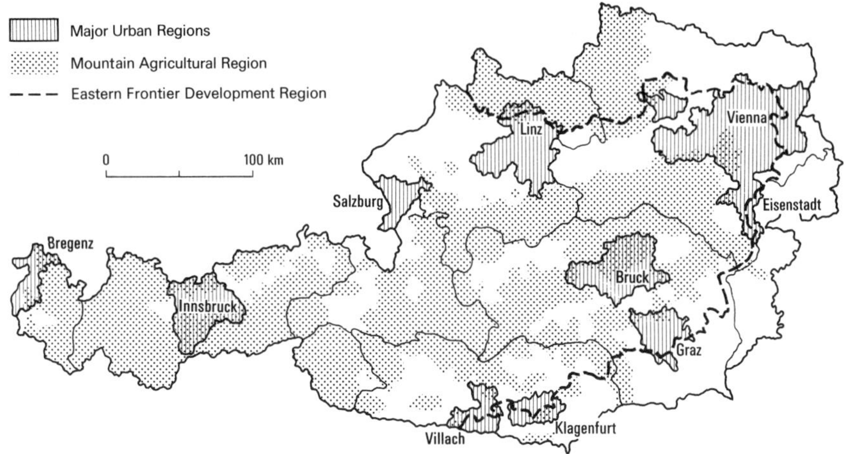

Figure 10.9 Regional development and growth zones in Austria (reproduced by permission of: Austrian Conference on Regional Planning; authors: R. Wurzer and R. Gisser)

In the following two chapters the city plans for a selection of West European cities will be discussed. The range of national, regional and urban planning policies outlined here have created a context for urban planning, sometimes encouraging urban growth while at other times and in other locations acting as a brake on urban development. Few urban planning strategies can be viewed in isolation from their national context. The basic distinctions between federal and centralized states, between ideologies of social democracy and conservatism and between city-centred and rural support policies will obviously colour the planning initiatives of the West European cities.

CHAPTER 11

Planning Major Metropolitan Areas

Plans aimed at the control of the growth of major metropolitan regions are by no means new. In West Europe, however, it is only during the last half century that a number of countries have made concerted efforts to direct the future growth and form of any major city. Such efforts have usually involved the planning of the capital city. In some cases the priority has been to curb its growth in an attempt to redistribute it and revitalize declining areas elsewhere in the country. For instance, the rapid growth of London and south-east England in the interwar period focused attention on the planning of the capital and its region, but at the same time gave rise to plans to inject new growth into ageing industrial areas such as Merseyside, South Wales and north-east England. In other cities, such as Paris, this secondary consideration linked to regional problems came later and the early plans in the 1930s sought merely to direct the manner in which the city was growing, particularly because uncontrolled development was rapidly absorbing the surrounding rural area. Copenhagen in the 1940s was presenting just such problems and a plan was introduced to harness the development of the city which was already overdominant within the urban hierarchy of Denmark. In this chapter the metropolitan scale of urban planning is discussed in terms both of the common characteristics which may be seen to run through many of the individual plans and of the distinctive approaches of each of the plans.

Peter Hall (1977) has contended that, 'Urban decentralisation is now a world-wide force in all highly industrialised countries'. It is difficult to challenge this contention and what is intriguing in a European context is the varying manner in which this force has been met, either through active promotion of decentralization policies or alternatively by strongly restrictive measures already discussed in the context of tertiary and quaternary activities (Chapter 4).

The planning of major metropolitan areas can be seen to have evolved through a number of distinct phases. Initially came the realization of the need to plan for future growth as these urban centres became increasingly dominant. Then specific plans were introduced to cater for this rapid urban development. The early plans, such as those for both Paris and London, envisaged the restriction of growth and the imposition of population limits on the metropolitan region under scrutiny. Later plans acknowledged that such approaches were not feasible and concentrated instead on directing growth along rational lines. There was considerable variation, however, in the way the newly acknowledged inevitable growth would be accommodated. In the event, many of these plans have been proved to be somewhat exaggerated in their population forecasts, bringing about a general reappraisal of their important underlying assumptions during the 1970s. This reappraisal marks the most recent stage in the evolution of metropolitan planning, and in some cases has given opportunity for new priorities to be established in the formulation of the revised plans. Priorities concerned with conservation in the broadest sense have replaced those concerned with providing the structure to accommodate vast new populations. In the process, it has enabled the organic tradition of planning, outlined in Chapter 2, to replace more dogmatic and tightly circumscribed forms of planning. It should be noted, however, that there are significant differences in the degree to which these new approaches have been adopted within West European states.

Not all cities have gone through these clearly defined phases in the production of their broad strategic plans. There can be little doubt, however, that the need for planning has changed rapidly from the postwar explosion of many of these centres, and the consequent need for stringent control and direction coupled with the desire to rebuild cities fit for the late twentieth century, to the need for a more measured adjustment of the urban system which characterizes today's planning of the major metropolitan areas. This is not to say that the urgency has been lost, but that it now stems from persisting imbalances within the urban system rather than from explosive growth.

Early Planning Directions—the Awakening to the Problems

In the case of many cities in West Europe, the interwar period demonstrated a clear need for measures to be taken to control their growth and logically the economic activities which gave rise to that growth. In Britain, the introduction of the Industrial Transference Board in 1928 and the Special Areas Act of 1934 introduced the concept of areas in need of special assistance to combat decline in the face of relatively strong economic and demographic growth in the south-east region in general and of the London area in particular. It was followed by the Barlow Commission Report in 1940 which was the background to the Distribution of Industry Act of 1945. McCrone (1970) regards the Barlow Report as ahead of its time because it introduced ideas that were not brought into perspective until the 1960s. In particular, 'it regarded the congestion problem of some cities and the unemployment of the depressed areas as different aspects of the same problem'. At the base of the 1945 legislation, as its *raison d'être*, lay the overwhelming dominance of London in the growth sectors of the economy and the need to evolve a more equitable distribution of economic activity.

The physical growth of London during the interwar period had also been dramatic, with the creation of vast areas of medium-density housing tripling the urbanized area between 1921 and 1939. The need for some degree of control was obvious and the possibility of planning the capital in some measure was given added impetus by wartime destruction. The control came in 1943 in the form of Patrick Abercrombie's County of London Plan. On the basis of official population estimates, the plan assumed that there would be no appreciable increase in population. It endeavoured, however, to provide for a lower density of urban development and some relief of inner city congestion. Outward growth was restricted by the establishment of the green belt, first defined by a parliamentary act in 1938. This belt was subsequently increased in extent so that it now encompasses a zone some nine kilometres in width. Such control had to be complemented by provision for some growth elsewhere and Abercrombie proposed the establishment of a series of new towns located beyond the green belt. These were to take a significant share of the 'overspill' of London, estimated by the plan to be in excess of a million. The concept of a green belt, with satellite new towns is very much in keeping with the utopian tradition of planning, although in practice there were obvious problems.

Abercrombie was incorrect in making assumptions based on growth forecasts utilizing trends of the 1930s on the growth of London, which was in the event much stronger than anticipated. Thus, far from his plan solving London's problems, it could do no more than impose a partially rational structure on the growth of the city as it continued to grow in the postwar period, both from natural increase and, at least in the early years of the period, by inmigration. Added weight was given to the planner to zone development following the 1947 Town and Country Planning Act.

The Parisian experience was not dissimilar to that of London, although its interwar growth was even more anarchic than that of London. London's new housing estates were sometimes elaborate in design, but they were served by improved arterial roads and by public transport routes such as those of the expanding underground and Southern Railway electrified routes (Hall, 1969). In contrast, uncontrolled development of Parisian suburbs with the purchase and development of indidual plots of land, *lotissements*, was commonplace. The uncoordinated development created the chaotic *système pavillonaire*, rarely served by any good public transport service and often not even provided with good made-up road surfaces. As early as 1928 a planning authority, the *Comité Supérieur de l'Aménagement et l'Organisation Générale de la Région Parisienne* (*CARP*) was charged with producing a general development plan for the Paris region. The result, the Prost–Dausset Plan gained government approval in 1939, its aims including the control of the development of *lotissements* through the designation of building zones. In practice, however, little was achieved before war intervened and eventually created new planning priorities in the whole of postwar France.

Note, however, that just as future growth predictions in London had certainly been conservative, so in Paris the relatively modest growth in the period before 1939 had led to expectations of a continuation in the low growth rate. By 1956, this optimism had been proved to be ill-founded and a new master plan was deemed necessary. The new plan, the *Plan d'Aménagement et d'Organisation Générale de la Région Parisienne* (*PADOG*), was approved in 1960 and contained proposals for a growth of a million in the population of the Paris region from 1960–70. It put forward proposals embodying some decentralization of employment and an improvement in the transport infrastructure, including the *Boulevard Périphérique*, completed in the early 1970s (Chapter 5). In addition, it proposed a massive urban renewal programme linked to the creation of new nodes of development within the existing urban area. However, it was to be supplanted within 5 years by a new plan for Paris, discussed below. One of the main reasons for the necessity for the new plan lay in the assumption of the *PADOG* that growth could be limited to an increase of population of 100 000 per annum in the decade 1960–70. It was the assumption of low, controlled growth which proved to be false. Indeed, the period 1962–64 saw the Paris region growing by an average of 165 000 per annum, of which 65 000 was by natural increase, 50 000 by internal migration and 50 000 by repatriation from Algeria (Hall, 1977). Plainly, the original aim of containing Paris within the limits of the existing conurbation would never have been achieved.

The postwar period saw the awakening of interest elsewhere. A series of reports in the 1940s and 1950s examined the problems of overconcentration of population within the western provinces of the Netherlands, centred on what came to be called the Randstad. In the case of Stockholm, active planning of the city started somewhat earlier. Municipal action was considerably eased by a policy dating from 1904 in Stockholm of bringing land into municipal ownership, so that by the mid-1960s the city owned approximately 70 per cent of the suburban land within its boundaries. A regional plan was formulated and approved by the city by 1959 and given national approval by 1960.

Stockholm's growth has been relatively slow by West European standards but sufficiently rapid to concern the city authorities: population growth of 1.95 per cent per annum 1965–70 far exceeded that for the country as a whole for the same period (0.77 per cent). A new plan was required within 10 years, actually approved in 1970, for the 29 municipalities which laid rather less stress on predictions and more on policy directions. In the Swedish context it is important to note that planning has been traditionally permissive rather than authoritatively directional. The instruments of planning are restricted to setting constraints on land-use and controlling transport development. Even now the municipalities have a surprising degree of autonomy in the sphere of physical planning.

Finally, Copenhagen illustrates the manner in which the mid-twentieth-century reassessment of the scale of the problem of growth in large cities came about. Until the 1930s the development of Copenhagen was relatively restricted. A parliamentary decision in 1930 led to the electrification of the suburban railways with the first subway trains (*S-bane*) running on the new system in 1934. The new-found accessibility to the city-centre via the *S-bane* led to major urban growth, particularly around the new *S-bane* stations. Private bus lines operating on the periphery of the built-up area further promoted urban growth. Having incorporated many surrounding districts into the municipality at the turn of the century, Copenhagen spread rapidly into the new suburban areas; consequently the population rose rapidly and reached a million by 1940. A clear need for a stricter control and direction of growth was established. Although the city continued to purchase land for future growth in the surrounding areas, the surrounding municipalities themselves wanted to retain their independence. Nevertheless, coordination of urban development was clearly necessary, and in 1939 a metropolitan committee was established with a brief to prepare a constitution to govern intercommunal relations in the Copenhagen metropolitan region. Politically that was no easy task and, in fact, a final constitution did not emerge until 1973. However, the stimulus for action was evidently there and a regional planning committee was formed, with some limited initial results in the area of recreational planning before the war. After the war, in 1947, a regional plan for Greater Copenhagen was produced, the renowned 'Finger Plan' (see Figure 11.2), which was to serve as an unofficial blueprint or guideline for the city for the period until 1960, when it was superseded by a new plan. The 'Finger Plan' was a bold attempt to channel growth along particular axes of development, following the *S-bane* routes. A new plan was eventually necessary, however, as growth exceeded expectations and, as elsewhere, the new mobility brought by private car-ownership, created new pressures on the intervening rural land.

The awakening to the problems had taken place and the plans had begun to emerge. Admittedly many were based either on unsound assumptions concerning the ability to restrict development, or on predictions of growth which proved to be inaccurate, or on both, necessitating their replacement by new plans in the late 1950s or the 1960s. We may note, however, at this stage, that the projections on which these plans were based were to be in their turn also questioned, some with remarkable rapidity. A further important lesson learnt in this early period related to the administrative machinery called upon to implement any plan. The multiplicity of authorities, in many instances, rendered effective planning at best inconvenient and at worst impossible. An essential prerequisite for effective metropolitan-scale urban planning was administrative reorganization and reform.

Local government reorganization has taken place in almost every major West European country since 1945. Generally this has resulted in a decrease in the number of small administrative units and the creation of larger more meaningful administrative units. An extreme example is that of Sweden which reformed its local government structure twice, in 1952 and 1964, progressively reducing the number of communes in the country from more than 2000 before 1952 to just over 1000, and to 282 in 1964. In respect to major metropolitan areas, however, the choice has generally been between amalgamation of existing units to form new units or systems involving voluntary cooperation between existing administrative bodies. Very often special attention has been paid to the metropolitan areas quite apart from the rest of the country. Thus, the Greater London Council was brought into being in 1965, 9 years before more general reform of local government in England and Wales. In 1971, a new county council for Greater Stockholm was created, although a considerable amount of local autonomy still rests with the local municipalities. Voluntary association may be illustrated by the Regional Planning Council for Copenhagen established in 1967 with representatives from the three metropolitan counties of Copenhagen, Frederiksberg and Roskilde together with the cities of Copenhagen and Frederiksberg. Perhaps the most complex reorganization was that which led to the new *départements* in the Paris region. Initially, in 1961, the *District de la Région Parisienne* was established, including within it the *départements* of Seine, Seine-et-Oise and Seine-et-Maine. Essentially, the new creation was a coordinating body for existing local authorities. Three years later, in 1964, two of the *départements* which had major problems on account of their size were subdivided into more manageable units to produce in the region as a whole a new administrative structure of eight *départements* including the *ville de Paris* as a separate *département* in its own right. Later, in 1966, the Paris region was designated as a higher level authority to coordinate regional activity, as part of a national system of planning regions. In 1972, it was renamed *la région de l'Île de France*. Local government reorganization has been a testimony to the fact that urban planning has had to look further than anachronistic boundaries of urban settlements to encompass the wider areas which need to be planned as a coordinated whole.

Characteristics of the Major Metropolitan Plans

The second generation of plans may be classified into three broad types although it should not be thought that these are mutually exclusive categories since some plans have characteristics typical of all three categories. First, there are those plans which have a series of preferential axes for new growth as their basic structure. An important accompanying advantage is the comparative ease of access to the open space between each major access, as well as the optimum use of transport corridors. A second category of plans may be termed polycentric, usually characterized by attempts to create a new pattern of urban centres through the designation of growth nodes, to counterbalance an overdominant centre. A third, more limited, category includes those where open space retention is the prime aim, governing all other characteristics of the plan, or at least severely restricting the available options. Examples of each of these will be examined in turn, drawing from the major cities which have been discussed in the first part of this chapter.

(1) Preferential Axes of Development

In the 1944 Greater London Plan, Abercrombie chose to limit the growth of London by the imposition of a green belt (HMSO, 1945). Later plans for directing growth on a broad regional scale of the whole of South-East England, but dominated by the metropolitan area, have generally emphasized the structural device of axial development. The green belt has remained as the most consistent element in the physical plans for the London region. In 1967, the concept of preferential axes of development were contained in the first report of the South-East Economic Planning Council, entitled *A Strategy for the South-East* (HMSO, 1967). It emphasized a series of sectors within the region, not with the intention of their being fully urbanized but to indicate the general direction of growth (Figure 11.1b). The proposals also incorporated the principle of growth centres originally introduced by the *South-East Study* in 1964 (HMSO, 1964) (Figure 11.1a). In the earlier document, new cities had been proposed at Newbury to the west of London, to the north at Bletchley and to the south-west in South Hampshire in the region of Portsmouth and Southampton. In addition, major town expansions were to be implemented at Stansted (Essex), Ashford (Kent), Ipswich, Northampton, Peterborough and Swindon. *A Strategy for the South-East* (1967) took a number of these and incorporated them into an axial structure with each axis terminating at a major node (see Figure 11.1b), some beyond the regional boundary. These plans in the 1960s were designed to house major population growth. For instance, the *South-East Study* was put forward on the assumption of an additional population of 3.5 million in the period 1964–81, two-

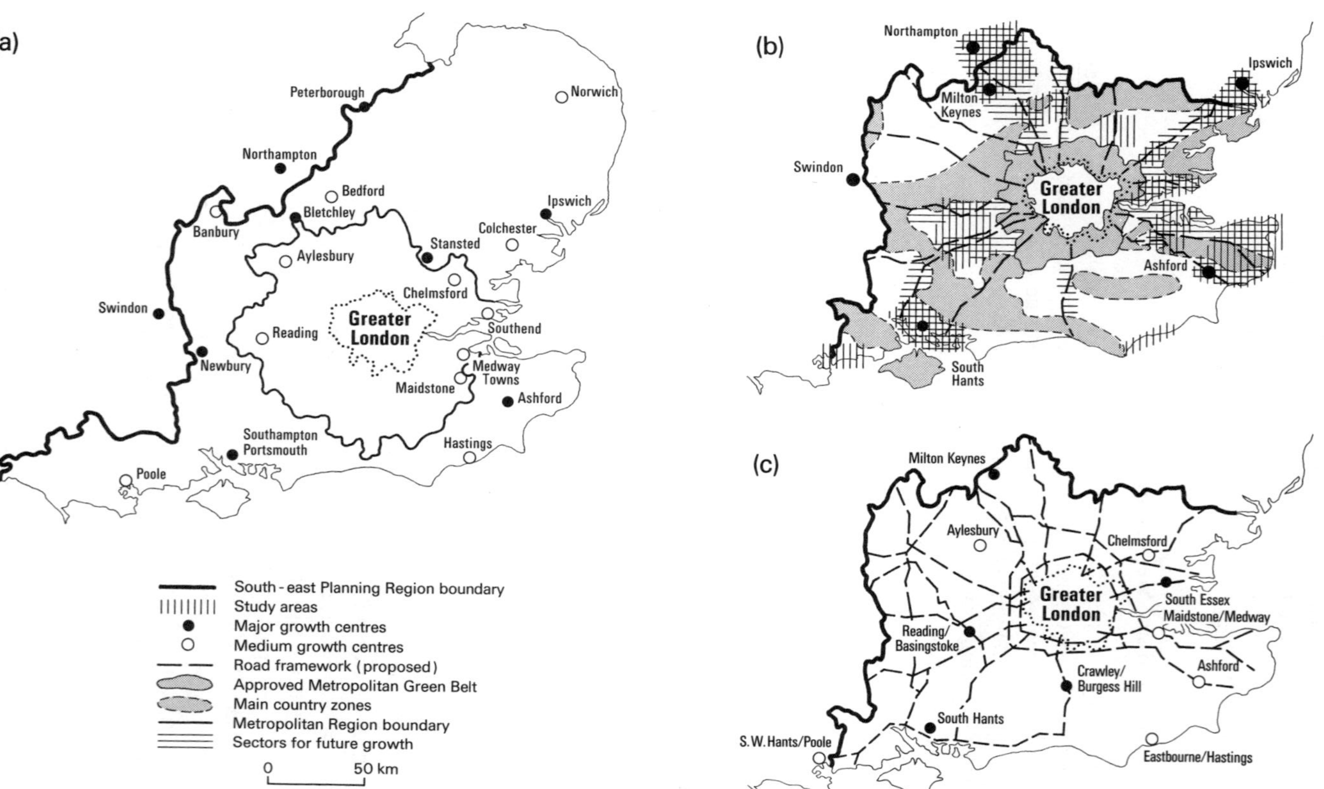

Figure 11.1 Plans for London and South-East England: (a) *South-East Study* (1964); (b) *Strategy for the South-East* (1967); (c) *Strategic Plan for the South-East* (1970) (all reproduced by permission of Greater London Council)

thirds of which would be through natural increases in the region. Later reappraisals were to revise such forecasts quite markedly.

The *Strategic Plan for the South East* (1970), compiled by the South East Joint Planning Team put its emphasis on a flexible framework but within the context of continued growth (HMSO, 1970). Individual urban areas were to be given clear identity and a limited number of major growth areas were to develop as more independent city regions. An improved regional transport network would be an integral part of such a plan as indicated in Figure 11.1c. The green belt, together with major tracts of rural land were to play an important role in maintaining a clearly identifiable structure of separate city-regions. In many respects, therefore, this plan continued to follow the basic principles of the earlier plans.

Rome experienced very rapid growth particularly in the outer suburbs in the period 1951–71. Between 1961 and 1971 the city's population grew by 27 per cent mainly as a result of inmigration from the south and Sardinia. Many settled in illegal settlements in the outer suburbs while most settled initially in the inner suburbs. The plans for future development have included a major axial development. It has been proposed to build a chain of new business centres 4 kilometres east of the city along a route linking the two ends of the *Autostrada del Sole.* The 'directive centres' which would upgrade the poorer eastern districts with offices, shops and hotels should relieve the centre where controls on commercial developments have existed since 1962. The eastern axis plan, despite its ambitious aims, is not meeting with much success mainly as a result of the illegal alteration of buildings in central Rome.

The original plan for Copenhagen accepted the notion of axial development from its earliest stages. Its 'Finger Plan' dating from 1947 was a clear attempt at confining growth to axes whilst leaving the intervening zones clear of major urban development (Figure 11.2). Whilst it was partially successful, the axes (or fingers)

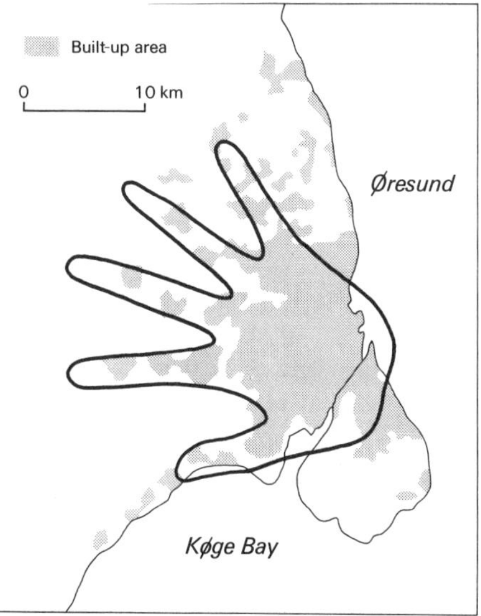

Figure 11.2 An outline of the 1947 'finger plan' for Copenhagen (reproduced by permission of Hovedstadsradet)

grew rather longer than originally planned and also broadened, partially destroying some of the advantages of axial development, particularly that of ease of access to open rural land. Thus, a new plan was prepared by 1960 entitled a *Preliminary Outline for the Copenhagen Metropolitan Region*, planning for growth through to 1980. It retained the concept of axes but implemented it in a more restrictive manner suggesting that the major part of the growth should be located in a main axis running south-westwards along Køge Bay. The growth was to be concentrated into two new towns, each with a population of 250 000. To the north, North Sjaelland was seen as an area to be preserved for recreational purposes. There is some departure from a purely axial structure in this plan. This comes firstly in the intention to establish two major nodes within the Køge Bay, and secondly in the proposal to create a new major urban centre of sufficient scale to relieve the city of Copenhagen itself of some of its functions. In the event, this part of the plan proved contentious and was not implemented, and in 1963 a modified provisional plan was agreed upon, termed the 'First Phase Plan'.

This plan stressed the importance of the development of the two axes from Copenhagen towards Roskilde and Køge. New subregional centres were also proposed at Høje–Tåstrup to the west and at Lyngby to the north. The Køge Bay development axis to the south-west was retained as an important element in the 'First Phase Plan', but with new growth concentrated not in two nodes but in ten new townships each with a population of 150 000. Unfortunately, two essential elements in the development of the axis, its rail and road transport links, were subject to considerable delays. The westward motorway, a key element in the entire plan, was not opened until 1973, while the new *S-bane* line was much delayed in its servicing of the entire length of the axis.

The axial plan, best epitomized by Copenhagen and by Stockholm with its similar pattern of new urban nodes along its *T-banen* system (Chapter 13), have obvious advantages of flexibility. Either axes can be developed in sequence as need dictates, or they may be extended to some degree to accommodate unexpectedly high growth. Recreational provision should be facilitated by ease of access to the interstitial open space. It might be noted, however, that there may be severe problems inherent in maintaining the separation of the axes and also of maintaining a viable farming structure in the face of close proximity of the urban area with associated problems of crop damage and trespass. Obviously, in order to be successful, such a policy requires strong planning measures to limit peripheral growth of the axes and coherent recreational policies to combine both viable agricultural use and recreational use of the intervening land. A further disadvantage lies in the potential for congestion towards the centre, where the axes converge. It could be argued that a strictly axial plan whose axes radiate from the central city is best suited to a medium-sized city such as Copenhagen or Stockholm, and elsewhere in larger metropolitan centres, other solutions have to be implemented.

(2) The Establishment of New Growth Nodes—Polycentric Plans

Certain plans for major centres have emphasized the need to restructure the distribution of urban functions by employing growth nodes into which a proportion of the new growth may be directed. The best example of this is undoubtedly that of Paris. It could be argued that the plan for Paris more properly fits into the previous section of plans dependent on preferential axes, but as we shall see there are good reasons for seeing it instead as a prime example of a polycentric plan.

The population growth rates in the early 1960s made it increasingly clear that a policy of restriction on the growth of Paris was impracticable. The *tâche d'huile* (oilslick) of Paris was inexorably spreading and required direction and, internally, a new structure. The new plan aimed at fulfilling these requirements was published in 1965 and superseded the *PADOG* described above. It was the *Schéma Directeur d'Aménagement et d'Urbanisme de la Région de Paris* (Figure 11.3a). There is little doubt that this plan was probably the most ambitious of its kind in the world. Set against the rapid economic growth of France of that period, it reflects a tremendous optimism that order could be brought to the chaotic urban pattern inherited from the interwar period, and that those mistakes would be forgotten as new development was carefully channelled into new and, in the event, often dramatic forms of urban development epitomized by some new town architecture (Chapter 13). It assumed a growth of population for the region from 9 million in 1965 to 14 million by the end of the century. It predicted particularly rapid rises in the tertiary employment sector and indeed the intervening period since 1965 has borne out that prediction to be accurate, since the Paris region now has approximately 40 per cent of French office jobs and about 60 per cent of its workers working in the tertiary sector. It foresaw a doubling of the urbanized area from approximately 1500 square kilometres to 2750 square kilometres. The need for new dwellings was exacerbated by the very high residential and occupancy rates prevailing in Paris as well as the need for new dwellings for the new growth in the population. Other priorities included an improvement in the transport network, which had already been the subject of close attention under the *PADOG* of 1960. It therefore proposed 900 kilometres of new urban motorways both circumferential and radial, together with the installation of a new express metro system, the *Réseau Express Régional* (RER), running both east–west from Marne-la-Vallée to St Germain-en-Laye and north–south through the region.

The direction for the new development contains two interrelated elements. Firstly, there is a clear attempt to orient development along preferential axes, for the advantages already described above. Secondly, however, the plan retains an element from the 1960 plan in its adoption of new suburban growth nodes. These take the two forms of *pôles réstructurateurs* in the existing suburbs and the more peripherally located new towns. While, as Figure 11.3 shows, the axes are important in giving directional structure to the plan, it can be strongly argued that at least thus far the establishment of the new towns and the suburban growth poles have been dominant in the implementation of the plan. The axes were selected to give a measure of reorientation to the dominant focus of Paris itself. Thus two axes were designated running tangentially to the existing agglomeration. One runs from the new town of Cergy-Pontoise in an east–south–easterly direction towards the second new town of Marne-la-Vallée. The other runs from the Seine valley near Mantes on the western

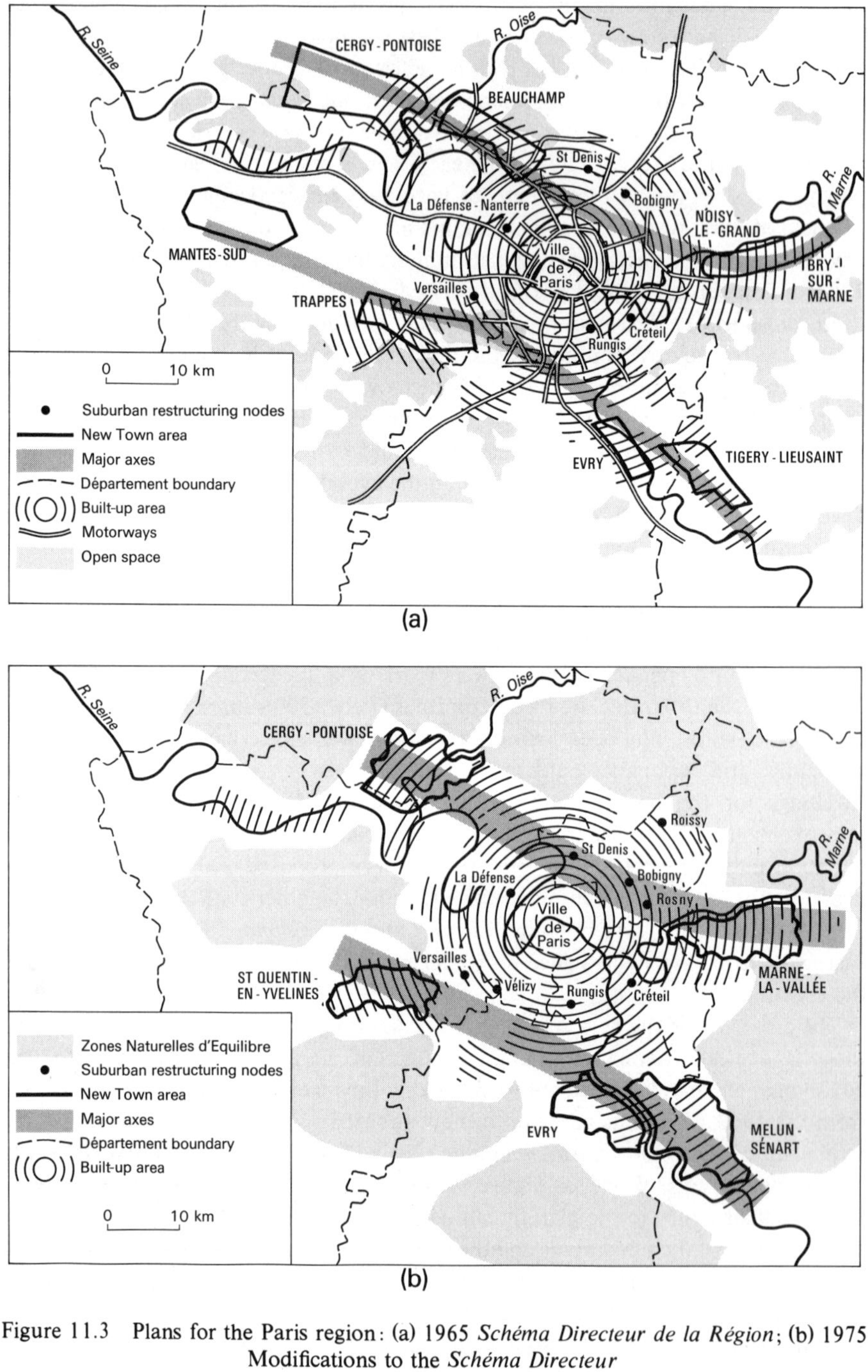

(a)

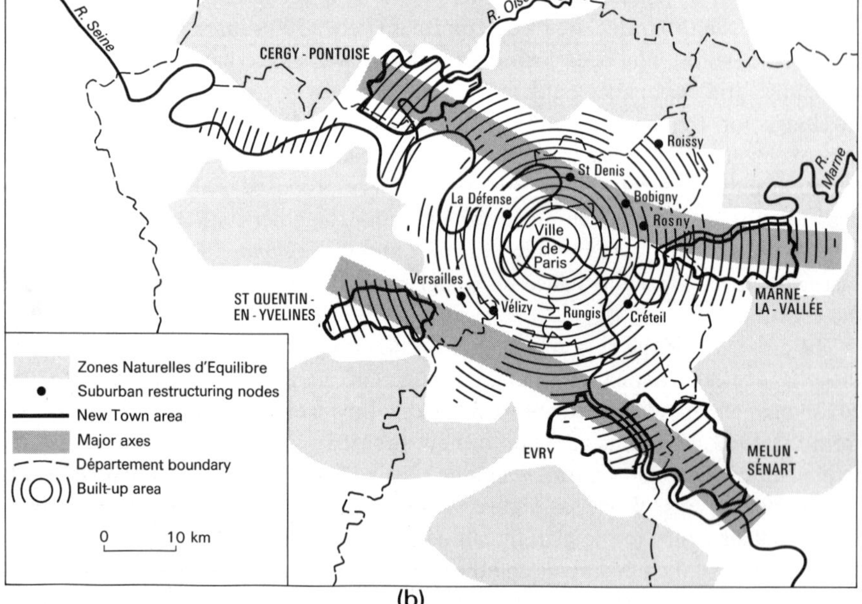

(b)

Figure 11.3 Plans for the Paris region: (a) 1965 *Schéma Directeur de la Région*; (b) 1975 Modifications to the *Schéma Directeur*

side of Paris, curving south-eastwards to terminate around the new towns of Evry and Melun-Sénart further upstream on the Seine from Paris itself. Both axes emphasize the broad regional direction of growth and the historic and future role of the Seine in guiding development and in a sense look westwards towards Rouen, the Lower Seine and eventually Le Havre. Nevertheless, as contended earlier, this is still essentially a plan based on the notion of polycentrism. The suburbs of Paris lacked almost completely the strong hierarchical structuring of service centres so characteristic of London or of many North American conurbations. The designation of new nodes has given to the city that essential structure and their creation has been a high priority in the past decade. They include La Défense (Chapter 4), Versailles–Vélizy–Villacoublay, which includes Versailles, one of the few obvious suburban nodes predating the plan, and St Denis, an industrial suburb to the north, located close to Le Bourget airport. Perhaps the most dramatic new suburban growth node is that of Créteil linked to Rungis and the new wholesale market complex to the west. Although the axes can be seen to link these and the new towns together (an exception being perhaps, La Défense), there can be little doubt that the principal tangible result of the 1965 *Schéma Directeur* will be the establishment of the embryonic polycentric structure for Paris. In fact, each of the new towns and suburban growth poles have been so effectively linked to central Paris, with few new or much improved transport links along the line of the axes, that it is difficult to see

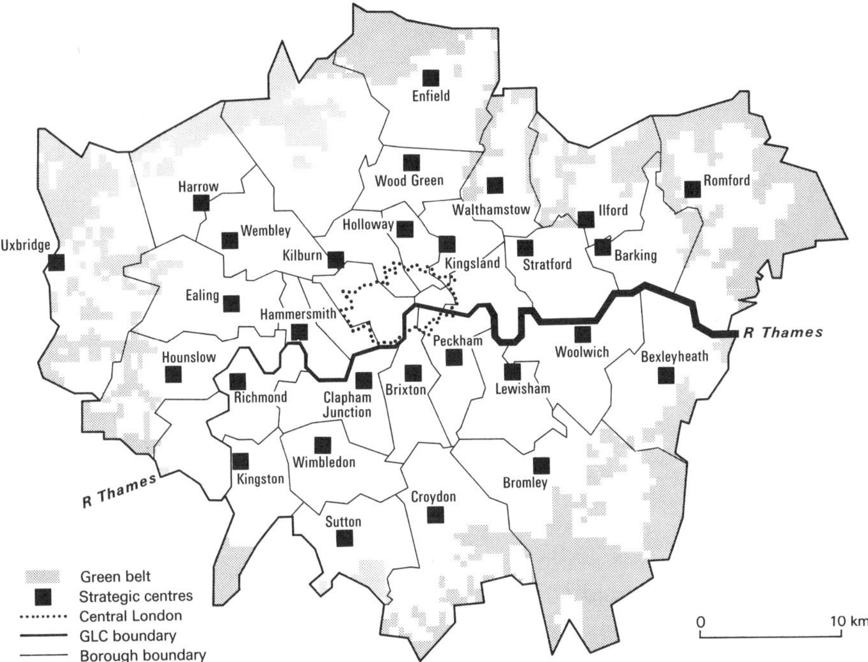

Figure 11.4 Strategic Centres in the *Greater London Development Plan* (reproduced by permission of Greater London Council)

their emergence as strong counter-growth currents to the magnetism of Paris itself.

The 1965 plan was first modified in 1969 when the number of new towns was reduced to five from the original eight. Mantes to the west was dropped from the original plan since Le Vaudreuil further down the Seine valley to the south-east of Rouen had been designated as a new town. Beauchamp to the north was similarly excluded as a new town in this first revision, whilst the two new centres at Trappes to the south were modified to form one, renamed St Quentin-en-Yvelines. A final new town modification was the redefinition of the site of Tigery-Lieusaint, to be renamed Melun-Sénart.

Although plans for South-East England, including London, were based on the definition of preferred axes of growth, a change of scale reveals a polycentric orientation for the detailed plans for London itself. The *Greater London Development Plan* (Greater London Council, 1969) contained from its earlier form the concept of strategic centres into which important new development such as offices could be directed. The distribution of such centres as they were proposed in the modified plan in 1976 are shown in Figure 11.4. They were chosen on the basis of serving a population of over 200 000 and had a 1961 retail turnover in excess of £5 million. Since that time, the new regional shopping centre at Brent Cross (Chapter 4) ensures its inclusion as a strategic centre.

Multicentred Metropolitan Plans

Polycentric plans are aimed at producing a series of centres, each sharing in growth rather than all growth being directed to a strong central focus. In some areas, however, a large number of centres already exist and require a plan for their future direction. Two such areas are the West Netherlands and the Ruhr, which are brought together under the broad heading of multicentred metropolitan plans.

(1) The West Netherlands

A primate city dominating the economic, political and social life of the nation in the style of London, Paris, Copenhagen, Brussels or Vienna did not develop in the Netherlands. Instead, a tradition of urban independence, and a physical geography that restricted urban development to a number of relatively small sites, produced a group of towns in the West Netherlands that shared the functions of a primate city between them. The slow growth of these towns until well into the modern period preserved this peculiar and untypical pattern of settlement in the Western provinces of North and South Holland and Utrecht. This inherited pattern gave the planners a set of both problems and possibilities quite different from those encountered in the great unicentred conurbations.

The idea of the Randstad (Dutch for rim-city) was propounded in detail in the first National Structure Plan of 1960. The concept had four main elements. First, the conurbation was to remain a distinct physical entity and not coalesce with the growing metropolitan areas of neighbouring countries. In the first 15 years after the war there appeared to be little threat to the substantial, if largely undefined, green

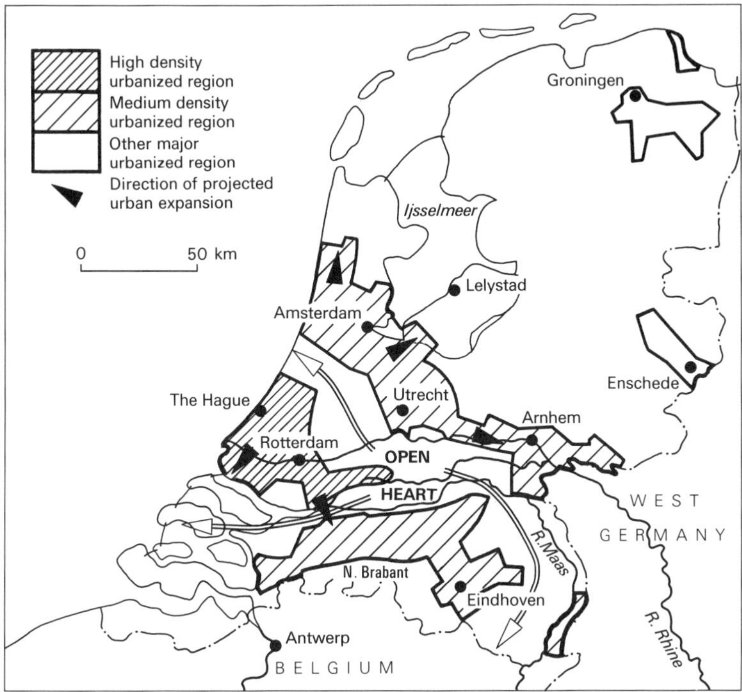

Figure 11.5 West Netherlands (Randstad), 1974: Second structure plan

belt that stretched all around the West Netherlands from Zeeland and Brabant in the south to Overijssel and Friesland in the east and north, that separated it from the towns of the Rhineland and the Schelde. Secondly, the towns of the West Netherlands were envisaged as lying along a narrow but almost continuous horseshoe that stretched from Amsterdam and the IJmond towns in the north, through the Gooi towns to Utrecht, and then down the great rivers through the *Drechtsteden* to Rotterdam and the Hague. On the map (Figure 11.5) the pattern was impressive. Thirdly, although the Randstad implied the existence of an urbanized belt, each of the constituent towns was to maintain its separate political, functional and physical identity. Finally, the urbanized *rand* enclosed a less densely peopled area with important agricultural, horticultural and recreational functions, to form what has been called, somewhat misleadingly, the 'greenheart metropolis' (Burke, 1966).

The Randstad may have been created by historical accident but it had to be defended as a political necessity. The threat to it came from the demands for space of a growing and increasingly prosperous Netherlands. The most fundamental pressure derived from the rapid growth in the Dutch population in the 20 years after 1945. West Europe's most densely peopled country also had its fastest rate of natural increase, and substantial net immigration. The West Provinces received the bulk of both the international and domestic migration. The demand for housing was fuelled by the population increase, an even faster growth in the rate of household formation and rising expectations of greater living space. As well as housing nearly half the Dutch population the West Provinces also accommodated an even higher proportion of the country's industrial capacity, and provided sites for the port-orientated industries that formed the vanguard in the drive for industrialization after the war. An increasingly affluent population also demanded space for leisure. Provision had to be made for the main centres of the country's foreign tourist industry, the main domestic beach holiday resorts, and day recreation for 5 million residents. Finally, the most pervasive threat to the integrity of the Randstad idea came from the rapid rise in car ownership which encouraged the dispersal of housing, employment and recreation, thus threatening to 'fill up' the 'open heart', cause a physical coalescence of the individual 'rim' towns, and eventually merge the West Netherlands with the Brussels–Antwerp conurbation to the south and the Rhine–Ruhr upriver to the east. In fact, it could be argued that the survival of the unique Randstad characteristics was only a fortuitous result of the remarkably low car-ownership levels that existed in the Netherlands until the early 1960s, and that this good fortune could not persist.

The second National Structure Plan of 1966 (Rijksplanologische Dienst., 1966) was designed to counter these threats, and was thus essentially defensive. Physical expansion was to be tolerated in five directions according to a policy of 'grouped deconcentration' (*gebundeld deconcentratie*). These were (Figure 11.5):

(1) northwards into Kennermerland;
(2) north-eastwards across the Flevoland polders to Lelystad;
(3) eastwards from Utrecht up the rivers to the Gelderland towns of Arnhem and Nijmegen;
(4) south-eastwards to link with the fast-growing industrial towns of Noord-Brabant that formed the *Brabantse Stedenrij*;
(5) southwards from Rotterdam into the Delta islands.

The urbanized horseshoe had now become two much broader east–west urbanized zones, called 'wings' (*vleughels*) by the planners. The northern wing stretched from the coast at IJmuiden through Amsterdam and Utrecht to Arnhem, while the southern stretched from the coast at The Hague–Scheveningen through Rotterdam to the Brabant towns. The 'open heart' and the buffer zones between the urban nodes remained theoretically inviolable, but the 'open heart' was now more accurately seen as a series of open corridors between the wings, running along the great rivers, south into the Zeeland Lake and north-eastwards along the IJsselmeer *randmeren*.

It appeared, therefore, that, on paper at least, the Randstad had been saved and the West Netherlands was not to succumb to the pressures and become 'merely another vast urban sprawl—a Dutch Los Angeles' (Hall, 1977). In reality, however, doubt could be cast not only on the policies that were intended to conserve the characteristics of the Randstad, but also on whether the Randstad had ever existed except as a concept in the imagination of the planners. The so-called 'open heart' was neither a sort of gigantic central park nor a rural agricultural region. It was in fact a district of small historical towns, like Woerden, Alphen or Gouda, suburban commuter settlements, intensive horticulture and some 'honeypot' recreation. Even its relative emptiness became increasingly questionable as, despite the strictures of the planners, many of its municipalities were growing much faster than the national average (Steigenga, 1968). Similarly, it was increasingly difficult to recognize the limits of Randstad, especially in the south and east. The expansion of Rotterdam southwards onto the Delta islands, and Antwerp down the Schelde, make it easy to conceive of the emergence of a single Delta port (Riley and Ashworth, 1975). Similarly, in the east the urbanized area had reached the German frontier at Arnhem–Nijmegen and threatened an eventual junction with the urbanized Rhine–Ruhr.

There was clearly a discrepancy between the concepts of the planners as expressed in the national planning documents and change as it was actually occurring. Dutch town planning has a longer tradition than most national planning systems in Europe but is stronger on ideas than on enforcement. There are, in fact, fewer restraints on the location of economic activity in the Netherlands than in France or Britain. The existence of three tiers of planning authority, national, provincial and municipal, was a further complication, especially when the interests of a municipality in growth contradicted a national proposal for restraint. (The Swedes face a similar problem in planning for Greater Stockholm.) Despite these misgivings, the town planners of the West Netherlands had by 1970 not only accommodated an increasingly numerous and demanding population, but had created an environment for living that was rightly the envy of their colleagues in Europe's unicentred conurbations.

(2) The Ruhr

The Ruhr region is the major metropolitan area where the problems of coalescing industrial centres were producing a massive urban industrial region stretching from Hamm in the east westwards to beyond Duisburg. Unlike the West Netherlands, the major problem has not been one of a rapidly increasing population within the area of the *Siedlungsverband Ruhrkohlenbezirk* (SVR) but one of a declining regional economy dependent on coal and metallurgy, a generally low-quality urbanized environment that had sprawled over the past century and a half, and a poor transport network. The SVR, which was designated in 1920, did attempt to create order within its boundaries in its original strategy published in 1960. But it has been forced to recognize that, in planning for the coalfield, it is planning for only a part of the large urbanized region that extends over a roughly triangular-shaped area from Bonn in the south to München Gladbach in the west and Hamm in the east including, therefore, the rapidly diversifying Rhine towns of Düsseldorf and Cologne. The Ruhr plan of 1966 (Figure 11.6) has a basic emphasis on the role of the green zones and belts separating the seven major north–south urban-industrial areas of the core, and a green buffer zone separating the core area from the newer urban industrial centres such as Marl, Wesel, Dorsten and Dinslaken in the northern region (Siedlungsverband Ruhrkohlenbezirk, 1966). Around the periphery are a series of recreation zones (Chapter 9). Pollution has been a major concern and the SVR has

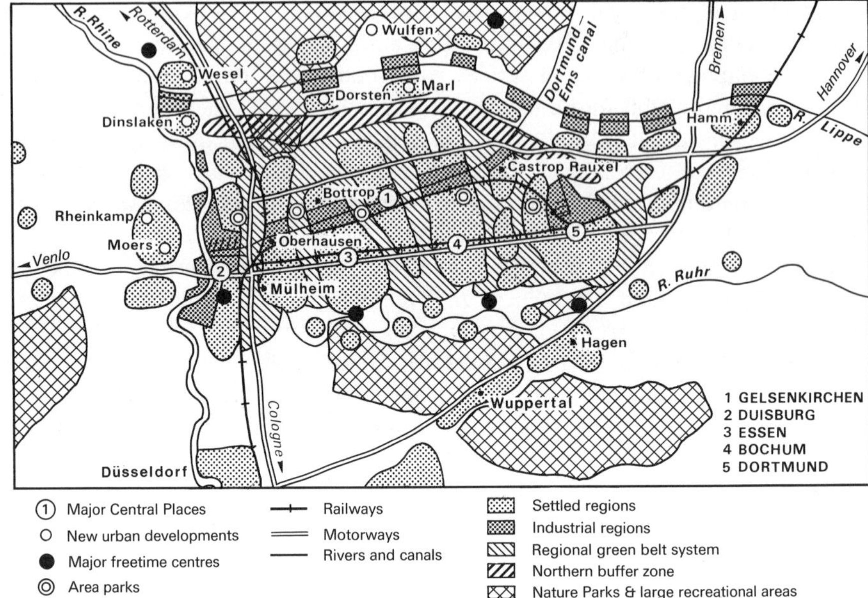

Figure 11.6 The Ruhr region structure plan (1966)

sponsored legislation to control atmospheric pollution. A new biological sewage plant has been constructed at the mouth of the Emscher to reduce the outfall of pollutants into the Rhine (Burtenshaw, 1974a).

Other aspects of the Ruhr plan are similar to the concepts discussed earlier. A hierarchy of central places and proposed growth centres for industry and services was part of the 1969 revision of the plan. These central places are now the foci for the integrated transport proposals including the *Stadtbahn* using existing rail-lines, and the tramlines which pass underground through the major centres. Other public transport feeds these major routes. In addition, a dense network of urban motorways now laces the region, some utilizing the opportunities for access provided by the green zones, and others such as the *Ruhrschnellweg* and *Emscherschnellweg* partly driven through the built-up areas as they traverse the region from east to west.

Today, however, the planning powers of the SVR are more limited and planning is seen much more in the context of *Verdichtungsraum Rhein–Ruhr*, the growth region designated in 1968, and the needs for balanced urban growth within the *Land* of North Rhine Westphalia (Burtenshaw, 1974b).

Reappraisals of the 1970s

The plans for major centres emphasized planning for growth during the 1960s, based on population projections predicting a continuing expansion of the urban population. In many cases, however, a reappraisal of these plans and a review of underlying assumptions was necessary. Predictions based on contemporary car-ownership trends foresaw a vast increase in personal mobility unhindered either by a shortage of petroleum or a slowing-down in economic growth rates. The *Schéma Directeur* (1965) for Paris took as one of its assumptions a fivefold increase in spending power, without being able to foresee the worldwide recession and stabilization of real spending power which have affected the western industrialized countries to a greater or lesser degree. Visions of urban population growth, coupled with an ever-expanding urban lifestyle necessitating large-scale planning, have had to be reviewed.

Other changes have been evident, both in terms of attitudes and contemporary processes, within the urban system. On the one hand, for instance, a stronger awareness of the environment, coupled with a more responsible attitude towards the exploitation of resources of all types, has been evident during the past decade. Hans Wohlin, chief planning architect for Stockholm, underlines this in a paper in 1977. He said (Wohlin, 1977),

> At the approach of both the 1970s and 1980s most municipalities had counted on a continuation of this rapid expansion. The hardening of the economic situation has come as a cold douche for many of them. Now we are in the process of readjusting ourselves from an almost unbridled expansion to a development where claims for reform must be dealt with on a strict priority basis. We must make better use of what we already have. We must learn to plan for more re-utilization.

We may certainly add that, despite the urban renovation, or homesteading movement in North America, European attitudes towards conservation at all levels have still attained a more practical result in terms of their reflection in urban policies, as shown in Chapter 6. A final reason for reappraisal lay in the unexpectedly rapid decline of the inner city, particularly noticeable in the case of London and the Ruhr towns and cities. A policy over the postwar period of economic decentralization in Britain, fostered initially by industrial development certificates, and from the mid-1960s by office development permits, had begun to take its toll. Dennis (1978) shows that population declined in Greater London by an estimated 9.4 per cent between 1966–74, while in the Inner London boroughs, the fall was 17.3 per cent. Even more startling was the decrease in manufacturing employment in Greater London with a 27 per cent decrease entailing the loss of 390 000 jobs to leave only 900 000 by June 1974. These figures may be compared to a national decline of 703 000 or 8.4 per cent over the same period. Obviously reappraisal was necessary and, in the following section, the impact of these changing circumstances on the plans for London and three other centres, Paris, the West Netherlands and Stockholm is reviewed, serving as illustrations of a more general current attitude.

London—Some Fundamental Problems in the 1970s

The early 1970s saw a degree of conflict in the two major plans published. One was at a regional level—the *Strategic plan for the South-East*, published in 1970 (HMSO,

1970). The second, dealing with Greater London itself, was the *Greater London Development Plan* (*GLDP*) (GLC, 1975). The *Strategic Plan* discussed earlier in this chapter, emphasized dispersal, clearly preserving the basic strategic approaches of the *South-East Study* (HMSO, 1964) and the *Strategy for the South-East* (HMSO, 1967) (Figure 11.1c). The *GLDP*, on the otherhand, was more concerned with taking measures to counter the decline both in employment and population which was becoming increasingly evident in the 1960s and into the 1970s. The principal problem was essentially one of balance, since within the South-East it was the centre, Greater London, which was losing relative to the outer metropolitan region. The inquiry panel which sat for a prolonged hearing of the case for the *GLDP* presented by the GLC rejected the view that policies should be implemented to retain population and jobs in London to counteract the drift from the city. Indeed, in rejecting the *GLDP*'s figure of a population between 7.0 million and 7.3 million by 1981, the panel saw no significant disadvantage in there being a lower population and, in fact, saw considerable advantages in terms of 'a more spacious environment for those that remain' (HMSO, 1973).

The scene was set, therefore, for a continuation of the outmigration of jobs to towns located at a medium range of about 60 kilometres from London, while the new growth centres envisaged in the *Strategic Plan* would also grow to populations in excess of a million. Certainly, if this process were to continue, then the emergence of a multi-centred urban region would be highly likely as the centre decreased in importance and the outer nodes increased. However, such a policy is not without its problems. Migration outwards is selective both in terms of people and jobs. The possibility of social polarization in the central city as middle-income earners move out, often to new office complexes in Reading, Croydon or Southend, is a real one. The decline in manufacturing jobs in the central city creates problems of unemployment. The new towns are selective in terms of population attracted from London (Chapter 13), taking white families rather than commonwealth immigrants.

The 1976 *Strategy Review* brought down the population estimates for the South-East region to 17.1 million from the figure of 19.8 million which was projected 6 years earlier (HMSO, 1976). It recognized that London itself would have a smaller share of the region's population than had previously been assumed. Since that time, as discussed in Chapter 4, some attempts have been made to retrieve the position lost by London. Current policies for both offices and large-scale regional shopping centres look towards attracting functions back to the capital and particularly to its inner city locations such as Stratford and Clapham. In this sense, GLC policy is closer to the original *GLDP* than to the *Strategic Plan* of 1970 or to the *Strategy Review* of 1976, but it remains to be seen whether planning powers even in Britain are sufficient to stem the tide whose flow was initiated by government policy, but whose momentum has proved difficult to stem.

The general change of views in the 1970s is best illustrated by a sentence from the *Greater London Development Plan: Written Statement* of 1976, following its modification. It states, 'The plan is not directed at an end-state for London in terms of bricks and concrete, but at imposing standards of life in London, a goal whose attainment will require continuous effort' (Greater London Council, 1976). The attainment of an organic planning framework, as discussed in Chapter 2, has perhaps been achieved through this approach. In contrast, the more authoritarian approach adopted by French planners, however, is still clearly discernible in the *Schéma Directeur* for Paris. Paul Delouvrier's plan of 1965, is almost as authoritarian in its direction as was Haussmann's over a century earlier. In the case of Paris, the review of the last few years has done little to change this approach.

Paris—a Decline in Growth Rates

Both population growth and increases in economic activity began to decline in the period after the 1965 *Schéma Directeur*. Population growth running at 2 per cent per annum between 1954 and 1962 fell away to 1.4 per cent per annum in the period 1968–75. The core of the city was losing population to the outer suburbs and the major problem lay in the balance of growth between east and west rather than merely accommodating growth itself. In the employment sector, manufacturing was giving way to tertiary employment, though once again the task was becoming one of correcting the inequalities between the relatively more prosperous west and the less well-endowed eastern sector. Even by 1969, the original *Schéma Directeur* had been modified to designate five rather than eight new towns. The outlines of the *Schéma Directeur* of 1975, however, remain broadly similar to those of the 1965 Plan. The transport links between the major nodes are to be strengthened, bringing with it a stronger likelihood of the eventual emergence of the two broad axes described earlier. One could conclude that the population shortfall will give to Paris the opportunity to redress imbalances and to make minor adjustments, as the city as a whole moves towards its polycentric form.

Normally it could be argued that a short-term shortfall in a predicted population should not invalidate a plan since, in time, as population does increase, albeit belatedly, the original provisions of the plan will still be required. This view, however, carries with it the suggestion that the underlying assumptions and objectives of the plan remain unaltered over time. As we will see, that would be an unfortunate suggestion in which to put a great deal of faith.

Reappraisal in the West Netherlands

As in the other major city regions already described, the 1970s was a period of change in both the realities of the city in the Netherlands and in attitudes towards planning and the city. Most fundamentally, the rapid decline in the West European birthrate succesively lowered the predicted population upon which the previous plans had been based, although this was compensated to some extent by the rate of household formation which continued at a high level. Concern for the conservation of the physical environment, for depleting energy resources, and for the renovation of the inner areas of the large cities, were not new in the Netherlands but they received a renewed emphasis. There was also a profound change, as has already been noted in other countries, in the philosophy and machinery of planning. The previous plans for the West Netherlands had been detailed, visionary blueprints of a fixed future at a stated time. The plans of the 1970s were more flexible and less detailed. They were indications of directions that could be followed and would need continuous monitoring. In addition, public participation in the planning process was mere consultation, limited to an involvement of citizens in the choice between alternative strategies.

The general pattern of urban and 'open' areas differs little from the 'wings' of the second Structure Plan (Figure 11.5). Quite different, however, were the four more detailed strategies presented to the public for consideration. These offered the consequences in terms of urbanized and open space in the three West Provinces of pursuing alternative policies of residential concentration or dispersal, dependence on public or private transport, renovation or demolition of the older city-centres, and degrees of severity in the containment of urban expansion.

In a country as small as the Netherlands it has become difficult to distinguish between town and regional planning, and the objectives and practice of the two have become inextricably linked. The goal of regional planning, since the 1950s, has been to stimulate the economic development of the northern, eastern and southern provinces, by encouraging counter-magnets (*tegenpolen*), most recently in Breda, Helmond, Zwolle and Groningen. The physical expansion of the western metropolitan area and the growth in car-ownership has drawn much of the south and east of the country into the orbit of the west. When viewed on the scale of Greater London or Paris almost all of the Netherlands, with the exception only of Limburg, Groningen and Twente, can be regarded as a single city-region, the regional growth centres as overspill towns on the urban periphery, and the remaining outer areas, such as the Friesian Lakes, Dreuthe, the Veluwe, Zuid Limburg, and the Brabant heaths, as an extensive green belt with largely recreational functions.

Stockholm—the New Priorities

Earlier regional plans for Stockholm had as their basic priorities the achievement of the optimum location for residential development with respect to jobs and transport provisions, together with recreational land preservation. The 1978 Regional Plan, however, marked a departure from these priorities. Economic and demographic changes necessitated fundamental changes of attitude, as illustrated earlier in this section.

The major debate has centred around the manner in which any new objectives might be achieved. The emphasis of the 1978 Regional Plan was to even out imbalances within the regional structure in terms of growth potential and resource discrepancies. In broad terms, this centred around a centre–periphery contrast and a north–south discrepancy with the north being relatively more advantaged in terms of resource endowment than the south. When the regional plan was originally presented to the Stockholm County Council it took the form of a careful, but by no means dramatic, deconcentration of activity. It was not accepted, however, by the ruling majority coalition of the council. Hence, two alternative plans were produced. The first plan, Alternative A, was the original. It provided for a move of

30 000–40 000 jobs from Stockholm to four major growth nodes in a fifteen-year period. This plan gained the backing of the conservative and liberal elements in the ruling majority and the social democrats of the minority parties. The alternative plan assumed the title Alternative C since it was advocated by the centre party of the ruling coalition, gaining support also from the communists of the minority parties. This plan envisaged a larger-scale decentralization in the order of 70 000 jobs from the centre of Stockholm over a 15-year period. It was most distinctive, however, in its move towards achieving, by job redistribution, an employment–residential balance in each of the municipalities of Greater Stockholm.

Thus the plan was against large-scale centralization and favoured instead small-scale development and self-containment. In this it was somewhat idealistic since, taken to its ultimate, agglomeration economies would be lost, and in any event such a pattern could not be achieved other than by major changes to the existing patterns. Whatever the outcome, however, this recent experience of Stockholm illustrates two major points concerning planning for large urban areas. First, previous assumptions concerning objectives and priorities are being increasingly questioned, and, second, that planning at this scale is more than a technical planning exercise, since it is also a major political issue.

The Lessons Learnt from the Metropolitan Plans

The necessity to produce large-scale plans in the postwar period was clearly established. Without them, many major European cities would have followed the path of cities in the United States with uncontrolled suburban sprawl leading to vast problems of servicing and a declining downtown with its deeply entrenched economic and social problems. Even if hindsight were to demonstrate that they had failed in the details of all of their objectives, the basic framework for control and the will to carry it through were important elements in shaping the developing urban form.

The postwar period has clearly demonstrated, however, the dangers of depending too much on long-term forecasts based on current trends. Demographic forecasts have proved to be particularly vulnerable in this respect, but economic predictions are not far behind. It seems probable that the surprisingly volatile nature of western economy and society, bringing with it population fluctuations, economic recession, and energy crises, together with an increasing number of questions concerning the nature of so-called ideal lifestyles in postwar Europe, renders large-scale 'blueprint' planning redundant. In its place, broad policy approaches with constant monitoring of the whole environmental system, seem best suited to coping with both short-term and long-term fluctuations.

CHAPTER 12

Planning for Non-primate Urban Centres

Within all the West European national urban systems there are a number of large and medium-sized cities whose plans for development are unsung. These are difficult to label in an all-embracing fashion. Their scale varies considerably from conurbations and cities of well over a million inhabitants such as Hamburg, Manchester, Milan and Barcelona to medium-sized cities such as Geneva, Rouen, Kiel and Norwich. Even the use of the term 'medium sized' is subject to various national interpretations. President Pompidou drew French attention to the medium-sized town (*villes moyennes*) which was seen as a settlement of under 200 000 persons such as Auxerre, Epernay, Cahors and Valence (Sauvy and Prud'homme, 1973). On the other hand the Dutch second Structure Plan of 1966 used the same concept (*Middlegrootstad*) to refer to towns with over and around 200 000 people. In West Germany the medium-sized city is more likely to be centres such as Mainz, Bremen or Stuttgart. For these reasons we have attempted to look at the plans for what we see as the non-primate urban centres or those cities and conurbations that are prominent but not dominant in the national urban hierarchies. The city structure plans that we have examined appear to group themselves into certain families of plans, each family depending more on one particular concept of a city's structure. Despite the use of more than one structure concept in some plans we have tried to isolate the major plan types in the examples used in the sections that follow. Families of plans have been identified as follows:

(1) City region plans
(2) City plans dependent on axial growth
(3) Plans dependent on central place concepts
(4) Axes and polycentric growth
(5) Plans utilizing a new town strategy
(6) Plans depending on publicized alternatives and participation
(7) City planning and the quality of life
(8) Cities where *laissez-faire* has dominated planning

City-Region Plans

As a result of the changed styles of living and working most planning proposals for cities in West Europe have concerned themselves more and more with the city-region rather than the more narrowly confined city. City-region plans have been commonplace for the primate metropolitan regions for nearly half a century. However, the non-primate cities have not concerned themselves with regionally based plans until the much more recent past when there has been a tendency to escape from the rigid confines of detailed planning proposals to the more generalized guidelines of structure planning with its requirement to adapt to economic and social developments. There are two types of plans for city-regions that we can illustrate: those for the single-centred regions of which Hannover and Geneva are examples, and those for the twin-centred and polycentric regions. In the latter case plans for Rhine–Neckar and Greater Manchester are two examples of a family of plans for the complex multicentred regions so common in West Europe.

(1) Grossraum Hannover

Grossraum Hannover is a unique city-region planning authority in West Germany founded in 1963 by the *Land* of Lower Saxony. Politically and spatially it is an intermediate tier between the *Land* and the *Kreis*. It embraces 2228 square kilometres including the city of Hannover (567 000 inhabitants) and the area of *Landkreis Hannover* with a further 556 000 people. A similar organization was established for Brunswick. *Grossraum Hannover* is administered by a council elected by the inhabitants and is responsible for regional planning within the guidelines set by the *Land*. Within the plan the authority is required to plan for the development of the area, the central places, the areas for the development and improvement of homes and workplaces, and recreational areas. *Grossraum Hannover* is also required to produce sectoral plans for hospitals, children's education, recreational arrangements, sewage and waste disposal and transport. It also has the responsibility for administering the federal government's frontier development region policy (*Zonenrandgebiet*) in those parts of the region that lie within 40 kilometres of the East German boundary.

The plans for the Hannover region contain many of the concepts developed by German planners in the postwar period besides that most German of all theories, the concept of the 'central place hierarchy' derived from the work of Walter Christaller. The basic format of the Hannover regional plan owes much to the ideas of Hillebrecht who was the city planner. In 1962 Hillebrecht designed his *Regionalstadt* using the Hannover region as his model (Figure 12.1). This showed a hierarchical development of centres within the region and the suburbs (Hillebrecht, 1962). One can also distinguish elements of Boustedt's scheme for the decentralized city (see Figure 3.3a) and the widely accepted definitions of the city-region that Boustedt put into diagrammatic form (see Figures 3.3b and 3.3c). Therefore, although the 1975 plan for the region obviously incorporates the views of the planners in the 1970s, there is an obvious debt to the planners of the previous two decades (Boustedt, 1967, 1970 and 1975).

The basic elements of the *Grossraum Hannover* plan are shown in Figure 12.2. The foundation of the region's development is the concept of a hierarchy of central places. Various central places (*Trabanten/Satelliten*) have been designated for expansion of housing, industry and service-sector employment. Thus the second-

Centre
Administration
Higher Education
Hospital
Exhibition Area
Airport
Urban Recreation and Rural Open Spaces
Neighbourhood Centre
Central Places beyond City
Planned Central Places
Residential Area with circles inversely proportional to population density
Industrial Area
Autobahn
Main Road
Railway
Rapid Transit Rail Transport
Waterway
40km
20km
10km

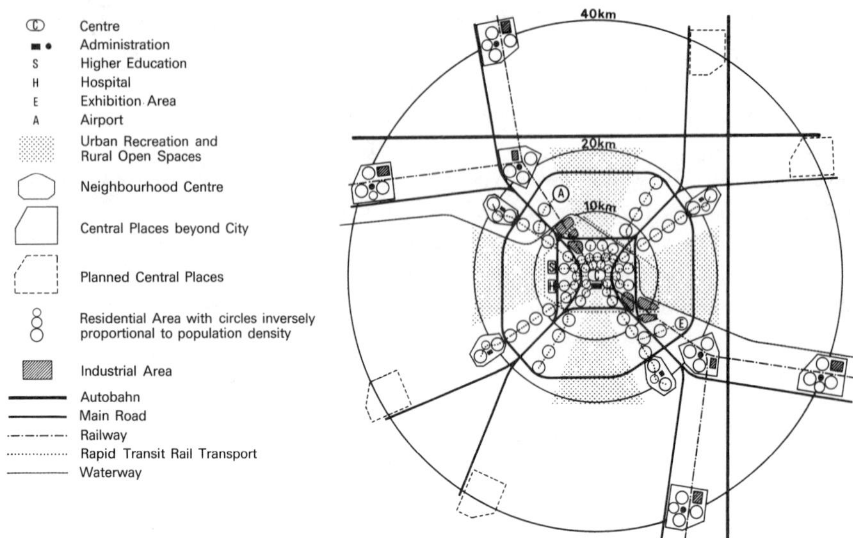

Figure 12.1 Hillebrecht's *Regionalstadt* (reproduced by permission of Dr R. Hillebrecht and Archiv für Kommunalwissenschaften)

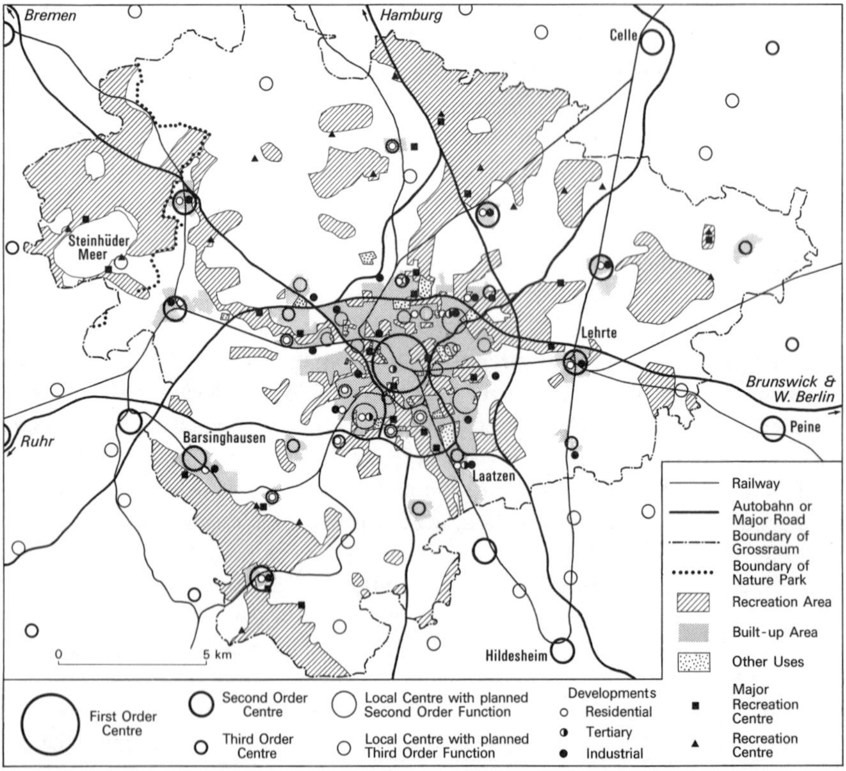

Bremen
Hamburg
Celle
Steinhüder Meer
Lehrte
Brunswick & W. Berlin
Peine
Ruhr
Barsinghausen
Laatzen
Hildesheim
0
5 km
Railway
Autobahn or Major Road
Boundary of Grossraum
Boundary of Nature Park
Recreation Area
Built-up Area
Other Uses
First Order Centre
Second Order Centre
Third Order Centre
Local Centre with planned Second Order Function
Local Centre with planned Third Order Function
Developments
Residential
Tertiary
Industrial
Major Recreation Centre
Recreation Centre

Figure 12.2 *Grossraum Hannover* structure plan (1975) (reproduced by permission of *Grossraum Hannover*)

order settlements such as Lehrte and Barsinghausen, will have both extra housing and new industrial sites. Many villages remain untouched or are only to expect new 'rural' homes. The second-order centres within the city of Hannover (*Nebenstadt*) will also have increased service-sector employment (*Grossraum Hannover*, 1975). Other centres beyond the region such as Celle (*Selbstandige Nachbarstadt*) are expected to grow as commuter centres. The major features of the regional transport plan include the development of the regionally integrated public transport network. There is a series of regional rapid transit rail links focusing on Hannover including park-and-ride facilities at 39 stations in the region. Several stations are also an integral part of purpose-built modal interchanges. In addition there are tramlines extending from the city to the outer suburbs. Already several lines pass underground through the city-centre converting ingeniously from street-level boarding to platform boarding of carriages like a conventional underground train. The third and most interesting developments in the plan is the expansion of the already well-developed regional provision of recreational areas, the most important of which is the Steinhüder Meer and its surrounding nature park. Provision is being made throughout the region for car-based visitors to the rural recreational zones.

Grossraum Hannover is not without its problems. The greatest difficulties are political and relate to the balance between the representation on the council between the rural fringe and the urban core. There is also concern that the whole concept could be abandoned by a *Land* government anxious to save on public expenditure on what is viewed as un unnecessary extra tier in the governmental structure that removes certain powers from the rural administrations in particular. Nevertheless the unique experiment has produced a set of comprehensive proposals for the city-region that are the envy of other cities.

(2) Geneva

We have already indicated in Chapter 10 that Geneva is an exceptional city because of its location. However, Geneva is a further example of a case of a city-region plan which, in this case, is the cantonal plan. This plan was first formulated at the same time as the concept of *Grossraum Hannover* and was updated in 1975 to take account of trends experienced in the previous decade. In this sense the Geneva plan has attempted to follow the tradition of organic planning.

The original 1965 plan was prepared in the age of spiralling expectations for population growth and even one of the present authors had commented on Geneva's problems in the light of the plan to accommodate 800 000 by the year 2015 compared with the 259 000 living in the city at that time (Burtenshaw, 1970). The fears for rapid city growth were dispelled in the succeeding decade when the ethos of zero growth overtook that of growth at all costs just as the birthrate stabilized and foreign immigration into the canton fell by 10 000 per annum. Thus the projections of a cantonal population of 800 000 by the turn of the century have been replaced by projections anticipating a mere 440 000 (République et Canton de Genève, 1975). At the same time the planners recognized that the city was one focal point of a region of 3 million people including five *départements* and two provinces of Italy. In the

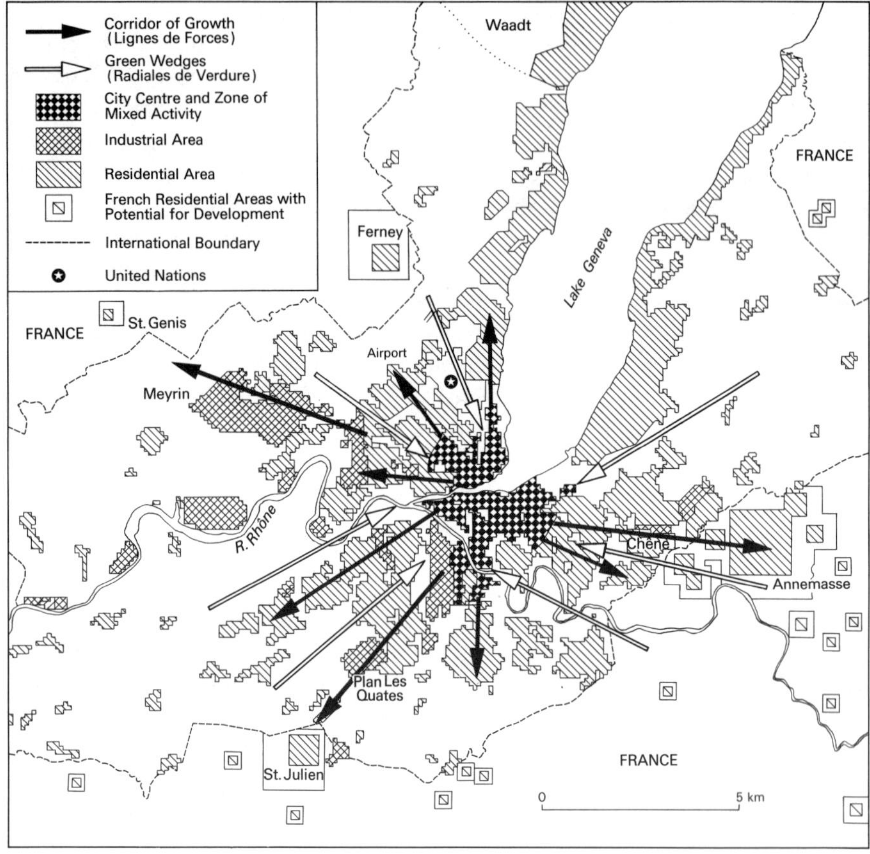

Figure 12.3 Canton Geneva structure plan (1975) (reproduced by permission of République et Canton de Genève)

immediately adjacent French regions population growth has been consistently higher than in the canton and plans envisage a continuing growth of transfrontier commuting to Geneva (République et Canton de Genève, 1974).

Given these changes, the 1975 cantonal plan has reaffirmed the concept of nine *lignes de force* (corridors of growth) extending out from the city into the region and, in the case of three corridors, to *pôles d'attractions* (poles of growth): (a) Servett, Meyrin and St Genis (French); (b) Grand Lancy, Plan-les-Ouates and St Julien (French) and Grange-Canal Chene and Annemasse (French) (Figure 12.3). In between the corridors, which will be structured into hierarchical units ranging from residential (1000–2000 inhabitants) to the sector (up to 40 000 inhabitants), are fingers of open land. These will be parkland, agricultural zones, sports areas and 'artificial zones' such as well-vegetated residential areas. Industrial zones will be concentrated in the corridors; tertiary employment would be spread throughout the new residential areas. At the same time the plan does attempt to ensure that development is concentrated within existing zones of construction and at a high density in order to conserve the need for infrastructural provision and to conserve the rural perimeter within the canton not as a landscape untouched by man, but as one that has acquired its character thanks to the work and intervention of man. This latter concern is a most Genevan adaptation of Swiss concern for the environment.

Thus by 1990 the city of Geneva will have grown in accordance with planned priorities for the directions of growth. The best-equipped areas will be developed first and industrial land and land for offices and shops is adequate for all forecast needs within the new areas. Socio-cultural facilities will be developed in relation to known involvement rather than hypothetical norms. The road system will be based on four zones of circulation penetrated by major roads but not motorways. Renovation of the existing fabric, particularly in the area of Les Grottes, is to take precedence over new developments.

Unlike Hannover, the Geneva plan is based on a longstanding political unit, including an enclave in Vaud, but increasingly there is a realization that the city-region is broader than the cantonal political unit. Attempts have been made therefore to fit the plan into the concept of an international city-region.

(3) Greater Manchester Structure Plan

Greater Manchester was created as an administrative unit as a result of local government reform in 1974. The new metropolitan county supersedes separate local authorities, many of which had traditionally looked to Manchester as the centre of the region stretching from Wigan to the Peak Park and from Rochdale and Bolton in the north to Stockport and Altrincham in the south. Given national control over certain policies the draft plan adopts a strategy that aims to balance the resources of the region emphasizing continued concentration of urban growth with the priority on areas suffering from social, environmental and economic stress. The resultant draft structure (Figure 12.4) places emphasis on modern housing needs both through additional housing and urban renovation and the government's inner area partnership programme. Retailing and office developments are to be maintained in existing centres. Transport improvements are to be coordinated and a series of open agricultural land riverine areas and areas of special landscape value have been maintained throughout the region.

The plan for the 2.6 million people (Greater Manchester Council, 1978) will both reduce the density of population and ease pressure on space in Manchester, Oldham and Salford which has resulted from the region's history. It will slightly add to the numbers in the other centres without changing the polycentric character of the region. On the other hand, positive steps will have been taken to improve the quality of the environment throughout the cities and towns in accordance with the central aim of the strategy.

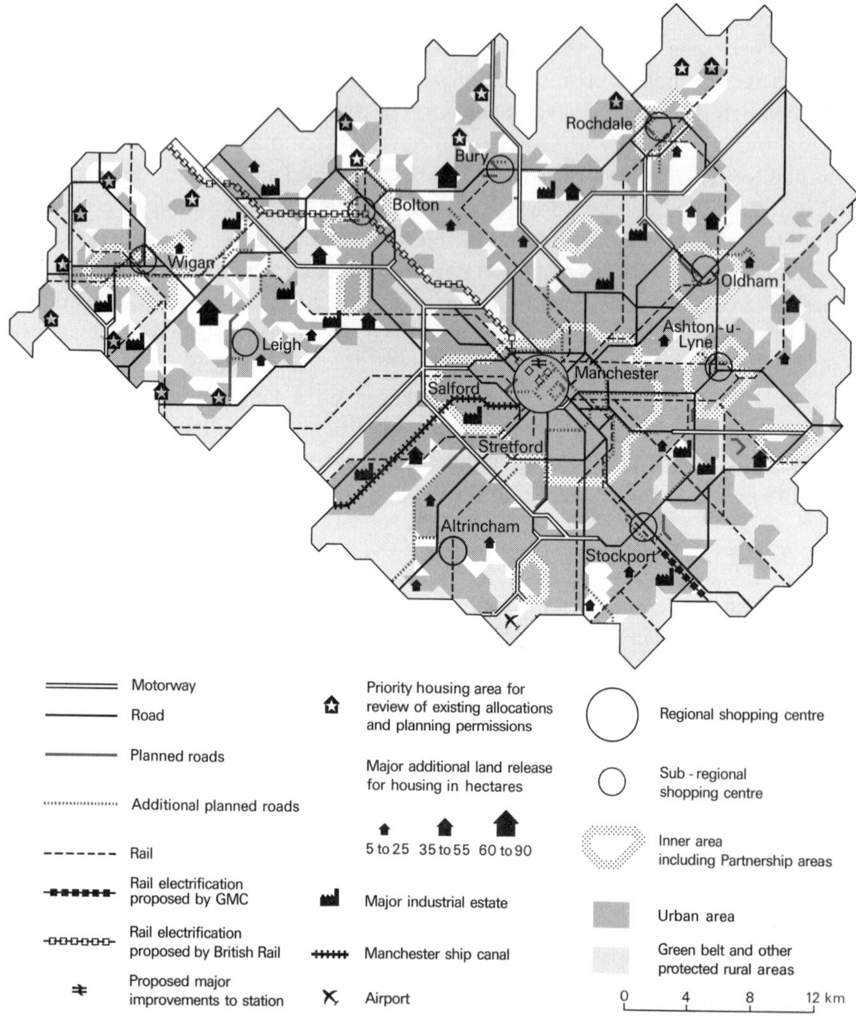

Figure 12.4 *Greater Manchester draft structure plan* (1978)

City Plans Dependent on Axial Growth

(1) Hamburg

The importance of transport as a factor stimulating and channelling city growth has been stressed in the context of the major metropolitan centres and their regions. Transport plans for London, Paris and the Ruhr (*Siedlungsverband Ruhrkohlenbezirk*, 1966) have been shown to be important determinants of the proposed structure of the future city regions. Other major centres such as Geneva have also utilized concepts of axes of growth, as we have already seen. Therefore the concept of

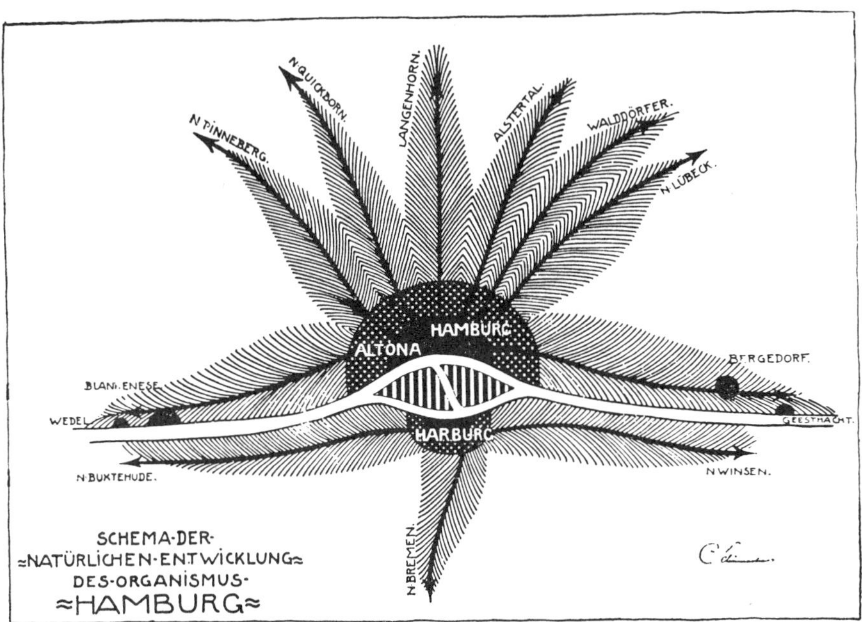

Figure 12.5 Schumacher's original axial plan for Hamburg

utilizing major axes of development for the future structuring of cities is a fundamental one. It is a tradition of planning that has appealed to many since Soria y Mata published his ideas for *Cuidad Lineal* a century ago. One of the best examples today of a city plan that has consistently embraced the concept of axes of growth centred on transport routes is Hamburg.

The original concept of axial growth for Hamburg was first proposed by the city planner Schumacher in 1921 (Figure 12.5). His original proposals have been much modified over the years to take into account the changing needs of the city. Nevertheless Hamburg has been able to plan consistently for over half a century on the basis of a series of radiating axes of growth (Albers, 1977). The basic structure of the 1969 plan is the form of eight regional axes extending out beyond the city boundary to towns within the region which, interestingly, had no fixed time-scale, a characteristic which has bedevilled so many plans for larger cities (Figure 12.6). The towns forming the axial end points such as Kaltenkirchen and Elmshorn to the north and Lüneburg to the south-east were linked by rail-lines that passed along the regional axes back to the city. The plan does distinguish between *Hauptachsen* axis routes where development could feasibly occur and *Hauptachsen* with an overwhelmingly recreational function. Thus the axis paralleling the Elbe to Stade is regarded as a line of development while two, those east to Schwarzenbek and to Buchholz, are part of a recreational zone. Once within the city boundary the axis becomes an urban axis and its form alters (Figure 12.7). There are also three major axes and four minor axes within the city confines (*Nebenachsen*).

Various changes in transport technologies have been incorporated into the axial plans for the city. Thus the current plans have laid emphasis on *autobahnen*

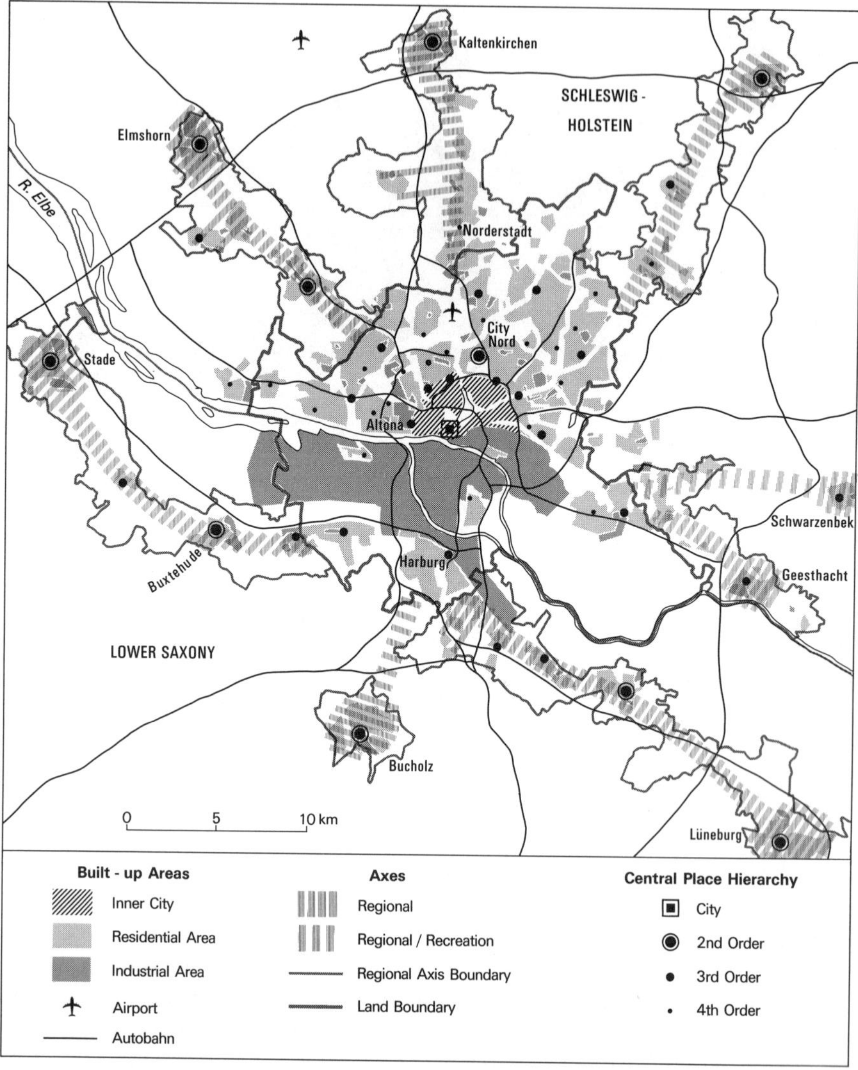

Figure 12.6 Hamburg region structure plan (reproduced by permission of Baubehorde-Landesplanungsamt, Hamburg)

following the axes. Because these have come relatively late onto the scene they have tended to be located on the fringe of the existing axes and have made use of the interstitial green wedges that penetrate deep into the city. The extensions of the *U-bahn*, rail improvements and bus routes have also been planned to function most effectively along the axes with bus routes feeding the fixed track network. More recently park-and-ride facilities have been provided on the rapid transit routes.

Nearly all other developments in the Hamburg region have been planned to fit into the overall concept of axial development. In theory, therefore, housing densities are related to distance from the main rapid transit stations (Figure 12.7). The plans for

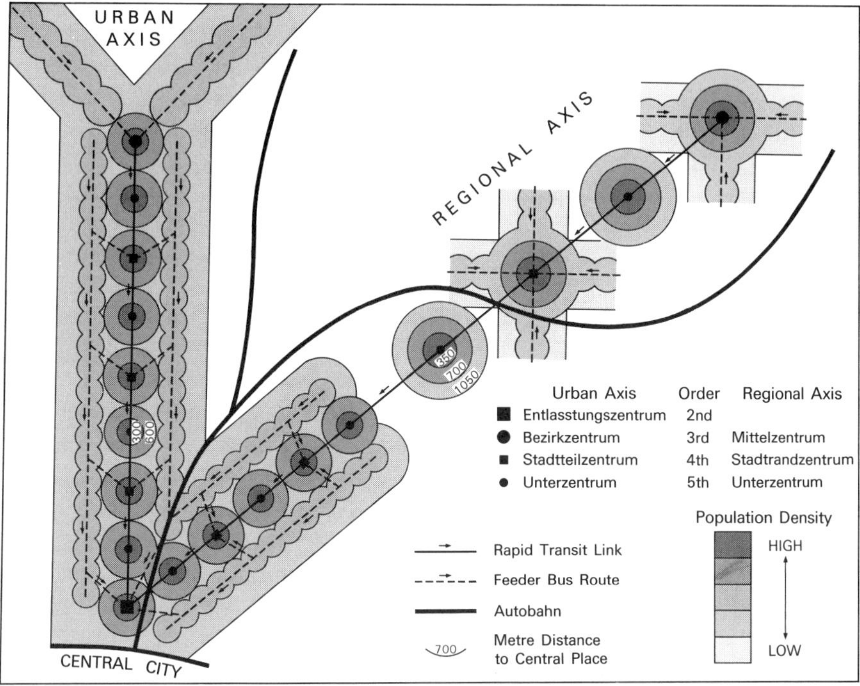

Figure 12.7 Detail of city and regional axes in Hamburg

new centres of office employment to relieve pressure on the city centre while seen as part of an overall framework of central places in the city, are located on particular axes. Thus the major office node City Nord (Chapter 4) is located on the primary axis extending to the present airport and beyond to Norderstedt and Kaltenkirchen, the site of the new airport. The second major office focus, in the city-centre of Altona, is located on one of the city axes. Harburg at the junction of three regional axes is a further proposed centre for office developments. In a similar fashion the new retail developments have been placed on the axes either as self-standing out-of-town shopping centres close to the *autobahnen*, or as new shopping centres placed at the interchange between the suburban rail-lines and the *U-bahn*. Further into the city, new office and retail developments such as Hamburgerstrasse have been located on the *U-bahn* and road routes leading to the centre.

Besides the important influence on axes within the Hamburg structure plan there is a secondary emphasis on a central place system which, as we have seen, relates to the federal scheme of central places. This system has also been devised to conform to the axes so that the more important centres are either at the meeting-point of regional axes or on the fringe of the centre while new centres can be developed at the outer fringes of the city proper. The axis also terminates in major centres (*Mittelzentrum*) within the region. Along the axes outside the city are fringe centres (*Stadtrandzentrum*) while district centres (*Stadtteilzentrum*) and local centres (*Unterzentrum* and *Kleinzentrum*) are located on the axes within the city (Figure 12.7).

Hamburg has been able to prepare plans for a city which could grow to become the centre for a city-region of 2.5 million people. Great emphasis has been placed on the technical solutions to the problems of movement which have been realized in part due to the vast financial resources that the German economy has been able to release for urban development and in particular for improvements in infrastructure. However, the problems of energy supply, coupled with Germany's decade-long low birthrate, have resulted in a fresh look at the bold vision of the future prepared by Schumacher. The priorities have moved sharply away from ever-increasing development along the axes to a greater consideration of the effects that growth has had on the older city districts. While not abandoning the axial concept, the city planners have dropped various proposals for new developments along the axes and concentrated more on renovating and improving the quality of life in the existing areas.

The changing demographic and economic prospects in the 1970s and the consequent slackening emphasis on physical growth at all costs, has also had a beneficial effect on the other problem that has been faced by the city, that of maintaining cooperation with the adjoining *Länder* (Bahr, 1976a). Schleswig-Holstein had always been more cooperative in planning matters than Lower Saxony, so more of Hamburg's growth had tended to be to the north although part of the reasoning has been the fact that the Elbe has formed a particularly strong barrier to south and westward expansion. The slackening of pressure for further urban growth and the formation in 1972 of the regional body to supervise recreational developments within 40 kilometres of the city (*Naherholung im Umland von Hamburg eV*), have reduced one potential area of inter-*Länder* friction (Bahr, 1976b).

(2) Bremen

Like Hamburg, Bremen has been faced with the problems of expanding within the *Land* area, which was the reason for the acquisition and development of Bremerhaven in the nineteenth century. The city of Bremen forms an elliptical area of up to 30 kilometres by 10 kilometres astride the Weser river although it is much more usual to see the city *Land* as the 600 000-person centre for the core of Weser–Jade region with its 1.9 million inhabitants. The development of the city has tended to be parallel to the river, particularly on the north bank as firms moved factories to the suburban fringes. A new university was built to the North east and the city built new housing areas west and east of the historic core such as Neue Vahr, Osterholz-Tenever and Kattenesch (Chapter 6) because of the constraints of the boundary and low-lying marshlands of Blockland.

The overall scheme of development of Bremen has attempted to reinforce these two primary axes of development within the broader growth area (Hollmann, 1977). The axes are not unlike those for Paris (Chapter 11) the first extending from Oldenburg in a crescent to Syke on the south-west side of the Weser and the second from Verden to Osterholz-Scharmbeck and on the north to Bremerhaven (Figure 12.8). There are other axes of varying strength within the urban region whose development has been agreed by the joint planning commission for Bremen and

Lower Saxony. Workers at the University of Bremen have measured the strength of existing and potential growth of the axes which is shown on Figure 12.8. The four most important axes extend towards Verden, Syke, Oldenburg and Osterholz-Scharmbeck. The axis towards Brake on the left bank is less strong although the planning commission sees this as being entirely within the growth region. Lesser axes are developing towards Delmenhorst and Rotenburg, and between Osterholz-Scharmbeck and Bremerhaven despite the existence of good rail and road links with the city.

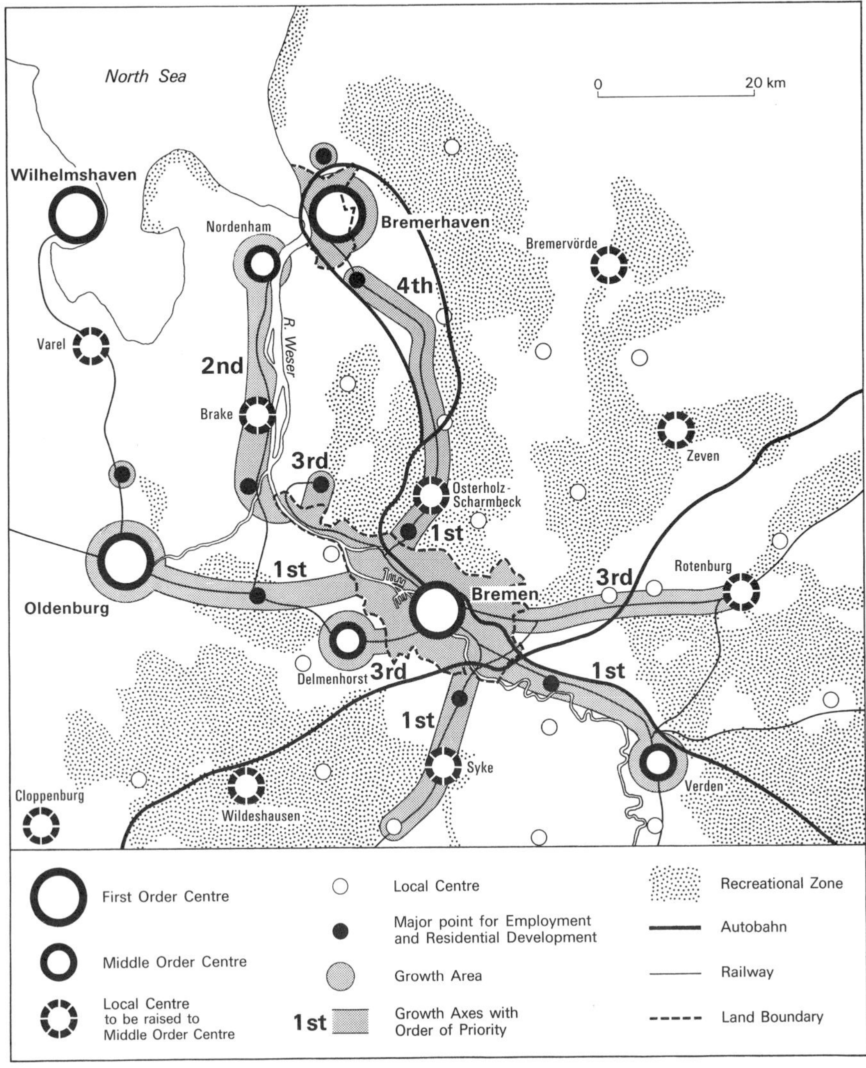

Figure 12.8 Axial planning and axis strength in the Bremen area (reproduced by permission of Senator für das Bauwesen, Stadt Bremen)

The other developments in the city and its region have been designed to reinforce the axial plan. Recreational zones skirt the city on both the north-east and south-west sides while the valley of the Weser provides a recreational space stretching upstream from the city. The location of recreation centres (*Freizeitzentrum*), which are generally within or adjacent to the major open spaces, has been planned for maximum access to the population by placing the majority of them adjacent to motorway access points. The integrated public transport system has been improved within the city in order to reinforce the basic north-west, south-east alignment while the commuter rail-lines have been used as the basis for eight of the axes of development. In order to promote the role of public transport in shaping city growth the transport plans give priority to public transport by building more routes, giving trains and buses priority at key points, rigidly controlling private vehicle parking both in provision and price, and by an extensive pedestrianization of the city-centre.

(3) Other Cases

Axial growth has also occurred where physical conditions have presented few alternative courses for expansion. Wuppertal is one of the classic cases where the linear nature of the settlement along an incised valley has been uniquely emphasized for over half a century by the famous monorail astride the course of river and the main road through the valley. Freiburg, St Étienne and Trier have also produced plans where the major extensions along valley axes are the sole means of accommodating the demands of space for industry and housing without the vast infrastructural costs of building out of the valley. The eastern end of Lake Geneva and the upper Rhône valley including the towns of Montreux, Vevey and Villeneuve has also had to look to the Rhône valley to provide an axis of growth (Barbier *et al.*, 1969). In the case of Middle Neckar focusing on Stuttgart eight axes of growth have been delimited and are partly confined by terrain so that the stronger growth can be expected along the Neckar valley north towards Heilbronn and to the south-east. A linear city has also been the basis of the structure plans for the *métropole d'équilibre* of Metz–Nancy–Thionville a 100 kilometre long urbanized area linked by the Metrolor rail link that would possess 'services and functions at a truly European level' (Burtenshaw, 1976; and Urbanisme, 1971). In the Loire valley regional planners have devised a plan that attempts to distribute the urban functions among the towns along the axis afforded by the valley thus permitting the growth of towns to be more linear and, thanks to improved transport, enabling the towns to be functionally interdependent.

Plans Dependent on Central Place Concepts: Cologne

In most cases where axial concepts have developed there has often been a second level of organization dependent on the establishment of a hierarchy of central places. This was most evident in the case of Hamburg. In the case of Hannover the central place hierarchy was part of a much broader city-region approach to the needs for urban development. In the case of Cologne, however, the central place hierarchy has dominated the structure plan for the city which was published in 1978 (Stadt köln, 1978). For a variety of reasons associated both with its political control and the personality of its early postwar administrators, Cologne was very late in producing a city-wide plan although this became more essential following local government reform in the early 1970s.

The Cologne structure plan has attempted to maintain the city as a polycentric urban area focusing on the city centre (*Innenstadt*). A four-tier hierarchy of places and areas was proposed in the plan as follows:

Area	*Place*	*Population*
Neighbourhood	Neighbourhood centre	5000–10 000
Second order	Middle centre	20 000–40 000
Urban area	*Bezirk* centre	75 000–200 000
City	City centre	>600 000

For each level of centre an area in the hierarchy was then established, the range of functions and services ideally needed given the size of threshold population required to maintain that service function, or the distance people are prepared to travel for that service. For each service or function there was an additional decision as to whether it should be in a centre, in the vicinity of the centre or elsewhere within the area served by a centre but not physically linked to it. The hierarchy of centres and areas was then defined with the help of a set of further criteria including existing administrative units, strong edges in the townscape such as the rail-lines, historical traditions, transport and ties of the residential population (Figure 12.9). For each designated area the size of population was predicted for 1990 and the deficiencies in service provision noted.

The concept of hierarchy was applied to most aspects of urban development in the city. Forecasts of employment shifts to the tertiary sector were used to propose that office space is dispersed throughout the central place hierarchy but also located in association with the major industrial zones of the city. Where areas were expected to develop, plans have been laid to upgrade the central place or places for that area to cope with the resultant demands.

Perhaps the most significant case of a new area is the district of Chorweiler which is frequently referred to as a 'new town' by the city planners. Here on 6700 hectares the city has planned a new urban district of 110 000 persons complete with its own shopping centre, its *U-bahn* link for the 10 kilometre (25-minute) journey to the city-centre, and an industrial zone which would link up with the already large-scale north Cologne industrial area including the giant Ford car plant. There is also a large area adjacent to the centre awaiting the development of an office park. The final element in the plan (Figure 12.10) is a large (4.8 square kilometres) recreational area separating the industrial area from the residential districts focusing on a large artificial lake produced by current gravel extraction. Chorweiler represents the modern creation of all that the planners feel should be constructed at the urban district level of the hierarchy.

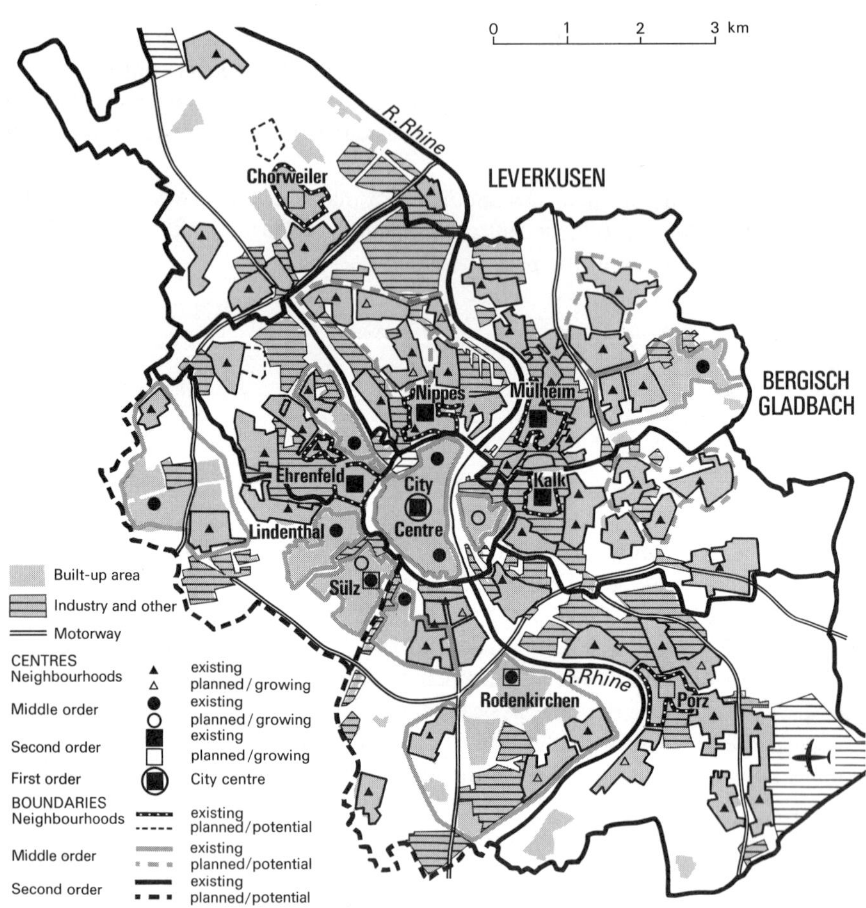

Figure 12.9 Cologne structure plan: central places (reproduced by permission of Amt für Stadtentwicklungsplanung, Köln)

At present the district contains just over half its population target, few new industries have arrived and the office park area is under agricultural use despite being available for development. Why has this district failed to date? The reason lies not in the concept of the central place hierarchy but in other political decisions and events beyond the control of structure planners. First the city decided to build a high-density mainly social housing development. Its stark pastel-shaded high-rise blocks and concrete walkways (even stone table tennis tables!) formed a very harsh environment right on the rural fringe of the city. They were developed at the time of the growing reaction against high-density living throughout West Europe. While there are other housing forms including old villages within the district they are not as visible. Thus the housing has proved to be less desirable than was hoped. Similarly, the slowing in the rate of economic growth has meant that new jobs either in industry, or in offices, have not come to the area but have been located on sites elsewhere, to the south and east of the city in closer proximity to the more desirable

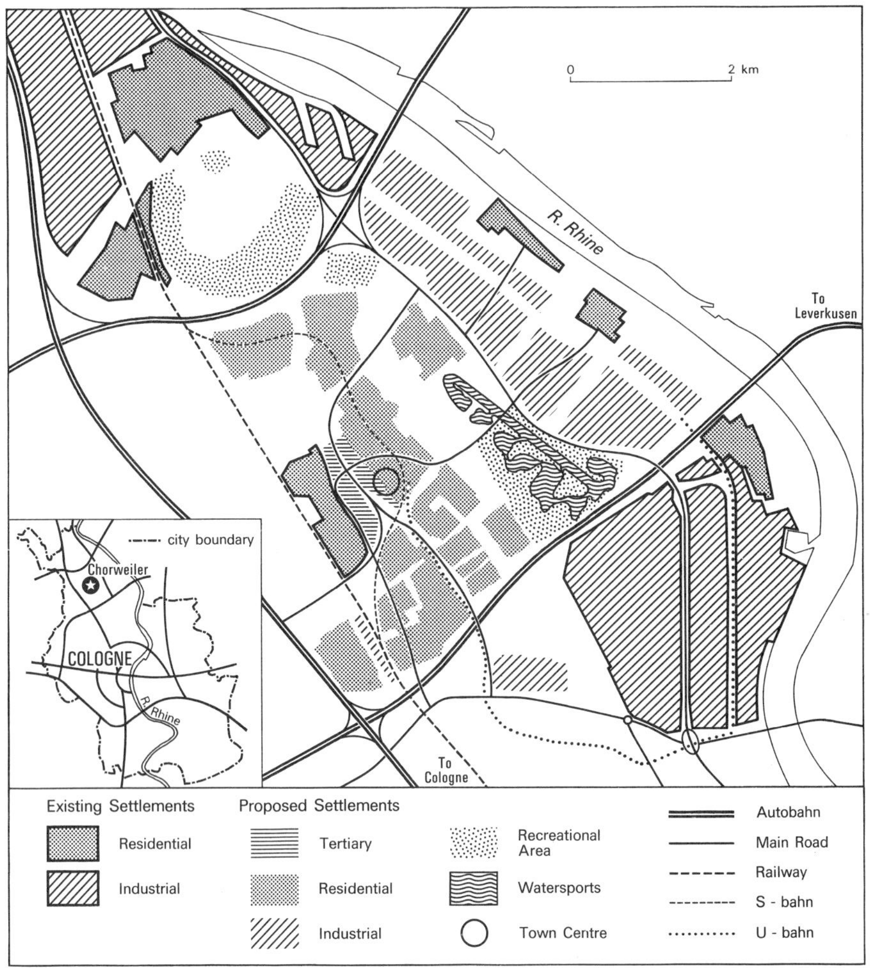

Figure 12.10 A new urban district, Cologne-Chorweiler (reproduced by permission of Hochbaudezernat, Stadtplanungsamt, Köln)

residential areas. Thus the lack of obvious success cannot be attributed solely to the planners but to external decisions, both economic and political.

Despite the problems faced by Chorweiler, Cologne has produced an integrated structure plan that best incorporates the existing city structure into a coordinated view of the future city. It is a plan that emphasizes the function of the historic core as a pivotal area around which the rest of the city evolves. For here the dominant tertiary sector of employment, the flourishing shopping precincts and the consequent demands on transport and parking, and the role of the city as a centre of tourism must be preserved without unnecessary invasion of the inner suburban areas (Stadt Köln, 1973). By recognizing the role of all the urban districts in the release of pressure for development of the centre, the planners are now able to encourage the upgrading of all facilities in the city centre, from housing to offices by, for instance, renovation and the installation of air conditioning so that it continues in the tradition of the West European city to have a dominant and living centre.

Axes and Polycentric Growth: Frankfurt

Frankfurt does appear to be the compromise solution between the more extreme axial and central place structures (Stadt Frankfurt, 1975). Here great emphasis has been placed on the expanding city centre and the role of the tertiary sector in overall city growth. The centre itself has expanded beyond the old core. Beyond the city the inner residential areas are separated from the outer suburbs by green belts and wedges (Figure 12.11). Much of the suburban expansion in the postwar period has been uncontrolled around village and small town nuclei, but this has now been controlled by the implementation of green zones so that the new industrial, office and retail centres are parts of existing suburban settlements linked by rapid transit in the form of *Stadtbahn*, *U-bahn* and *autobahn* to the major centres of employment. The sole case of a new centre and district has been Nordweststadt, a new town of medium-rise, high-density social housing.

The speed with which growth has occurred within the region surrounding the financial capital of West Germany has resulted in a polycentric growth pattern along

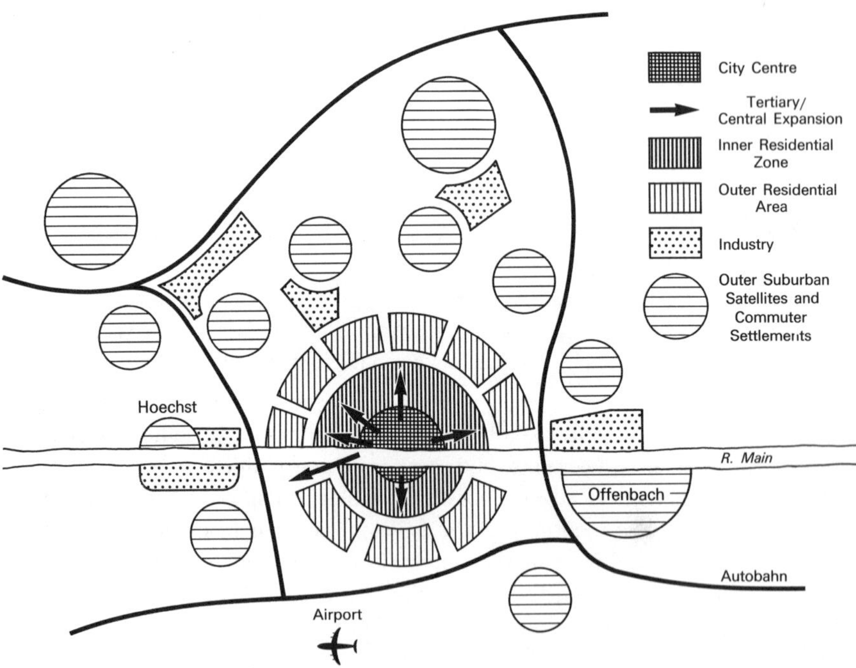

Figure 12.11 Frankfurt structure plan (reproduced by permission of Dezernat Planung, Frankfurt-am-Main)

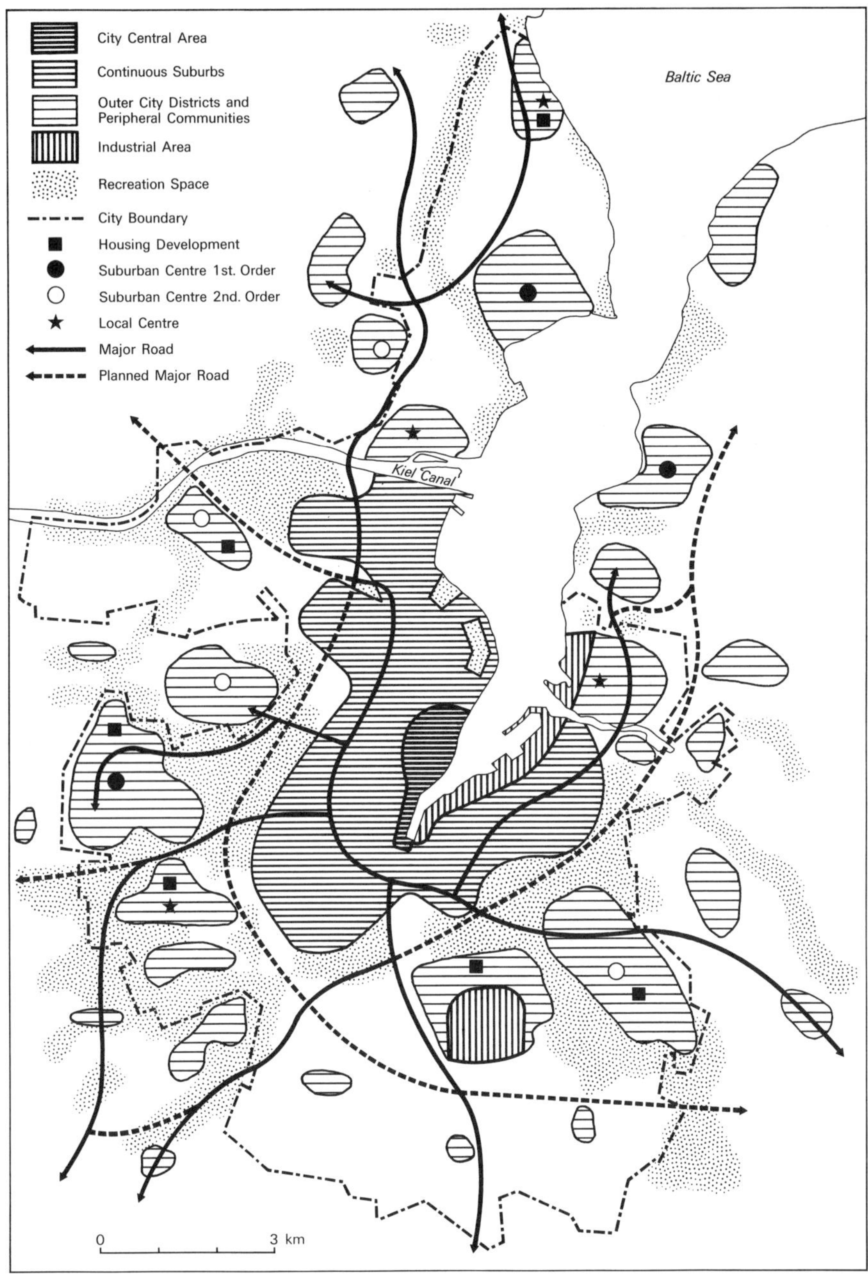

Figure 12.12 Kiel polycentric structure plan (Magistrat der Stadt Kiel, Amt für Entwicklungsplanung)

major routes which the 1975 plan attempts to control more rigidly in the future. Polycentricity is a characteristic of the broader region, so the basic concept is not unfamiliar. The concept of polycentric growth of areas along major routes beyond the continuous built-up city has also been utilized in Kiel's proposals (Figure 12.12) (Stadt Kiel, 1977).

Plans for Utilizing a New Town Strategy

In the case of Cologne and Frankfurt the planners referred to Chorweiler and Nordweststadt respectively as new towns and they compared the concentration of people in similar schemes in other West German cities to the English new towns, acknowledging immediately the vastly different location *vis-à-vis* the core city. There are non-primate cities elsewhere in West Europe that have deliberately utilized the new town strategy as a part of their controlled growth. While it is not the purpose of this chapter to discuss new towns in detail (see Chapter 13) it is valid to see the new town as part of a legitimate strategy for reducing urban congestion in a number of towns.

In the United Kingdom the new towns of Cumbernauld and East Kilbride have been built to relieve the pressures on Glasgow, and at Cramlington and Killingworth for Newcastle. In France, Le Vaudreuil is part of a planning strategy for the lower Seine valley around Rouen. L'Isle d'Abeau and Lille Ascq are new towns built to structure the growth of Lyons and Lille respectively. In 1970 the Spanish government passed the *Acturs* programme which was to enable new towns to be developed outside Barcelona, Valencia, Seville, Zaragoza and Cadiz although the National Regional Economic Development Plan of 1972–75 has tended to contradict these schemes (Wynn and Smith, 1978; Richardson, 1975).

(1) Lyon–St Étienne–Grenoble

The new town idea has been embodied in the structure of the Lyons–St Étienne–Grenoble OREAM (Organisation d'Étude d'Aménagement d'Aires Métropolitaines). The original *schema d'aménagement* in 1970 foresaw two new towns, Pont d'Ain and L'Isle d'Abeau, being created 35–40 kilometres to the east of Lyons, as two new urban industrial centres that would relieve pressure for growth in Lyons and enable the Lyons region to function as a polycentric conurbation. L'Isle d'Abeau has been planned to accommodate 12 000 inhabitants by the year 2000 in a series of ten relatively low-density residential areas on either side of the valley containing the open space at the centre (Figure 12.13a). Besides attracting firms from Lyons the new town has been able to divert other investments away from Lyons in both the industrial and tertiary sector. Pont d'Ain has not in fact achieved new town status but it has been the focus of urban-industrial development and is regarded as an urban growth pole rather than a new town (Bonnet, 1975).

In Grenoble, the original OREAM proposals did refer to the concentration of growth in the Echirolles district as a *ville neuve* although it has never been listed as a new town. The objective was in many ways similar to that of Chorweiler and several

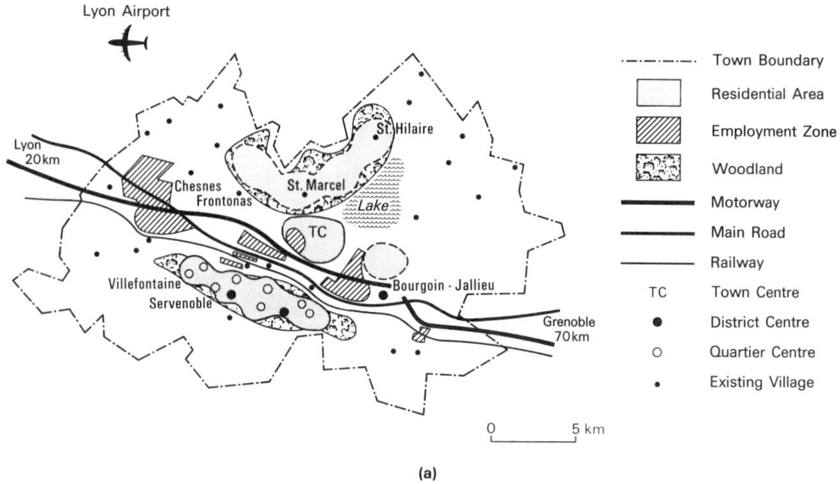

(a)

(b)

Figure 12.13 Cities with new town developments: (a) Lyon and l'Isle d'Abeau; (b) Lille and Lille Ascq

British new towns, namely that of providing a new urban area to combat the tendencies for centrifugal urban growth, to ease congestion at the heart of the city and to create a functionally integrated and basically self-contained urban area rather than a mere suburb.

In the case of the Lyons conurbation the new town strategy was seen as best adapted to the characteristics of the site, and the nature of urban growth associated with high technology industries and the tertiary sector. As a result Lyons was to change from being a single city in a three-centre region to become an integral part of a polycentric urban complex of which L'Isle d'Abeau was just one centre (Bonnet, 1975).

(2) Lille

Lille Villeneuve d'Ascq is another case where a city government has taken the decision to focus expansion in a new town (Figure 12.13b). The decision in principle was made in 1967 and work began in 1971. A new town strategy was decided upon because in this way the growth that was already taking place in the area could be controlled and organized more effectively to create an urban environment of quality. It would also achieve greater cohesion in the area between Lille and Roubaix if it was to be a plan for the *métropole* of Lille–Roubaix rather than a large suburban addition to Lille. Much of the growth was to be structured around the university campus of Lille III being built in the area, the result being an influx of jobs in the tertiary sector. The town now faces problems, however, first with its inability to attract industrial investment from centres other than Lille itself, and second with the declining birthrate (Bruyelle, 1976).

(3) Rouen

Le Vaudreuil is a third French case of a new town strategy to relieve pressure on an urban centre, Rouen. In this case the new town, like that of L'Isle d'Abeau, is in a growth region and is an attempt to give structure to the inexorable growth in the lower Seine valley that focuses partly on Rouen. The other similarity to the Lyons case is that there are marked physical constraints on the growth of Rouen and the designated area of Le Vaudreuil has a valley site that enables it to be at a new crossroads of development along the Seine with a north–south route.

(4) British examples

On the whole, the British provincial city plans that have included new towns have been in regions where the problems are similar to those of Lille. In the case of Newcastle-upon-Tyne, Cramlington and Killingworth were built as small-scale new towns to provide a more attractive living and working environment than that commonly believed to exist by industrialists in the declining north-east of England. Likewise the development of Cumbernauld and East Kilbride as alternative locations to Glasgow, with new twentieth-century images, was an attempt to bring growth to a declining industrial region. Coleraine and the New University of Ulster is an even closer parallel to Lille Ascq, but even more than its French counterpart, there have been problems of attracting people and firms either from Belfast or from further afield.

(5) Languedoc resorts—La Grand Motte

A new town type of strategy has also been used in another form on the Mediterranean coast of Languedoc where an attempt has been made to structure and control the growth of resort settlements and the existing urban areas such as Montpellier and Narbonne between the mouth of the Rhône and the Spanish border. In this case the new town strategy is not one of accommodating overspill from existing urban centres but of developing new settlements to accommodate the demand for both permanent and seasonal homes that was threatening to overwhelm other more developed stretches of the Mediterranean coast. The continuing growth of existing ports and resorts such as Sète, Perpignan and Port Vendres was one possibility, along with the explosive growth of other small settlements such as Le Grau du Roi and the very rapid expansion of the major centres such as Montpellier, which was one of the fastest-growing French cities in the 1968–75 intercensal period. On the other hand, the concentration of growth into new resort towns was an attractive alternative that appealed to the government planners in the mid-1960s and subsequently architects and tourists alike. The result has been the creation of a series of 'new towns', La Grand Motte, Cap d'Agde, Port Carmargue. By far the best developed and most famous is La Grand Motte, 15 kilometres south of Montpellier, sufficiently close to perform the role of a satellite to its older neighbour (Figure 12.14). Here the settlement has a distinct French new town flavour with its imposing pyramid apartments and hotels. It does possess a small developing commercial core and the types of accommodation which will house a projected population of 42 000 are zoned, including camping zones on the fringes.

Plans Depending on Publicized Alternatives and Participation

One increasingly dominant theme in city planning has been that of the need for plans to be more flexible both in their reactions to public criticism and their ability to respond to future changes in economies and societies. To fulfil at least the first of these objectives, there has been a marked attempt in an increasing number of countries to have more effective public participation in urban planning. To enable the public to participate more effectively and in a more informed manner, many city authorities have utilized publication of a number of alternative strategies on which public comment is invited.

(1) Lausanne

A very early example of such a strategy was the initiative of the canton of Vaud into the potential growth of Lausanne (Barbier *et al.*, 1966). The study of the Lausanne region was no more than an investigation into various problems and possibilities for the structuring of urban growth but it did contain illustrations of three alternative forms of growth: unconstrained, growth within a green belt, and growth along fingers or axes (*doigts de gant*) separated by green wedges (Figure 12.15 a to c). For each alternative the advantages and disadvantages for Lausanne were outlined. The

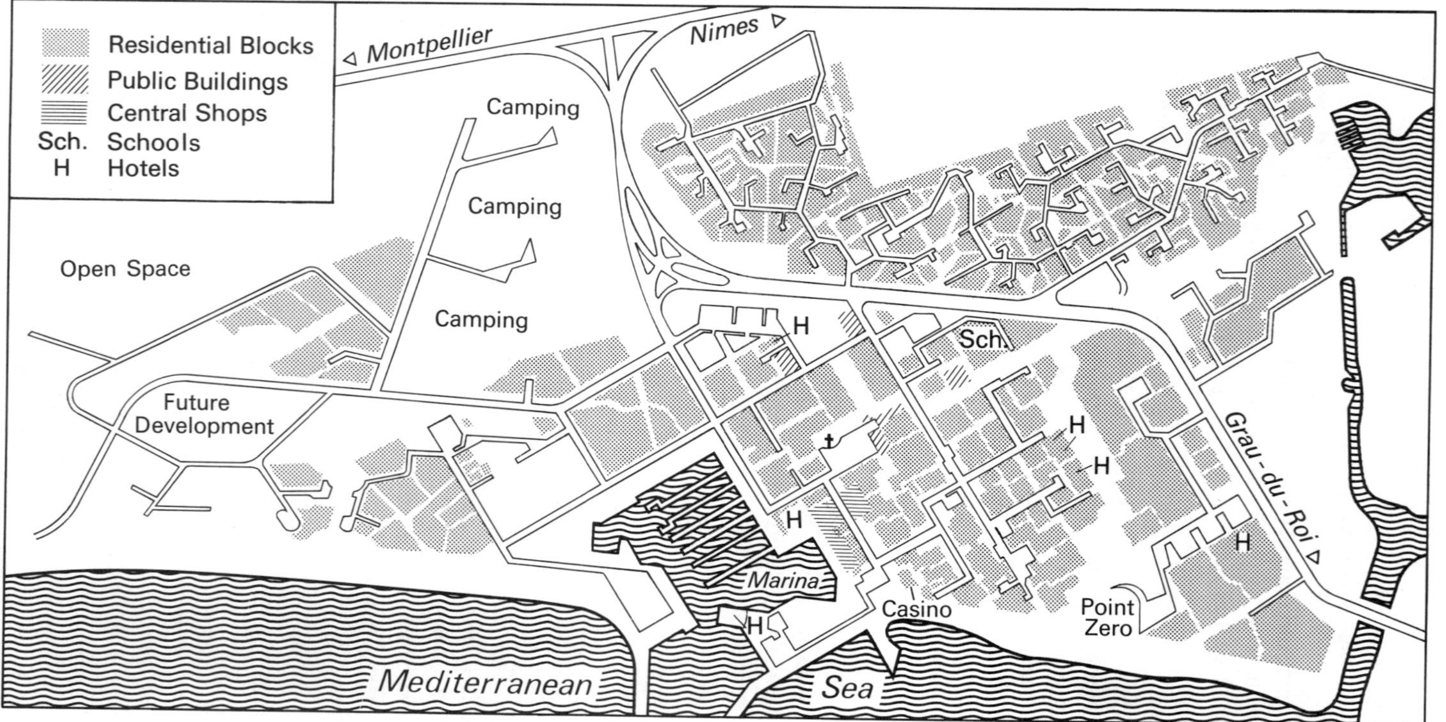

Figure 12.14 La Grand Motte

plans for Linz in Austria, prepared in 1969, also presented three alternative strategies involving (a) two corridors of growth; (b) three growth points including Linz; and (c) greater deconcentration involving the spreading of growth through nine settlements in the region. These particular planning exercises are not uncommon in many countries today.

(2) South Hampshire—Southampton–Portsmouth

In South Hampshire, one of the earliest of the structure planning exercises following the 1968 Town and Country Planning Act and the Skeffington Report on public participation involved the publication of a series of alternative strategies. These were designed to be completely different from each other by proposing a different urban structure and by stressing different elements such as conservation. Thirty-one original structures were eventually grouped into four 'families' which reflected stages in a continuum from concentration to dispersal. The best representative from each family was then published for public comment and detailed evaluation (South Hampshire Plan Advisory Committee, 1972). Strategy A (Figure 12.16a) entailed concentration of almost all growth in a new separate city, a proposal not unlike those for Lille or Lyons. Strategy B (Figure 12.16b) consisted of a series of smaller satellite settlements around Portsmouth and Southampton. Strategy C attempted to control the growth of the two cities in a more orderly form while Strategy D was a more dispersed development on either side of the M27 axis between Portsmouth and Southampton (Figure 12.16c and d).

Each plan was tested to assess its performance against defined planning aims and was the subject of public debate and assessment. Members of the public either by sample selection or voluntary contribution and their local government representatives were able to rank the plans in order of preference. The preferences were generally in favour of a mixture of Strategies C and D although the cities, not unsurprisingly, voted for Strategy C. The proposals that emerged as part of the structure plan therefore concentrated growth in areas on the fringes of the two cities and in four growth areas both along the M27 and extending out as axes from the cities (Figure 12.17).

There are problems involved in such an approach. First the public reaction and that of their representatives tends to be conservative. Therefore, as we have seen in the South Hampshire case, the more radical solutions are frequently rejected. Second, many people feel that the majority of the public do not really see their city as a whole in the way that a structure plan is required to do and, in addition, most people do not think sufficiently far ahead in the terms that a structure plan might demand. Therefore public reaction can be confined to small points about localities rather than a consideration of the broader strategic issues. Thus many do feel that structure planning alternatives are more difficult to debate although participation at a more local level in alternative plans does seem to be more successful. In Swedish cities there are joint consultations on major planning matters and lay people are encouraged to work with the experts in a study group. Field offices and the training of planners in the techniques of consultation and demonstration have been instituted.

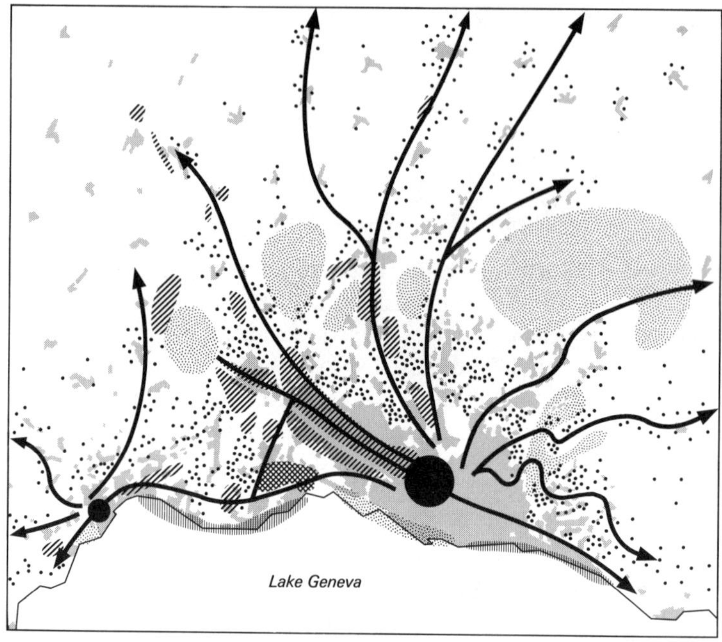

(a)

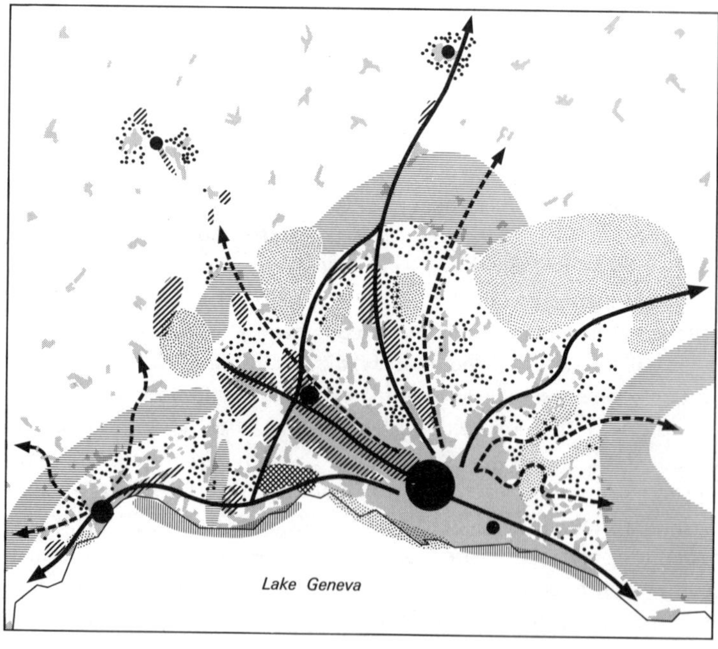

(b)

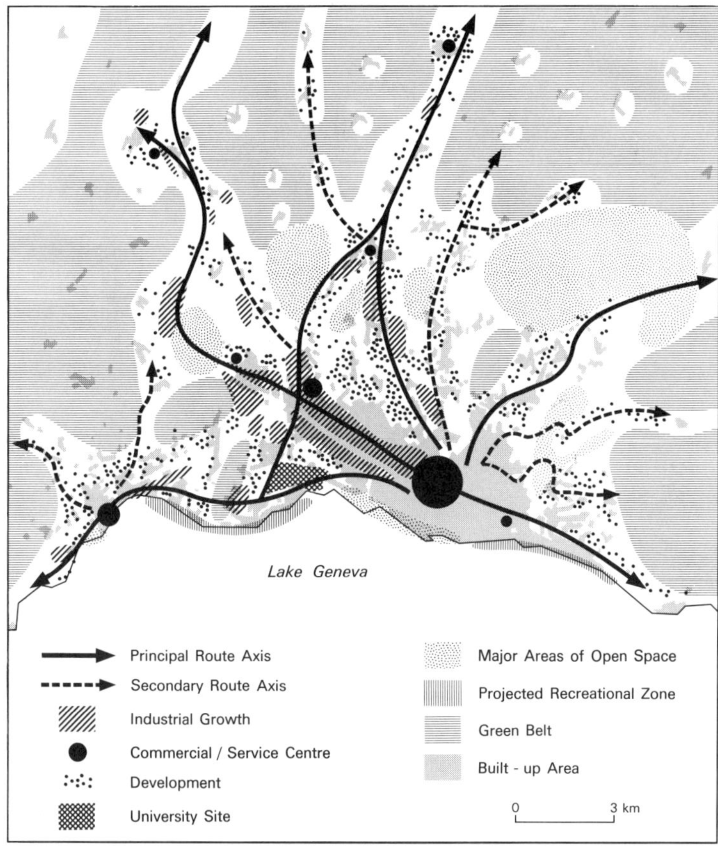

Figure 12.15 Lausanne development alternatives (1966): (a) uncontrolled growth; (b) Green belt controlling growth; (c) Green wedge and fingers of growth (*doigts de gant*) (reproduced by permission of Groupe d'études de la Région Lausannoise)

Hamburg has used its own employees as 'devil's advocates' to make sure that any participation exercises, especially in immigrant areas, are not dominated by the more articulate nationals. In these ways there has been greater responsibility given to areas of the city to respond to alternative strategies for development.

French studies of participation in planning confirm that the participation is effective mainly at a local level (Dupuy, 1977). There are four types of participation initiated by: (a) inhabitants; (b) local planners; (c) central authority; and (d) very localized initiatives. The first type is often concerned with management of an estate rather than planning and is also found in Swedish and British cities in the form of the neighbourhood council. There are cases of new areas of Alençon and renovation schemes in Marseilles where participation is on local initiative. The second type is the local planners' attempts to involve the inhabitants in the plan. Usually it is the

Future built - up areas
Major road network
Winchester
0
8 km
S
P
Isle of Wight
THE SOLENT
MJD

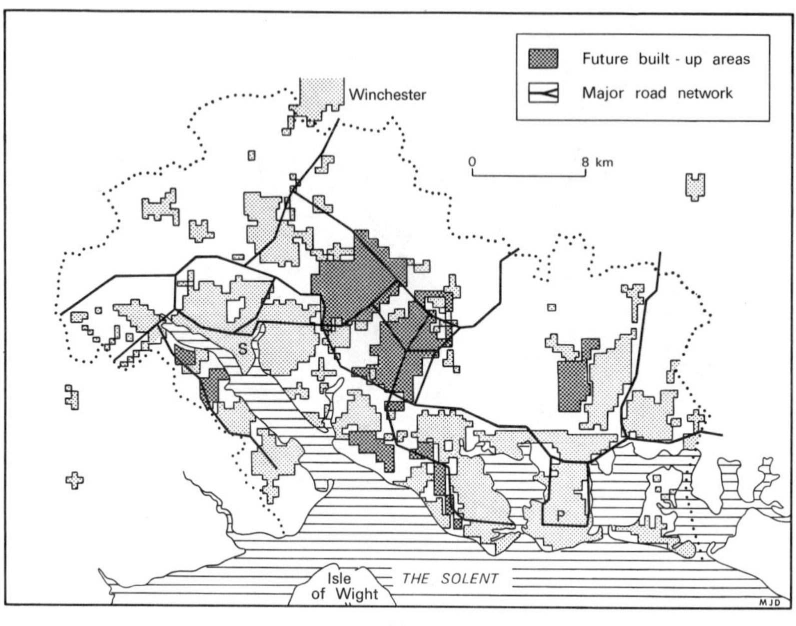

(a)

Future built - up areas
Major road network
Winchester
0
8 km
S
P
Isle of Wight
THE SOLENT
MJD

(b)

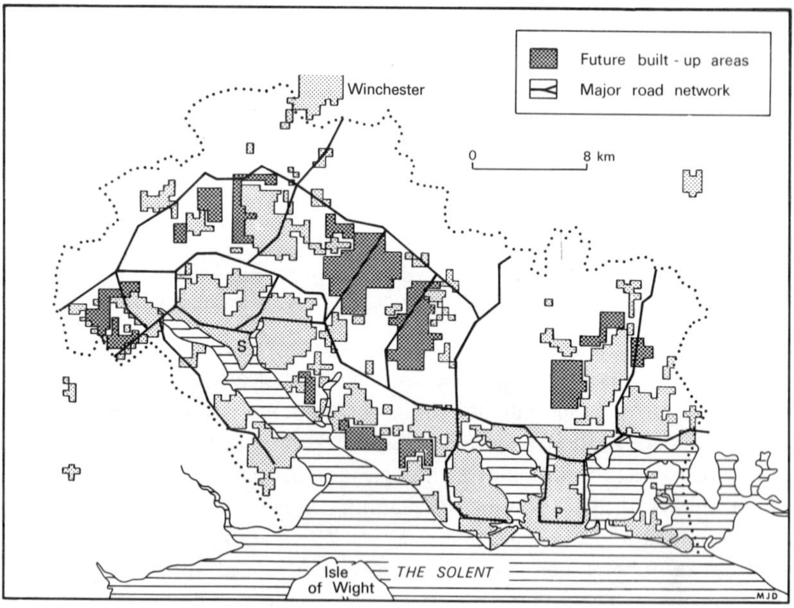

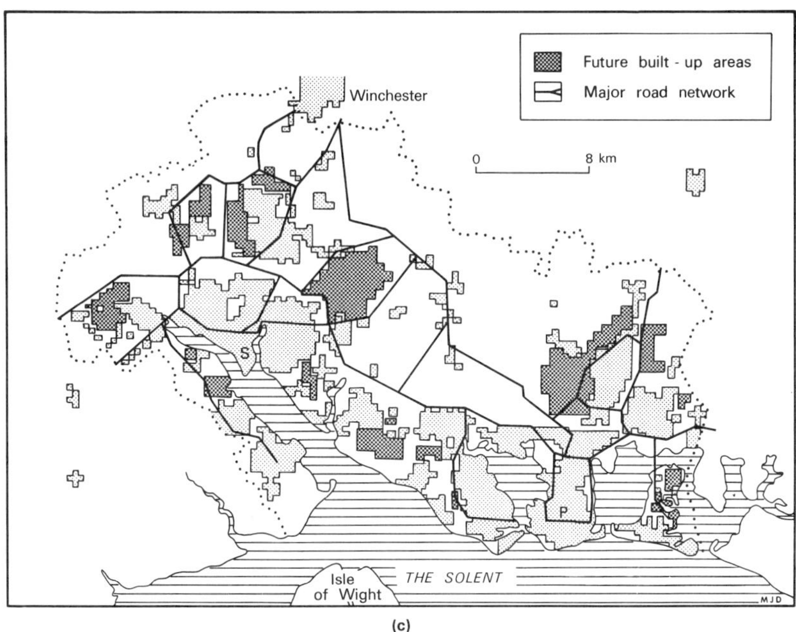

(c)

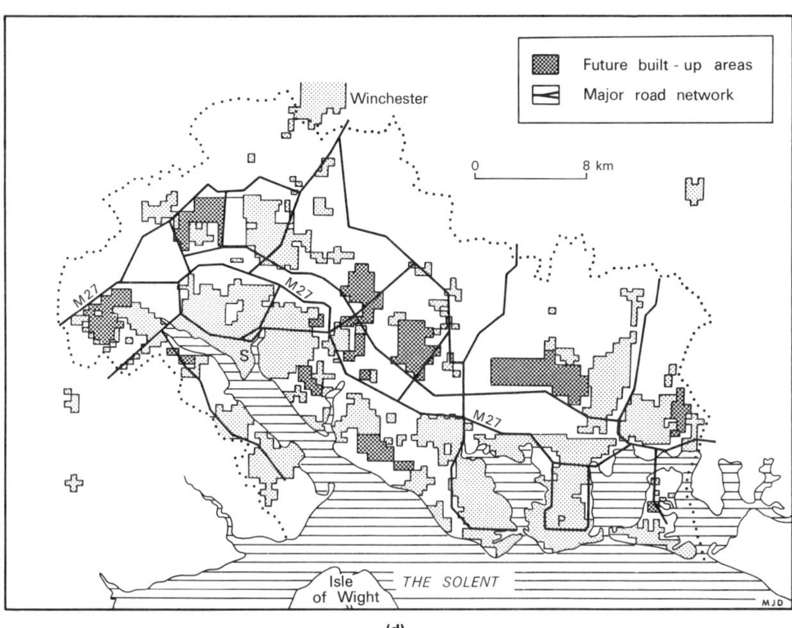

(d)

Figure 12.16 South Hampshire structure plan alternative strategies: (a) Strategy A—concentration in a new city; (b) Strategy B—satellite settlements; (c) Strategy C—continued growth of major settlements; (d) Strategy D—M27 axial growth (reproduced by permission of Hampshire County Council)

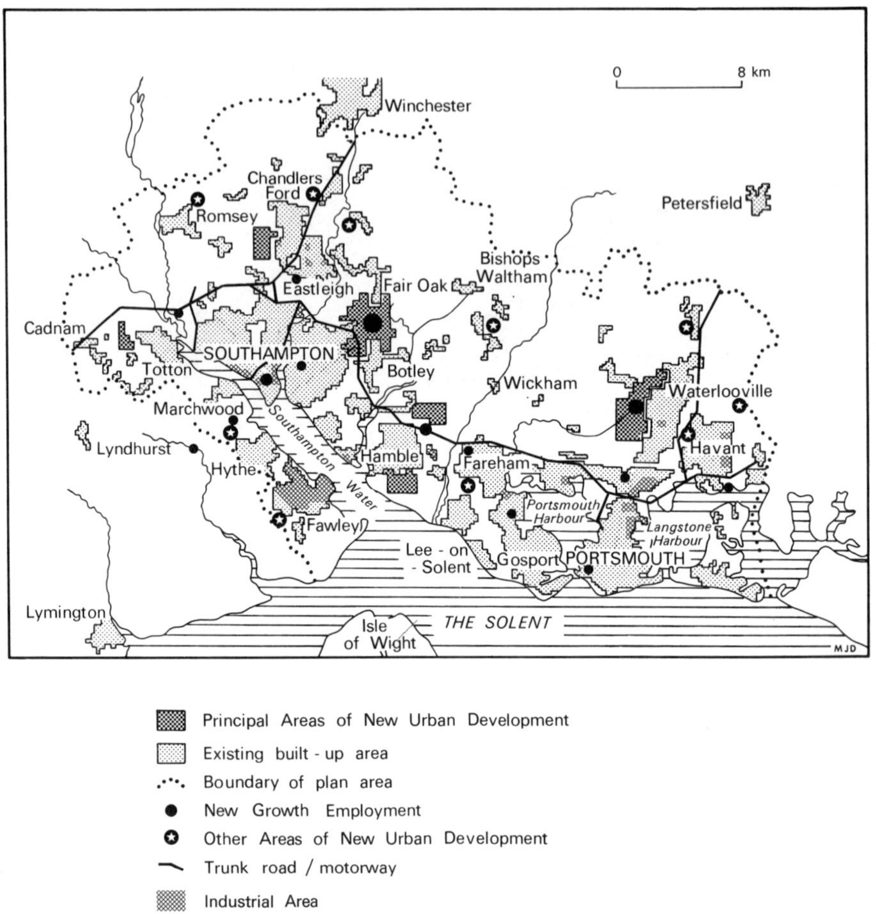

Figure 12.17 South Hampshire structure plan preferred strategy (reproduced by permission of Hampshire County Council)

initiative of the city as in Dunkirk, Rennes and St Étienne, or it can be the new town authorities particularly the more recent authorities of Le Vaudreuil, L'Isle d'Abeau and Villeneuve d'Ascq. Alternatively the administration can request participation as happened in Bordeaux and Saumur. Finally, central government initiatives have been experimental but encouraged in the hope that they will justify existing unique plans at Autun, Angers and Givors. The final type is very small in scale and involves very localized planning such as the construction of groups of homes. Participation of the second and third form is within the spirit of participation in city planning rather than local planning.

The list of other cities that have published alternative models includes Hannover with proposals for concentrated, axial and the preferred central place model, and Rouen which published a set of alternative proposals for the tertiary sector. Greater

Manchester also had alternative strategies prior to its Draft Written Statement, examined above. The three stages were: (a) a relative decentralizing strategy; (b) a middle-of-the-road strategy arising from the balanced spread of resources and benefits; and (c) a relatively concentrated strategy slowing down decentralizing trends and putting an emphasis on areas of economic, social and environmental stress.

City Planning and the Quality of Life

The more recent planning proposals have placed far greater emphasis on the quality of life in cities than previously attempted. Obviously there are variable expectations both between and within countries as Monheim's studies showed with reference to residential preferences (Chapter 6). Nevertheless, the most recent plans do contain more statements on the quality of life as a guiding principle. While it is difficult to put quality into a cartographic, diagrammatic or photographic form, there are several instances where quality of life is stressed directly. Wohlin (1977) feels that much of this reaction by the professional planners is the result of the influence of the environmental movements which grew out of Vietnam protests and student revolts in the 1960s, and began to demand control of motor vehicles and roads, the conservation of energy, refurbishing dwellings, more green for the pedestrian.

Greater Manchester placed the quality of life at the centre of its draft strategy and from this stemmed a series of policies that were to change the region's townscapes, for the good of all (Greater Manchester Council, 1978). Likewise the introduction to Munich's development plan gives as its first priority the coordination and concentration of effort to maintain the attractiveness, quality of life and life chances for the inhabitants. The plan then goes on to spell out how this primary aim can be achieved through a set of broad policies for investment, urban growth, recreation and management (Stadt München, 1975). The rise of specific recreational plans for many cities, particularly in German-speaking and Scandinavian countries has further emphasized the importance of the non-working hours of a citizen's life which far exceed working hours. The specific resort plans of the French have also recognized that quality of urban life is important even on holiday.

Cities Where *laissez-faire* has Dominated Planning

Obviously there appears to be a contradiction in any reference to so-called *laissez-faire* planning, but an examination of cities in West Europe suggest that there are examples of cities where planning has not taken place in any conventional or legal meaning of the term. Perhaps it would be more truthful to say 'There has been no lack of planning research and legislation ... but the lack of management bodies with economic and judicial power to make a significant impact on the urban scene has led to an "urbanism of tolerance" on a large scale' (Wynn, 1979).

The comment above was made with reference to post-1953 planning in Barcelona. Despite a long tradition of planning dating back to Cerda's plan of 1859, the city has grown in an uncoordinated fashion, particularly in the outer suburbs where immigrants are almost encamped in the *barracas* and recent residential estates in an area that the 1965 *Plan Director* saw as being organized into decentralized townships. In the old city, decay continues because no renovation is taking place. The city is being developed piecemeal by private speculators and public bodies. Since the fall of the Franco regime there have been moves to rectify the situation by public participation and better control and management which will hopefully prevent the continuation of 'urbanism of tolerance' and all its attendant economic and social ills.

A very similar situation existed in Portugal up to 1974 with the result that there was very little planning of urban development even in Lisbon and Oporto, despite the well-meaning statements in the national plans. Even the ideas of promoting new growth centres inland from the country's two urban foci never got beyond the stage of general designation of centres. As a result developments were uncoordinated even in the largest cities. Despite the revolution of 1974 and increased public participation little progress seems to have been made to rationalize urban planning (Gaspar, 1976; and Lewis and Williams, 1980).

It has already been noted with reference to Frankfurt that planning was slow to have an effect in that city and its region where the problems of the federal structure of the state placing planning powers in the hands of *Gemeinden* resulted in the piecemeal growth of urbanized communities in the outer suburbs. A similar situation occurred more dramatically in Bonn–Bad Godesberg. Until 1971 Bonn was officially the temporary capital of West Germany, a status it had achieved in competition with Stuttgart, Kassel and Frankfurt thanks to the intervention of Chancellor Konrad Adenauer. As a result there was always a strong undercurrent of thought which maintained that in time the capital functions, and hence much of the pressure on the region, would disappear. However, as the federal state grew in strength so did the supporting needs of the civil service, parliament, the diplomatic corps and the host of institutions that feed off the government. All these pressures resulted in the Bonn region achieving the fastest population growth in the 1960s in an area still characterized by small communities (*Gemeinden*) with autonomy in building and planning. The result was the sprawl that characterizes Bonn–Bad Godesberg today because each small *Gemeinde* could and did encourage building. Federal ministries are scattered around the urban area interspersed with offices, residential areas and farms that have resisted the pressure to sell. The large residences of the elegant spa of Bad Godesberg house many of the embassies, and the new part of this flourishing suburban centre has government research offices over the shops. There is an attempt to provide a government quarter around the parliament buildings, but until recently the quality of the buildings hardly matched the status of modern West Germany in the world. Along the arterial road linking the government quarter to Bad Godesberg runs part of the new tram/*U-bahn* passing by government buildings, quality residences, old farms, car sales areas, party political offices, abandoned farmland and the end of a partly completed motorway. It is only within the past decade, with local government reform and the official recognition of capital status, that a belated effort is being made to control the inevitable growth of the city. The cosmetic planning to date has been of a prestige nature relating to the new tram/*U-bahn* and pedestrianization whereas the real tasks of producing a coherent structure model for the capital lie ahead.

Conclusion

Every city is unique in its location, evolution and planning. However, we have attempted to show with the aid of sets of case studies that it is possible to group the plans of the non-primate urban areas. Increasingly, city plans are regional in their scope, no longer confining themselves to the built-up area and its immediate vicinity. Administrative reform has ensured that this is the case in many cities. Given that there is a regional interest, two types of fundamental models of growth have underpinned most structure plans, the concept of axial growth and the concept of a central place hierarchy. Frequently today the two concepts are linked although in this chapter we have tried to select cities that rely more heavily on one or other model. Where the site conditions are more constrained either by physical barriers or by past economic developments then new towns have been proposed as the major means of accommodating future growth. The reaction, though, to some of the more rigid early plans and their subsequent failures or miscalculations has been a demand for more public participation and alternative structure plans for public debate. Although costly, public discussion of planning has a growing part to play in the West European city because, in this way, the continued pride of place that distinguishes so many cities is maintained and strengthened. Nevertheless there are cities where the lack of a controlled view of the future serves as a salutary reminder of the dangers of the 'non-plan philosophy'. Glaswegians still 'belong to Glasgae' but Bonn has to promote belonging with its 'love Bonn' campaign!

CHAPTER 13

The New Town

In many West European countries, new towns are a testimony to two distinct facets of urban planning. On the one hand, they bear the imprint of the theorists and the philanthropists of the nineteenth century which culminated in Ebenezer Howard's garden city movement at the turn of the century (Chapter 2). The second distinctive strand which interweaves with this inheritance is the fact that they reflect in part the national ideology of the society which created them. In this respect they contain a particular blend of authoritarian, utilitarian, utopian, technocratic utopian, organic or socialist traditions which happened to be prevalent at the time and place of their creation. Thus it could be argued that in early postwar Britain, Crawley bore the imprint of Howard and a utopian tradition of urban planning. In contrast, Evry new town (Paris), focused on its modern Agora of commercial and recreational facilities surrounded by high-density pyramidal residential structures, owes more to a utopian technocratic tradition.

Further differences exist between new towns with respect to the functions that they have been required to fulfil. In some cases new urban centres, though very varied in form, have been part of a more general policy of restructuring major urban regions such as Paris, London or Stockholm. In other cases new towns have been designated as new economic growth points or as foci for economic revitalization of declining regions. New towns have also varied considerably in their internal morphology. This variation is apparent both between countries of West Europe and as their development has progressed through time. For instance the early emphasis in postwar British new towns on socially mixed, relatively self-contained neighbourhoods has frequently been replaced by other priorities such as one of maximizing internal mobility.

Because of their role in the general development of urban planning, the importance of new towns outweighs that which might be expected from the proportion of the population which actually lives in them, although in passing we may note that in the United Kingdom in 1977 a population slightly in excess of 2.2 million were living in urban centres newly created since 1945. The new towns have in the recent past been subject to a major reappraisal of their role and their priority in national urban planning policies. For instance, in Britain the inner city has emerged as a new focus of attention, causing the new town to be more carefully scrutinized.

This analysis of West European new towns is divided into four sections. The first examines new towns both in the context of the traditions of urban planning discussed in Chapter 2 and in the light of the 'conventional wisdoms' prevalent at the time of their designation. The second moves to a discussion of the varied functions of new towns, including an appraisal of the success of new towns in fulfilling these functions. The variation in the internal morphology of new towns is examined in the third section, while the concluding section examines new towns in the light of current urban planning priorities.

New Towns and Urban Planning Traditions

In the early phases of new town building, the legacy of the utopian tradition of Howard was strong. His first garden city at Letchworth in 1903 had a strong commitment to urban open space and to self-containment of the garden city and other proposed satellite communities which would have existed in his ideal plan. The first generation of new towns in Britain clearly bore the imprint of this thinking. Following the enabling legislation of the New Towns Act 1946, the new towns, whatever their purpose, had relatively small populations and it was intended that they develop a strong local economy. Abercrombie in 1944 had proposed satellite towns as a part of his plan for the growth of London. The proposal eventually came to fruition with eight new towns, occupying sites different from those suggested by Abercrombie, but nevertheless designed to channel some of the growth of the capital away from London itself, into economically viable new towns (Figure 13.1). Their siting was determined by the need to preserve good agricultural land (a high priority in wartime and early postwar Britain), to have good communications links with the capital and to have a pre-existing centre to act as an initial nucleus for the new town. There was a strong intention to discourage commuting from the new town back to London, an intention which clearly relates to the aim of self-containment, characteristic of Howard's garden city. In practice, no new town has ever been economically self-contained, least of all the eight original new towns around London which are now very easily within the comuting zone of the metropolitan area.

The new towns around Paris illustrate a more realistic aim in respect of self-containment and move away from this particular ideal. In these new towns, there has been an attempt to achieve a high job ratio (number of jobs available as a proportion of the employed resident population). It is clearly acknowledged, however, that this is no more than the net situation after commuting both into and out of the new town has been taken into account. Elsewhere, the concept of self-containment has been debated. In the case of Stockholm, the role and form of new urban centres has been discussed over some 30 years. The initial debate in the 1940s centred on the concept and the precise nature of the satellite town including its degree of self-containment. Thus, in 1945, the first broad planning document for Stockholm advocated satellite towns in the form of relatively independent urban units with a balance of homes and workplaces. They were to be subdivided into distinct urban units, with a suburb of 10 000 population comprising a series of smaller units each with a population of about a thousand. It was never the intention, however, to produce self-contained satellite towns. In this case, the power to shift economic activity or to determine its location has always been rather more limited than in Britain. Faced with this fact there has been no concerted effort to create new

Figure 13.1 New towns in the United Kingdom

employment growth points in the new urban centres. Instead the new centres have been planned with good public transport links to the central city and its employment base. Thus the utopian tradition of creating new towns as part of a new urban beginning complete with a variety of employment, but lacking in polluting industries, has been adopted in only a very limited sense. Even in Britain, by the 1960s, the principle had been abandoned with the acknowledgement that a new town such as either Washington or Milton Keynes would be a part of an extended commuting network incorporating both surrounding settlement and occasionally rather more distant urban centres.

The garden city introduced open space into new urban developments. Indeed in Letchworth, the original site was almost 10 000 hectares, later increased to just over 11 000 hectares. Of this, only 3700 hectares was to be used for the town itself and even this was to be built at a low density. The intention was to create a town where trees would grow and open space would be available for recreation and its aesthetic value. This facet of Howard's garden city certainly lived on in many new urban centres. Vällingby, the first of the Stockholm new suburban centres was spacious in layout, utilizing natural vegetation cover where possible, considerably aided in its landscaping by the occurrence of natural rock outcrops. In Britain new towns outside London also adopted this approach. For instance two new towns in County Durham in north-east England have each paid close attention to the effect of landscaping. In the early stages of its development the new town of Peterlee, set amongst the mining communities of East Durham, commissioned Victor Pasmore, the artist, to advise on the general design of the town and its open spaces. In Washington, a decade later, landscaping and the introduction of open space in an area scarred by a century of coalmining were understandable priorities.

The utopian tradition has been a strong one but by no means the only one. It could be argued that the high-density development of central Evry or the business node of Noisy-le-Grand in Marne-la-Vallée are reminiscent of the limited resurgence of authoritarian planning in Gaullist France, discussed in Chapter 2. Certainly the *grands ensembles* of the 1960s were part of this tradition. They often took the form of architecturally bizarre implantations in the suburbs, such as that at Grigny in southern Paris. Nowhere, however, have new urban centres been planned to match the new towns of East Europe in terms of an authoritarian approach.

In fact, many new urban developments in France owe as much to the utopian technocratic tradition as to any authoritarian tradition. Certainly it is the new town in the Paris region which of all European new towns has moved further away from neatly ordered garden city style of planning. The original plan to link Cergy-Pontoise to Paris by an *aerotrain* although later abandoned, suggested the style of planning prevalent at the time of the designation of the new towns for Paris in the late 1960s and early 1970s. The public transport orientation of Evry, and more particularly the manner of its translation on the ground in the first part of the town to be developed in the form of segregated bus lanes passing through the base of pyramidal residential structures close to the centre, linking these and lower-density development further out with the centre and the main railway station, suggests a strong input of the utopian technocratic tradition. A similar scheme was first introduced in Runcorn in north-west England where public transport was given a segregated route system. It took the shape of a 'figure of eight', centred on the town centre, with residential, development and employment centres closely allied to this segregated system (Figure 13.2). The increasing acceptance of new technology in new town planning has been

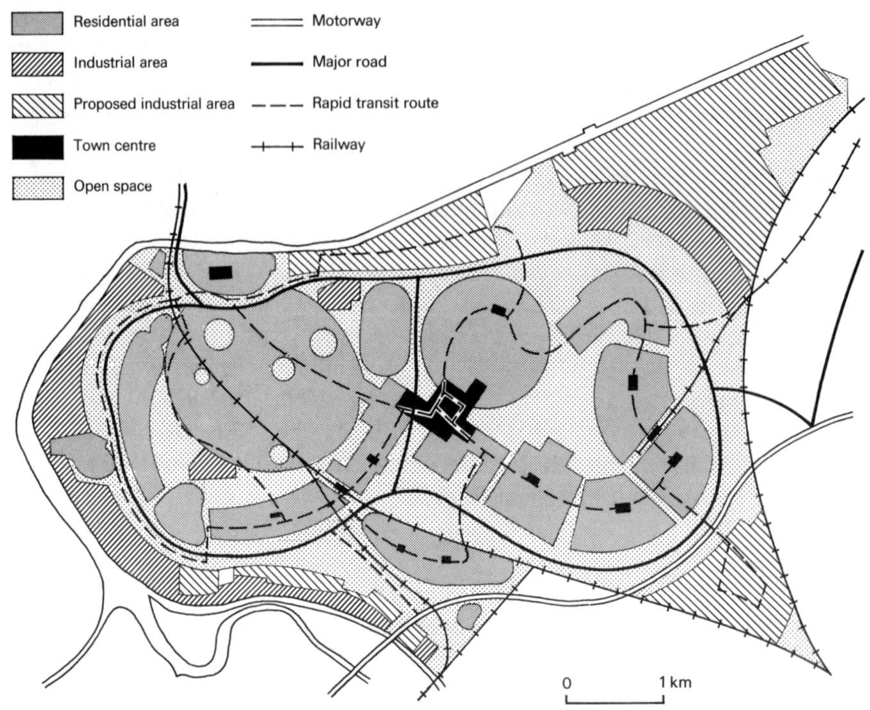

Figure 13.2 Runcorn new town, United Kingdom

evident, although it should be noted that despite early expectations no new town has been created with a completely new high-technology rapid transit system. It would appear that the major reasons for this is one of economic viability given the relatively restricted size of new towns.

It is a matter of some debate as to how far a tradition of socialist planning has been evident in West Europe's new towns. The original ideas of social balance within neighbourhoods in British new towns were soon proved to be excessively idealistic. Indeed today social segregation along socio-economic and occasionally racial lines can be seen to be as complete as in any other town. The early postwar planning of new towns in Britain, under the new Labour government of that period was frequently criticized as being socialist in concept. In its eventual execution, however, there is no real difference in these terms between a new town and any other urban centre.

A final tradition which deserves consideration is that of the organic tradition of planning. A continuing problem, but one only recently recognized, has been that of producing a plan for a city of perhaps a quarter of a million population. Its eventual completion date may well be a quarter of a century distant, yet attempts have been made to produce a master plan for a greenfield site without any input from the eventual population. Events in the last ten years, however, have frequently created the need for a new approach involving both monitoring and a flexibility of approach.

The building of Milton Keynes on a grid-square basis with an expectation of high personal mobility may yet prove to be unfortunate, but it is difficult to alter the basic plan. Other new towns, however, have had a greater degree of flexibility built into them. Examples are Le Vaudreuil, near Rouen in France, and Warrington in north-west England. Certainly the rigid urban blueprint has proved to be an outmoded instrument of urban planning both for new towns and larger existing centres. Increasingly the choice has been taken to keep possible options open for the future in the development of new towns. In this respect, almost by necessity the utopian tradition which was so very strong in the early phases of new town building has been superseded by a more pragmatic organic tradition.

Role and Purpose of New Towns in West Europe

While many new towns have been developed as satellites, accommodating growth from a major centre, others have had very different functions. These have ranged from stimulants to growth in areas of economic decline to growth points in areas of new economic development. The situation is complicated by the fact that although many of the early new towns had a single clearly defined role, be it satellite or growth node, later designations frequently had more than one purpose. In still other cases, the original *raison d'être* of the new town has dissipated since its designation, requiring a change of function for the new town.

New towns as overspill centres or satellites are numerous in West Europe. Both Copenhagen and Stockholm, as a part of plans to channel growth into well-planned new urban sectors, adopted new town satellites. For instance in Copenhagen in 1947, the so-called Finger Plan (Chapter 11), served as guidelines for the growth of the city. The 'fingers' of development stretching out from central Copenhagen took the form of linear axes of small townships along the *S-bane* lines (or subway routes). Later, in 1960, the scale of new towns increased just as it had in the United Kingdom by that time. It was proposed at that time that the growth of Copenhagen for two subsequent decades should be housed in two new towns each with a population of a quarter of a million. Although this proposal was not carried out it plainly illustrated the strength of the notion of new urban centres as satellite centres. As suggested previously the new towns, or perhaps more properly new suburban centres, of Stockholm emerged with rather less emphasis on economic structuring than their British counterparts. Nevertheless they were clearly satellite developments, catering for a growing Stockholm. Since the first such developments, however, the new suburban centres changed considerably in form as we shall see in the following section of this chapter.

In Britain the first London new towns were certainly satellites designated to take overspill from the capital. Similarly, following the planning initiatives of the 1960s (Chapter 11), other satellite new town designations were made. Milton Keynes, Peterborough and Northampton all fit into this category. Elsewhere in Britain, early satellites included East Kilbride and then Cumbernauld, catering for Glasgow. Telford was designated as a new town to take excessive growth from the West Midlands, but here we see the ambivalent position in which these new towns now exist. The local authorities of the West Midlands were initially eager to see the new town relieve some of their growth pressures. By the 1970s, however, when their own economies were being stretched in an economic recession, they were rather less enthusiastic to lose manufacturing employment. Demographically a similar situation exists in Milton Keynes, where a labour shortage threatened the growth of the new town as population predictions for the south-east fell short of earlier predictions. The major problem appears to be that new towns have usually been designated in growth periods, either demographic or economic, with the clear expectation that these trends will continue. When there are unexpected declines in growth, the new town is particularly vulnerable.

The new towns of Paris may also be classified as satellite towns, although their role is undoubtedly somewhat more sophisticated than being merely reception areas for excessive growth. The eight original new towns formed one of the essential elements in the emergence of a new bi-axial development for the Paris region (Chapter 11). Thus the five new towns that remain of those originally proposed are integral parts of the two new axes. Cergy-Pontoise and Marne-la-Vallée form part of the northern axis and St Quentin-en-Yvelines and Evry, with neighbouring Melun-Sénart, are part of the southern axis (see Figure 11.3b). Besides accommodating growth, however, they share the responsibility, with the new growth poles planted in the inner suburbs (*pôles restructurateurs*), of bringing to the Parisian suburbs a strong service-centre structure with alternative nodes of employment. It was noticeable that as a part of this policy both Cergy-Pointoise and Evry early in their development had new *préfectures* for two of the new *départements* of the Paris region, Val d'Oise and Essonne respectively. (Note that a new *préfecture*, that for the *département* of Val-de-Marne, was established in Créteil, one of the very large new suburban growth poles). In addition new regional shopping centres were also situated in the new towns. It could be argued therefore that the Paris new towns are rather less vulnerable in terms of achieving their original purpose even though population growth has declined; they have already brought impressive new service centres to the previously underequipped Paris suburbs. The population targets for the new towns of the Paris region were considerably larger than those of the original London new towns. The latter now have targets of between 29 000 (Hatfield) and 130 000 (Basildon), while later London designations have higher targets, such as Milton Keynes with 200 000, Northampton (180 000), or Peterborough (160 000). Those for Paris had original target populations closer to half a million population, and already by 1979 a total of 393 000 people were living in the five new towns of Paris. Nevertheless, the original targets have had to be considerably decreased as population growth slackened.

In the Netherlands, the new town of Zoetermeer is a new satellite town modelled consciously on the British pattern. It is situated 10 kilometres from The Hague which makes it much closer to its 'parent' city than those of London or Paris, each of which are up to 40 kilometres from the main city. It has a target population of 100 000 for 1985. Zoetermeer is by no means self-contained, and indeed has been planned for commuters to The Hague with no house more than 500 metres from a train station, and access to the special commuter train the 'Sprinter', which links the new town to its parent city. In both Paris and Amsterdam large-scale developments have been undertaken which are akin to satellite new towns, although not strictly new towns as usually defined. Bijlmermeer with a target population of 80 000 serves Amsterdam, whilst the *pôles restructurateurs* of Paris are similar developments in terms of scale, although much more a part of the existing city.

Serving two functions in a similar fashion to the Paris new towns are the new towns of the Flevoland polders. The early Dutch new towns on the polders, such as Emmeloord on the north-east polder, were purely new regional centres built to service the new settlement of the polders. The newer towns closer to Amsterdam, however, have been subject to different pressures. For instance, both Lelystad and Almere on the southern IJsselmeer polders (Flevoland), were originally planned as regional centres, with population targets by the end of the century of 100 000 and 250 000 respectively. However by the late 1960s and early 1970s they were assigned a new role as overspill centres for Amsterdam.

While the original concept of a new town was principally as a satellite centre, some new towns have been designated for economic purposes. Wulfen and Marl in the northern Ruhr were to accompany expansion of the mining industry. Despite the opening of a new mine at Wulfen, however, it is unlikely that it will be a sufficient economic base for a new town (Burtenshaw, 1974). A similar problem faced Glenrothes on the Fife coalfield in central Scotland since a change of policy in the coalmining industry deprived it of its primary role of a new mining town and assigned it instead to a more general role of a new town in a region of economic assistance. In contrast to these new towns, Corby in Northamptonshire was designated in 1950 as a new town in an attempt to widen its economic base which was heavily dependent on the iron and steel industry. In the event, the town has still proved to be economically vulnerable in its dependence on one industry and still requires considerable economic diversification. With the imminent closure of the iron and steel works in 1980 the town has been granted development area status in an effort to bring some balance to its employment structure. In the case of one of London's five new towns, Basildon, designated in 1949, the opportunity was taken to provide a solution for another planning problem besides that of the growth of London. In this case it was sited in an area of considerable rural dereliction so it was intended that the new town would give a new structure to a poorly planned area.

In Britain many new towns have been established as a part of a regional development policy. Cwmbran (1949) in South Wales, Newton Aycliffe (1947) (now simply Aycliffe), and Peterlee (1948) were amongst the early ones. They were followed by others which had various purposes but still had a major regional policy component in their designation. Skelmersdale (1961), designated in part to provide new housing for Merseyside, and Washington (1964), intended to provide good land for industry, overspill facilities for Tyneside and to set a standard for the urban environment, fall into this category.

Success or Failure of the New Towns

At this stage it is worth considering the success of new towns in carrying out these varied roles since it can scarcely be claimed that all new towns have been unconditionally successful. In the case of overspill or satellite new towns in Britain, there have been some disturbing conclusions concerning the general ability of new towns to cater for those in greatest need in the 'parent' urban community. For example, it has been suggested in Glasgow that the new towns have done little to alleviate the problems of multiple deprivation, and that by providing houses primarily for those employed in the new town they have been selective in taking only one segment of the urban population. Although the argument can become circuitous, in an analysis of urban deprivation the new towns score best since their housing stock, being newer, is automatically of a higher standard, and in addition unemployment is generally lower than in the central city.

A similar view has been put forward concerning London's new towns by Deakin and Ungerson (1977). In a study of the impact of the new towns on the inner London borough of North Islington, they offer support for the contention that the inner cities have been socially and economically damaged by the development of new towns. Predominantly it has been the young, the skilled and the white population which has been attracted to the London new towns. As a result, an analysis of the ethnic composition of the new towns shows that only 1.1 per cent of the population of the eight first generation London new towns were of New Commonwealth origin at the last census in 1971, compared to 5.7 per cent in Greater London. This type of discrepancy is only part of the reason for the more general reappraisal of British new towns discussed in the final section of this chapter.

If one attempts to measure the economic success of the British new towns then the contrasts are stark. Generally those whose prime function was overspill facility for London have been more successful than those elsewhere with a similar function or those created for purely economic reasons, although admittedly this is a generalization which should be treated with some caution.

Crawley, as an example of a London satellite new town, has been economically successful. In contrast to many new towns outside the south-east region, it has attracted not only manufacturing jobs but also offices. For instance between 1947 and 1978, 73 986 square metres of office space was completed. Other new towns attracted even more, such as Northampton, with 148 500 square metres between 1968 and 1978, and Bracknell, 111 117 square metres from 1949 to 1978. These figures may be compared to the 5946 square metres of offices built in Aycliffe from 1947 to 1978 or the 9633 square metres in Peterlee over a similar period.

Crawley was particularly fortunate, however, with the location on its northern boundary of Gatwick airport, which has emerged since the 1960s as London's second airport. This has generated a considerable amount of service employment in Crawley and together with vigorous economic growth gave rise to a major shortage of land for new residential development by the late 1960s.

The economic contrasts are all too apparent in a comparative examination of some of the new towns designated in development areas in Britain. Peterlee, in County Durham, for instance, although primarily designated in order to improve the residential stock of the (then) Easington Rural District, also had to attract new industry. In this aim Peterlee met with comparatively little success for a number of reasons. One was its inaccessibility, sited in the east of the county away from the main north–south line of communication. Second, it had to withstand the opposition of neighbouring local authorities, such as Hartlepool to the south, which were anxious to improve their own weak economic base. Finally, there were problems of land subsidence arising from its location on a coalfield which was being actively worked (see Thomas (1969) for a fuller discussion of the problems of this and other new towns). The net result is that Peterlee attracted industry providing only 5067 jobs between 1948 and 1978 compared to the 19 782 new jobs created in Crawley during the same period. The importance of location within a region is illustrated by the fact that Washington, designated in 1966, has been much more successful than Peterlee in attracting industrial jobs, though it shares the same inability to attract service employment. Washington is on the main north–south axis of the region, alongside the A1(M) motorway, close to Tyneside and Wearside, and in this location has attracted 9200 jobs between from 1964 and 1978.

New towns outside south-east England have demonstrated their vulnerability in terms of economic decline at times of more general economic recession. Expanding companies attracted to the new towns in the development areas by a range of financial inducements may well locate only a branch plant in the new town location. At times of economic stress these plants are the most vulnerable to closure. Skelmersdale in Lancashire has had a particularly troubled history in terms of its employment base. Designated in 1961 with the primary aim of solving some of Merseyside's housing problems, and particularly those of inner Liverpool, it developed a vulnerable economic structure, heavily dependent on two major manufacturers, Thorn (making television tubes), and Courtaulds (a major textile company); in 1975 these two companies employed 20 per cent of the town's workforce. A total of 10 000 new jobs had been created between 1965 and 1975, many of these in the small 'nursery' factory units of less than 800 square metres (7000 square feet) provided by the development corporation. By mid-1977, however, both major factories had closed and unemployment levels were in excess of 20 per cent. After the closure of one factory, *The Times* (1976) summarized the plight of the new town thus, 'it may be that the crisis that Skelmersdale now faces, in terms of both employment and confidence, may lead to fresh thinking and that for some considerable time to come, the effort will have to be directed towards restoring and consolidating the new town within its present limits, rather than looking for big new growth'. Later events confirmed the reappraisal not only of Skelmersdale but of all British new towns.

The success of new towns as instruments of the restructuring of large urban areas varies considerably. The new town or new suburban developments of Stockholm have certainly given a logic to the structure of that city. At the same time they have ensured the viability of public transport since they are specifically oriented to the *T-bahn* (subway) system, in a similar fashion to those of Copenhagen. A more fundamental restructuring such as that attempted in Paris via the new towns has proved to be rather more difficult. The example of Marne-la-Vallée illustrates the difficulties of fulfilling the roles assigned to the new towns.

Situated 10 kilometres from the centre of Paris, Marne-la-Vallée comprises three

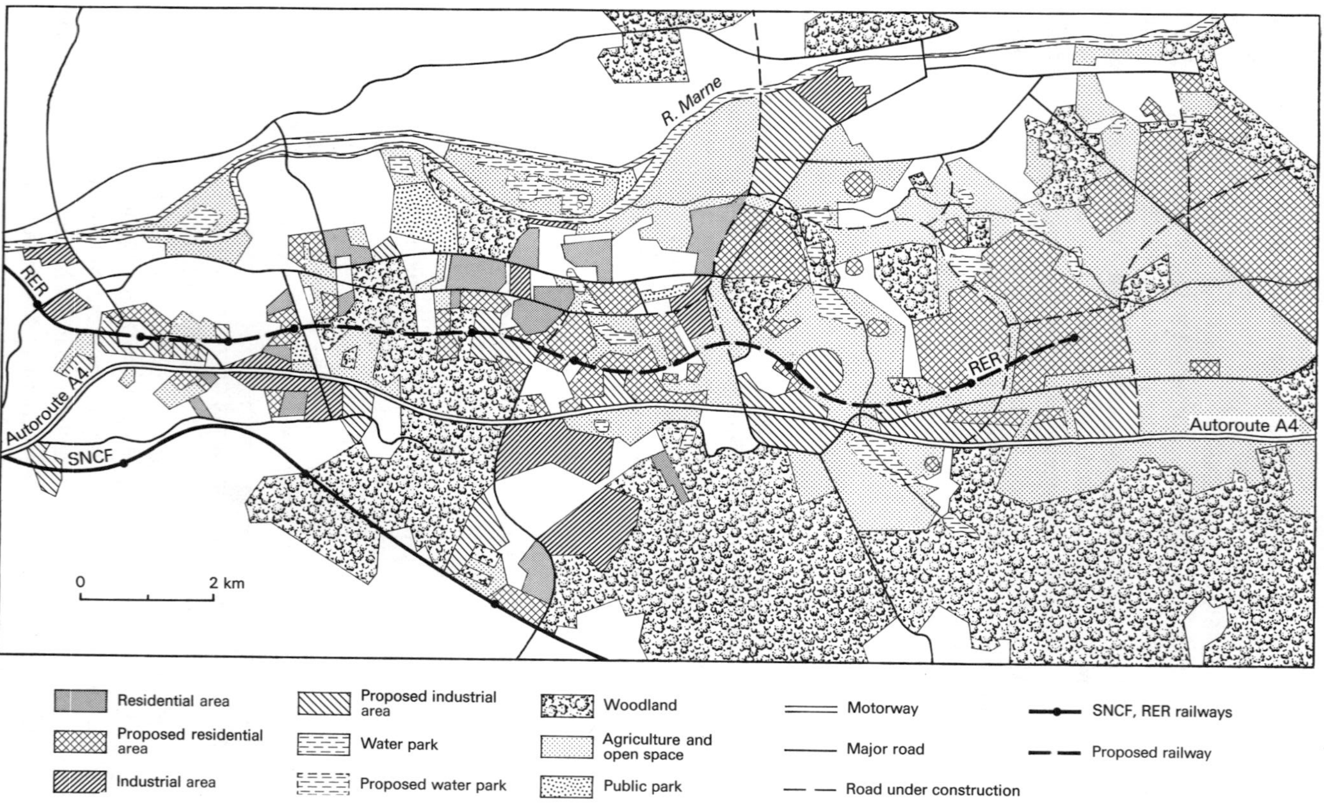

Figure 13.3 Marne-la-Vallée new town, France

distinct sectors extending west to east, linked together by the new RER line . *Express Régional*) and by the A4 *autoroute*, which runs through the southern sector of the new town (Figure 13.3). The new town is seen as having a major role in correcting the east–west imbalance of the Paris region in terms of economic growth. Thus its western sector, centred on Noisy-le-Grand is essentially a part of the inner suburban ring of communes in eastern Paris. The development of a large commercial complex with a regional shopping centre and 117 000 square metres of offices has gone some way to providing a better service base for the eastern inner suburbs. This location within the pre-existing suburban zone has brought with it obvious problems of creating a clear identity for the new town. The second and third sectors of Marne-la-Vallée, located further eastwards have progressively lower densities of development and are more akin to 'conventional' new towns with small-scale groupings of new residences and associated facilities separated by recreational land.

Thus Marne-la-Vallée has succeeded in giving a new structure to the eastern suburbs though perhaps at the cost of a clear identity for itself. It is more questionable whether the new towns of the Paris region can effectively help to create the new axes of growth described both in the *Schéma Directeur* of 1965 and its modification in 1975. It is already apparent that a major initial priority was to forge an effective link with Paris itself rather than with each other or along the lines of the new axes. However, such an assessment may well be premature, and it may be that given time the Paris region will emerge as a more polycentric region than it has been in the past as the new towns develop further.

Indeed any assessment of success or failure of all West European new towns may be equally premature. We are assessing the development of towns over a relatively short period and in many cases it would be naïve to expect short-term results. Short-term economic failure may be transient, and large-scale aims may take several decades to fulfil.

The Morphology of the New Towns

The internal layout of new towns in West Europe has been the subject of continual reappraisal. Early new towns, following the first British examples, were predominantly oriented towards neighbourhood planning with a degree of traffic segregation. The neighbourhood size was determined by school catchment areas and each neighbourhood centre had a small range of convenience-goods stores. Increasingly, however, this stereotype of the new town has been questioned and new forms of the town have emerged. The development and continuous reappraisal of the form of the new suburbs for Stockholm, for example, indicate the degree to which change has been apparent.

The form of the first development was to have small communities of 2000 population, which in their turn were grouped into suburbs of 10 000 which then went to form larger units of up to 50 000 population. These may be termed successively 'suburban elements', 'suburbs', and 'districts' and the conceptual plan is well illustrated by Vållingby conceived in the 1940s (Figure 13.4). Developments such as the Vållingby group were termed ABC groups where work (*arbeiter*)

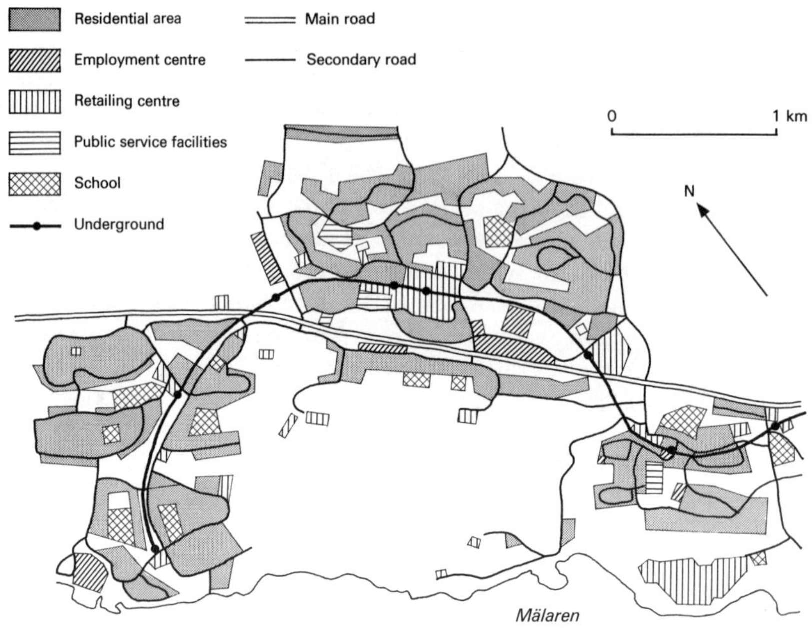

Figure 13.4 Vållingby suburban group, Stockholm

combined with residences (*boståander*) and focused on the centre (*centrum*). In practice the work component was rather belatedly incorporated into the plan. Experience with these first-generation new suburbs suggested that some improvements were needed particularly with regard to the adaptability of these new developments. There were three specific problems. First, it was shown that the age structure differed over time from the original population, requiring an adaptability in service provision. Second, the Swedish school system was reformed and with it the catchment areas, necessitating a change in the size of the suburban clusters. Finally, the changes in retailing in the 1950s and 1960s, bringing an increase in the scale of operation and the decline of the small shop, favoured the development of larger suburban shopping centres, serving not one, but several suburban areas. Thus the 'pearls on a string' development which had characterized early developments in Stockholm were superseded by much larger suburbs. The first-stage subdivisions at the lowest level, between 'suburban elements' and 'suburbs' were omitted and the centre was one of regional importance. Thus the Skårholmen group was developed (Figure 13.5), comprising Bredang, Såtra, Skårholmen and Vårberg, with its retailing centre designed to serve not only these districts but also the neighbouring communes of Huddinge and Borkyrka. In the event, the retailing centres were not as successful as anticipated and further changes in plan design took place.

In 1967, the first inhabitants moved into another type of suburb at Tenstra and Rinkeby, which were the forerunners of a major new development of the 1970s. These two districts were characterized by high-density development, with a belt of service facilities including schools and retailing running through the centre of the

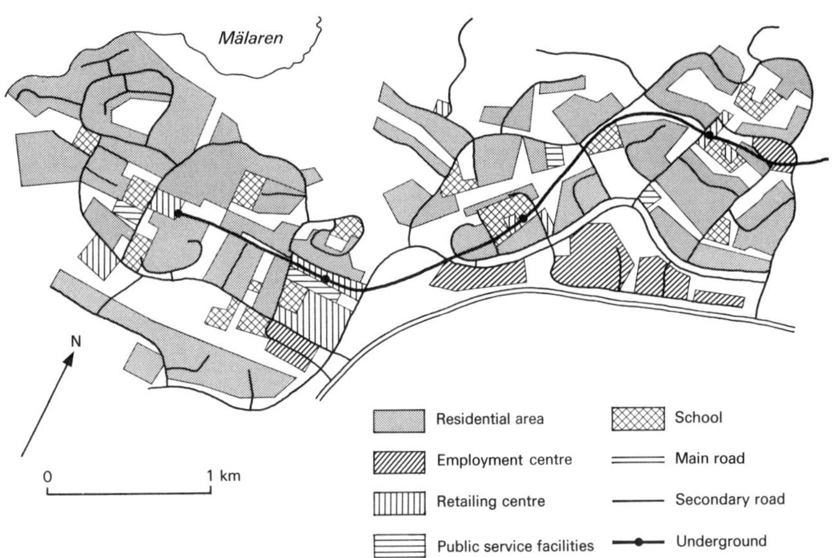

Figure 13.5 Skårholmen suburban group, Stockholm

suburb along the line of the *T-banen* route. This axial development now adopted in the Nórra Järvafältet development, contrasts with the small nuclear settlement patterns of the Vållingby group. The Nórra Järvafältet group (Figure 13.6), comprising Kista, Husby and Akalla, has an axis of service development with high-rise development closest to this axis and progressively lower density development away from it. Although it is intended that this arrangement ensures that services are equally available throughout the length of the axis, one centre, Kista, has a larger retailing unit than the others, in the form of a covered shopping mall, but with direct access to the *T-banen* system. The adoption of this style of development following the rejection of the Skårholmen pattern was made partly on the grounds of flexibility but also because of the opposition to the larger-scale planning epitomized by Skårholmen.

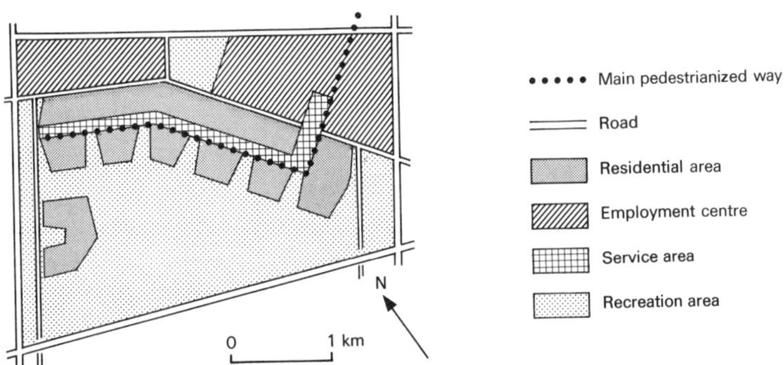

Figure 13.6 Nórra Järvafältet suburban development, Stockholm

While the planning of the new suburban centres of Stockholm illustrates changing attitudes in the planning of new urban areas, elsewhere in West Europe new towns demonstrate a number of approaches, reflecting a variety of priorities which may be either socially based or, increasingly, mobility based. The plan for Runcorn in 1964 was an important milestone in new town planning. No longer was the cellular pattern of neighbourhood units adopted as the basic morphological pattern for new towns. In its place was an emphasis on public transport with adoption of its segregated bus track mentioned earlier. This concept was subsequently extended in the planning of the central zone of Evry, Paris, where the pyramidal apartment blocks frequently straddle a segregated bus route network (Figure 13.7).

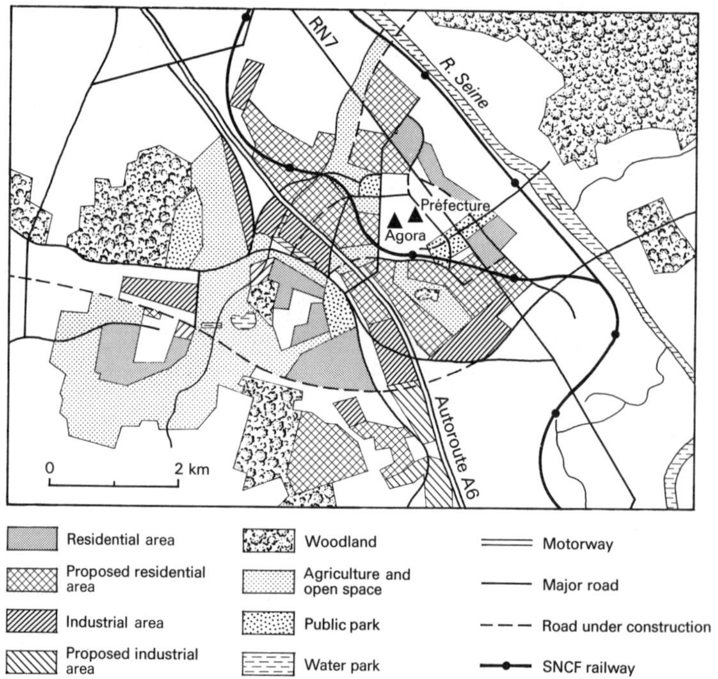

Figure 13.7 Evry new town, France

A concern for mobility also characterized the planning of two contrasted new towns in Britain, Milton Keynes and Washington. Both date from approximately the same period as Runcorn, and both master plans were prepared by the same design partnership. However, the contrasts in the plans for the two new towns are important since they illustrate the nature and extent of the reappraisal of the neighbourhood unit which had been so important to the earlier new towns.

A prime design objective of Milton Keynes was to provide freedom of choice for the individual. It was felt that the neighbourhood unit, by providing a central focus of services and encouraging social interaction at that level, inhibited such freedom. For this reason, the neighbourhood was rejected. In its place, a grid pattern was adopted as shown in Figure 13.8, in order to facilitate mobility within the new city. The service facilities were then located on the primary route network rather than being centrally positioned within the residential zones. A high level of mobility for the inhabitants by bus or private car thus ensured their freedom of choice between competing facilities. Such a plan, fostered also by Melvin Webber's notion of 'community without propinquity' (Webber 1964) is almost a symbol of a high energy-consuming society, particularly unfortunate in terms of its reliance on private transport.

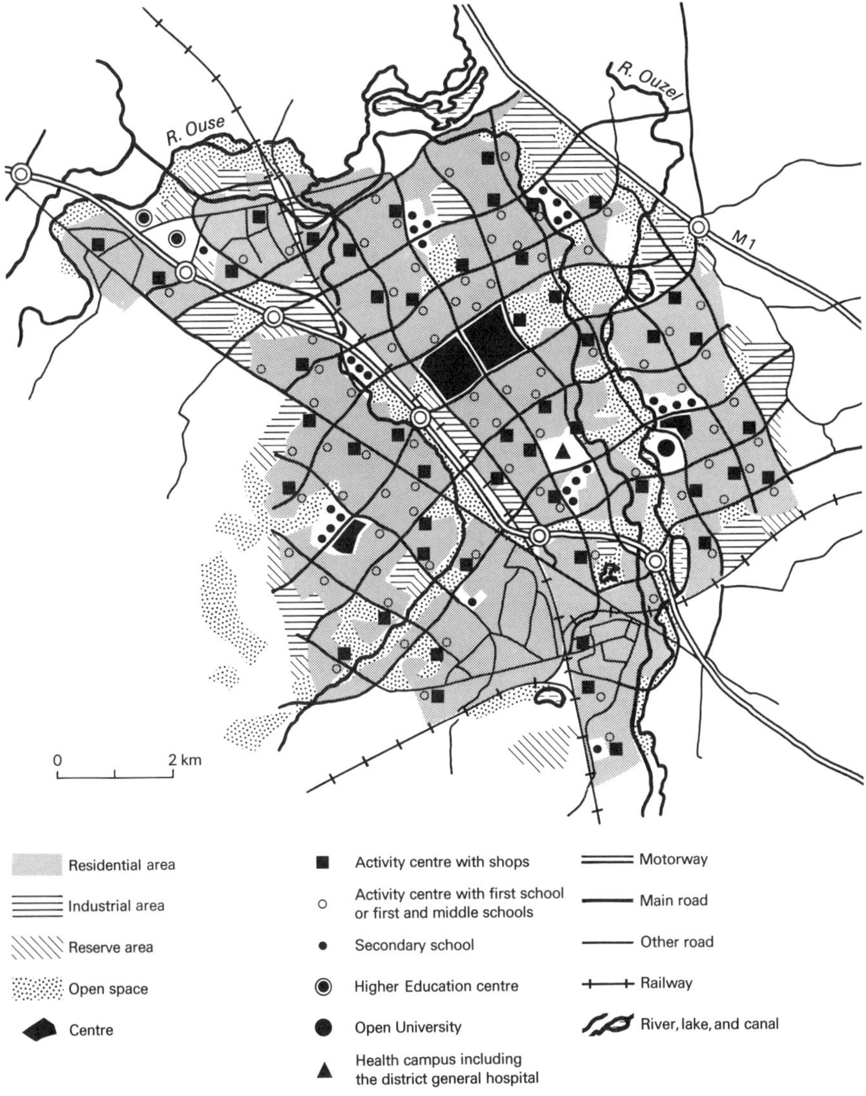

Figure 13.8 Milton Keynes new town, United Kingdom

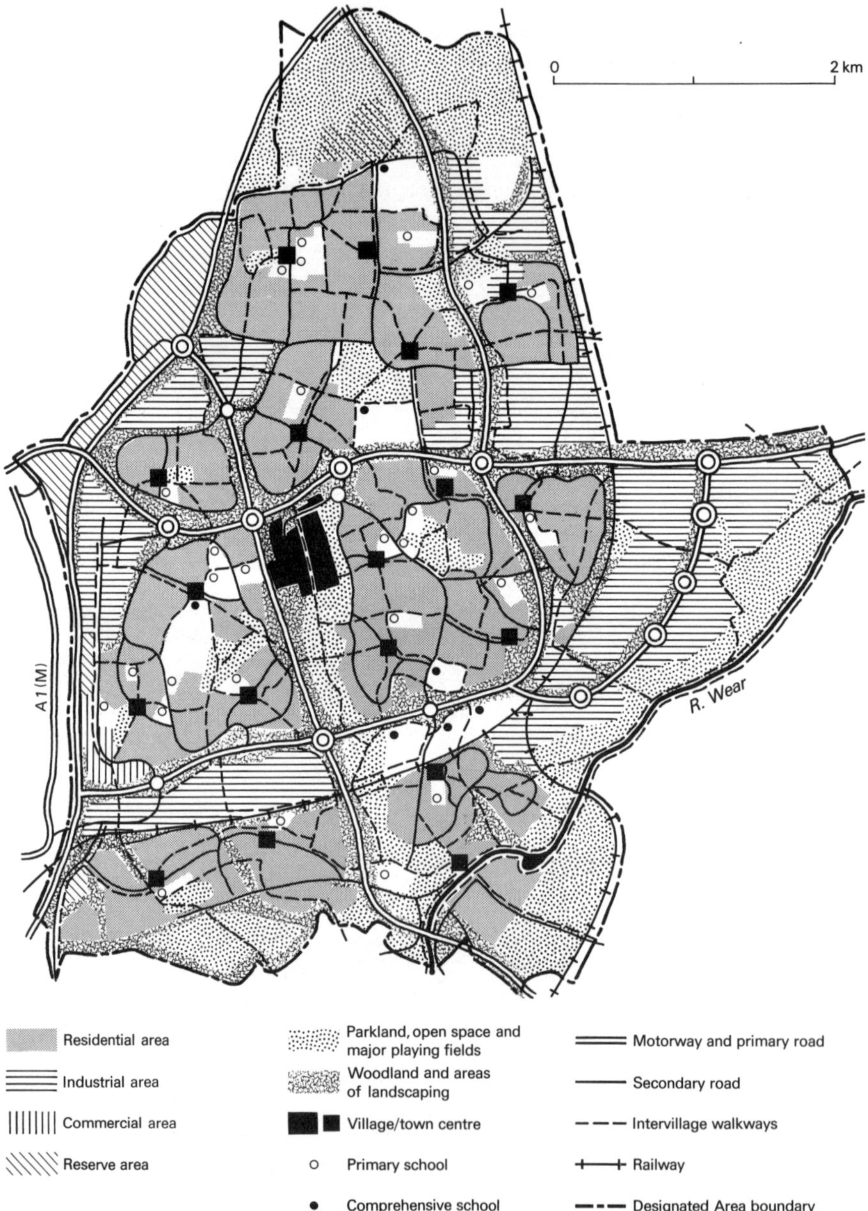

Figure 13.9 Washington new town, United Kingdom

A similar grid pattern of primary distributor roads formed the basic transport network for Washington new town (Figure 13.9). In this case, however, the social planning component was much more traditional. It involved the development of eighteen villages with approximately 4500 people in each. At this level, such a development reflects the local structure of the mining communities of the region in which Washington is located, some of which were included in the designated area of the new town. Each village is subdivided into 'places' of between 200 and 600 families in which it is expected that the inhabitants would best develop a feeling of local identity or 'sense of place'. Finally, the 'places' are subdivided into groups of between 24 and 50 dwellings, often around a common facility such as a shared garden or play space. This closely structured pattern is in sharp contrast to the Milton Keynes design. In its planning of industrial zones, Washington is also very traditional. Industry has been located in a number of small estates, providing opportunity for one village to forge particularly strong links to one industrial estate. Furthermore there is provision for small-scale workshop industry to be incorporated into village centres. Washington, then, is more a traditional new town than Milton Keynes. It does reflect the traditional patterns and residential–employment relationships of its region, although the plan acknowledges the likely role of longer-distance commuting between Washington and the neighbouring centres of Sunderland and Newcastle upon Tyne. Milton Keynes, on the other hand, alongside the M1 motorway—a major growth zone—is perhaps more symbolic of the urban expectations of the last quarter of the twentieth century, before the energy crisis lowered such expectations.

Reappraisal—the New Priorities

The 1970s have seen a reappraisal of the place of new towns in overall strategies of urban planning. In Britain the slowing down of population growth has raised questions concerning the need for new cities such as Milton Keynes. In France the new towns of the Paris region will not reach their original population targets, at least in this century. In both countries there has emerged a competition for resources which has affected the new towns. For instance in France, it has been suggested that the *métropoles d'équilibre* designated in 1966 to act as regional nodes for growth, have been neglected in favour of the new towns and the replanning of the Paris region (Berry, 1973). In Britain, however, the reappraisal has been much more fundamental and dates from government policy statements from the mid-1970s. For instance, in late 1976 Peter Shore, the Secretary of State for the Environment (responsible for urban planning), suggested in a speech in Bolton, Lancashire that the emphasis on dispersal to new towns and overspill areas had been directly responsible for 'daunting problems' faced by older urban areas with a declining industrial and economic base. Well-established local authorities in the vicinity of Central Lancashire New Town such as Bolton, and even closer ones such as Blackburn, were opposed to the new town when they themselves were faced with major problems of urban rejuvenation (*The Times*, 1976).

The major policy change came in April 1977 when the government cut back dramatically on the new town programme and particularly on the Central Lancashire new town project. The urban programme with particular responsibility for the inner city was transferred from the Home Office to the Department of the Environment with an increased budget from £30 million per annum to an eventual

£125 million by 1979–80. It was felt that the reversal of emphasis away from the new towns to the inner city would aid the revitalization and economic regeneration of the latter. The inner city areas to benefit at that time were the London districts of Lambeth and the Docklands, and the inner areas of Liverpool, Birmingham and Manchester–Salford, with Glasgow as the subject of separate provision later. This list is somewhat selective and indeed certain medium-sized cities also have their share of inner city deprivation. Apart from this, however, there is a further point of contention concerning the policy change. Milton Keynes, for instance, claimed that only 10 per cent of its population comprised 'planned migration' from London (*Sunday Times*, 1977). In fact the new policy affected only Central Lancashire new town on a large scale, with the growth of the other new towns to be tapered off in the 1980s; thus Telford would have a population of 186 000 by 1986 instead of its originally planned population of 220 000.

These reappraisals coupled with a considerable slowing down in growth generally have brought to a standstill new town designations throughout Europe. The 30 years of active development of new towns in West Europe have clearly reflected much wider issues of urban planning. Current problems demonstrate the problems of planning large-scale new cities in an era of economic and demographic uncertainty and a rapidly changing energy supply situation. New towns may be seen as current victims of this reappraisal which has affected all urban planning in West Europe. Their special role and place in planning has been replaced by a colder more detached appraisal inevitable in the conditions likely to prevail in the last two decades of the century.

CHAPTER 14

Conclusion

We began by an examination of the Europe city as a distinct entity, a product of ideology and history, and we must end by an assessment of how far the cities in Europe have remained distinctly European while retaining within the European urban system a rich internal diversity. How far have the European urban visionaries been forgotten, as the city in West Europe, so rich in culture and fruitful as a place of interchange and exchange, has moved into the second half of the twentieth century, coping with reconstruction, refurbishment and growth? Has the last quarter of a century added to the richness which is European urbanism, or has it systematically procured its dissipation? We conclude with an attempt to identify the trends in Europe which are forming the city of the year 2000. That magical landmark in time is no longer the distant milestone that 1984 was to George Orwell, or even to the more recent projects of urban futures such as Peter Hall (1969 and 1977). Nevertheless, prediction is a hazardous process, and we must plead that uncertainty overrides confidence as economic frustration, social change, recurring energy crises and changes in political control cloud rather than clarify even the comparatively near future.

The nineteenth and twentieth centuries were periods of rapid growth which transformed many cities. Indeed the scale and pace of change was such that many cities lost their essential character as centres of urban culture and were shaped by the forces of economic rationality alone. The 'property machine' rode roughshod over other aspects of urban culture (Ambrose and Colenutt, 1975). The industrial revolution dehumanized small towns and transformed them into thriving cities, all too frequently characterized by poor housing. Twentieth-century growth frequently gave rise to amorphous, asocial suburbs, the very antithesis of the urban centres advocated by the early generation of European planners who had been so anxious not to repeat earlier mistakes. In this sense Europeans cannot claim to have been faithful to the ideas of the urban utopians, many of whom proposed smaller-scale, more intimate urban forms than those created in postwar Europe. Most of them, however, shared the common characteristic of being both expensive and incapable of tackling problems of the scale encountered. In practice the choice was often between a high quality of provision for the few, or mass-produced standardized facilities for the many. Before condemning out of hand the towerblock and prefabricated estate the critic must show how else the homeless millions of postwar Europe could have been provided with the basic necessities of shelter.

The need to refocus attention on the inner city may be taken as an admission of the failures of urban planning in the last few decades, as part of the spatial fabric of the urban system became progressively neglected and then, inevitably, fell into decay. Some towns have found adaptation a difficult process, especially so in the case of uni-functional towns such as the coalmining towns of Europe or other products of the industrial revolution. Even architectural 'gems', such as the eighteenth century spa of Bath developed in a short period of time, have had to face similar problems. These urban centres lack the rich inheritance of many periods of town growth which characterize many West European cities—Hall's 'repositories of the irreplaceable past' (Hall, 1977). This legacy has in many ways equipped them the better for further change. Development has always been the hallmark of cities such as Rotterdam, Lyons, Milan, Munich or Zurich, acquiring new development from successive centuries including the present. But the twentieth century has brought a more difficult development for Lille, Glasgow or Essen and other products of the industrial revolution. Nowhere is this better illustrated than in the small textile towns of Europe, where the decline of the staple industry has stripped the urban centre of its single dominant function. The textile towns of Greater Manchester such as Rochdale and Bolton, or Anny, Enschede and Hengelo in the Twente district of the Netherlands, München Gladbach or Rheydt west of the Rhine in West Germany, and Verviers in Belgium, all demonstrate the specific problems of adaptability in such mono-industrial urban centres.

The scale of the planning response to urban growth has frequently been dramatic. The interwar suburban estates in Britain or even more marked, the *Grands Ensembles* of postwar France, were faithful to Corbusier's 'machine for living' rather than to the more human scale of traditional building. Public housing schemes in almost every country have had to pay heed to economic reality and in the process have suffered, as we have seen in Chapter 6. All too often they have become second-class places of residence instead of living examples of contemporary urban planning at its best. One of the reasons for this lies in our obsession with access to one resource, that of housing, with scant regard to access to the other facilities which add up to an urban culture. The current movement back into the inner city on a class-selective basis is a clear demonstration that many have realized what the city in its totality offers. Access to all its varied facilities and opportunities is important and was denied to the inhabitant of Sarcelles (Paris) or Wythenshawe (Manchester) or Osterholz-Tenever (Bremen). The reasons for the preoccupation with the provision of housing are not difficult to find. The acute postwar housing shortages, and the continued growth of Europe's largest cities as a result of high natural increase of population and steady immigration, combined to establish the priority of satisfying the massive demand for new residential space. Even in the early new towns the complete package of urban functions and opportunities was all too frequently missing for a full urban lifestyle. In any event, the creation of a new town within one generation cannot hope to provide the cultural variety and the diversity of social and economic opportunity which is the product of many centuries of growth in other European cities. In that sense, although certainly great improvements on a lifeless culturally barren suburbia, they could not hope to compete with established towns. Given the same residential opportunities, there would be few Englishmen who would prefer to live in Stevenage than Norwich, few Frenchmen who would take Evry before Chartres and few Dutchmen who would not live in Leiden, dominated by its magnificent history, rather than in Zoetermeer, for all its planned precision. So thus both the scale of provision and its priorities have been open to criticism.

It could be argued that materialism in postwar Europe has meant that society as a whole has not been willing to pay for an ill-defined higher 'quality of life', meaning a fruitful and productive urban environment in both social and economic terms. An increase in the scale of building has usually meant a decrease in unit costs and in a period when politics have been increasingly important in the whole sphere of urban planning, costs may be equated with taxes which, when increased, cost votes. Perhaps then, our mistakes are merely a reflection of our communal priorities. We may take this argument somewhat further by pointing to the fact that the mistakes are not necessarily those of the planners, but more usually those of politicians expressing these communal priorities through their vote. A distinctive feature of the city in West Europe has been the degree of democratic control, which brings with it a strong control over the freedom of the planner. The planner prepares a plan which has to be politically acceptable in such a system, and it is then the community which ultimately makes the decisions and must be held responsible for both successes and failures.

To dwell on the problems and failures, however, would be to give a distorted picture, because there is much in contemporary urban planning to ensure the survival of the European city. The realization of the value of the past, which has given rise to the urban conservation movement throughout Europe has been not only timely, but vitally important, as demonstrated in Chapter 7. It has meant that despite the increasing omnipresence of Shell, C and A, Marks and Spencer, and now on an intercontinental scale combining to give a 'sameness' to many urban cores, MacDonald's, Col. Sanders', and Woolworth, the underlying diversity will be retained. It may be too late to prevent the emergence of new retailing or office centres which could be equally at home in Chicago, Sydney, Cologne or Paris, but the existing urban cores are being increasingly protected against an encroaching insensitive commercialism, for it is the centre which has been most at risk. Despite postwar developments the towns of West Europe are still more characterized by their variety than their similarity and the urban conservation movement will ensure the continuation of this. There are a number of other reasons for this optimism. One lies in the importance of tourism to so many European cities (Chapter 8). That function can thrive only if accompanied by careful and sympathetic treatment of the urban landscapes which are part of the European cultural heritage that is itself the tourist industries' main resource. The creation of pedestrian precincts in the centres of many cities of major historical interest in the last 20 years, has been one technique adopted to enhance their tourist attraction. To be able to walk the medieval streets of York, Chambéry, Bruges or Regensburg, free of vehicles, is an obvious advantage. In these surroundings one can see few signs of the European urban environment being under attack. The main danger is perhaps the opposite of this, that cities, or at least their historic cores, may be preserved as museum exhibits, incapable of undergoing the change and modification which has happened through the ages.

The new town movement in Europe, for all its faults, was a demonstration, to at least the rest of the western world, that modern urban development could be more than unimaginative accretions tacked on to the edge of the growing city. The opportunity was taken in many countries to demonstrate that a high standard of urban environment could be created in the twentieth century side by side with economic growth. The active role of the public sector in the new town movement and the frequent motive of achieving a social balance have often attracted envious glances, particularly from North America. Furthermore the new towns have reflected individual national identities in many subtle ways. The carefully toned down appearance of the Scandinavian new town, using much of the natural landscape of evergreens and rock outcrops is not the same as the colourful vitality, perhaps even the brashness, of Evry or Marne-la-Vallée, which appear to be so much the products of the new technocrats who have emerged in France since 1960. Similarly the confident planning of Lelystad in the Dutch IJsselmeer polders is very different from Washington or Runcorn implanted into industrial northern England or Wulfen in the Ruhr.

In European cities, the tide of deconcentration generally turned before urban functions flowed from the city to the suburb in the wake of the population. Nevertheless, it was not always the case and the plight of the inner city is a very real one and can paradoxically be related to the very success of the new town planning. No city can withstand the loss of employment opportunities at the rate of 30 per cent in the six years between 1966 and 1972, which is what took place in Manchester (Lloyd and Mason, 1978). The European urban crisis, however, is by no means on the scale of that in North America. There are a number of significant differences which are worth recounting. Firstly, there is little evidence to suggest that any European city has ceased to be governable, with the possible special exception of Belfast, or that any are facing recurrent financial crises which threaten their existence. The general policy reorientation towards the central city is likely to see such possibilities recede even further. Secondly, the deconcentration of activity from the West European city, eroding its tax base and filtering away its vitality, has not been on the same scale of that in North America. Admittedly within West Europe the strength of policies aimed at preventing the decentralization of functions such as retailing varies considerably, but the dangers of excessive deconcentration are universally acknowledged. Thirdly, the spatial extent, and therefore the dependence on the automobile, is more restricted in West European cities than in those of North America. The energy crisis therefore, although very real, does not have the same inherent dangers as it does for the operation of the North American city. The problems posed by an overdependence on the car and the lorry, and the consequent decline in public transport provision, was realized at a much earlier stage than in North America (Chapter 5). Policies to redress the balance were introduced before private transport could create urban structures which only it could serve.

If these arguments are accepted, are we then correct to talk of an urban crisis, in which the city and especially its inner areas are particularly vulnerable? It would be naïve to deny problems that undoubtedly do exist. The poor, frequently neglected housing of so many inner cities, often inhabited by low socio-economic groups or by immigrants, is a devastating indictment of the ability of our new European society to cope with the problems which manifest themselves within the inner city. In every country in West Europe, the gradients of material affluence within its cities can still be remarkably steep. Poverty, violence and racial tension still breed off each other in pockets of deprivation. The West European city is still as much Glasgow's Blackhill or Edinburgh's Craigmillar as Venice's Piazza San Marco or Paris's Place Henri IV.

The crisis exists, then, but it is recognized and an increasingly large share of resources are being expended to try to reach a solution. Its very existence, however, has demonstrated a new crisis, that of a crisis of confidence in the planning system. In most, although not all countries, has come a realization that the bold planning approaches of postwar Europe were not solving all the urban problems and may indeed be creating new ones. With this realization has come a more careful approach involving a continuous monitoring of the impact of the planning system on not only the built environment but also the wider social and economic systems. Some countries, such as France, have had to take a rapid step back from the confident planning of the 1960s, while others such as Sweden and Denmark have realized the need for a more cautious approach.

The decision-making process itself has changed dramatically in the last decade. The planners of the immediately postwar generation saw themselves as responsible professional experts who were custodians of the 'public interest'—impartial referees who adjudicated between the claims of commercial interests. They operated upon the city for the city's good, but would no more consult the citizen than a surgeon would consult a patient about how he should proceed. In the last 20 years, however, the word 'participation' has taken on increasing significance, as a result both of popular demand and subsequent legislation. Officials channels of public consultation and on occasion even public decision by referendum, have been built up in most countries, as a supplement to the normal processes of representative democracy. The cost has been heavy in terms of the time taken to reach decisions, and the opportunities presented by public participation have understandably been exploited most effectively by articulate groups in society who may not be representative of society as a whole. Nevertheless public opinion has become a powerful and immediate influence on planning decisions in a way that was unknown a generation ago.

The need for this reappraisal stems also from our inability in postwar West Europe to make accurate predictions in the vitally important spheres of demographic change and economic growth. Quite apart from that, the social revolutions in even the last two decades in much of industrialized West Europe have emphasized the dangers of formulating long-term plans on the basis of contemporary trends and opinions. Who, in 1945, would have predicted the vast increase of women in the employment market, or the movement of over 2 million foreign workers moving into a relatively few German cities by the early 1970s? The planners who swept the trams from the streets of so many European cities could hardly have foreseen the cry for their reinstallation as a form of 'light rail rapid transit' 20 years later.

This leads us to the opinion that the planning of cities in West Europe may have to follow a more flexible path, sensitive to priorities which may change over time.

Long-term goals and objectives may still be desirable, but rigid blueprints may have to give way to written policy statements on the general direction of change. This has already occurred, of course, with the recent change to structure planning. Indeed in many spheres this approach is being adopted. Nevertheless, it is not without its dangers. Without a major plan, there may well be a reluctance on the part of politicians to cross major thresholds of expenditure. The expansion of a drainage system or the installation of a rapid transit system may well be jeopardized in an atmosphere of step-by-step incremental planning. At times, however, urban government is called upon to take a significant step and to cross such a threshold. In many cases, such expenditure may already have been delayed, thereby depressing the quality of life in an urban environment. Therefore the spending can only make good past deficiencies. In other cases, it may be necessary in order to provide a viable framework for future urban development without the quality of the contemporary city being put at risk. Given the new atmosphere of more careful monitoring the timing of such delicate decisions should be made less difficult than it was in the past.

What of the future spatial form of the city of West Europe? West European cities have been subjected to a degree of urban sprawl, with minor urban centres being incorporated, with the addition of successively high-order centres, until a multicentral urban system emerges. In some cases, such as Paris, positive planning policies have the polycentric city as an ultimate aim. It seems unlikely, however, that any European city will decant sufficient functions from its core to fundamentally reorient the focus of the city. Nevertheless the agglomerations of Rhine–Ruhr and the West Netherlands stand as good examples of multicentred urban regions. Indeed, on a wider scale a case could be made out for recognizing one vast urban region comprising many centres within north-west Europe. It would stretch from Paris to Amsterdam, and from north-west England to Frankfurt with an extension to Stuttgart and Munich. Even though the physical spread of the urban environment is by no means complete there are few areas which are not essentially characterized by an urban lifestyle or operating under an urban influence.

The emergence of a European Community city within this heartland of the Community is by no means farfetched. It contains the 'European' cities of Brussels, Luxembourg and Strasbourg and the only highly developed parts of the Community excluded from it are to the north Copenhagen and Hamburg, and to the south, the Rhône Valley from Lyons to Marseilles and the north Italian industrial concentration of Lombardy—Piedmont. These latter areas are increasingly included within the 'extended golden triangle' of West European urbanization as a result of the increasingly rapid development of the Mediterranean cities from Barcelona through Languedoc, the French Riviera to North Italy, and perhaps including Switzerland, southern Bavaria and western Austria. Rapid population growth in the cities and large towns, the concentration of research and development activities and 'new' industries are making the southward extensions of the 'golden triangle' a form of 'sunbelt' urbanization. If the enlarged Community continues to prosper at the rate experienced by the original six in the 1960s, this urban heartland is likely to command an even more dominant position in Europe. Already the distances between the major centres have been shrunk by good transport links. A suggestion that Schipol international airport near Amsterdam could serve as London's much debated third airport further underlines the intricate and close links within this region.

The European tradition of urbanism has been a strong one. The emergence of an urban system spanning national boundaries has become a reality. There would seem to be clear indications that the city in Europe is being controlled and not being overwhelmed by poverty as are the cities in the Third World, or conversely by the misdirected affluence suffered by North American cities. Its traditions of planning are well established and have given a guiding framework to the developing urban system. Despite the past mistakes, the West European cities will retain their diversity. The pressures of the twentieth century may have been the catalyst for a reassessment of the strengths of the European urban tradition.

We must end with an affirmation of faith. Despite the concentration of serious social problems in the city and the mountain of literature that describes them, and despite the recent crisis of confidence that has turned planners from olympian idealists into timid fad-blown conformists, the West European city remains today, and will remain for our children, as much the democratic fount of civilized values as it was in Socrates' Athens, Dante's Florence, or Erasmus' Rotterdam. Above all it will remain the most congenial living environment ever designed by man.

Our future task is to ensure that our urban culture is not accessible merely to the rich or the aristocratic as it has been all too often in West European history. Instead the rich resources of the European urban culture which are being enhanced year by year must be made available to all Europeans.

Bibliography and References

Chapter 1

Ambrose, P. and Colenutt, B. (1975). *The Property Machine*, Penguin, Harmondsworth.
Berry, B. J. L. (1973). *The Human Consequences of Urbanisation: Divergent Paths in the Urban Experience of the Twentieth Century*, St Marins, New York.
Blacksell, M. (1968). 'Recent changes in the morphology of West German townscapes', in *Urbanization and its Problems* (eds. M. Beckinsale and J. Houston), pp. 199–217, Blackwell, Oxford.
Castells, M. (1976). 'Is there an urban sociology?', in *Urban Sociology: Critical Essays* (ed. J. Pickvance), pp. 35–59, Tavistock Publications, London.
Castells, M. (1978). *City, Class and Power*, Macmillan, Basingstoke.
Gravier, J. F. (1947). *Paris et le Désert Français*, Flammarion, Paris.
Hall, P. (1977). *Europe 2000*, Duckworth, London.
Harvey, D. (1973). *Social Justice and the City*, Edward Arnold, London.
Holzner, L. (1970). 'The role of history and tradition in the urban geography of West Germany', *Ann. Assoc. Amer. Geog.*, **60 (2),** 315–339.
Jones, E. (1966). *Towns and Cities*, Oxford University Press, London.
Kormoss, I. (1976). 'Urban extensions in Belgium', in *The Environment of Human Settlements, Vol. 1* (ed. P. Laconte *et al.*), pp. 177–186, Pergamon, Oxford.
Langton, J. (1978). 'Industry and towns 1500–1730', in *Historical Geography of England and Wales* (eds. R. Dodghson and R. Butlin), pp. 173–198, Academic Press, London.
Lefebre, L. (1968). *Le Droit et la Ville*, Paris.
Lichtenberger, E. (1972). 'Die Europäische Stadt—Wesen Modelle Probleme', *Raumforsch. Raumord.*, **16,** 3–25.
Lichtenberger, E. (1976). 'The changing nature of European urbanization', in *Urbanization and Counter Urbanization* (ed. B. J. L. Berry), pp. 81–107, Sage, Beverly Hills.
Mathieu, H. (1977). 'L'écologie contre l'urbanisme?', *Urbanisme*, **46 (160),** 45–49.
Pirenne, H. (1925). *Medieval Cities* (translated by F. Halsey), Princeton University Press, Princeton.
Sacco, G. (1976). 'Morphology and culture of European cities', in *Europe 2000, Project 3 Volume 1* (ed. M. van Hulton), pp. 162–187, Nijhoff, The Hague.
Sjoberg, G. (1960). *The Pre-Industrial City*, Free Press, New York.
Vance, J. (1977). *This Scene of Man*, Harper and Row, London.
Vance, J. (1978). 'Institutional forces that shape the city', in *Social Areas in Cities*, (eds. D. T. Herbert and R. J. Johnston), pp. 97–126, Wiley, London.

Chapter 2

Abercrombie, P. (1945). *Greater London Plan 1944*, HMSO, London.
Albers, G. (1977). 'Stadtbauliche Konzepte im 20 Jahrhundert—ihre Wirkung in Theorie und Praxis', *Berichte Raumforsch. Raumplan.*, **1,** 14–26.
Boustedt, O. (1970). *Stadtregionen, Handwortenbuch der Raumforschung und Raumordnung*, Akademie für Raumforschung und Raumordnung, Hannover.
Castells, M. (1972). *La Question Urbaine*, Maspero, Paris.

Castells, M. (1977). 'Towards a political urban sociology', in *Captive Cities* (ed. M. Harloe), pp. 61–78, Wiley, London.

Castells, M. (1978). *City, Class and Power*, Macmillan, London.

Castells, M., and Godard, F. (1974). *Monopolville: L'Enterprise, L'État, L'Urbain*, Mouton, Paris.

Cerdà y Suñer, I. (1867). *Teoria General de Urbanizacion*, Madrid.

Choay, F. (1969). *The Modern City Planning in the Nineteenth Century*, Studio Vista, London.

Curl, J. (1970). *European Cities and Society*, Leonard Hill Books, London.

Dahne, R., and Dahl H. (1975). *Die Berliner Strasse*, Senator für Bau und Wohnungswesen, Berlin (West).

Doxiadis, C. (1968). *Between Dystopia and Utopia*, Faber and Faber, London.

Geddes, P. (1915). *Cities in Evolution*, Ernest Benn, London.

Gubler, J. (1975). 'Hans Bernoulli et le "Modele Helvetique" de cité-jardin', *Werk/Oeuvre*, **12,** 1049–1051.

Gutkind, E. (1969–72). *International History of City Development*, Collier-Macmillan, London.

Hall, P. (1969). *London 2000*, Faber and Faber, London.

Hillebrecht, R. (1962). *Die Stadtregionen, Grossstadt und Stadtbau*, Schwarz, Göttingen.

HMSO (1935). *Report of the Departmental Committee on Garden Cities and Satellite Towns*, HMSO, London.

HMSO (1940). *The Report of the Royal Commission on the Geographical Distribution of the Industrial Population: Barlow Report*, Cmd. 6153, HMSO, London.

HMSO (1946). *New Towns Committee: Reith Report*, Cmd. 6876, HMSO, London.

HMSO (1964). *South-East Study 1964*, HMSO, London.

HMSO (1967). *Strategy for the South-East 1967*, HMSO, London.

HMSO (1970). *Strategic Plan for the South-East 1970*, HMSO, London.

Houghton-Evans, W. (1975). *Planning Cities: Legacy and Portent*, Lawrence and Wishart, London.

Howard, E. (1946). *Garden Cities of Tomorrow*, Faber and Faber, London.

Kirk, W. (1953). 'The geographical significance of Vitruvius' "De Architectura" ', *Scot. Geog. Mag.*, **69,** 1–10.

Lavedan, P. (1959). *Histoire de l'Urbanisme, Renaissance et Temps Modernes*, Vincent, Freal, Paris.

Le Corbusier (1964). *The Radiant City*, Faber and Faber, London (translation of *La Ville radieuse* (1935)).

Mackinder, H. J. (1902). *Britain and the British Seas*, Heinemann, London.

Manuel, F. (1966). *Utopias and Utopian Thought*, Houghton Mifflin, Cambridge, Mass.

Marx, K. (1968). 'Critique of the Gotha Programme' (1875), in *Selected Works 1*, Lawrence and Wishart, London.

Merlin, P. (1969). *Les Villes Nouvelles*, Presses Universitaires de France, Paris.

Meyerson, M. (1961). 'Utopian tradition and the planning of cities', *Daedalus*, **1961,** Winter, 180–193.

Mumford, L. (1961). *The City in History*, Penguin, Harmondsworth.

Pahl, R. E. (1969). 'Urban social theory and research', *Environ. Plan.*, **1,** 143–153.

Pahl, R. E. (1977). 'Managers, technical experts and the state: forms of mediation, manipulation and dominance in urban and regional development', in *Captive Cities* (ed. M. Harloe), pp. 49–60, Wiley, London.

Pickvance, C. (1976). *Urban Sociology: Critical Essays*, Tavistock, London.

Reau, L., *et al.* (1954). *L'oeuvre du Baron Haussmann*, Presses Universitaries de France, Paris.

Sant Elia, H. (1914). *La Nuova Città*, Milan.

Sartoris, A. (1935). *Gli Elementi dell'Architettura Funzionale*, Hoepli, Milan.

Sitte, C. (1965). *City Planning according to Artistic Principles* (translated by G. Collins and C. Collins), Phaidon, London.

Sutcliffe, A. (1970). *The Autumn of Central Paris: The Defeat of Town Planning*, Edward Arnold, London.
Unwin, R. (1909). *Town Planning in Practice*, Ernest Benn, London.
Vance, J. (1977). *This Scene of Man: The Role and Structure of the City in the Geography of Western Civilization*, Harper and Row, New York.
Whittick, A. (1974). *Encyclopedia of Urban Planning*, McGraw-Hill, New York.
Williams, P. (1978). 'Urban managerialism: a concept of relevance?', *Area*, **10**(3), 235–240.
Wynn, M., and Smith, R. (1978). 'Spain: urban decentralisation', *Built Environ.* Vol. **4**(1), 49–55.
Wurzer, R. (1976). 'Anlass, Ziele Durchfuhrang und Verlwirklichung von Städtebaulichen Planungen im 19 Jahrhundert', *Berichte Raumforsch. Raumplan.*, **1,** 3–20.

Chapter 3

Abrams, P. (1978). *Work, Urbanism and Inequality*, Weidenfeld and Nicolson, London.
Andritsky, M., *et al.* (1975). *Labyrinth Stadt*, Du Mont Aktuel, Cologne.
Ashworth, G. J. (1978). *Gelderland Field Guide, 2nd Edition*, Geography Department Portsmouth Polytechnic.
Boal, F. (1970). 'Social space in the Belfast urban area', in *Irish Geographical Studies in Honour of E. E. Evans* (eds. N. Stephens and R. Glassock), pp. 373–393, University of Belfast.
Boal, F. (1972). 'The urban residential sub-community—a conflict interpretation', *Area*, **4,** 164–168.
Boal, F. *et al.* (1974). *The Spatial Distribution of some Social Problems in the Belfast Urban Area* Northern Ireland Community Relations Commission, Belfast.
Borja, J. (1971). 'Urban movements in Spain', in *Captive Cities* (ed. M. Harloe), pp. 187–211, Wiley, London.
Boustedt, O. (1967). 'Zum Beteulung des Dichtebriffes in der Raumordnung und Landesplanung', *Mitteilungen der Deutschen Akademie für Städtebau und Landesplanung, Heft* 11.
Boustedt, O. (1975). *Grundriss der Empirischen Regionalforschung Teil III Siedlungsstrukturen*, Schoedel, Hannover.
Boyle, M. (1978). *Aspects of Spatial Cognition in Sunderland* (unpublished PhD, University of Manchester.
Braun, P. (1976a). 'Sozialräumliche Gliederung des Hamburger Raumes', *Deutscher Planungsatlas*, Band 8 Hamburg, Lieferung 9, Akademie fur Raumforschung und Landesplanung.
Braun, P. (1976b). *Die Sozialräumliche Gliederung Hamburgs* (mimeo), PLANCO Consulting Gesellschaft mbh, Hamburg.
Buursink, J. (1977). *De Hierachie van Winkelcentra*, Institute de Geographie, Groningen.
Castells, M. (1972). *La Question Urbaine*, Maspero, Paris, translated (1977) as *The Urban Question*, Edward Arnold, London.
Castells, M. (1973). *Luttes Urbaines*, Maspero, Paris.
Castells, M. (1978). *City, Class and Power*, Macmillan, Basingstoke.
Castells, M. and Godard, F. (1974). *Monopolville: L'Enterprise, L'État et L'Urbain*, Mouton, Paris.
Damer, S. (1974). 'Wine alley: the sociology of a dreadful enclosure', *Sociol. Rev.*, **22,** 221–248.
De Jong, D. (1962). 'Images of urban areas: their structure and psychological foundations', *J. Inst. Amer. Planners*, **28,** 276–286.
De Lannoy, W. (1978). 'Enkele Aspecten van de Residentiele Differentiatie in de Brusselse Agglomeratie', *De Aadrijkskunde*, **3,** 251–262.
Dennis, N. (1972). *Public Participation and Planners Blight*, Faber and Faber, London.
Drewe, P., *et al.* (1974). *Segregation in Rotterdam*, Paper Presented to the 9th World Congress of Sociology, Research Committee 24, Uppsala, Sweden.

Durr, H. (1972). 'Empirische Untersuchungen zum Problem der Sozial Geographischen Gruppe: Der Aktionsraumliche Aspekt', *Münchener Studien zur Sozial- und Wirtschaftsgeographie, Band* 8.

Elkins, T. H. (1975). 'Style in German cities. Urban development since World War 2', *Geog. Mag.*, **48 (1),** 17–23.

Eyles, J. (1969). *The Inhabitant's Images of Highgate Village*, Discussion Paper 1095, Department of Geography, London School of Economics, London.

Ford, J. (1975). 'The role of the building society manager in urban stratification', *Urban Stud.*, **12,** 295–302.

Friederichs, J. (1977). *Stadtanalyse*, Rowohlt, Hamburg.

Gehring, J.-M. (1977). 'Le Luxembourg', *Mosella*, **7** (1 and 2).

Gisser, R. (1969). 'Okologische Segregation der Berufschichten in Grossstädten', in *Soziologische Forschung in Osterreich* (eds. L. Rosenmayer and S. Hollinger), pp. 199–220, Bollaus, Vienna.

Gittus, E. (1964). 'The structure of urban areas: a new approach', *Town Plan. Rev.*, **35,** 5–20.

Gordon, G. (1971). 'Status areas in Edinburgh' (unpublished PhD), University of Edinburgh.

Gould, P. and White, R. (1974). *Mental Maps*, Penguin, Harmondsworth.

Hamm, B. (1975). *Untersuchungen zur Sozialen Wirtschaftlichen und Baulichen Struktur der Stadt Bern*, M.S. Bollingen.

Hammond, E. (1968). *London to Durham*, Rowntree Research Unit, University of Durham.

Harloe, M. (1977). *Captive Cities*, Wiley, London.

Herbert, D. T. (1967). 'Social area analysis: a British study', *Urban Stud.*, **4,** 41–60.

Herbert, D. T. (1970). 'Principal components analysis and urban social structure', in *Urban Essays: Studies in the Geography of Wales* (eds. H. Carter and W. Davies), pp. 79–100, Longmans, London.

Herbert, D. T. (1976). 'Social Deviance in the City', in *Social Areas in Cities*, Vol. II, (eds. D. T. Herbert and R. J. Johnston), pp. 89–121, Wiley, London.

Herlyn, U. (1975). 'Beitrage zum Problem der Suburbanisierung', *Veroffentlichungen der Akademie fur Raumforschung und Landesplanung: Forschungs und Sitzungsberichte, Band* 102.

Herlyn, U. (1977). 'Infrastrukturausgleich als Sozialpolitische Aufgabe', in *Soziologie und Sozialpolitik* (eds. C. von Ferber and F. Kaufmann), pp. 577–590, West Deutscher Verlag, Opladen.

Iblher, P. (1977). 'Andwendungsmoglichkeiten Sozialer Indikatoren in der Raumplanung', *Wirtschaftsdienst*, **57(6),** 313–320.

Johnston, R. J. (1978). 'Residential area characteristics: research methods for identifying urban sub-areas, social area analysis and factorial ecology', in *Social Areas in Cities* (eds. D. Herbert and R. Johnston), pp. 175–217, Wiley, London.

Jones, E. (1960). *A Social Geography of Belfast*, Oxford University Press, London.

Jones, P. (1970). 'Some aspects of the changing distribution of coloured immigrants in Birmingham 1961–1966', *Trans. Inst. Brit. Geog(.*, **50,** 199–215.

Klingbeil, D. (1976). *Aktionsraume im Verdichtungsraum München*, Dissertation, Technische Universität, München.

Kutter, E. (1973). 'Aktionsbereiche des Stadtbewohners', *Ark. Kommunalwissenschaft*, **12,** 69–85.

Lichtenberger, E. (1970). 'The nature of European urbanism', *Geoforum*, **4,** 45–62.

Lichtenberger, E. (1972). 'Die Europaische Stadt—Wesen Modelle Probleme', *Raumforsch. Raumord.*, **16,** 3–25.

Lichtenberger, E. (1976). 'The changing nature of European urbanisation', in *Urbanisation and Counterurbanisation* (ed. B. J. L. Berry), pp. 81–107, Sage, Beverly Hills.

Lob, R. and Wehling, H. (1977). *Geographie und Umwelt*, Hain, Mesenheim.

Mann, B. (1965). *An Approach to Urban Sociology*, Routledge and Kegan Paul, London.

Matti, W. (1972). 'Das Wahlverhalten der Hamburger Bevolkerung bei den Burgerschaftswahlen 1966 und 1970', *Hamburg in Zahlen, Sonderheft* 1.

McElrath, D. (1962). 'The social areas of Rome: a comparative analysis', *Amer. Sociol. Rev.*, **27,** 376–391.

Milgram, S. and Jodelet, D. (1976). 'Psychological maps of Paris', in *Environmental Psychology: People and their Physical Settings, 2nd Edition* (eds. H. Proshansky, *et. al.*), pp. 104–124, Holt Rinehart and Winston, New York.

Mischke, M. (1976). *Faktorenökologische Untersuchung zur Raumlichen Auspragung der Sozialstruktur in Pforzheim*, Karlsruhe Universität, Karlsruhe.

Morgan, B. (1971). 'The residential structure of Exeter', in *Exeter Essays in Geography* (eds. W. Ravenhill and K. Gregory), pp. 219–236, Exeter University.

Morgan, B. (1975). 'The segregation of socio-economic groups in urban areas: a comparative approach', *Urban Stud.*, **12,** 47–60.

Moser, C. A. and Scott, W. (1961). *British Towns: A Statistical Study of Their Social and Economic Differences*, Oliver and Boyd, London.

Nellner, W. (1976). 'Die Innere Gliederung Stadtischer Siedlungsagglomerationen', *Forschungs und Sitzungsberichte Akademie fur Raumforschung und Landesplanung*, **112,** 35–74.

Niemeyer, G. (1969). 'Braunschweig—Soziale Schichtung und Sozialraumliche Gliederung Einer Grossstadt', *Raumforsch. Raumord.*, **27,** 193–209.

Pahl, R. E. (1970). *Whose City?*, Longman, London.

Peach, C. (1975). 'Immigrants in the inner city', *Geog. J.*, **141,** 372–379.

Pfeiffer, U. (1973). 'Market forces and urban change in Germany', in *The Management of Urban Change in Britain and Germany* (ed. R. Rose), pp. 45–52, Sage, London.

Pocock, D. (1976). 'Some characteristics of mental maps: an empirical study', *Trans. Inst. Brit. Geog., New Series*, **1 (4),** 493–512.

Rees. P. H. (1968). *The Factorial Ecology of Metropolitan Chicago* (unpublished masters thesis) University of Chicago.

Rex. J., and Moore, R. (1967). *Race, Community and Conflict*, Oxford University Press, London.

Richardson, H., Vipond, J., and Furbey, R. (1975). *Housing and Urban Spatial Stucture: A Case Study*, Saxon House, Farnborough.

Robson, B. (1969). *Urban Analysis*, Cambridge University Press, London.

Robson, B. (1975). *Urban Social Areas*, Oxford University Press, London.

SAS (1976). *Zeitbudget und Aktionsraume der Bewohner von Zwei Neubausiedlungen*, Hamburg Universität, Hamburg.

Schaffer, F. (1971). Prozesstypen als sozialgeographisches Gliederungsprinzip, *Mitteilungen der Geographischen Gesellschaft München*, No. 56.

Schriefer, B. (1977). *Die Sozio-okonomische Struktur der Stadt Bremen: Eine Faktorökologische Untersuchungen* (mimeo), Bremen Universität, Bremen.

Smith, D. (1979). *Where the Grass is Greener*, Penguin, Marmondsworth.

Sweetser, F. (1965). 'Factorial ecology; Helsinki 1960', *Demography*, **1,** 372–385.

van Engelsdorp Gastelaars, R., and Beek, W. (1972). 'Ecologische Differentatie Binnen Amsterdam', *Tijd. Econ. Soc. Geog.*, 63, 62–78.

Vilsteren, G. J., and Everaers, P. C. J. (1978). Factor-Ecologie van Arnhem, *Nijmeegse Geografische Cahiers*, No. 12.

Williams, P. (1976). 'The role of institutions in the inner London housing market', *Trans. Inst. Brit. Geog., New Series*, **1 (1),** 72–82.

Williams, P. (1978). 'Urban managerialism', *Area*, **10 (3),** 236–240.

Woessner, R. and Bailly, A. (1979). 'Images du centre-ville et méthodes d'analyse factorielle: le cas de Mulhouse', *Environ. Plan.*, **11,** 1039–1048.

Chapter 4

Bennison, D. and Davies, R. L. (1977). *The Local Effects of City Centre Shopping Schemes: A*

Case Study, Paper presented to PTRC Summer Annual Meeting, University of Warwick.
Burtenshaw, D. (1981). 'Austria', in *Regional Development in Western Europe* (ed. H. Clout), forthcoming 2nd Edition, Wiley, London.
Daniels, P. W. (1975). *Office Location, An Urban and Regional Study*, Bell, London.
Davies, R. L. (1977). *Marketing Geography, With Special Reference to Retailing*, Methuen, London.
Department of the Environment (1972). *Development Policy Control Note, 11*, HMSO, London.
Department of the Environment (1977). *Development Policy Control Note, 13*, HMSO, London.
Eurostat (1976). *Regional Statistics*, European Community, Brussels.
Goodall, B. (1972). *The Economics of Urban Areas*, Pergamon, Oxford.
Groupe Balkany (undated). *Parly 2, Chevry 2, Velizy 2, Rosny 2*, Groupe Balkany, Paris.
Hardman Report (1973). *The Dispersal of Government Work from London*, Cmd. 5322, HMSO, London.
Lendrai, P. (1979). 'Vienna', *Financial Times Survey*, 23 August, London.
Merenne-Schoumaker, B. (1970). 'Evolution récents de la distribution de shopping centres', *Bull. Soc. Geog. de Liège*, **6,** 91–119.
MPC and Associates Ltd. (1974). *Retailing in Europe*, MPC, Worcester.
Spork, J. (1972). 'Les nouvelles implantation commerciales dans la métropole Liègeoise', *Travaux Geog. de Liège*, **159.**
van Hecke, E. (1977). *De Lokalisatie von de Tertiare Sector in de Brusselse Agglomeration*, Universiteit Leuven, Leuven.
Vlassenbroeck, W. (1975). 'De Grootwinkelbedrijven in Belgie, Enkele Structurele Kenmerken en Spreidingsbeeld', *Publ. von het Seminaire voor Menselyke en Econ. Geog., RU Geal* 11.
Wood, D. (1976). *The Eastleigh Carrefour, a Hypermarket and its Effects*, Department of the Environment Research Report, 16, HMSO, London.

Chapter 5

Abercrombie, P. (1945). *Greater London Plan 1944*, HMSO, London.
Acton, P. (1979). 'Glasgow's Clockwork Orange', *Surveyor*, **153,** C1–C7.
Bendixson, T. (1974). *Instead of Cars*, Temple Smith, London.
Blake, J. (1974). 'How Londoners travel to work', *Surveyor*, **144,** 34–35.
Città di Torino (1976). *Programma di Intervento*, Torino.
Cottle, R. (1973). 'The experience of cities in the improvement of the pedestrian environment', *Bull. Env. Educ.*, **24,** 1–14.
Economic Commission for Europe (1973). *Role of Transportation in Urban Planning Development and Environment*, Brussels.
Greater London Council (GLC) (1971). *Greater London Development Plan. Report of Public Enquiry*, GLC, London.
Greater London Council (GLC) (1966). *London Travel Survey*, GLC, London.
Halsall, D. (1978). 'Rapid transit in Merseyside', *Area*, **10(3),** 212–216.
Heeger, H. (1977). 'Government policy with respect to passenger transport and the traffic circulation plan of some Dutch cities', *Plan. Devel. Nether.*, **9(1),** 3–15.
Heggie, I. and Bailey, J. (1977). 'Declining public transport, is car ownership to blame?' *Surveyor*, **149,** 9–11.
Kupka, K. (1979). *Bologna, Modelgemeente voor de Stadsvernieuwing. Onderzoekrapport.*, Universiteit van Amsterdam.
Meyer, J., *et al.* (1965). *The Urban Transportation Problem*, Harvard University Press, Cambridge, Mass.
Milne, R. (1974). 'Minitram, Croydon or Sheffield first', *Surveyor*, **144,** 10–13.

Ministry of Transport (1963). *Traffic in Towns*, HMSO, London.

Moseley, M. J. (1979). *Accessibility: the Rural Challenge*, Methuen, London.

Netter, J. (1977). 'Transports, circulation, stationnement, une politique pour les villes', *Urbanisme*, **160,** 3–7.

Organization for Economic Cooperation and Development (OECD) (1974). *Streets for People*, OECD, Paris.

O'Sullivan, P. (1978). 'Issues in transportation', in *Issues in Urban Society* (eds. R. L. Davies and P. Hall), pp. 106–131, Penguin, Harmondsworth.

Poole, S. (1976). 'The bus in urban Sweden', *Buses*, **27,** 226–238.

Préfecture de la Région Parisienne (1972). 'Plan global transports', *Bull. Inform. de la Région Parisienne.*

Republique et Canton de Genève (1977). *Some Aspects of Town Planning in Geneva*, Deptartment of Public Works, Geneva.

Richards, B. (1966). *New Movement in Cities*, Reinhold, New York.

Rijksplanologische Dienst (RPD) (1976). 'Derda Nota over de Ruimtelijke Ordening', Deel 2 *Verstedelijkingsnota.*

Thomson, J. (1977). *Great Cities and their Traffic*, Gollancz, London.

Tumiati, P. (1972). 'Verdict on Rome's free buses', *Financial Times*, 11 January.

Chapter 6

Angotti, J. (1977). *Housing in Italy: Urban Development and Political Change*, Praeger, New York.

Apelroth, J. (1974). 'The Cooperative Movement in Danish Housing', in *Public Housing in Europe and America* (ed. J. Fuerst), p. 88–98, Croom Helm, London.

Barlow Report (1940). *Royal Commission on the Distribution of the Industrial Population*, Cmd. 6153, HMSO, London.

Becker, H. and Kein, K. (1977). *Gropiusstadt: Soziale Verhaltnisse am Stadtrand*, Kohlhammer, Stuttgart.

Bengtson, S. (1974). 'Housing and planning in Sweden', in *Public Housing in Europe and America*, (ed. J. Fuerst), pp. 99–109, Croom Helm, London.

Bird, H. (1976). 'Residential mobility and preference patterns in the public sector of the housing market', *Trans. Inst. Brit. Geog., New Series*, **1 (1),** 20–33.

Blacksell, M. (1968). 'Recent changes in the morphology of West German townscapes', in *Urbanization and its Problems* (eds. M. Beckinsale and J. Houston), pp. 199–217, Blackwell, Oxford.

Boddy, M. (1976). 'The structure of mortgage finance: building societies and the British social formation', *Trans. Inst. Brit. Geog., New Series*, **1 (1),** 58–71.

Borja, J. (1977). 'Urban movements in Spain', in *Captive Cities*, (ed. M. Harloe), pp. 187–212, Wiley, London.

Bremische Gesellschaft (1977). *Sanierung Ostertor*, Bremische Gesellschaft fur Stadterneuerung, Stadtentwicklung und Wohnungsbau mbh.

Cribier, F. (1970). 'La Migration de rétraite des fonctionnaires Parisiens', *Bull. Assoc. Geog. Français*, **381,** 119–122.

Daun, Å. (1976). 'The ideological dilemma of housing policy', in *Plan International—Habitat 76* (ed. G. Corlestan), pp. 21–30, Swedish Society for Town and Country Planning, Stockholm.

Department of the Environment (1974). *Urban Guidelines Studies, Sunderland, Oldham and Rotherham*, HMSO, London.

Duclaud-Williams, R. (1978). *The Politics of Housing in Britain and France*, Heinemann, London.

Fuerst, J. (ed.) (1974). *Public Housing in Europe and America*, Croom Helm, London.

Gatzweiler, H. (1975). 'Zur Selektivitat Interregionaler Wanderungen', *Forsch. zur Raumentwick., Band* 1.

Ginatempo, N., and Cammarota, A. (1977). 'Land and social conflict in the cities of southern Italy. An Analysis of the housing question in Messina', in *Captive Cities*, (ed. M. Harloe), pp. 111–122, Wiley, London.

Gray, F. (1976). 'Selection and allocation in council housing', *Inst. Brit. Geog. Trans., New Series*. **1 (1),** 34–46.

Greater London Council (GLC) (1974). *A Strategic Housing Plan for London*, GLC, London.

Green, E. (1959). 'West German city reconstruction', *Sociol. Rev.*, **7,** 231–244.

Green, E. (1964). 'Politics and planning for reconstruction', *Urban Stud.*, **1,** 71–78.

Hallett, G. (1977). *Housing and Land Policies in West Germany and Britain*, Macmillan, London.

Headey, B. (1978). *Housing Policy in the Developed Economy*, Croom Helm, London.

Info Service (no date). *The Future of the Old Housing Stock in the Netherlands*, Ministry of Housing and Physical Planning Information Service, The Hague.

King, J. (1971). 'Housing in Spain', *Town Plan. Rev.*, **42,** 381–403.

Koch, R. (1976). 'Altenwanderung und Raumliche Konzentration Alter Menschen', *Forsch. zur Raumentwickl., Heft* 4.

Lagarde, J. (1968). 'Les Grandes Ensembles douze ans après', *Urbanisme*, 106, 30–34.

Law, C. and Warnes, A. (1973). 'The movement of retired people to seaside resorts. A study of Morecambe and Llandudno', *Town Plan. Rev.*, **44 (4),** 373–390.

Lawson, R. and Stevens, C. (1974). 'Housing allowances in West Germany and France', *J. Soc. Policy*, **3 (3),** 213–234.

Manchester and Salford Inner City Partnership Research Group (1978). *Manchester and Salford Inner Area Study*, Manchester and Salford Partnership.

Ministry of Housing (1976). *Current Trends in the Field of Housing, Building and Planning* (mimeo), 1b, 3.363, August, Copenhagen.

Ministry of Housing and Physical Planning (1976). *House Building and Planning in Sweden* (mimeo), Stockholm.

Ministry of Local Government and Labour (1976). *Current Trends and Policies in the Field of Housing, Building and Planning* (mimeo), H 1024, Oslo.

Monheim, H. (1972). 'Zur Attraktivitat Deutscher Stadte', *Berichte zur Regionalforsch., Heft* 8.

Monehim, R. (1979). 'Wohnungsversorgung und Wohnungswechsel', *Geog. Rund.*, **31 (1),** 17–28.

Nationwide (1979). *Housing and Housing Finance in the European Economic Community*, Nationwide Building Society.

Notes et Études Documentaire (1976). 'Lille et sa Communauté urbaine', *Notes et Études Documentaire*, 4297–4299.

Ottensen (1977). *Urban District Development in Hamburg Illustrated with Ottensen as an Example*, International Union of Local Authorities World Congress, 1977.

Power, A. (1976). 'France, Holland, Belgium and Germany, a look at their housing problems and policies', *Habitat*, **1 (1),** 81–103.

Racine, E. and Creutz, Y. (1975). 'Planning and housing in France', *The Planner*, **61,** 83–85.

Rappoport, A. (1968). 'Housing and housing densities in France', *Town Plan. Rev.*, **39 (4),** 341–354.

Shankland Cox. (1971). *La Vie Dans un Grand Ensemble*, Shankland Cox, London and Cergy-Pontoise.

Smith, M. (1973). 'Housing in Amsterdam', *Housing*, May, 9–15.

Theunissen, A. (1974). 'Housing policy in Europe', *Housing*, May, 10–13.

Thomas, W. S. G. and Tuppen, J. (1977). 'Readjustment in the Ruhr—the case of Bochum', *Geography*, **62,** 168–175.

United Nations (1973). *Urban Land Policies and Land Use Control Measures Volume 3, West Europe*, United Nations, New York.

United Nations (1974). *Compendium of Housing Statistics 1971*, United Nations Department of Economic and Social Affairs Statistical Office, New York.

Urbanisme (1978). 'Renovation urbaine', *Urbanisme*, **46 (162–3),** Thematic Issue.
Vance, J. (1977). *This Scene of Man*, Harper and Row, London.
Watson, C. (1971). *Social Housing Policy in Belgium*, Occasional Paper 9, CURS, Birmingham.
Wendt, P. (1962). 'Post-World War 2 housing policies in Italy', *Land Econ.*, **38 (2),** 113–133.
Williams, A. (1980). 'Conservation planning in Oporto: an integrated approach in the Ribeira–Barredo', *Town Plan. Rev.*, forthcoming.
Wilmott, P., and Young, M. (1973). *The Symmetrical Family*, Routledge and Kegan Paul, London.
Wilson, H., and Wommersley, L., *et al.* (1977). *Change or Decay: Final Report of the Liverpool Inner Area Study*, HMSO, London.
Wohlin, H. (1977). *Framework for Urban Development in Sweden* (mimeo), Department of Planning and Building Control, Stockholm.

Chapter 7

Aldous, T. (1972). 'The Continuing Battle of Bath', *Built Environ.*, **1 (7),** 480–484.
Angotti, T. (1977). *Housing in Italy: Urban Development and Political Change*, Praeger, New York.
Barnett, W. and Winskell, C. (1977). *A Study in Conservation*, Oriel Press, Stocksfield.
Cervellati, P. and Scannarini, R. (1973). *Bologna: Politica e Metodologia del Restauro nei Centri Storichi*, Bologna.
Council of Europe (1974). 'The future of our past', *Ekistics*, **39,** 139–142.
Culot, M. (1974). 'The rearguard battle for Brussels', *Ekistics*, **37,** 101–104.
Dobby, A. (1978). *Conservation and Planning*, Hutchinson, London.
Engels, F. (1935). *The Housing Question*, Martin Lawrence, London.
Esher, Viscount (1969). *York. A Study in Conservation*, HMSO, London.
Fabre-Luce, H. (1976). 'SOS Paris', *Urbanisme*, **153–4,** 104.
Fawcett, J. (1976). *The Future of the Past: Attitudes to Conservation*, Thames and Hudson, London.
Fay, S. and Knightley, P. (1976). *The Death of Venice*, Deutsch, London.
Ford, L. (1978). 'Continuity and change in historic cities', *Geog. Rev.*, **68 (3),** 253–273.
Fried, R. (1973). *Planning the Eternal City: Roman Politics and Planning Since World War 2*, Yale University Press, London.
Hall, P. (1977). *Europe 2000*, Duckworth, London.
HMSO (1969). *Bath. A Study in Conservation*, A Report to the Ministry of Housing and Local Government and Bath City Council, HMSO, London.
Insall, D. and Associates (1969). *Chester. A Study in Conservation*, HMSO, London.
Kain, R. (1975). 'Urban conservation in France', *Town Country Plan.*, **43,** 428–433.
Lottman, H. (1976). *How Cities are Saved*, Universe Books, New York.
Lynch, K. (1972). *What Time is this Place*, MIT, Cambridge, Mass.
Oaks, R. (1974). 'Conservation in Italy', *Town Country Plan.*, **4,** 270–275.
O'Riordan, N. (1975). 'The Venetian Ideal', *Geog. Mag.*, **47 (7),** 416–426.
Piasentin, U., Costa, P., and Foot, D. (1977). 'The Venice problem—an approach by urban modelling', *Reg. Stud.*, **12,** 571–602.
Rogatnick, A. (1971). 'Venice, Problems and possibilities', *Archit. Rev.*, **149 (891),** 261–273.
Shaffrey, P. (1975). *The Irish Town: An Approach to Survival*, O'Brien Press, Dublin.
Stungo, A. (1972). *The Malraux Act 1962–72*, Royal Town Planning Institute, London.
Sutcliffe, A. (1970). *The Autumn of Central Paris: The Defeat of Town Planning*, Edward Arnold, London.
UNESCO (1975). *The Conservation of Cities: Studies Commissioned by UNESCO*, Croom Helm, London.

Chapter 8

Ashworth, G. (1976). 'Distribution of Foreign Tourists in the Netherlands', *Department of Geography Occasional Papers*, 2, Portsmouth Polytechnic.
Central Bureau Statistiek (Annual). *Statistiek van Vreemdelingenverkeer*, Staatsuitgeverij, The Hague.
City of Westminster (1972). *Hotels and Tourism*, London.
Eastbourne Tourist Board (1977). *Eastbourne Tourism Study*, Eastbourne District Council.
English Tourist Board (1975). *Hove Tourism Survey*, English Tourist Board, London.
Greater London Council (1971). *Tourism and Hotels in London*, GLC, London.
Greater London Council (1978). *Tourism. A Paper for Discussion*, GLC, London.
Lavery, P. (1975). 'Is the supply of accommodation outstripping the growth of tourism?', *Area*, **7 (6),** 289–296.
Sandles, A. (1978). 'Question marks overhanging British tourism', *Financial Times*, 9 December.
Stadt Nürnberg (1976). *Nürnberg—Plan, Teil 1: Bericht zur Entwicklung der Altstadt.*
Union of Dutch North Sea Authorities (1971). *De Nederlandse Kust als Recreatiegebied.*
VVV Delft (1972). *De Ontwikkeling van het Vreemdelingenverkeer, 1972–1976.*
Young, G. (1972). *Accommodation Services in Britain 1970–1980*, University of Surrey, Guildford.
Young, G. (1973). *Tourism, Blessing or Blight?*, Penguin, Harmondsworth.
Youngson, A. (1966). *The Making of Classical Edinburgh*, Edinburgh University Press, Edinburgh.

Chapter 9

Bonnain-Moerdyk, R. (1975). 'L'éspace gastronomique', *L'Éspace Geog.*, **2,** 113–126.
Bowler, I. and Strachan, A. (1977). *Parks and Gardens in Leicester: A Survey*, Recreation and Cultural Service Department, Leicester City Council.
Burgess, E. W. and Park, R. (eds.) (1925). *The City*, University of Chicago Press, Chicago.
Burke, G. (1966). *Greenheart Metropolis, Planning the Western Netherlands*, Macmillan, London.
Cargill, S. and Hodgart, R. (1978). *A Strategy for the Provision of Squash Courts in the Lothian Region*, Department of Geography, University of Edinburgh.
Chadwick, G. (1966). *The Park and the Town*, Architectural Press, London.
Christiansen, M. (1978). *Park Planning Handbook*, Wiley, London.
Conseil de Paris (1971). *Les Éspaces Verts de Paris*, Paris.
Davidson, J. (1978). 'Growing importance of the urban fringe', *Surveyor*, **151, (4479),** 19.
Dower, M. (1965). 'Fourth wave', *Archit. J.*, **141 (3),** 122–190.
Edinburgh District Council (1977). *Planning Department Report*, Research Section, Edinburgh.
Glasgow County Council (1975). *Open Space and Recreation*, Planning Policy Report, Glasgow.
Greater London Council (1967a). *Greater London Development Plan*, GLC, London.
Greater London Council (1967b). *Greater London Development Plan Enquiry*, GLC, London.
Hampshire County Council (1978). *Policy Review Recreation*, Hampshire County Council, Winchester.
Hampshire County Council (1976). *Policy Analysis and Review, Recreation Programme Areas*, Hampshire County Council, Winchester.
HMSO (1960). *Report of the Committee on Youth Service in England and Wales*, Cmd. 929, HMSO, London.
HMSO (1975). *Sport and Recreation*, Cmd. 6200, HMSO, London.

Jacobs, J. (1962). *The Death and Life of Great American Cities*, Jonathan Cape, London.
Leusse, M. (1976). *Le Quotidien*, 20 April.
Lever, W. (1973). 'Recreation space in cities', *J. Town Plan. Inst.*, **59,** 138–140.
Mennell, S. (1976). *Cultural Policy in Towns*, Council of Europe, Strasbourg.
Mennell, S. (1978). *Strategy for the New Project*, Council of Europe, Strasbourg.
Mercer, C. (1976). *Living in Cities. Psychology and the Urban Environment*, Penguin, Harmondsworth.
Ministry of Housing and Local Government (1962). *The Green Belts*, HMSO, London.
Molyneux, P. (1972). 'The context for planning indoor sports centres', *Built Environ.*, **1 (8),** 523–526.
Préfecture de la Région Parisienne (1975). *Schéma Directeur d'aménagement et d'urbanisme de la Région Parisienne*, Paris.
Provinciale Bestuur van Zuid-Holland (1967). *Vrije Uren in de Vrije Natuur*, Rotterdam.
Provinciale Planologische Dienst Zuid-Holland (1969). *Rotterdamers op Zondag.*
Rijksplanologische Dienst Netherlands (1965). Den Haag.
Roberts, R. (1974). 'Planning for leisure', *Building*, **15 (3),** 98–102.
Robertson, I. M. L. (1978). 'Planning for the location of recreation centres in an urban area: a case study of Glasgow', *Reg. Stud.*, **12 (4),** 419–428.
Shakespeare, W. (1978). 'Henry VI Part I', in *The Complete Works of William Shakespeare*, Abbey Library, London.
Siedlungsverband Ruhrkohlenbezirk (1966). *The Ruhr Plans, Progress and Prospects*, Siedlungsverband Ruhrkohlenbezirk, Essen.
Sociografischdienst gewest Arnhem (1975). *Stadsverniewing Arnhem*, Arnhem.
Stadt Köln (1978). *Stadtentwicklungsplan, Freizeit, Sport, Freiraumplanung*, Cologne.
Stadt Mannheim (1977). *Grunordnung und Stadtplanung in Mannheim*, Mannheim.
Steigenga, W. (1968). 'Recent planning problems of the Netherlands', *Reg. Stud.*, **2,** 105–118.
Ulfert-Herlyn, V. (1977). 'Soziale Ungleicheiten in der Stadtischen Freiraumversorgung', *Landschaft und Stadt,* **9 (2),** 49–57.
Ward, B. (1976). *The Home of Man*, Penguin, Harmondsworth.
Weber, M. (1958). *The City*, Heinemann, London.
Windle, R. (ed.) (1981). *Records of the Corporation 1966–1974*, Portsmouth City Council, Portsmouth. Mimeo.
Wippler, R. (1966). *Vrije Tijd Buiten*, Economische, Technologische Institut, Groningen.
Wolfenden Committee of Sport (1960). *Sport and the Community*, Central Council of Physical Recreation, London.

Chapter 10

Abress, H. (1974). 'An outline of the federal German government's regional and urban development policies', in *The Role of Transportation in Urban Planning, Development and Environment*, 03.023 Schriftenreihe des Bundesministirium für Raumordnung Bauwesen und Städtebau.
Ashworth, G. (1979). 'Language, nationality and the state in Belgium', *Area Stud.*, **1,** 28–32.
Bahr, G. (1976). 'Raumordnungsvorstellungen der Vier Norddeutschen Lander', *Veroffentlichungen der Akademie fur Raumforschung und Landesplanung*, Deutscher Planungsatlas, Band VIII, Hamburg, Lieferung 11.
Barlow (1940). *The Report of the Royal Commission on the Geographical Distribution of the Industrial Population*, Cmd. 6153, HMSO, London.
Bourne, L. (1975). *Urban Systems*, Oxford University Press, London.
Burtenshaw, D. (1970). 'Switzerland's Planning Priorities', *Planning Outlook, New Series*, **8,** 55–68.
Burtenshaw, D. (1976a). *Saar–Lorraine*, Oxford University Press, London.

Burtenshaw, D. (1976b). 'Problems of frontier regions in the EEC', in *Economy and Society in the EEC* (eds. R. Lee. and P. Ogden), pp. 217–231, Saxon House, Farnborough.

Burtenshaw, D. (1981). 'Austria', in *Regional Development in Western Europe* (2nd edn), (ed. H. Clout), Wiley, London.

Buursink, J. (1971). 'De Nederlandse Hierarchie der Regionale Centra', *Tijd. Econ. Soc. Geog.*, **62,** 67–81.

Chaline, C. (1978). *New Departures in Regional Planning—France* (mimeo), Paper presented to Regional Studies Association Conference, 19 May.

Conseil Économique et Social (1973). *Rapport 13*, 7 August, Paris.

de Jong, F. (1969). *De Economische Betekenis van de R. V. Groningen voor de Provincie*, R. V. Groningen.

DATAR (1973). *Paris Ville International, Travaux et Recherches de Perspective*, DATAR, Paris.

Elasser, H. (1979). *Siedlungs Struktur und Raumplanung in der Schweiz*, and *Regional Politische Problem der Schweiz* (mimeo), Papers presented to Geographische Instituut Rijksuniversiteit, Utrecht.

Gravier, J. F. (1947). *Paris et le Désert Français*, Flammarion, Paris.

Hansen, J. (1972). 'Regional disparities in Norway with reference to marginality', *Trans. Inst. Brit. Geog.*, **57,** 15–30.

Hammond, E. (1968). *London to Durham*, Rowntree Research Unit, University of Durham.

Hollmann, H. (1977). 'Grenzuberschreitende Landesplanung Bremen/Niedersachsen', *Raumforsch. Raumord.*, **35,** 218–224.

Kormoss, I. (1976). 'Urban extensions in Belgium', in *The Environment of Human Settlements, Volume 1* (eds. P. Laconte *et al.*), pp. 177–186, Pergamon, Oxford.

Knox, P. (1973). 'Norway: regional policies and prosperity', *Scot. Geog. Mag.*, **89,** 180–195.

Lajugie, J. (1974). *Les Villes Moyennes*, Editions Cujas, Paris.

Michael, R. (1979). 'Metropolitan development concepts and planning policies in West Germany', *Town Plan. Rev.*, **50 (3),** 287–312.

Michels, D. (1976). 'Das System der Entwicklungsachsen und Verdichtungsschwerpunkte in Nordwesteuropäischen Kernraum', *Forsch. zur Raumentwick.* **Nr 3.**

Ministry of Environment (1975). *A Survey of Norwegian Planning Legislation*, Oslo.

Ministry of Housing (1976). *Denmark's National Report to Habitat*, Copenhagen.

Ministry of Housing and Physical Planning (1976). *Housing Building and Planning in Sweden*, Stockholm.

Nanetti, R. (1972). 'Urbanization in France and Italy', *Council of Planning Librarians Exchange Bibliography*, 340.

Norway (1977). 'The main features of the new Planning Act', *Norwegian Official Reports Series*, **1.**

Pinder, D. (1978). 'Guiding economic development in the EEC.: the approach of the European investment bank', *Geography*, **63 (2),** 88–97.

République et Canton de Genève (1975). *Plan Directeur Cantonal*, Directeur de l'Aménagement—Division de l'Équipement, Geneva.

République et Canton de Genève (1977). *Some Aspects of Town Planning in Geneva* (mimeo), Department of Public Works and Town Planning, Geneva.

Rijksplanologische Dienst (1976). *Verstedelijlsnota*, The Hague.

Riley, R. C. and Ashworth, G. J. (1975). *Benelux, An Economic Geography of Belgium, The Netherlands and Luxembourg*, Chatto and Windus, London.

Second Structure Plan (1966). *Second Report on Physical Planning in the Netherlands*, The Hague.

Tamsma, R. (1972). 'The Northern Netherlands: large problem area in a small country, small problem area in a large economic community', *Tijd. Econ. Soc. Geog.*, **63,** 162–179.

Verbeck, V. (1973). 'Het Benelux Middengebied', *Stadebouw en Volkshuisvesting*, **10,** 372–380.

Chapter 11

Burke, G. (1966). *Greenheart Metropolis*, Macmillan, London.

Burtenshaw, D. (1974a). 'Regional planning in the Ruhr', *Town Country Plan.*, **42(5),** 267–269.

Burtenshaw, D. (1974b). *An Economic Geography of West Germany*, Macmillan, London.

Dennis, R. (1978). 'The decline of manufacturing employment in Greater London, 1960–74', *Urban Stud.*, **15,** 63–73.

Greater London Council (1969). *Greater London Development Plan: Written Statement*, GLC, London.

Greater London Council (1975). *Modified Greater London Development Plan*, GLC, London.

Greater London Council (1976). *Greater London Development Plan: Written Statement*, Approved by the Secretary of State for the Environment, 9 July, 1976.

Hall, J. (1976). *London: Metropolis and Region*, Oxford University Press, London.

Hall, P. (1969). *London 2000*, Faber and Faber, London.

Hall, P. (1973). *The Containment of Urban England*, Allen and Unwin, London.

Hall, P. (1977). *The World Cities* (2nd edn), Weidenfeld and Nicolson, London.

Hellen, A. (1974). *North Rhine–Westphalia*, Oxford University Press, London.

HMSO (1964). *The South-East Study*, HMSO, London.

HMSO (1967). *Strategy for the South-East*, HMSO, London.

HMSO (1970). *Strategic Plan for the South-East*, HMSO, London.

HMSO (1973). *Greater London Development Plan*, Statement by the Rt Hon. Geoffrey Rippon, QC, MP, Secretary of State for the Environment, HMSO, London.

HMSO (1976). *Strategy for the South-East: 1976 Review*, HMSO, LOndon.

Lynch, K. (1961). 'The pattern of the Metropolis', *Daedalus*, Winter.

McCrone, G. (1970). *Regional Policy in Britain*, Allen and Unwin, London.

Rijksplanologische Dienst (1966). *Tweeda Nota over de Ruimtelijke ordening in Nederland*, The Hague.

Riley, R. C. and Ashworth, G. K. (1975). *Benelux: An Economic Geography of Belgium, the Netherlands and Luxembourg*, Chatto and Windus, London.

Siedlungsverband Ruhrkohlenbezirk (1966). *Gebietsentwicklungsplan 1966*, Siedlungsverband Ruhrkohlenbezirk, Essen.

Steigenga, W. (1968). 'Recent planning problems of the Netherlands', *Reg. Stud.*, **2,** 105–115.

Wohlin, H. (1977). *Framework for Urban Development in Sweden* (mimeo), Department of Planning and Building Control, Stockholm.

Chapter 12

Abercrombie, P. (1945). *Greater London Plan 1944*, HMSO, London.

Albers, G. (1977). 'Stadtbauliche Konzepte im 20 Jahrhundert—Ihre Wirkung in Theorie und Praxis', *Berichte Raumforsch. Raumplan.*, **1,** 14–26.

Bahr, G. (1976a). 'Raumordnungsvorstellungen der Vier Norddeutschen Länder', *Veroffentlichen der Akademie für Raumforschung und Landesplanung*, Deutscher Planungsatlas, Band VIII, Hamburg, Lieferung 11.

Bahr, G. (1976b). 'Die Landesplanerische Zusammenarbeit mit den Nachbarlandern', *Veroffentlichen der Akademie fur Raumforschung und Landesplanung*, Deutscher Planungsatlas, Band VIII, Hamburg, Lieferung 10.

Barbier, J., *et al.* (1966). 'La Région Lausannoise de Lutry à Morges', *Cahiers de l'Aménagement Régional*, 2, Office Cantonal Vaudoise de l'Urbanisme, Lausanne.

Barbier, J., *et al.* (1969). 'Haut-Leman Chablais', *Cahiers de l'Aménagement Régional*, 7, Office Cantonal Vaudoise de l'Urbanisme, Lausanne.

Bonnet, J. (1975). 'Lyon et son agglomeration', *Notes et Études Documentaires*, 4207–4209, La Documentation Française.

Boustedt, O. (1967). 'Zum Bedeutung des Dichtebegriffs in der Raumordnung und Landesplanung', *Mitteilungen der Deutschen Akademie für Stadtbau und Landesplanung, Heft* 11.

Boustedt, O. (1970). 'Stadtregionen', *Handwortenbuch der Raumforschung und Raumordnung*, 3207–3237, Akademie für Raumforschung und Landesplanung, Hannover.

Boustedt, O. (1975). *Grundriss der Empirschen Regionalforschung, Teil 3, Siedlungsstrukturen*, Schroedel, Hannover.

Bruyelle, P. (1976). 'Lille et sa communauté urbaine', *Notes et Études Documentaires*, 4297–4299, La Documentation Française.

Burtenshaw, D. (1970). 'Switzerland's Planning Priorities', *Planning Outlook, New Series*, **8,** 55–68.

Burtenshaw, D. (1976). 'Problems of frontier regions in the EEC', in *Economy and Society in the EEC* (eds. R. Lee and P. Ogden), pp. 217–231, Saxon House, Farnborough.

Dupuy, G. (1977). 'Aménagement et participation', *Urbanisme*, **46 (160),** 68–77.

Gasper, J. (1976). 'Regional planning, decentralisation and popular participation in post-1974 Portugal', *Iberian Stud.*, **5,** 31–34.

Greater Manchester Council (1978). *Greater Manchester Structure Plan, Draft Written Statement*, Greater Manchester.

Grossraum Hannover (1975). *Regionales Raumordnungsprogramm Grossraum Hannover 1975, Grossraum Hannover* Informationsstelle.

Hillebrecht, R. (1962). *Die Stadtregion—Grossstadt und Stadtbau*, Schwartz, Göttingen.

Hollmann, H. (1977). 'Grenzuberschreitende Landesplanung Bremen/Niedersachsen', *Raumforsch. Raumord.*, **35,** 218–224.

Lewis, J. and Williams, A. (1980). *Regional Uneven Development on the European Periphery: The Case of Portugal, 1950–78*, Paper presented to the Conference of Institute of British Geographers, Lancaster.

République et Canton de Genève (1974). *Plan Directeur Cantonal*, Département des Travaux Publics, Geneva.

République et Canton de Genève (1975). *Plan Directeur Cantonal Étude de Mise à Jour*, Département des Travaux Publics, Geneva.

Richardson, H. (1975). *Regional Development Policy and Planning in Spain*, Saxon House, Farnborough.

Sauvy, A., and Prud'homme, R. (1973). 'La mode des villes moyennes', *Urbanisme*, **42 (136),** 18–32.

Siedlungsverband Ruhrkohlenbezirk (SVR) (1966). *Gebietsentwicklungsplan 1966*, Siedlungsverband Ruhrkohlenbezirk, Essen.

South Hampshire Plan Advisory Committee (1972). *South Hampshire Structure Plan, Report*, Hampshire County Council, Winchester.

Stadt Frankfurt (1975). *Konzepte zum Flachennutzungsplan*, Dezernat Planung, Frankfurt on Main.

Stadt Kiel (1977). *Entwicklungsplanung, 1977–1981*, Landeshauptstadt, Kiel.

Stadt Köln (1973). *Köln Innenstadt*, Hochbaudezernat Stadtplanungsamt, Cologne.

Stadt Köln (1978). *Stadtentwicklungsplan, C1 Raumlich-funktionale Ordnung*, Stadtplanungsamt, Cologne.

Stadt München (1975). *Stadtentwicklungsplan 1975*, Referat fur Stadtforschung und Stadtentwicklung, Munich.

Urbanisme (1971). 'Schéma d'aménagement de la métropole Lorraine', *Urbanisme*, **40 (125),** 44–55.

Wohlin, H. (1977). *Framework for Urban Development in Sweden* (mimeo), Department of Planning and Building Control, Stockholm.

Wynn, M. (1979). 'Barcelona: planning and change 1854–1977', *Town Plan. Rev.*, **50 (2),** 185–203.

Wynn, M. and Smith, R. (1978). 'Spain: urban decentralization', *Built Environ.*, **4 (1),** 49–55.

Chapter 13

Berry, B. J. L. (1973). *The Human Consequences of Urbanisation: Divergent Paths in the Experience of the Twentieth Century*, Macmillan, London.
Burke, G. (1971). *Towns in the Making*, Edward Arnold, London.
Burtenshaw, D. (1974). 'Regional planning in the Ruhr', *Town Country Plan.*, **42(5),** 267–269.
Deakin, N., and Ungerson, C. (1977). *Leaving London, Planned Mobility and the Inner City*, Heinemann Educational, London.
Sunday Times (1977). 'Will trimming a town save a city?', *Sunday Times*, 10 April.
The Times (1976). 'Rethinking strategy on new towns', *The Times*, 1 November.
Thomas, R. (1969). *Aycliffe to Cumbernauld: A Study of Seven New Towns in their Regions*, PEP, London.
Webber, M. (1964). *Explorations into Urban Structure*, University of Pennsylvania Press, Philadelphia.

Chapter 14

Ambrose, P., and Colenutt, B. (1975). *The Property Machine*, Penguin, Harmondsworth.
Hall, P. (ed.) (1977). *Europe 2000*, Duckworth, London.
Hall, P. (1969). *London 2000*, Faber and Faber, London.
Lloyd, P., and Mason, C. (1978). 'Manufacturing industry in the inner city; a case study of Greater Manchester', *Inst. Brit. Geog. Trans., New Series*, **3(1),** 66–90.

Place Name Index

Maps are in italic.

General Index

Entries in italic indicate references to figures on the page numbers given.